LIBRARY LIT. 4-
The Best of 1973

edited by
BILL KATZ
and
SHERRY GAHERTY

The Scarecrow Press, Inc.
Metuchen, N. J.   1974

ISBN 0-8108-0702-5
Library of Congress Catalog Card Number 78-154842

Copyright 1974 by The Scarecrow Press, Inc.

CONTENTS

Introduction   v
Acknowledgments   vii

Part I. LIBRARIES AND LIBRARIANS

The Contact Factor (S.D. Neill)   1
That Inordinate Passion for Status
    (Raleigh DePriest)   13
Books, Libraries, Librarians--European and
    American Style (Herman Liebaers)   27
Humorrhoids--The Big Slipcase (Henry Beard)   36
Expanding Library Horizons: The Significance for
    Academic Learning (Robert Vosper)   41
How I Got My Library Job Good
    (Joseph McDonald)   57
The Changing Role of Directors of University
    Libraries (Arthur McAnally and Robert B.
    Downs)   64
Information Science As an Emergent Discipline:
    Educational Implications (D.J. Foskett)   100
Three Peas in a Pod: A Hero and Two Heroines
    (Caroline E. Werkley)   117
Who Runs the Library? (Edward G. Holley)   130
Libraries, Love, and the Pursuit of Happiness
    (Arnold P. Sable)   141
Selling the President, Architecturally
    (Ada Louise Huxtable)   155

Part II. TECHNICAL SERVICES/READERS'
          SERVICES

Cataloguing in Publication (Verner W. Clapp)   161
Protection of Libraries (Oscar M. Trelles)   177
Distributing Books (Dick Higgins)   213
Who Invented Dewey's Classification?
    (John Maass)   225

Part III. COMMUNICATION AND EDUCATION

Such Good Friends (Richard Kluger)	237
Humanization of Cartography (Denis Wood)	253
Perspectives on Media (Peggy Sullivan)	266
Reading Habits and Library Experiments in Sweden (Bengt Hjelmqvist)	271
Is Tomorrow a Four Letter Word? (Jean Karl)	279
Biography: The Bad or the Bountiful? (Patrick Groff)	288
Black English: The Politics of Translation (June Jordan)	298
Modern Trends in Book-Collecting (Anthony Rota)	307
Why We Hardly Have Any Picture Books in the Children's Department Anymore: A Brief Fantasy (Eva Nelson)	319
Audio-Visual Aids: Fallout from the McLuhan Galaxy (William R. Eshelman)	323

Part IV. THE SOCIAL PREROGATIVE

Kid Porn v. the Burger Five (John Leonard)	327
Book Selection in Philadelphia (S. J. Leon)	331
The Concept of "National Security" and Its Effect on Information Transfer (I. M. Klempner)	360
Freedom of the Press--American Style (Harriet F. Pilpel)	370
Notes on Contributors	381

INTRODUCTION

This is the fourth year of an anthology which a number of librarians and students report they find useful as a compilation of good to excellent articles by and about librarians. The purpose, as before, is to acknowledge the "best" writing in this field by selecting articles published in magazines over a one-year period, in this case between November 1972 and November 1973. The articles are gathered from some 200 magazines, most of which are library oriented, although a few are representative of general or other specialized fields. This year the initial gathering consisted of 121 articles which were gradually reduced to a manageable number by the editors and the jury. Many entries were suggested by librarians who seem to follow this series. As an added help, the library school students here at Albany assisted in the first go-around of selection.

It is apparent to the librarians who make suggestions for this series, as well as to the students, jurors, editors and writers, that there is no single method by which an article may be considered "best" or "better" and ultimately end up in this collection. No one is ever totally satisfied with the final selection, and this is never so evident as when the jurors meet to evaluate and to choose. Aside from perhaps a half dozen articles, there is no consensus. The final result is a bit of compromise, of give and take between the jurors and the need for an anthology of this type to be representative not only of the best, but of the field as a whole.

There are numerous reasons for compiling an annual effort of this type. At a minimum it gives readers an overview of a field and makes it possible to avoid much worthless material. Also, it is a time-saver for students who may be assigned many of these readings and, searching for the original magazine, inevitably discover the article or even that issue missing. Then, too, it is by way of a slight reward and a major recognition to those authors who took the pains and the imagination to commit themselves to paper.

Beyond the rather obvious rationale, one more is suggested. Perhaps the cumulative effect of the now over 100 entries will help to dispel the notion that librarians are automatically social and intellectual duds. The pejorative use of "librarian" is a bit overdone; and to compare a would-be assassin to a "librarian" is the ultimate put-down--e.g., the following, from the magazine section of The New York Times (September 2, 1973, p. 26), may be the quote of the year: "De la Tocnaye's (the prototype for the Jackal in The Day of the Jackal) feelings about Bastine-Thiry (a fellow assassin) were mixed. 'When I met him,' he recalls, 'I was surprised. He didn't look like a colonel. He looked like a librarian. His face was puffy. I wondered what that type of fellow was doing in our type of action."

Well, in the "type of action" variously described in this collection there are neither visible killers nor puffy faces, although there may be a colonel or two, not to mention a few privates and corporals. Beyond that, let the present collection speak for itself.

William A. Katz
Sherry Gaherty
Albany, New York
December 1973

ACKNOWLEDGMENTS

Jurors: The editors wish to thank the jurors who assisted in the selection of the articles: William R. Eshelman, editor, Wilson Library Bulletin; Karl Nyren, associate editor, Library Journal; Jane Stevens, former editor of Library Literature; and Eric Moon, president, Scarecrow Press.

Editors and Authors: And thanks to the editors of the magazines who were kind enough to allow reprinting; and to the authors whose works are honoring this anthology and the literature as a whole.

Consultants: The editors, also, wish to thank the many librarians who once again suggested entries. And particular thanks should go this year to students at the Albany library school for helping in the initial selection.

Part I

LIBRARIES AND LIBRARIANS

THE CONTACT FACTOR*

S. D. Neill

> "Efficiency is no longer effective in an
> electric society that requires informal
> participation and involvement as a basis
> for any operation whatever."
> Marshall McLuhan

In a comparatively recent issue of the journal of The American Society for Information Science, the lead article complained that the conference of 1970 on unsatisfied needs for information of various segments of our society was disappointing. Evidently, only a few papers clearly focused on the problem. The author of the article had hoped "that more of us would have suggested how we could apply the expertise we have developed during the last twenty years to perhaps less important (i.e., less important than such things as the information gap between Congress and the military), but nonetheless still serious problems now confronting an information-conscious but information-poor society." (1, p. 71)

While it would be interesting to debate the values behind the phrase "less important," I would rather, at this time, try to supply a reason for this admitted inability to "apply the expertise" to problems the size or importance of which might be appropriately classified as being within the human scale.

The failure of the information scientists to provide solutions to the information problems of ordinary people is a result of their failure to provide results beyond "low effectiveness" for the specialized users of existing retrieval

---

*Reprinted by permission from the January-February 1973 issue of Canadian Library Journal, pages 48-54.

systems. (2, p. 139) The reason for this failure has been present in information science from the beginning, when the decision was made to ignore the human element. The decision has been expressed in many ways, but it has remained constant over the years. Three examples follow:

1. Leon Brillouin, one of the early and important writers in the field of information theory, in describing the parameters within which he was working, both in the first and second editions (1956 and 1962) of his book Science and Information Theory, says:

> The methods of this theory can be successfully applied to all technical problems concerning information: coding, telecommunication, mechanical computers, etc. In all of these problems we are actually processing information or transmitting it from one place to another, and the present theory is extremely useful in setting up rules and stating exact limits for what can and cannot be done.
> But we are in no position to investigate the process of thought, and we cannot, for the moment, introduce into our theory any element involving the human value of information. This elimination of the human element is a very serious limitation, but this is the price we have so far had to pay for being able to set up this body of scientific knowledge. The restrictions that we have introduced enable us to give a quantitative definition of information and to treat information as a physically measurable quantity. This definition cannot distinguish between information of great importance and a piece of news of no great value for the person who received it.... All these elements of human value are ignored by the present theory. (3, x-xi)

2. Gerard Salton, creator of the SMART system, and author of a major text in the field, does not use the phrase "human element," but I believe that that element is directly responsible for the difficulties in those theoretical problems regarding meaning which are noted in the following:

> This text, then, is an attempt to examine the principal technical and intellectual problems arising in information processing and to determine the extent to which they are amenable to solution by

automatic or semi-automatic methods. The structure and properties of scientific information are of principal concern, as reflected in a semantic content analysis of the documents (but not a qualitative evaluation concerning their accuracy, veracity, or conciseness).

In many ways, a study of the analytical aspects of scientific information in a mechanical environment must appear as a hopeless endeavor, because so many of the important theoretical problems are unsolved. What exactly is the content or meaning of a document? To what extent can individual words, or word groups, in a text be said to carry and maintain a well-defined, controlled meaning? How can one isolate the content-bearing units if they exist? And so on.

Since the answers to these fundamental questions are nuclear, it becomes impossible to justify the text-manipulating procedures introduced in this volume for purposes of content analysis other than as ad hoc devices. (4, p. 2-3)

3. While Salton continued to work with theoretically unjustified procedures, other information scientists tried to found a discipline on the same basis. In this next quotation we have a repeat of Brillouin's position, with the application to man left to some ultimate point in time: (4, p. 2-5)

Man sets the limit to what can be done with information. As ultimate user and, in many cases, as generator of information, his information processing capabilities determine the usefulness of information systems to him individually and collectively. This statement concerning man as the point of reference applies even to the functions of hypothesized supermachines exhibiting artificial intelligence exceeding that of exceptional human performance.

It must be recognized, however, that the complexity of man's relation to information and of his information processing, prevent man, at this time, from being the test bed for information sciences. The theories forming the body for the metascience of information may have to evolve slowly. They have to be based on elementary information conditions in manmade form and environment. The application of these fundamental laws and relations in more and more complex systems ultimately have to be applicable to man and always have to serve man. (5, p. 92)

We have here an unbelievable situation. Brillouin recognizes the "very serious limitation" of ignoring man, Salton does so as well, but continues to work at a "hopeless endeavor," and Otten and Debons reluctantly struggle with the development of an argument for a metascience which must, seemingly of necessity, do without its "point of reference" and its limiting factor--man. Is it any wonder that the "expertise" of such a peculiar "science" should be inapplicable to a society made up of human kind. Certainly the results must be invalid for any viable type of library service that I know, and how anyone could even expect them to be valid seems to me to be just plain bad thinking.

There is hope, however. Some small steps toward including man have been taken. Garfield[1] is concerned about the common man's information needs, da Solla Price (6) with the need for humility of the elite (including, I presume, some information scientists), and Shera (7) with the impact of the content of the library on society.

These after dinner musings are given some solid support in two other articles in the same issue. Saracevic reports on a four-year project inquiring into the testing of information retrieval systems. The first of his general conclusions simply identifies the importance of the human element which information scientists have always known about but have chosen to ignore: "The human factor, i.e., variations introduced by human decision-making, seems to be the major factor affecting the performance of every and all components of an information retrieval system." (2, p. 138) In the other article, McAllister and Bell (a couple of IBM boys), actually attempt to identify "human factors" and to design a system for total library management. They are, of course, concerned with a very narrow range of man's activities, but it is a step in the right direction. Their final sentence in the following paragraph is an apt comment on the Brillouin-Salton dilemma:

> Yet system designers and programmers really know very little about what happens when a person sits down in front of a terminal. Generalized models of man-machine communications are often limited in scope. Skirting the complex problems

of experimental control of statistical analysis of
this kind of interaction, theoreticians sometimes
produce equally complex equations based on purely
hypothetical systems. (8, p. 104)

The information science people are concerned now
because science in general is in disfavour. There are undoubtedly a number of reasons for this, but one of them is
the lack of obviously successful results relevant to the
quality of life on this planet which would give to us primitives the chance of making what Charles Erasmus calls a
"frequency interpretation." (9, p. 31) Perhaps it would be
better to say that there are some obvious examples of disasters resulting from the scientific-industrial enterprise.
We are also looking askance at education, which has laid
claim to at least a pseudo-scientific method for decades, and
has had a good bash at a revolution in schooling during the
last ten years. Paradoxically, there are now too many
teachers for a system that has been pushing independent
study and individualization techniques for the child-centred
school. No thought has been taken for serving people as
people, only as learners to be guided to specific objectives,
or users of thesauri and sample document stores. Basing
much of their thinking on the model of programming, educators and information scientists seem to have fostered a
two-bit mentality, and this has brought them to the present
confrontation with that "human element" that was set aside
for some future, ultimate consideration. Among the educators, of course, only the radicals have realized that anything was missing at all. The human element just doesn't
seem to fit into the context of tests and measurements and
controlled experiments. Nor are librarians immune to this
mental block, especially when a revered statesman among
them can even suggest that the status of the library profession is observable "in its cataloging rules." (19, p. 450)

Another reason for the present search for the human
factor is not unrelated to the first, and that is the cry by
the taxpayer for accountability. It is now obvious that poor
results in any information system, even the highly controlled,
have been because man has been ignored. In education, of
course, poor results and failures are described as having
no significant difference. Garfield sees even the mediocre
results of costly IR systems research as being possibly in
the wrong sector. Thus his query regarding what information scientists have done to improve the telephone book.
Indeed, the whole matter of concern for the information-

conscious/information-poor society could be summarized as the yellow pages problem--the result of undue submission to the pressure of the research grant and the project number.

However, this incredible state of affairs is merely a symptom of a much wider problem, which I will now attempt to identify. To begin with, I think we must ask an entirely different question from those we seem to have been concerned with up to now. It is not a question like how much information, or what kind of information (which assume that people want information), but an open question like what it is that people want that we can give?

Peter Drucker cites an interesting method for analysing a potential market in a process he calls innovative marketing, (11, p. 52) and the questions he uses provide a means for us to approach the people problem. The first question --what is the unfulfilled expectation of typical members of the community?--is my main concern in this inquiry; for the answer to it is needed before the answers to the other two questions can be attempted. The second question, reworded for library purposes, is: Can the members of the community afford the service? Aspects of the answer might entail, for instance, the cost of hiring more librarians against the cost of computerizing in an interactive library system. The third question is: Who decides what is borrowed (or used in the library)? Answering that question today, for illustrative purposes, one might be tempted to say the individual. But with so many students using the library, and so many adults taking courses, the answer could well be educational institutions. For other patrons, the answer might be service organizations or business interests.

What _are_ some of the unfulfilled expectations of members of a community vis-à-vis the library? I suppose a questionnaire or some other sort of survey is called for at this point, but let me quickly rough in some ideas and their implications. A little pre-thinking, like a little pre-soaking, helps get out those stubborn stains that ordinary procedures tend to ignore.

I doubt if there are any unfulfilled expectations with regard to the quantity of information, either in Brillouin's absolute sense of the word, or in the broader meaning, which librarians have traditionally defined as inclusive of: information (as a datum or fact), recreation, education, and inspiration. We are a data-dominated society, mauled by messages dumped on us from all directions and by many means, from mass media to mass education; from brochures to billboards to libraries. The quality of this information depends on conditions bounded by space, time, mood, and mind. There is no lack of either quantity or quality. What is lacking is communication, if that be interpreted as a two-way process. And I don't mean communication by means of public library group programs. I mean one-to-one, face-to-face communication with a specific individual about his specific requirements--the quantity and quality of the materials he needs set in the context of the quantities and qualities of all the materials available. The mass media provide no such feedback. Our educational establishments provide limited choice both quantitatively and qualitatively. Neither of these massive institutions, by the very nature of their underlying purpose and philosophy and in spite of their efforts, can ever organize themselves for the kind of personal contact I mean. Their aim is to reach society en masse. Their methods are compulsion and monopoly. There are, of course, and there always will be, pockets of human concern in every large organization, philosophical or practical, operating in a pluralistic democratic system, but somehow these seem to be exceptions--islands in a vast waste of recall/relevance ratios and <u>standard</u> deviations.

There is, however, an established, public institution in the information field that is not based on these principles. Only in the dreams of its wildest enthusiasts has the public library ever been thought of as an attraction for the mass, and although it is publicly tax-supported, its use is voluntary. Libraries have always supported the freedom of the individual to make his own way and his own choice, or not to do so at all. Perhaps it is this emphasis that has, in its extreme form, persuaded librarians to move away from efforts to guide their clients in any but an impersonal manner. In these times of shifting values, censorship is an enemy librarians see around every corner. This could be one factor in the trend away from personal contact. Another factor influencing our mental set in this respect is the general technological invasion of privacy, accompanied by the anti-computer complex generated by the problems of man-machine interface and the high-and-mighty braggadocio about hypothetical and artificial superbrains.

Western man is in an era of insecurity caused by the seeming necessity of unpopular wars, information overload, and public and private debt, and has become disillusioned

with the old faiths of church, science, and education. The
unfulfilled need of our time is the satisfaction that comes
from the warmth and intimacy of personal contact. This is
not the involvement in participatory democracy so much as
it is the awareness of the human face as the kinesthetic
communication medium par excellence. Marshall McLuhan's
insights into the sensorial wholeness we are regaining because
we are "back in acoustic space," cannot be ignored by
those who seriously intend to understand society and help to
fulfil, as far as possible, mankind's expectations.

This does not mean that libraries should store more
books on group therapy or hobbies, but that the librarians
must get into dialogue with their customers in such a way
that the customers will know it, which is not possible when
they interface with the card catalogue, or the circulation
desk, or even an interactive computer terminal. Personal
satisfaction in a communication process can only come from
contact with persons--thinking, talking, and breathing.
That's what Shera's "lady librarian" knew instinctively and
by experience, (7, p. 79) and what used to be practised in
the services of the reader's advisor. (12) If my argument
is valid, then we must plan for informal personal contact
now. Future needs <u>might</u> be different, but we should be
prepared to serve present needs, which are so much more
difficult to define because we incorporate our own prejudices
into the definition. I would think that in any time period
more emphasis ought to be placed on the present, otherwise
we will be considered irrelevant by our contemporaries and
they will pass that message on to the future.

A service of personal contact will need more librarians
at the interface, capable of interdisciplinary action, prepared
to listen, to assist, and even to teach; for what better
conditions are there for individual study and continuous
progress. Personal contact librarians are the kind who can
engage all varieties of people in sympathetic and intelligent
book talk: young and old, ignorant and scholarly. This
necessitates a high standard in the librarian's knowledge
base and in his understanding of the learning process.

Library administrators have seen the need for contact
and participation in the planning and policy-making functions
within the library itself--where the price of ignoring
the human element is low morale and disputatious personnel.
The same principle applies to the public; although ignoring
them and their need to be consulted is not as immediately

nor as personally felt.

Young librarians who complain that their work does not fulfil their expectations, and library school students who are unhappy because their interest in books and people is ignored, and who are then encouraged to invest their enthusiasm in cataloguing rules and computer applications, will understand the necessity of emphasizing the contact factor. It is here that the great satisfactions of librarianship lie-- librarianship defined as service to people. We are not in the "data" market. We are in the idea business.

The analogy to business can be useful. I have heard librarians compare their libraries to supermarkets. This comparison fits well with the hands-off-the-reader's-choice philosophy. Even the library floor plan is similar to a supermarket's, with its administrative module like the librarian's office (but often more accessible), and the turnstiles like the circulation procedures. The only concession the supermarket makes to the need for personal service is at the meat counter, and that they advertise this aspect is a significant commentary on the psychological situation we are now discussing.

Sitting at a reference or inquiry desk, the concession made by libraries to customer contact, is too passive. It is necessary to be obviously mobile, or to be present at the places where the users make decisions. Information Canada's brochures advertise their centres as follows: "One thing you'll notice is that they have no counters. That is because they have been designed with people in mind: Instead of sitting behind a counter, the centre's information officers will stand beside special information consoles--and will be encouraged to meet citizens face-to-face." Whether this happens or not, there is still a recognition of what should be happening. Large department stores take an interesting hold on the problem by placing counters arranged by type of goods over the floor area, each counter island having one or two persons "on location" with the time and the knowledge to talk to each client, something like providing numerous corner stores. This has the necessary qualities to make it a suggestive model for library designers.

While business can say satisfaction guaranteed or your money refunded, libraries cannot. The librarian can't guarantee satisfaction from reading a specific book. In our business, satisfaction is not in the product, but in the complex results of using the product. The results are ideas and emotions, and unless the client is a recluse, the real satisfaction in having ideas and emotions is in communicating them to others.

Admittedly, the client can communicate with many others, not librarians, but surely to divorce the dealer from the idea content, the satisfactions of his product, its long-run, in-depth meaning for the customer, is to provide half a service only, and that half the least important in the user's mind. No wonder our patrons have seen us as dried-up prunes. We are seemingly not interested in what interests them. Those who sell such relatively meaningless items as soft drinks and tooth paste are well aware of the necessity to <u>provide</u> a meaning that goes beyond the utilitarian uses of their product--quenching thirst and cleaning teeth. Life, love, and the pursuit of happiness (indeed, the finding of happiness) are "written-into" the product. For librarians, these qualities are already in their goods; for they are about life, love, happiness, and unhappiness, and they provide ideas for the pursuit of quality or dignity in these more or less unavoidable events. Our product, in this sense, <u>is</u> life, and if we would rather not claim to be qualified to discuss <u>that</u> with our customers, there is no reason why we cannot prepare ourselves to talk about ideas of life as presented in the individual opinions and examples found on our counters.

The human element is a factor not only at the catalogue, the circulation desk, and in technical services. It is <u>the</u> factor in our materials. It's what our materials are all about. If Saracevic can come to the conclusion that the human factor seems to be the major one affecting the performance of all the components of an information retrieval system, how much more does the human factor apply to that other component, the client himself. It is noteworthy that Saracevic nowhere includes the librarian in his model, and although he makes a concession to using personal knowledge to supplement thesaurus terms, he has some doubts about interviewing users in "question expansion." Significantly, he also concludes that: "Without doubt a retrieval system needs to have designed into its operations elaborate procedures and adequate capacity in terms of people, cost, time, etc., for the handling of questions." (2, p.139) If we expand the handling of questions to field theory size, we have one-to-one contact about the user's interests that could cover the entire universe of knowledge, never mind

Saracevic's minuscule "vector-borne tropical diseases."
Anyway, I doubt the possibility in any library of separating
the question itself from the total context in which the user
asks it, i.e., what he's thinking, how he's thinking, and
why he's thinking it--not if one wishes to understand the
meaning and not just the syntax of the question.

Saracevic notes that other large-scale evaluations of
IR systems support his conclusions. The danger the IR
boys face (and librarians following them) is that they will
interpret the human factor to mean the subjectivity in semantic interpretation of index terms and interrogative speech
acts. They will seek some standard vocabulary to ensure
precision or relevancy. We are not in the precision business. We're in the thinking business, and one man's
thoughts can range from the data to cure tropical diseases,
to his sore toe, to his favourite TV show, to the morality
of art, each having some bearing on the other.

Communicating is the key word, and the librarian
and his customer can only communicate by personal contact
and lots of it. Since his business is all knowledge and all
emotions, it is the librarian's job to help the user make
the relationships across the disciplines and within himself,
and this only happens in loose discussion, in slow time,
face-to-face.

In the context of outreach activities, librarians have
been accused of doing nothing to get books and other resources to the people out there. Social activists have said
this in the past few years (see the proceedings of the
Change Institute held at the University of Maryland's library
school in 1969 (13)). One of the reasons why librarians as
a group are not seen to be acting on outreach principles is
because they react as individuals, ad hoc, almost reacting
on impulse to some felt pressure or bandwagon hysteria.
The profession does not move as a body because no rationale
for action has been developed. There is no theory to justify the program--only a wind-blown waving of the arms to
ward off disaster or extinction. This brief essay has attempted to provide at least the beginnings of the needed
foundation for more librarians to encourage more interaction
between library personnel and library users.

REFERENCES

1. Garfield, Eugene. "Information Science and the Information-Conscious Society." Journal of the American Society for Information Science, 22:2 (Mar.-Apr. 1971), 71-73.
2. Saracevic, Tefko. "Selected Results from an Inquiry into Testing of Information Retrieval Systems." J.A.S.I.S., 22:2 (Mar.-Apr. 1971), 126-139.
3. Brillouin, Leon. Science and Information Theory. 2d ed. New York: Academic Press, 1962.
4. Salton, Gerard. Automatic Information Organization and Retrieval. New York: McGraw-Hill, 1968.
5. Otten, K., and A. Debons. "Towards a Metascience of Information: Informatology," J.A.S.I.S., 21:1 (Jan.-Feb. 1970), 89-94.
6. Da Solla Price, Derek J. "Some Remarks on Elitism in Information and the Invisible College Phenomenon in Science." J.A.S.I.S., 22:2 (Mar.-Apr. 1971), 74-75.
7. Shera, Jesse H. "The Sociological Relationships of Information Science." J.A.S.I.S., 22:2 (Mar.-Apr. 1971), 76-80.
8. McAllister, Caryl, and John M. Bell. "Human Factors in the Design of an Interactive Library System." J.A.S.I.S., 22:2 (Mar.-Apr. 1971), 96-104.
9. Erasmus, Charles. Man Takes Control. Minneapolis: University of Minnesota Press, 1961.
10. Lubetzky, Seymour. "1976 minus 6... 5...." Library Journal, 96:3 (1 Feb. 1971), 450-451.
11. Drucker, Peter F. The Age of Discontinuity: Guidelines to Our Changing Society. New York: Harper and Row, 1968.
12. Money, Darlene. "Whatever Happened to Readers' Advisory Service." Ontario Library Review, 55:1 (Mar. 1971), 14-16.
13. School of Library Services, University of Maryland. Frontiers in Librarianship: Proceedings of the Change Institute, 1969. Westport, Conn.: Greenwood Pub. Co., 1972.

THAT INORDINATE PASSION FOR STATUS*

Raleigh DePriest

While the last decade has witnessed considerable articulation among librarians in favor of faculty status, there have been opponents as well: Kenneth Kister, who describes what he sees as librarians' attempt to imitate the faculty and their blurring of the distinction between librarianship and teaching at a time when they ought to be earning their status as librarians only;[1] Daniel Gore, who rates the idea as farcical;[2] Richard Thompson, who believes librarians need faculty status no more than do physicians, nurses, accountants, or policemen;[3] Lawrence Clark Powell, who evidently thinks the way to status is simply hewing away at the job in hand and keeping one's nose clean;[4] and Robert Blackburn, who marvels at what he calls the librarian's "inordinate passion for status."[5]

In this paper I should like first to comment on the positions taken by these writers and then to make some suggestions as to why I believe the librarian's concern for status is "inordinate"--if indeed such is the case.

As I understand them, each of these writers either questions faculty status for librarians altogether or the method librarians use to accomplish it, but each in so doing raises one or more serious questions about his own position.

As I understand Kister, teachers are educators; librarians are not. Teachers deal with substance and are concerned with the <u>why</u> of a given matter; librarians deal with procedures, the <u>how</u> of the matter. Teachers make value judgments about subjects, but librarians are relatively

---

*Reprinted by permission from the March 1973 issue of <u>College and Research Libraries</u>, pages 150-158.

neutral toward subjects. However, if librarians claim they are educators they thereby may have some leverage in attaining faculty status, and this is why they attempt to ape the faculty.

The spirit of Kister's piece suggests that only those who are habitual classroom teachers are involved intellectually with learners. He does admit that the staff members give "casual" instruction to readers and sometimes are invited to lecture in classes. But he never specifically recognizes those whose everyday activities involve them in instructing, guiding, advising, encouraging, demonstrating, and interpreting in bibliography, grammar, logic, documentation, vocabulary, statistics, or simply the language of the printed page in face-to-face relations with all seekers, even the faculty. Kister all but ignores the reference librarian, readers' advisor, and subject specialist. In fact, however, if the librarian in this vortex of academic inquiry is merely concerned with procedures and the how, then he quite clearly does not belong there; nor does he belong there if he does not qualify, or is not working on his qualification, in a subject other than library science on the graduate level, since his business is not administrative but instructive.

Not only is he involved in value judgments in advising readers and researchers, but in his selection of general and special reference tools, as well as books of his specialty in the general collection, his quest necessarily ranges far. Thus Kister, who charges some with blurring the distinctions between teaching and librarianship, evidently does some blurring of his own. In his ardor to show how teachers and librarians are unlike, he fails to account for the distinction between those positions that are administrative and those that are instructive.

One would also believe from Kister's piece that a library is a mysterious entity interpreted by skilled information specialists, who, however, are neither concerned with nor cognizant of the aims, purposes, and procedures of the very clientele they serve. Kister's stand in granting to the librarian a service function but prohibiting for him any kind of role as educator apparently indicates a radical disregard of the very nature of the academic library. He appears not to recognize that here we are not dealing with any old library, but a significant unit of an institution of higher learning whose sole purpose is the support of that institution, whose every important move is to be made not simply for the sake of general service, no matter how clever or magical, but in terms of a college service--a specific kind of college with a specific kind of patron, specific curricula, course offerings, aims, methods of teaching, level of teaching, ratio of graduates to undergraduates, and a specific overall philosophy of education.

If we can agree that the library is, or ought to be, at the vortex of academic inquiry--a learning tool for the student who does his most serious work investigating a specialized field--then how are we to furnish this kind of service unless we are concerned with and cognizant of the subjects that are studied, the educational policies being observed, the methods underlying our teaching, the plans of courses being taught, the general academic planning being done, and the very aims of higher education itself? In other words, the library generally, and the readers' service staff particularly, appear to have no choice but to be closely involved with the educational process as special educators. Yet this seems to be the very role that both Powell and Kister deny them.

Again, Kister quoting Powell says "Unless librarians do what faculty do--teach, research, publish--they will not achieve true faculty status. If they do then they are faculty, not librarians."[6] While Kister evidently thinks there is something unusual about librarians teaching, researching, and writing, certain evidence seems to point in a somewhat different direction. Anita Schiller's study of 2265 academic librarians indicated that 15 percent of her respondents taught courses for credit, and Perry D. Morrison showed in his study of 707 librarians, that one-third of the respondents had previous teaching experience.[7] None of this of course includes the noncredit informal teaching with which most reference librarians are involved, nor the day-to-day individual instruction in reference and research which they do regularly.

Publishing? One only has to scan the literature of the field to see that considerable writing--much of it important--is being done, or to check the index, Library Literature, to see the great number of periodicals devoted to librarianship alone, or to check Morrison's study which shows that over 70 percent of respondents on the average among several categories had at least published something.[8]

Research? Both catalogers and reference librarians

do some research as a regular task, either in order to
identify and verify the description of various elements of
the materials being processed, or to satisfy the degree of
evidence needed in research questions. If we examine the
character of articles and reports being published by librarians continually, we would see also that many of them could
not have been published without extensive research.

Thus it is not strange to say that many librarians
teach, research, write, and publish, yet they are not teachers in the strict sense. What are we to call them? The
truth is there are laggards in both occupations. Some librarians write, research, and publish; some do not. The
same is true for teachers. There are poor librarians and
able ones, poor teachers and able ones; but quite a few
scholars emerge from both occupations. Why hold up teaching alone as a sacred standard of scholarship, especially
when some of our most famous professors do little teaching? The universities honor them by actually relieving them
of their teaching tasks so that they can do research, write,
and publish. One trouble with Kister's and Powell's position seems to be its rigidity; the formula is much too pat.

Richard C. Thompson asks in effect that, since physicians, accountants, architects, and policemen, connected
with the university, are not designated as faculty, then why
would librarians be designated as such?[9] I can only say
that while these worthy occupations could not be dispensed
with by the university, they represent identities all their
own and their functions are not even remotely analogous to
library work. How is the accountant, the architect, the
physician, or the policeman involved directly and steadily in
the development of the minds of students, a function assumed generally to be the raison d'etre of the institution,
itself? If one is asked how librarians are so involved,
then one can say simply and without exaggeration that they
acquire and organize the very record of civilization and
guide students and faculty in its use.

A problem in Thompson's position apparently is that
he is trying to compare occupations that are incommensurable. To keep the business office abreast of its annual expenditures, debits, and credits, is one thing; to guide a
student in English to the discovery that Ralph Waldo Emerson made his most significant contribution to world literature by way of profound Oriental thought is quite another.

Mr. Powell tells us that librarianship is "an opportunity to serve people, learn from them, and love them. And perhaps gain status thereby."[10] The general spirit of his piece indicates that devotion to one's task and relentless execution of work on the job is the way to win status. Precisely. Men have done the same for centuries in all endeavors. Let us hope that that opportunity will never die, because it is a last vestige of desirable individualism we have. What we have to do now is to protect that individuality and give it identity. Virtue may be its own reward, but it alone does not get bread for the belly or provide a condition of employment in which one can serve himself and his institution best. The message of that virtue must be said loud and clear enough that administrations will be caused to recognize it. The one way it can be protected is by official academic recognition from administration, and the means of carrying the message in this brash world is through the collective voice of teaching faculty and librarians together. They need each other.

Since Powell however would have the librarian pay his price for status only by individual effort--each one pulling himself up by his own bootstraps--then how should the teachers earn theirs? If he would have the teachers possess their status by fiat but the librarians theirs by sheer individual struggle, perhaps with a measure of boot-licking, then a serious question of academic principle and justice arises.

Daniel Gore, now rather well-known for his sport of baiting librarians, may have been pecking at the wrong people. His "Mismanagement of College Libraries" and "A Modest Proposal" are rather similar in that they both deal with the unprofessional aspect of library work, the first scoring the librarian for what Gore thinks is frittering away time in menial tasks while pretending his work is important academically; the second proposing that the college do away with most librarians, hire clerks, and retain a skeleton-work of professionals to direct the clerks.[11] In short, what Gore has been concerned with is that a considerable part of library work is clerical and the ratio of professionals to clericals is too high. His first assumption is true; the second too, but it seems to be improving.

The record indicates however that librarians themselves have long been striving to get a balance between clericals, semiprofessionals, and professionals. Some problems of personnel in universities and colleges, for instance, may be beyond any remedy available to the local administration, and many times complements of personnel offered may be too few or imbalanced.

The individual staff member, after spending some seventeen or eighteen years in preparation for his occupation, is not likely to allow idealistic notions of what is or is not professional stand between him and his employment; he is more likely to accept the situation with the hope that better times may lie ahead. So he performs a combination of professional and nonprofessional tasks, especially in public services, where the show must go on. In this context librarians are merely straw men set up by Mr. Gore, who fails to get at the real problem--that of top management in the matter of personnel.

Gore, in his schoolboyish piece, "Faculty Status for Librarians at Arbuthnot," continues to belabor the menial tasks done by librarians.[12] If we employed a lawyer, physician, or accountant yet gave him some subprofessional work to do, we could very well expect him nevertheless to demand a recognition of all his time spent as professional time, it being up to us to furnish work appropriate to his level of preparation. Why should librarians act differently? Mr. Gore merely describes the symptoms; he never gets at the disease.

Robert Blackburn is concerned with what he believes to be the inherent differences between teaching faculty and librarians, both professionally and psychologically; he sees a condition detrimental to student use of learning materials. In his thoughtful article he says that one of the characteristics of the librarian is "an inordinate passion for status.... Faculty rank seems to be a sought after goal, almost as an end in itself."[13]

There is some truth in what Blackburn says, but there are reasons for status other than its being an end in itself. I suggest two basic reasons why I believe the concern for status has occupied the minds of librarians: (1) the need for a trade-union, bread-and-butter security, and (2) the need for full academic recognition in order to play a more effective role in the academic program.

For the first I shall give some accounts of libraries in state-supported colleges in Pennsylvania. Here the personnel, except laborers, are divided into two groups: the academic group consisting of teaching staff, deans, librarians, and counselors on one side, and the civil-service group consisting generally of such personnel as those handling the business end of the institution--clerks, secretaries, bookkeepers, and business managers.

Librarians in the public schools of Pennsylvania have for many years belonged by public law in the category of teachers, and state college regulations mainly have followed the same pattern.[14] At Mansfield State College, for example, the staff have not been aware that they were ever treated in any way different from the teaching staff. Staff enjoy tenure, take sabbaticals, serve on faculty councils, and have all the other advantages that faculty have. Their ranks range from that of instructor to associate professor and they are employed on a nine-month basis, with options for summer employment. However, there can be cause for anxiety, for no matter how hard-won or desirable the condition of employment, it can prove not to be exactly safe from modification. Recently the head librarian, along with counselors, was placed in the administrative category rather than the academic. This was not only an about-face in the traditional policy of status for the head librarian--often more likely to have faculty status than others on the staff--but it left the rest of the staff in an ambiguous position.

There are other sources of concern, and librarians' reactions reflect it. Thus when a team of consultants made a year's study of state personnel in 1969, and recommended a separation of librarians and others from the teaching faculty, several papers from librarians of the state colleges and from Indiana University in Pennsylvania made their appearance, totally rejecting the proposal.[15] In this they have been supported by the Association of Pennsylvania State College and University Faculties and help has been offered by AAUP, both of which have librarians in their membership.

Further, since the entrance to professional librarianship in Pennsylvania state-supported colleges has demanded a greater amount of preparation than the entrance to teaching in the same institutions, librarians see any alternative to faculty identity impossible, especially since any alternative could mean civil service classification and removal from academic effectiveness.[16]

In short, affiliation with faculty, both in their work and in the faculty associations, provides an umbrella of protection in a very real and material sense for that comparatively tiny group of specially-prepared academic people in Pennsylvania. As they see it, remove that umbrella and anything can happen.

The second factor in the concern for status involves identity and professionalism, both of which are related to the librarian's educational background, his personal interest, his activity in the profession, and the manner in which he views himself in the academic world. Morrison, studying 707 academic librarians, found a wide range of personal characteristics, but as a group they were cultured and intelligent, with a high mean score of self assurance, from families of high social and educational status, but not necessarily economic, a lack of drive or anxiety over status more befitting the upper class than the middle class, a majority (59 percent) of them possessing more graduate credit than the first professional degree, about one-third having previous teaching experience, over 70 percent having published, and much less likely to regret entering their occupation than others in other occupations.[17]

Anita Schiller's study of 2265 academic librarians showed that 85.5 percent had at least the first professional degree; that 25 percent, in addition to the first professional degree, held advanced nonlibrary degrees as well. As noted before, about 15 percent of Schiller's subjects were teaching credit courses and two-thirds belonged to national, state, or regional associations.[18]

Some data indicating how academic librarians see themselves in the academic community was recently given by Josey in his study of 101 academic librarians in the state of New York.[19] About 98 percent of these responded positively to the opening statement of the ACRL Standards, which says in effect that librarians should have all rights and benefits that teaching staff have, and 90 percent viewed themselves as faculty of their respective institutions.

Thus there is some evidence that academic librarians may believe--with considerable justification--that they have something worthwhile to offer. Believing in themselves, knowing that a solid academic program cannot exist without them, they evidently feel that academic potential deserves academic recognition, if such potential is ever to realize its worth.

However, this does not fully answer the question raised by Kister, Powell, and others, namely, why do librarians demand to be faculty the same as teaching staff, since relatively few of them spend a great proportion of their time in formal classroom teaching? I now wish to examine briefly the question of status concern as related to professionalism.

Carroll DeWeese has discussed a study that sought to distinguish between library staff members of a low concern for status on the one hand and members of a high concern for status on the other among thirty-nine professionals in a large midwestern, land-grant university library.[20] The librarian of high status aspiration tended to be more professionally oriented and more concerned with professionalization of librarianship; he desired more autonomy for his profession and greater recognition for his work, and he more often mentioned work as a main satisfaction in life than did those of low status concern. His inability or unwillingness to leave his profession was linked with high status concern within that profession.

The librarian of high status concern was also more likely to see professional associations as important and he experienced more conflict with the faculty than those librarians of low status aspiration who reported relatively little difficulty. The last named characteristic appears especially significant, because it indicates a pattern which evidently links a felt need for status with the concomitant conditions that cluster with or about it--professionalism, autonomy, authority, responsibility, and, as a related issue, professional preparation. With professionalization the librarian becomes something of an "authority," but it must be a recognized authority or it is nothing. Without it, "cooperation" with patrons becomes confused with groveling, and groveling in this case is not merely a matter of inverted pride. In this connection, I cannot agree with Powell who implies that the patron is always right, because such a policy if acted upon would violate the very principle upon which professionalism rests. Ultimately we must act according to what we know the customer needs, not what he vaguely feels that he wants.

Further investigation, no doubt, would shed further light on library-faculty tensions. A review of library literature will reveal that professors once ran the library; that some of them do believe that librarians for the most part

are merely technicians; and some professors would still like
to run the library, with librarians of course doing the work--
the most serious point for conflict of authority imaginable.21

Thus a belief in one's profession, devotion to and
satisfaction in the work, and certainty that it is important in
the academic sense, all accord with the wish for a freedom
to exercise those convictions so that one's real responsibility
can be met, so that the library may proceed on an even
keel, not subject to every buffet or pressure from faculty,
administration, or students, for the benefit of all concerned.
In this context I believe faculty and administration may rest
assured that, by the very nature of professionalism, there
will be few free-loaders who demand status, because status
ultimately goes with professionalism and professionalism
logically demands devotion to one's work and a much greater
overall responsibility.

Let me illustrate concretely the implications of status,
autonomy, authority, and responsibility. If I plan and execute
a teaching program in bibliography exactly as that which
I have in mind and which includes student responsibility to
me, I have no doubt that it will succeed, since my past experience
indicates such to be true. But as soon as I begin
compromising with the English staff--each one wanting something
different--a whole new ball game begins developing;
and if I now face the possibility of a mere tour of the library
and a few handouts, or some other equally trivial
plan, all of which I disapprove, then indeed do doubts assail
me, because eventually the manner of my very presentation
is affected adversely. Thus, not only do I become the goat
of the project, but, more important, students are betrayed.

The teaching staff generally has all the authority
needed by academic fiat, but in the same area--many times
even where the librarian has a bona fide faculty status--the
librarian has only whatever authority the instructor of the
class he is visiting gives him, and the students, even if
compelled to attend his meetings, know that what he has to
offer for them is a take-it-or-leave-it proposition. If I resist
the demands of faculty in this instance, tension is more
than likely to result.

In the problem above then why should I be subservient
if I have both the bibliographic competence plus even
more credit in the humanities than in library science, plus
teaching experience, plus faculty status? I do not try to

tell the English professor how to teach Melville and Faulkner. Why should he dictate to me how to teach bibliography, either in the general area or in the humanities? As far as academic integrity is concerned, I am a professor the same as he and can resist legitimately any encroachment on my freedom to instruct as I see fit. Further, I cannot afford to be merely separate and equal, because I know of no group other than faculty that affords the essential protection of the freedom I must have in such matters. Thus, only faculty status allows me to meet the responsibilities I know are mine in the task of making the library a place worthy of scholarly practice and its patrons adept in one of the most mature and useful academic endeavors they will ever engage in--independent investigation.

It has been my purpose, then, to indicate that the concern for status among academic librarians is perhaps more than simply an anxious preoccupation with academic social climbing, justified by the droll argument that one is what one is not. The question of status is not a mere figment of the imagination, but as real a problem as any in the academic world, and it is rooted in the very purpose and philosophy of higher education.

However, in the end, the question of status eligibility is not really whether one teaches or how much one teaches in a classroom--even though such function might lend academic weight--but whether one renders a direct scholarly service to the academic program. Moreover, if the conscientious, well-educated librarian, live to books and ideas and people, conscious of the undeniable opportunities of his library, appears to be "inordinately" concerned with status, then it behooves us to look deeper than surface evidence for the cause of this concern.

REFERENCES

1. Kenneth Kister. "A View from the Front; A Blast at the 'Library College' Idea from a Working Librarian." Library Journal, 96 (Oct. 15, 1971), 3283-8.
2. Daniel Gore. "Faculty Status for the Librarians at Arbuthnot; A Farce in One Scene." American Libraries, 2 (Mar. 1971), 283-95.
3. Richard Thompson. "Crutches and Crying Towels," a letter. Library Journal, 95 (Apr. 1, 1970), 1260.
4. Lawrence Clark Powell. "Shoe on the Other Foot."

Wilson Library Bulletin, 45 (Dec. 1970), 384-9.
5. Robert L. Blackburn. "College Libraries; Indicated Failures; Some Reasons and a Possible Remedy." CRL, 29 (May 1968), 171-7.
6. Kister, op. cit., p. 3285. He refers to Lawrence Clark Powell's quotation in Powell's article [see 4 above].
7. Anita Schiller. Characteristics of Professional Personnel in College and University Libraries. Final Report. Washington, D.C.: U.S. Dept. of Health, Education, and Welfare, 1968; 119p. Perry D. Morrison. The Career of the Academic Librarian: A Study of the Social Origins, Educational Attainments, Vocational Experiences, and Personal Characteristics of a Group of American Academic Librarians. Chicago: ALA, 1969; 169p., biblio. This is a condensation of Morrison's doctoral dissertation in library science, accepted at the University of California, Berkeley, 1960.
8. Morrison, op. cit., p. 64.
9. Thompson, "Crutches," p. 1260.
10. Powell, "Shoe on," p. 389.
11. Daniel Gore. "The Mismanagement of College Libraries." AAUP Bulletin, 52 (Spring 1966), 46-51. "A Modest Proposal for Improving the Management of College Libraries." Educational Record, 48 (Winter 1967), 79-86.
12. Daniel Gore, "Faculty Status."
13. Thompson, "Crutches."
14. Purdon's Pennsylvania Statutes Annotated, title 24, sections 11-1141, reads in part "'Teacher' shall include all professional employees and temporary professional employees, who devote fifty per cent (50%) of their time or more to teaching or other direct educational activities, such as classroom teachers, demonstration teachers, museum teachers, counselors, librarians, school nurses, dental hygienists, home and school visitors, and other similar professional employees ... certified in accordance with the qualifications established by the State Council of Education."
15. A Personnel Program for Selected Faculty Employments in The Pennsylvania State Colleges and University. Chicago: Public Administrative Service, 1969; 41p. Appendix.
16. The minimum entering requirement for teachers with the rank of instructor is a bachelor's degree plus

fifteen semester hours of graduate credit. The entering minimum requirement for librarians--if they are to be employed in professional capacity and with the same rank--is the master's degree in librarianship.

17. Morrison. The Career of the Academic Librarian. One must keep in mind that the gathering of Morrison's data could not have occurred later than the late fifties. In the matter of status concern of librarians, Morrison himself noticed a changing pattern of personnel toward a more ambitious mood for professional advancement. Thus, after twelve or fifteen years, we might see that his librarians of upper class mentality may now have changed radically to that of middle class aggressiveness.

18. Schiller. Characteristics of Professional Personnel. Since broad rather than narrow concentration in subject fields has traditionally been advised for librarians, nondegree credit may be the rule rather than the exception. Some extra hours are studied for the immediate value of understanding or skills on the job. One of Schiller's subjects reported earning nine hours' credit in law expecting the study to enable her to organize materials in that area more efficiently. Thus, in library science, particularly, the very nature of one's strength which is relevant may go unrecorded in some educational records such as that found in college catalogs.

19. E. J. Josey. "Full Faculty Status This Century." Library Journal, 97 (Mar. 15, 1972), 984-9.

20. L. Carroll DeWeese. "Status Concerns and Library Professionalism." CRL, 33 (Jan. 1972), 31-8.

21. F. W. Bateson complained that few university librarians in America are scholars in their own right. His specific problem was the need for a bibliographer in the humanities, specifically in his own field, English. He proposed two alternatives: one, a member of the English staff be assigned the task with partial relief from teaching; two, assignment of a librarian, actually the first choice, according to Bateson. But he asked where one could find a librarian to fit this scholarly requirement. Librarians, he believed, suffered from a "bogus preoccupation" with "library service." "Degrees and diplomas are even accorded in this bastard discipline and often become a union card, the shibboleth that permits entry into the profession.... Library science, I am told, can be

learned in a fortnight." It is interesting to note that Bateson, a well-known English professor and scholar, is holding in contempt the idea of service, while Kenneth Kister, a librarian, whom we have discussed in this paper, used the same idea for his forte in his article "A View from the Front...." For Bateson's discussion see F. W. Bateson, "Function of the Library in Graduate Study in English," Journal of General Education, 13 (Apr. 1961), 5-17.

BOOKS, LIBRARIES, LIBRARIANS--
EUROPEAN AND AMERICAN STYLE*

Herman Liebaers

When a European librarian speaks or writes for an American audience, he must first try to answer these questions: Why is American librarianship more advanced than its European counterpart? Why do American libraries have larger and better collections than European institutions? Why do American librarians have a more professional approach to the problems of librarianship than we do?

When North America became independent nearly two hundred years ago, it had already drained from Europe a group of enterprising people who had blown up their bridges behind them and consequently were forced to look ahead. The pioneering spirit has been for many generations a cliche, but it still is the best characteristic from a point of view which seeks a conscientiously adopted mixture of foresight and hindsight. In the nineteenth and twentieth centuries, power gradually moved from Europe to the United States, and expressions like "the old world" or "the new society" became household words. To put this too-general statement in a strictly professional framework, I would say that an American network of outstanding libraries became a much more powerful ingredient of progress than a series of venerable and isolated institutions in the aging social context of Western Europe.

The areas in which the American profession has surpassed the European constitute an impressive inventory: professional training, collection building, the place of libraries in society, and so on. But such tremendous gains

---

*Reprinted by permission from the January 1973 issue of Journal of Library History, Philosophy, and Comparative Librarianship, pages 18-22. This article was originally a speech given at the UCLA Library in January 1971.

may also hide some small losses. And I wonder if this is not the basic reason why the views of a European are always welcome in the United States--because, fundamentally, his audience is not interested in these small losses of some human values resulting from that epic passage from Europe to America.

I am always very careful when it comes to critical statements about the United States; I am accustomed to say that a European is always too late when he wants to criticize because a genuine American patriot--in the etymological sense of the word--has always done it before him, and often in more violent terms than a foreigner would dare to use. Actually, this violence is one of the main sources of worry for a friend from abroad.

Are libraries not natural walls of protection against this violence? They certainly are, here and elsewhere, but a library is as much a product of the society to which it belongs as a factor in molding this society. There is no doubt that any American librarian is more aggressive in tackling his problems than any of his opposite numbers, in France, for instance. No one, and certainly not I, would confuse aggressiveness with violence, but somewhere in the back of my mind I see a historical link between both.

The relationship between collection building and human values is probably a topic where the differences between the United States and Europe are, fortunately, small indeed. If you take rare book collections, for example, you will find that in both parts of the world they exist as both public and private libraries, while there is a more visible difference when it comes to collections of current books. In this connection, the private library is still more in use in Europe than in the United States. It is not unusual to run into a European scholar who never uses his university library, because he has enough books at home--or he thinks he has. (This is often, also, the type of professor who thinks that students are a nuisance.) However, one may wonder whether being the private owner, in your own house, of the books with which you have to work daily might in the long run influence in different ways the values upon which you try to build your life. Does the use of a smaller quantity of books lead to a more critical attitude towards their contents? I fear I have to leave it with a question mark.

Whatever may be the advantages or disadvantages of this more outspoken European private library system, it certainly is linked with the image of the isolated, nearly ivory-tower scholar which is disappearing in Europe, actually under American influence. Modern science would not have made its spectacular progress without the research team's replacing the individual scholar. The direct implication of this trend for libraries has undoubtedly been an increase of the importance--as spectacular as for science itself--of the large public research collection. I would say that this challenge has been understood extremely well in the United States.

When modern science invaded libraries at the turn of the century, European librarians did not understand the challenge to build up collections to match the requirements of research carried out in teamwork, while the American librarians responded immediately. As a result new, dynamic institutions were created in Europe, apparently outside the profession, which actually were libraries but which had very good reasons to avoid this obsolete word, still proudly used by backward-looking institutions. Let me parenthetically add that these venerable libraries, some of them centuries old, did a good job within their nineteenth-century terms of reference. The new European institutions, which called themselves "documentation centers," were actually libraries which tried to serve the needs of modern science, equated more or less with natural, physical, and applied sciences.

The antagonism between the two cultures has therefore been sharper in Europe than anywhere else. The major weakness of the professional evolution in Europe has been precisely this antagonism, which for three-quarters of a century has drawn far too much energy--energy which in the United States has been used in a positive way. Although the European scene, as described here, has nearly become history, there are still in both camps--if I may use a military term with which all European librarians have grown up--representatives of what I once tried to describe as follows: "some librarians still think that documentalists are barbarians who have replaced words by figures, and some documentalists still do believe that librarians are unsuccessful novelists who live from books written by others." This antagonism is nearly over in Europe also, at least in Western Europe, because on its Eastern borders "les frères ennemis" are still in good shape. Here is a quotation from a serious book issued under the title Theoretical Problems of Informatics, published recently by FID in Moscow: "a library is an archive of mostly literary documents." In all fairness I must add that the author is French and, characteristically, completely unknown to the profession in France.

It would be a nice divertissement if I went on now to talk about the semantics of the word "informatics," but I must revert to more serious matters. With many reservations I raise the question of whether the much better answer of American librarians to the challenge of modern science does not have its own weakness too, whether this weakness is not actually part of the great anxiety which marks American society today and for which Big Science itself may be partially responsible. The United States has never been as powerful and rich as it is today, and yet Americans have never questioned as thoroughly as today the very roots of their society. Libraries have grown to meet the demands; librarians have improved their techniques to cope with the sophistication which has been part of this quantitative growth, and they have done it better than anywhere else in the world. But....

In Europe we have painfully followed the American example. The European scholars came back from the United States, and no matter what their field of research, it was always the same story that we librarians heard: American libraries are better organized, have better collections, give better service. Our protective arguments were that we did not have the same financial means at our disposal and that our authorities were not as library-minded (actually, there is no French equivalent for "library-minded," neither is there one for "computer-based"). Could I say here, with the hope that I shall never be quoted at home, that I sometimes thought that the resistance of the authorities and the lack of money were not an absolute disadvantage? The slower growth, the sharper arguments forced us or gave us an opportunity to view retrospectively and critically this new mythology of Big Science, within which the research libraries tried to establish their own patterns.

European scholars returning from the United States and blaming European librarians are only a part of the picture. The point of view of American scholars working in European libraries should also be mentioned. Accustomed as they are to their outstanding university libraries, they always begin in Europe with a big disappointment. Since

they have no books in their suitcases they have to use these
old-fashioned local libraries, which most of the time have
an arrangement as old as the buildings and places which
normally house them. After some time the American scholar
discovers that the European librarian is more evident and
available, and occupies personally a more important place
between the books and their users. This is important when
the catalogs are poorer, and even more important when the
librarian and the user happen to work in the same field.

This brings me, of course, to a major distinction
between the two groups of librarians: the subject background
of the European librarian still is more often of importance
than for his American opposite number. Unfortunately, this
subject background will very often be limited to the humanities. Also, his strength in subject background is often set
off by his lack of professional training. His professional
techniques are always weaker, but, rightly or wrongly, he
has a tendency not to be ashamed of this. As one American
scholar once put it to me, "European librarians are much
better than European libraries!"

The shared cataloging program is a good point at
hand. Weakness in subject background and also a lack of
knowledge of foreign languages--another aspect which could
lead to interesting comments--were two considerations which
led the profession in the United States to set up an ambitious
centralized program actually going against an old established
American tradition of decentralization--offically called the
National Program for Acquisitions and Cataloging. The result is a collection-building system of a magnitude unknown
to the world outside the United States. We in Europe may
have proportionally more linguists among the librarians or
more subject specialists, but we do not transform this potential wealth into an improvement of our professional organization. We even have a tendency to be complacent about
ourselves, and when we consider a program like Shared
Cataloging--americain par excellence--we wonder if such aggressive collection-building does not hide some weaknesses.
And it does, of course. It has been voiced, on the old
continent, that the Shared Cataloging program puts quantity
before quality. Of course, no major book escapes such a
widespread net, but the price paid to bring in heaps of junk
as well is too high indeed. Shared Cataloging already proves
to be a tremendous impetus to renewed professional thinking
in every corner, an example of which is the critical reexamination of the various national bibliographies which may

eventually lead to a true Universal Bibliographical Control.

In this paper I am, of course, trying to stress differences and consciously avoiding similarities, which twice distorts the real situation. This also forces me to oversimplify in saying that the vast, monolithic United States, in contrast to the infinitesimally small, diversified, and divided Europe, creates two different thinking habits. The United States is not a monolithic bloc, I know, and yet the very size of the country and the use of the same language over such a wide area have specific influences. I would say that Americans are not so much attracted by differences as Europeans are. This gives to Americans a natural generosity, where Europeans have a no less natural scepticism--let us say more specifically a critical generosity in America and a generous scepticism in Europe. You have no idea how much we Europeans like to look for borders, for dividing lines. In Europe we have countries with books but no libraries; we have other countries with librarians and no books; and we also have countries with nothing at all when it comes to the things we are interested in. This game can go on, and you can make any combination of the words books, libraries, and librarians, putting each time the name of a specific country under it.

My own country of Belgium is a wonderful observation post for this European puzzle, and it is the meeting point of the two major civilizations in Europe: the Latin one from the south and the Germanic one from the north. Historically, this small country has been a middle land, un pays d'entre-deux, and we have benefited from both cultures. We have paid a high price for this privilege because we have also been, with the same historical benediction, the battlefield of Europe. But, being a Belgian, I am a good enough observer to see a strange professional border running through Europe from west to east and following roughly the northern out-skirts of the Catholic world. This border is not as visible as the iron curtain, but it certainly is as real. South of this border you find countries with centralized institutional systems where everything has come from the government. North of the line, where the American influence is much stronger, library associations have a real influence on the development of the profession. As always, both systems have their advantages and disadvantages, but if you look at the actual institutions providing library services there can be little doubt that one system has more advantages than the other and, since I live under one such

Libraries and Librarians 33

system, it is not surprising that my sympathy is with the other one.

In a completely different context I would like to return once more to the trilogy: books, libraries, and librarians. Until now I have looked at their relationship from a geographical point of view, but besides space there is also the factor of time. When I was a young librarian, books came first, then libraries, and finally librarians. Now it is exactly the contrary: librarians first and books last. I often wonder why. A quarter of a century ago I had the feeling that with books alone I could enter into the profession; now books help me to escape from too much professionalism. A quarter of a century ago when I wanted to work with books I never said that I was a librarian when I visited a library; now I meet only librarians and I always try to avoid visiting libraries. The only exception, but a rewarding one, remains my interest in the new acquisitions of books by the librarian I happen to meet. I know by experience that the man who is showing you his recent additions to the collection is a happy man, and it is always good to be in the company of happy people. Most of these acquisitions are rare books, which should not detract from the importance of adding to the general collections. In a recent excellent book, Great Libraries, the author, Anthony Hobson, systematically links examples of great books to the collections to which they genuinely belong. It is a source of unlimited satisfaction when a librarian is lucky enough to add to his collection not just a book which happens to be expensive, but that book which fills an old gap in the stacks of one's library.

I would like to cite two such examples which have enriched my own experience. For years I had been put under pressure by excellent staff members to buy systematically the lavish modern French books called livre de peintres, which are published in Paris--and when it rains in Paris, then you open your umbrella in Brussels. You know these books with a series of original lithographs or etchings by famous artists like Picasso, Matisse, and Dali, the text of which is of no importance, and even if it were, the size of the book would make it unreadable anyhow; most of the copies are bound for their owners by a famous binder who does not carry out the work himself--what the British call "non-bindings for non-books." I resisted the pressure because I think that such books can only be bought when you have a liking for them and that such a criterion should not

be applied when you buy with public money. Since these
books are, however, an important socio-economic and esthetic phenomenon of our times, they should be available
for study in a public collection, and to solve this dichotomy
I tried to convince my people that they should be offered to
us, because they were too expensive to be bought. When
such a gift materializes after many years of patient arguing,
you understand the deeper meaning of that innocent phrase
that "books are different" indeed. (For the record, I am
referring to the fairly complete collection of <u>livre de
peintres</u> which was offered in 1962 to the Royal Library of
Belgium by Madame Louis Solvay, who had collected them
during a lifetime; many copies were individualized through
artists' corrections, inscriptions, dedications, bindings, etc.)

    Another example of what I would call the genuine enrichment of a collection is a quite different one. We have
in our small country a city, Liège, which wants to be different from all other Belgian cities and which actually is
different and, the local people say, better. One of the
blows to the reputation of that city, which had already produced outstanding manuscripts in the tenth century, was that
typography was introduced only as late as 1560. This late
date had to be accepted by everybody, until quite recently
when a unique copy of a meaningless six-page booklet appeared, with Liège in the colophon and with worn-out typefaces which undoubtedly put the date of the book around
1500. When such a book enters the collection you feel that
justice has finally been done to a city which did not deserve
to wait until the second half of the sixteenth century to have
its print shop.

    It is something of this kind of satisfaction, I guess,
that a librarian may rediscover when it comes to the dedication of a new building. And, since that is the immediate
cause of my putting together these observations, let me
close with a reference to this aspect of our libraries in
Europe and in America. Before the librarian reaches that
stage he has to line up, exactly as with an acquisition, resources among which goodwill and competence are the most
important ones. Goodwill inside and outside the library,
competence inside and outside the library. I am not going
to talk about the relation between the architect and the librarian, but I have experienced that when a librarian has
carefully explained to an architect what a colophon exactly
means and when a librarian has really understood how an
architect has calculated the strength of his materials, they

can use the same language in planning a new building.

When, as I look around such a new building, I gain the feeling that the dialogue was a fruitful one, and that the architecture conveys the meaning of the contents of the building, this seems to me of the greatest importance. It also means that the librarian could explain outside the profession, the fundamental meaning of these contents.

For the last time, I am going to mention a difference between America and Europe. You have a tradition in new library buildings, and we have only beautiful old buildings to look at. You have architects who have built libraries over and over again; we have a few architects who will have built a library but once in their lifetime. You should not ask who is better off.

HUMORRHOIDS--THE BIG SLIPCASE*

Henry Beard

> ... Once again, Mr. Simpkins ("Super-sleuth" to his colleagues) is eyeball to eyeball with his prey. He speaks. "Excuse me, sir," he says, "I'm from the public library. It's about all those overdue books." When they hear that, they know the game is up. Mr. Simpkins is one of the best of that unsung band of men from libraries everywhere who chase down stolen and overdue books--the library fuzz.
>
> Wall Street Journal

"It's no good, Jimmy," said Sammy "Sam the Blot" Incunabula, crouching lower behind a pile of <u>Readers' Guide to Periodical Literatures</u>. "They got us boxed in tighter than a complete set of Dickens."

There was a tinkle of breaking glass and the sharp "thwuck" of a bullet burying itself in a two-volume French novel. Jimmy Folio, alias Jimmy "the Thumb," alias Jimmy Novella, lit a cigarette and sighed. "It sure looks like ZAR to ZZZ," he said, counting the cartridges left in his pocket. There were twelve. "One for each book of the <u>Aeneid</u>," he thought grimly.

"Come out with your hands up," blared a megaphone from the street. "Come out or we'll come in and get you." Jimmy stiffened. "I know that voice," he said. "Yeah," said Sammy. "It's Simpkins. That goddamn glue-shoe."

---

*Reprinted by permission from the February 1973 issue of <u>National Lampoon</u>, pages 30 & 32.

Folio inched along the wall and peered out the window. He jumped back. "Christ, they've got a bookmobile out there," he croaked. "We haven't got a chance. The only way we're leaving here is in a slipcase."

"Take it easy, kid," said Sammy. "We'll make it. We always made it before." "Yeah," whispered Folio, "but we never hit a federal lending library before. You know the rap--five dollars a book and ten cents a day. And for what? A lousy set of Thackeray and ten years' worth of Who's Who." " I thought it was an encyclopedia."

"Who's Who for Christ's sake. You could have picked up the whole set of Great Books of the Western World." "Hey, lay off. This job was your idea, remember?" "Yeah, yeah."

Sammy paused. "Say, kid," he said finally, "how did you get into this racket? I mean, now me, I was doing fine in 'Subjects' in a nice little library in Michigan, and then everything went 'Alphabetical by Author.' It was rough. I couldn't make the change. They gave me my endpapers, and I figured I'd get even. I started small, Bees of Jamaica, Portuguese Furniture of the Middle Ages, William Glintz: Mariner, stuff nobody misses. Slap a fake bookplate in there--Francis X. Libris, something like that-- fence it for a dime or two bits in one of those Any-Book-for-a-Buck stores, no questions asked. After that, I was a second-copy man for a while--you know, grab one copy, they catch you, you say, 'Look this one's mine,' they find they've got one and apologize, you're home free. Then I got into a gang that was working the biographies in Detroit. I was out of circulation for a while and I swore I'd go straight, but it was no good. But you, you got education. I mean, you coulda been a librarian."

"Shelve it," said Jimmy, grinding his cigarette out in a jar of book paste. But he couldn't help remembering....

She was smart, she was pretty, and she read a lot. Jesus, she read a lot. I guess I should have known then that she was a "worm," thought Jimmy, but it was spring and we were both young--no creases, no stains....

They had met in the card catalogue at the university library. She was looking for Herzog, and he was looking for "Hemingway, Ernest." In the wrong file, of course. Her hand had trembled. He had thought her fingers looked awfully black. "You come here often?" he asked. "Constantly," she breathed.

It began so simply. She had taken out all the books she could that month and she wondered, could she borrow his card? Just this once? She had this term paper and two book reports--she'd see everything got back on time. Jimmy said yes, of course it was all right. She read me like a book, he thought bitterly.

The notices started coming in about two weeks later. First the green LATE, then the yellow OVERDUE--two of those--then the pink FINE. He tried to reason with her, make her understand but they fought. She tore up his library card, cried. That was it for almost a month, then he got to thinking, "What a stupid thing--to get so riled up over some dumb books." He called her, they made up, and the world was a fifty-dollar Christmas art book with hundreds of illustrations, many of them in color.

They had a date, he took her home--an apartment in an old house on the edge of town. They went to her room. It was filled with books. Floor to ceiling. There must have been a thousand of them. He picked one up and a public library slip two years old fell out. She smiled weakly. "I thought you knew," she said quietly.

"You--you're speeding," said Jimmy. "I mean, you're really hooked, aren't you? Haven't you ever tried to put it down?" She sat down on a stack of atlases. "I tried--once. Four years ago. I went to a special camp in Maine. Nothing for miles around--no 'print,' no 'pulp,' no 'slick.' I went crazy. I was reading No Hunting posters, pup-tent instructions, candy-bar wrappers. I can still remember to this day what's in a Milky Way: dextrose, caramel, vanilla extract, molasses, whole milk, eggs, cocoa, artificial flavoring--"

He slapped her, hard. She started to cry. "Look," he said, "there must be a place for people like you, somewhere you could go." Suddenly, he realized he loved her.

"There is," she said, a strange tone creeping into

Libraries and Librarians

her voice. "There are these two big stone lions outside...."

After that, it was all he could do to support her habit. He stole everything: best sellers, histories, plays, poetry. He forged library cards, slipped books under his jacket and dropped them out of windows. But the checkers at the doors were more thorough, more suspicious. And she was more demanding than ever.

"I've got to have the real stuff," she said one day. "Encyclopaedia Britannica. I've got to have it." Jimmy protested. "That's thirty volumes. And anyway, the library doesn't have it. They have a Collier's Encyclopedia, but that isn't even complete," he said, looking around the room. "I know a place that does," she said.

It was the biggest library he had ever seen; it was like a railroad station. They caught him on volume 18. Tar paper, tarpaulin, tarpon, Tarquin, tarsal, tarsier. There was a hearing, and he was let off with a lecture and a stiff fine. When he got back to the university, he saw a stoop-shouldered instructor going into her apartment with the complete works of Milton. He kept walking.

He couldn't pass his exams. They wouldn't let him near a book. After he flunked out, he turned to the only trade he knew....

"It's awful quiet," said Sammy. "No coughing, no sneezing, no nothing." Jimmy started. "Yeah," he said.

"If I ever get out of this," said Sammy, "I'm going to retire. I got a nice little place upstate, with about twenty years of National Geographics stashed away. Maybe I'll work the clubs for a while, but this is my last job."

The door flew open and a short man in a slouch hat and a faded dust-jacket burst in. He had a mean-looking 23.05 Dewey Decimal in his hand and behind him was a heavyset policewoman with a pair of glasses around her neck on a string. "For once you're right, Incunabula. Both of you, drop those guns and reach for the top shelf."

"Simpkins," hissed Sammy. Two guns clattered to the floor. "Don't try anything funny, either of you, or you'll get it in the glossary."

"Creep, crumb, cuss, fink, heel, knave, louse, rogue, stinker," spat Jimmy. "Any of the family Rodentia, especially the common, or Norwegian, rat!"

"File it, Folio," said Simpkins sharply. Sammy glared. "All I can say is when I get out, your life ain't gonna be worth a dime, even if it's in two volumes and bound in leather."

"I'm too worried. By the looks of it, you two will be making bookplates for a long time to come." Simpkins smiled. "O.K., Miss Reilly," he said "take 'em down to the main branch and write 'em up."

Simpkins watched as the policewoman put the three-ring binders on them and led them away. He lit a cigarette and idly picked up a book. It was Butterflies of Angola. Damn, he thought, if it had been Crime and Punishment I could have said something really swell.

EXPANDING LIBRARY HORIZONS: THE SIGNIFICANCE FOR ACADEMIC LEARNING*

Robert Vosper

One of the magnificent but little known sagas of American history is the growth of our libraries. This is true of all manner of libraries, municipal libraries for the general reader and imaginative library services for children, as well as the libraries I will emphasize today, those that support scholarship and learning. The story of this unparalleled flourishing is a creative aspect of American institutional history that deserves to be more widely recognized, for it has been an essential component, or even proponent, of the flowering of American cultural and intellectual life, especially in the twentieth century.

Unhappily right at this moment, for reasons more political than statesmanlike, the present administration in Washington seems inclined to abandon to the scrap heap, or at least sharply to modify, the well-spring of federal support for library development that has been so influential and promising in recent years--just as is the case with many other social and educational programs that bear the taint of initiative under previous administrations. In the opinion of the ALA, present policy in Washington is "dimming the lights on the public's right to know."

In my opinion, however, the thrust of social need is so imperative, the recent nationally-oriented library development so logical, and the potential horizons for library growth and service so exciting that we face today merely a temporary roadblock in the way of an inevitable movement--

---

*Reprinted by permission from the July 1973 issue of PNLA Quarterly, pages 9-19. This article was originally "A University Lecture in honor of the retirement of Carl W. Hintz as Director of Libraries at the University of Oregon, May 24, 1973."

a temporary roadblock, that is, if we can rally concerted effort behind the forward movement. The library lights must not be dimmed.

All the more reason to recall, particularly for an academic audience of new voters, the significant library progress we have already made, to point out the remarkable opportunities within our grasp, and to state the case for libraries in urgent terms.

In 1853 at the first conference of American librarians the Rev. Samuel Osgood of the Providence Athenaeum remarked that not a single library in America, not even Harvard's, "affords the requisite means for the thorough study of any topic of recondite learning, even if of practical science. Any scholar who tries to investigate any ancient or historical subject will find, to his regret, that no library in the country has a plummet that can sound its depths."

That was in 1853, but as recently as 1919 (if I may call that recently--and for my purposes it is a very significant date), E. C. Richardson presented an important paper on "The Poverty of American Libraries in the Matter of Research Books." Dr. Richardson was no casual commentator, for that speech was made toward the end of a long and distinguished career as the librarian of Princeton University. He had been president of the American Library Association in 1905; he was a notable pioneer in national and even international library cooperation; and he was the promoter and co-editor of the initial volume, that for 1902, of the basic and still-continuing annual bibliographical series called <u>Writings on American History</u>. Thus, it was out of detailed experience that he made this damning statement in 1919: "Already in 1905 it had been for a good many years evident to research workers, and those who are charged with furnishing them the means of research, that our American libraries, in spite of their wonderful growth on the educational side ... were so deficient in research books as to make it a serious problem to the average college professor...." He went on to state that in the majority of lines of research it was necessary to go abroad to study in foreign libraries, and that this was true not just in the case of unique books and manuscripts but even in the case of standard reference and research books. This situation still held in 1919, Mr. Richardson said, as it had in 1905. But by 1919, with the ending of the great war in Europe, the problem had become a minor national scandal. Mr. Richardson's appraisal was supported, for example, by Yale's librarian, Andrew Keogh, who spoke of the "regrettable conditions of our scholarly libraries" with regard to the primary and secondary sources of research, the lack of "the unusual books in ordinary subjects and the best books in unusual subjects."

The meagerness of American library resources in those earlier days, and the dismay this engendered, are of course not surprising. On the one hand the reference point of comparison and envy was of course Western Europe, with its rich and ancient heritage of medieval monastic libraries, the princely library foundations of the Italian Renaissance, and the royal libraries of the seventeenth and eighteenth centuries. As the Rev. Osgood indicated in 1853, "we cannot expect soon to rival the great libraries of Europe." On the other hand the energizing forces behind the remarkable growth of research libraries in this country did not come into play until well into the present century; they were in fact just beginning when E. C. Richardson made his 1919 analysis.

One essential moving force, quite obviously, was the flourishing of graduate education and research, both academic and industrial, that metamorphosed American universities beginning in the 1940's. Another primary factor was the metamorphosis of several great private libraries into public institutions during the previous two decades, the 1920's and 1930's.

The powerful and steady growth of book collections in individual American university libraries, particularly during the mid-twentieth century, has been a major achievement in American educational history. It both matched and even fostered the ebullient and questing intellectual life of the universities themselves, and it has been a marvel to many foreign observers.

The Report of the Shackleton Committee on University Libraries at Oxford, issued in 1966, for example has this to say: "Oxford's library expenditure, large though it is in comparison with the expenditure of most other British universities, is still considerably less than the expenditure in a large number of American university libraries. A remarkable feature of American universities since the war has been the unfaltering growth of even the largest libraries. This can be seen both in the rate of book acquisition and in the rate of expenditure. Such comparisons are disheartening.

It is a national disgrace that British university libraries are so starved of money for books. Indeed it can be demonstrated that the present state of most university libraries constitutes emergency." Similar comments could well have come from any European country, excepting perhaps only Russia.

Outside observers are equally struck by the considerable numbers of American university libraries that, in a relatively short lifetime, have achieved high levels of distinction and vitality. This phenomenon of rapid numerical growth in holdings as well as qualitative growth in breadth and depth is exemplified particularly in such eminent state universities as Illinois, Michigan, Berkeley, and Cornell, since except for Michigan they, like the Northwest, are barely a century old. Thus they confirm the ambitious commitment of a pioneering American society to a new view of higher education as being tax supported, and thereby broadly available to aspiring young people, and as being devoted at once to traditional academic excellence as well as to the unique new conceptions of the Morrill Act of 1862.

Not only does each of these libraries today have total collections rapidly exceeding the three and four million volume range (by way of the annual intake of well over 150,000 volumes and the regular receipt of 35,000 or more journals), but all are unquestionably judged by scholars here and abroad to be qualitatively among the greatest research libraries of the world and of high distinction in a wide range of disciplines (historical ones as well as those concerned with contemporary scientific and social problems). The university libraries mentioned above are nearly equalled in these levels of excellence by a number of others, including Indiana, Minnesota, UCLA, and Wisconsin.

Berkeley's East Asiatic Library is one of the greatest of its kind in the world. The collections of original works in the history of science at Wisconsin and Cornell are exceeded no doubt by those of Harvard, but hardly matched elsewhere. Perhaps nowhere else, not even in Great Britain, would a scholar find in one place so rich a Milton collection as at Illinois or so extensive a collection of nineteenth-century English fiction as at UCLA. Indiana's Lilly Library, Berkeley's Bancroft, Michigan's Clements, and UCLA's Clark are all, in their fields of concentration, probably non pareil.

These are but examples of peaks of highest eminence which come readily to mind; an inventory would reveal many others. But the striking thing about these great modern state university libraries is the diverse and extensive range of disciplines in which each library supports research with impressive collections as well as lively services. In this wide-ranging and optimistic approach to knowledge these university libraries, of course, have reflected, interacted with, and even at times stimulated their parent universities, which have been of an omnibus intellectual style that hardly exists outside this country and Canada. Each year hundreds of Ph.D. candidates in scores of fields find in their own institutions a sufficiency of published material, and even manuscripts, to support their dissertations. In each of these libraries large numbers of the world's greatest scholars, including émigrés and visitors from all over the world, can conduct seminars and pursue research, often in highly abstruse areas of knowledge, with but occasional or tangential reference to other libraries. The frame of reference is virtually unlimited as to historical time, language, or geography. Each of these libraries is indeed a phenomenal institution when viewed in the setting of world cultural history.

This dramatic growth in size and quality of individual university libraries, has, of course, been the result of an optimistic, even aggressive--and some would go so far as to say "piratical"--approach to collection building on the part of both scholars and librarians. Book selection has generally been on a wholesale and opportunistic basis, rather than proceeding from classical selection policies or criteria involving a precise evaluation of the worth of each book. As J. P. Danton pointed out in his <u>Book Selection and Collections</u>, an illuminating comparison of German and American university library practices, this American style of collection building is in full contrast with long-standing tradition of academic librarianship in Germany as well as other parts of Europe. Whereas the American style has been gross and accumulative, the German style has been carefully designed and engineered to assure a rigorous review of the fundamental scholarly importance of each book added to the collections. One could perhaps relate this sharp difference in professional style to certain obvious national characteristics, but more particular factors can be suggested.

American universities themselves have until recently operated within a competitive laissez-faire system wherein distinguished faculty members have been attracted from one

institution to another by higher salaries and also by promises
of forcefully developed book collections. One recognized
measure of prestige among universities has been this very
matter of aggresive library growth; thus when the American
Council on Education issued Allan Cartter's An Assessment
of Quality in Graduate Education in 1966, there was included
a careful rating of libraries--with particular attention to
total size of collections and the richness of the current intake of both books and journals--because "no other single
non-human factor is as closely related to the quality of
graduate education."

The American tradition of libraries and of education
in general, including higher education, has emphasized the
values inherent in local control and autonomy rather than
centralized direction or pattern setting through a system of
strong national ministries, as in Europe, or even such a
moderating body as the British University Grants Committee.
The strength of this open American system, if it can be
called a system, has been in terms of diversity and variety
as well as in the encouragement for change, experimentation,
and growth that is fostered by competition. Yet the evidence
of wastefulness and low capacity for long-term planning has
been sufficient in these recent years to force a noticeable
shift, for both higher education and libraries in general,
toward greater national and state participation in both planning and financing.

Economics has assuredly been another factor in the
American style of collection building, for until quite recently
and earlier during the Great Depression years, American
academic librarians have operated in a bullish economy, assuming and arguing for continually expanding book funds.
Universities themselves have proceeded on the assumption
of a steadily increasing public and private investment in
higher education. Only very recently have these assumptions been seriously questioned, and only very recently has
it been generally argued that the federal government must
bear a larger and larger share of the costs of education and
of libraries, with all the hazards of control and interference
that this may involve. To be sure the present administration is pointing the finger of responsibility at the states, but
I am certain that the argument for federal support will continue hot and heavy.

The very style of scholarship in American universities has also been a significant factor in the style of li-

brary collection building. In contrast with the British experience, which until quite recently has given relatively little attention to research or to graduate (doctoral) and professional education, American universities for the past century, and with a powerful impetus in the years following the Second World War, have greatly emphasized these activities. The emphasis has occurred, moreover, in large numbers of institutions serving extensive populations of faculty and graduate students, as well as research workers in industry and government. The consequent pressure for mushrooming library collections has been great. Another influential aspect of American scholarship, alluded to earlier, has been the long-standing concern with the newer disciplines and particularly the social sciences, including the social aspects of historical and literary studies. For at least two generations, for example, American historians have wanted ready access to newspaper files and ephemeral publications as bodies of evidence, and literary scholars have wanted access to "popular" literature as well as to classical landmarks. All of this has been, at least until quite recently, in contrast with the European and British traditions of respectable scholarship and library collecting policy.

Moreover, American academic librarians have been led to build their own self-sufficient local collections with relatively little attention to the availability of resources elsewhere because of the very difficulty in this extensive country of assuring their scholars that books essential to research work can in fact be secured quickly and precisely from another source. This is partly the consequence of the size of the country and the very large population of users; it is also the consequence of inadequate tools and mechanisms for assured external access. In Germany, by contrast, the system of regional union catalogs and interlibrary lending for academic users has been remarkably efficient. And in so small a country as Great Britain, a central lending library for scientific and technical journals has been able to operate speedily and effectively.

In response then to these several stimuli, American university librarians have pursued a course of collection building that can fairly be described as imaginative and resourceful, often imprudent and risk taking, and remarkably successful. All told, as an episode in bibliothecal history this experience can be compared with the widespread Renaissance search for manuscripts and the development of the great princely libraries in Italy. Moreover, many of the forceful collecting methods and attitudes of university librarians in the mid-twentieth century parallel those of the great private collectors of the nineteenth and early twentieth centuries.

From among the roster of American private collectors who applied nineteenth-century entrepreneurial wealth and entrepreneurial bravura to book collecting, I would remind you particularly of J. P. Morgan, Henry E. Huntington, William L. Clements, Henry Clay Folger, and William Andrews Clark, Jr. Not only did they match and even overreach the earlier book and manuscript ingathering of European princely and royal families, but they converted their private hobbies into well-endowed public research institutions. Thus they were a major factor in turning the tide of library development in the United States. The Henry E. Huntington Library was created in New York by deed of trust in 1919 (the very year of E. C. Richardson's desperate speech) and opened to the public in the magnificent new building at San Marino a few years later; the Clements Library was opened at the University of Michigan in 1923; the Morgan Library was chartered as a public institution in New York City in 1924; William Andrews Clark, Jr. declared his intention in 1926 to bequeath his library to UCLA and the estate transfer, including a new library building and an endowment, was effected in 1934; and the Folger Shakespeare Library was founded in Washington in 1932. With these names can be linked that of J. K. Lilly, Jr., who turned his superb library over to the University of Indiana as recently as 1966. But it was in the brief span of the 1920's and early 1930's that this major aspect of American research librarianship, as we now know it, burst into flower.

As Dr. Louis B. Wright, distinguished American historian and emeritus director of the Folger Library has indicated, "No other nation has seen such a rapid proliferation of research libraries which are the enterprise of dedicated and intelligent book collectors who have utilized their interests, knowledge, and money for the public good;... Nowhere else in modern times has such a development occurred."

Thus in the relatively short period of the half century since the 1920's, between the energy of university libraries and the generosity of private collectors, the tide of library events shifted from Great Britain and Western Europe to the United States. And the further point to be

noted here is that this library development was a major
factor in shifting the center of scholarship from Europe to
this country.

Yet despite this great flourishing, the research collections of American libraries have by no means kept pace with either the expectations of their users or the ambitions of their librarians. Both have been outpaced by economic inflation as well as inflation in the publishing and information market--that is, by the steady increase throughout the world in the amount and variety of significant publications and other types of information stores. Harvard's librarian was obliged to report in the early 1960's that with 7,000,000 volumes the Harvard Library was more frequently reminded of its inadequacies than it had been sixty years earlier when it had only 1,000,000.

In fact, thoughtful academic librarians, as well as the directors of the great national libraries of the world, have long realized that the concept of the self-sufficient and all-encompassing library is only a myth. Faced with this realization of inadequacy the American research library community has forcefully undertaken a number of large-scale, voluntary joint actions that would supplement the capabilities of individual libraries, particularly through national programs, and thus enhance overall service to scholarship. Princeton's E. C. Richardson early in this century foresaw the need and suggested generally some of the necessary structures, but practical, large-scale voluntary efforts in behalf of national book collecting needs were fostered especially toward the end of, and following on, the Second World War. They were developed then in parallel with the great period of growth for individual libraries that has already been mentioned. In fact, that War, with the consequent blockade of European libraries and book distribution sources, shocked the librarians and scholars of this country into action.

At least as early as the 1920's American library leaders had proposed the ideal of "providing somewhere, somehow, in American libraries, at least one copy of every book that may be needed for research." This ideal was finally adopted as a necessary and practical goal by the Association of Research Libraries in the mid-1940's, when it devised a massive cooperative effort, known as the Farmington Plan, to bring currently published European books into this country and distribute them among American research libraries on a subject specialization basis. This cooperative approach at the national level was given particular emphasis and meaning through a crucial statement in 1945 by Archibald MacLeish, then Assistant Secretary of State and formerly the Librarian of Congress, "that the national interest is affected" by the collective holdings of American research libraries. That generous statement opened up a new era of American academic librarianship and set a tone that was heard with increasing clarity over the subsequent years, and with a great crescendo in 1965.

During the 1950's it became increasingly clear that this goal of bringing into the country an adequate selection of current foreign books, as well as certain other library goals then aspired to, could not be reached by voluntary local efforts alone. Thus the MacLeish doctrine of "the national interest" was invoked during the Johnson Administration to bring the federal government into a significant partnership role in the development of a genuine national library program in this country. 1965 saw the enactment of an impressive package of federal laws providing financial support for public library services, elementary and secondary school libraries, medical libraries, and college libraries. The intention was both to improve the general level of quality and to equalize library services throughout the country.

Imbedded in the Higher Education Act of 1965 was a seemingly modest and technical provision entitled Title II-C, which provided the Library of Congress with authorization and funding for: "(1) acquiring, so far as possible, all library materials currently published throughout the world which are of value to scholarship; and (2) providing catalog information for these materials promptly after receipt and distributing bibliographic information by printing cards and other means." It might be noted that another Princeton University librarian, William S. Dix, was a key figure in the promotion of that legislation.

Here then the dream of the 1920's and the aspirations for the voluntary Farmington Plan of the 1940's were finally established as a truly national effort, now called the National Program for Acquisitions and Cataloging. The speed and precision with which the Library of Congress put into action this intricate, global program deserves forthright praise. It is now fully operative for most of the countries of Eastern and Western Europe, Great Britain, Canada, Australia, New Zealand and Japan. Through regional acquisitions offices in East Africa, Southeast Asia, and Latin America a beginning program is under way in these areas. Since June 1966 over 500,000 new titles have been handled by the new shared cataloging procedures. The Congress is being asked in the present session to extend funding and thus coverage to other countries in the coming years. Unhappily though, I must report to this audience that Oregon's distinguished Congresswoman is thwarting this effort because of self-serving pressure from a local commercial firm. I venture to suggest that both parties to this mean effort stand thereby to lessen their public reputations.

An important additional element in Title II-C, beyond the rapid procurement of currently published foreign books, is that little requirement for providing prompt bibliographical information to any interested library about these newly acquired books. Behind this apparently technical library function is a powerful instrument of information control as well as economy of effort.

Librarians and scholars since the earliest days of printed books have dreamed of, and several times abortively attempted, a world-wide record of currently published books. By way of Title II-C and an operative mechanism called "shared cataloging" the Library of Congress quite unexpectedly, and almost without design, provided a modern key to unlocking that age-old problem. It works something like this. American academic librarians had included the prompt cataloging element in Title II-C so that the expensive intellectual and technical task of clearly identifying new books in a multiplicity of languages could be done once and for all, for any library, thereby reducing to a considerable degree the wasteful duplication of effort we have all been engaged in by way of separately cataloging and re-cataloging the same book. In order to secure that essential bibliographical information quickly for new foreign books, the Library of Congress took the significant step of entering into contracts and treaties with national libraries abroad, or similar bodies, to provide the information about their own national publishing output, that is in "shared cataloging." This multinational flow of up-to-date bibliographical information was then to be coordinated by, and made available from, the Library of Congress.

The fortuitous capabilities of computerization gave an added dimension to the program. The Library of Congress undertook to store and transmit the accumulated information not just by way of printed catalog cards but also by way of

computer tapes, using a programming format (MARC) that is
rapidly being adopted as an international standard by many
foreign countries. This happy congruence of technical innovation, intended originally just to serve the needs and efficiencies of American libraries, was quickly seen by librarians elsewhere as a remarkable opportunity for international
collaboration.

In 1966 at an international library meeting in The
Hague, the director of the British Museum, Sir Frank
Francis, stated with something other than British understatement, "when I first discussed with the Librarian of
Congress and his colleagues just twelve months ago, their
proposals for adopting a system of shared cataloging (on a
truly international scale) to enable them to meet the new
assignment laid on them by the United States Congress, I
was electrified by the prospect which this new development
opened up. I felt we were at last on the edge of the most
important breakthrough in the realm of information."

The effort still proceeds at that same level of international enthusiasm. A colleague of mine has just returned
from a conference in Bogotá that will foster congruent
multi-national Latin American participation in this shared
cataloging and distribution effort. At a time when United
States relationships with many Latin American countries are
less than cordial, this Bogotá proposal has symbolic as
well as practical importance. It suggests that intellectual
collaboration is still feasible in a multi-lingual and multi-political world, and it suggests, moreover, that librarianship is a truly international profession. We have long assumed this to be true, but the power of the idea and the
mechanism of Title II-C is giving added reality to the belief.

It is of more than passing interest that today librarians in the newer and developing countries of the world--Africa, Southeast Asia, the Caribbean, and Latin America--are
eagerly vocal about the need for international collaboration
and mutual library support. Early in December 1972, as
the culminating program in the United States observance of
1972 as International Book Year, a group of influential economists, government planning officials, educators, publishers,
and librarians were brought together at the Mohonk Conference Center outside New York City, to "assess the role
of books and other educational materials in both educational
and economic development." These representatives from
Colombia, Brazil, England, France, Indonesia, Thailand,

Libraries and Librarians 53

USSR, Ghana, Nigeria, and Argentina agreed that "an essential part of the total educational resources of any country is a library program which can motivate, and make possible, life-long learning on the part of every individual." A leading participant, Chief S. O. Adebo of Nigeria particularly expressed the hope that the necessary "advice and guidance" would be made available to any interested country. He spoke against the background of the developing countries, "where hundreds of millions of literates have no meaningful access to books or libraries and 900,000,000 persons are illiterate altogether--a number that is growing, not diminishing."

Thus far this evening I have emphasized particularly the expanding horizons, nationally and internationally, of university and research libraries in the service of academic learning, but the Mohonk statement about basic book and library needs in developing countries--a statement that is destined, I am confident, to be a landmark in modern library history--has meaning for us in the United States as well, for we have our own underdeveloped areas and problems of literacy. So let me take a few moments now to just suggest some other library and learning horizons that we can lift our eyes to.

A few months ago an official of the Department of Health, Education and Welfare stated that the Nixon Administration had lost confidence in public libraries because they had done nothing useful for the underprivileged groups in American society. My interpretation is that the statement represents just one more rationalization on the part of the administration in its decision to jettison any program touched with the imagination of the Great Society. Let me just mention two recent reports about library service in one of the more notoriously underprivileged parts of this country, the Watts district of Los Angeles.

Last December the Los Angeles Times carried a feature story about a seventeen-year-old black youngster named Stanley Houseton, a senior at Crenshaw High School, who had produced a startling short documentary, "The Gang Story," about the desperate teen-age street life in that black community. The son of an impoverished divorcee who had put herself through nursing school, young Houseton made the film with $200 he had earned selling hamburgers at a drive-in, and he learned his craft from library books. "If I'd run into problems," he said, "I'd go back to the books."

Stanley Houseton is clearly no average youngster in any society, but his library experience is probably not unique. Recently Barbara Clark, the energetic and articulate senior librarian in charge of the Watts Branch of the Los Angeles Public Library was given one of four City Employee Service Awards by her fellow city workers for her imaginative and successful efforts to make that library a lively community center for children, young people, and adults. Mrs. Clark had started her own library career as a trainee, and then she worked her way through professional school, with time out to have a daughter. All of her local library program required imagination, and not all of it required special funding--for example, tricycle races for preschoolers, a guinea pig under a table of children's books, and crochet classes for grandmothers--but she was materially helped along by extra federal funds provided under the Library Services Act, which is now being phased out by Washington.

American public libraries have a long, honorable record of providing this kind of stimulation and encouragement for underprivileged people, young and old. At quite another extreme in American society, Mr. Elmer Holmes Bobst recently financed the spacious new library building of New York University with an $11 million gift, because, said he, "I am paying off a life-long debt to libraries." Mr. Bobst claims he got his education "with books borrowed from local libraries."

In these days of experimental, non-traditional, self-paced, and out-of-school education, the public library is a key institution ready to hand. Public libraries were considered "the people's universities" in the nineteenth century and were central to the mechanics institute movement of an earlier day. It is both understandable and heartening therefore that the College Entrance Examination Board, sponsored by the Council on Library Resources, the National Endowment for the Humanities, and the U.S. Office of Education, has just established the Office of Library Independent Study and Guidance Projects. The purpose is to assist public libraries in extending their capacities as "people's universities," as dynamic community learning centers providing planned independent learning experiences for adults. In Dallas, for example, credit arrangements are being worked out with local colleges for "open university" work in the public library. Long before today's college students began talking idealistically about "experimental colleges" and "free universities," the open-access public library was affording precisely this kind of life-long learning opportunity for self-propelled individuals and groups, outside the structured formality of the regular school system. If the potentials of two-way cable TV are properly developed in the public interest and linked to libraries as information and learning centers, providing a kind of public information utility, the functions of "the people's university" can be multiplied tremendously.

As I said at the beginning, it is shocking that the present administration seems inclined to withdraw its encouragement and support just as these heartening new learning horizons come into view for academic libraries as well as for public libraries. But we should not despair. We still have the impetus of social need and potential before us. Moreover, as an enduring bequest of the 1965 Great Society legislation, we now have for the first time in this country a National Commission on Libraries and Information Science. Librarians had long seen the need for some body of organized intelligence that could speak authoritatively to government and to the public about the library needs of the country and give guidance and planning effort to the work ahead. The Commission, fortunately chaired by the American Council of Learned Societies, who is a kind of missionary in behalf of libraries, has just finished its first year of investigation. One can hope that the Commission will help keep our national sights on the right horizons. But if the library lights are not to be dimmed in this country, we will particularly need the open support of users and friends of libraries, such as yourselves.

Archibald MacLeish, the senior American poet and senior American librarian, declared in a 1972 essay that would seem to reply to the political and mechanistic critics of libraries:

> No, it is not the library, I think, that has become ridiculous by standing there against the dark with its books in order on its shelves. On the contrary the library, almost alone of the great monuments of civilization, stands taller now than it ever did before. The city--our American city at least--decays. The nation loses its grandeur, becomes what we call a 'power,' a Pentagon, a store of missiles. The university is no longer always certain of what it is. But the library remains: a

silent and enduring affirmation....

I trust that you and the other friends of the library will be vocal in its behalf.

HOW I GOT MY LIBRARY JOB GOOD*

Joseph McDonald

When I first thought of offering my experiences for publication, I conceived an expanded Jack Anderson-type exposé on the library flesh market of 1972. Visions of trustees and vice presidents and deans and selection committees dangling helplessly at the end of my skillfully wielded rapier tipped with a potent venom of satire and ridicule flowed through my head with such regularity that they sustained me in those dark hours when no jobs were offered and prayer, that crutch for the weak and hope for the strong, eluded my convulsed and dying faith.

Then I received a job offer, and I figured, what the hell, things are not too bad after all. Well, that is not quite true. Anyone who has recently looked for a job or is now doing so can testify, with a spat on the ground and blue invective, that things are damned bad. No, it is true, things are not as bad as they are for teachers. (I am told, reliably, that there are 3000 applications for 11 vacancies in the West Chester, Pennsylvania, Area School District.) But that is little consolation for the experienced librarian and absolutely none whatsoever for the new graduate faced with finding a decent job.

A lecture on the reasons for this discouraging state of affairs lies beyond the scope of this article. Instead, I propose here to deal with job-hunting existentially. And more specifically, to generalize from my recent soul-shaking experience in the field (swamp is more appropriate) trying to bag a job. Not just any job, mind you, but one that

---

*Reprinted by permission from the February 1, 1973 issue of Library Journal (pages 388-390), published by R. R. Bowker Co., a Xerox Education Company. Copyright © 1973 by Xerox Corporation.

met what I expected in a (as library school placement folks say) professional appointment. I hope this will help fellow hunters, if not to land a job (pardon the mixed metaphor), at least to stalk in the right places and to use the proper ammunition. I should add, my remarks are made with experienced librarians in mind. I can offer nothing for new librarians except what may be extrapolated from my findings. When a cataloging position was announced recently in a prestigious suburban Philadelphia community college, the hundreds of applicants ranged from directors who had finally achieved their Peter Principle level of incompetency to newly minted library journeymen (journeypersons?). A new graduate was appointed.

Ideally, the last task in job hunting is a letter of resignation. This is usually an intellectual endeavor analogous to a Roman legionnaire marching into Podunkum or Vespa or somewhere with his long-haired, blue-eyed slaves clanking behind him. Done correctly, a resignation letter subtly informs a supervisor just how stupid he was to have allowed things to have come to this pass. It also announces triumphantly that one will from henceforth be employed by the best possible of all employers in the best part of the world at the best possible salary. If it can be done with a straight face, it is good to replace "with regret" with the more poignant "with sorrow"; or if one subscribes to the correspondence theory of truth, one, perhaps should say, "It is with considerable pleasure that I ... etc."

Unfortunately, regardless of how well we brush our teeth and shine our shoes, it is not granted to all of us to savor the sweetness of revenge a properly written notice of resignation can provide. For some of us (many of us?) job hunting begins somewhat abruptly when we are (why mince words?) fired. This is known variously as a demand for resignation, a nonrenewal of contract, a dismissal, or for the more circumlocutious deans, a discontinuation. This condition has the unfortunate tendency to alter one's hormonal balance, which in turn can create odd desires such as a craving for prostitutes or, in the other sex, a need for pickled cauliflower at breakfast.

There is a third category of library job-seeker: the stupid one. And, alas! I must so label myself. This person says, "My God! I cannot stand this job any more. I was hired to file addenda to loose-leaf services and, behold! here I am organizing students' term papers. I must leave forthwith or my professional sensibilities will be blunted beyond recognition." Accordingly, he writes a resignation letter ("selling life insurance is preferable to continuing in a position where my best efforts are not encouraged and where I cannot contribute to the fullest extent of my ability") and casts about for a job; eventually, any job.

I did all this well before my contract expired, vainly assuming I would find a suitable job in a month or so and could leave my somewhat traitorous institution high and dry for a while by demanding an early release from the contract.

But it did not work that way, and I also hazard to guess it will not for anyone else. Especially for one who has definite ideas of what he wants to do. The hirers are not begging any more; which means the hirees must scratch and plead or go sell Volvos in Parsippany.

Résumés, finding the openings, gaining an interview, and signing the blessed contract are the necessary ingredients for job-hunting fulfillment. A lot of pious nonsense has been written about the whole process, somewhat in the same spirit as a library administration textbook. Actually, library job-hunting is like fish reproduction. Many eggs are spawned, somewhat fewer are fertilized, even fewer hatch, even fewer fish yet survive into maturity.

The résumé is critical, unless your committeeman is willing to pull strings for you. Ideally, the best résumé is one written specifically for a given vacancy. But except for a few choice positions, the effort involved in this is not rewarded commensurately. But care must be taken in duplicating the résumé. A sloppy photocopying job, and you are in the wastebasket. I have so treated many applications when I had occasion to squeeze the tomatoes. Printing is cheap; or, if you have unlogged access to a photocopying machine and are willing to fiddle with the settings, a photocopy can be made to appear typewritten, especially if you substitute decent bond paper for the traditional copy paper. It is worth the effort.

There are enough how-to-do-it résumé books around to check for style and format. A one-page document is ideal, but an uncluttered two- or three-page offering is usually received with favor. My résumé is five pages, and I suspect frequently deters otherwise interested employers. All of which leads to content.

Ideally, again, a résumé's contents will reveal an orderly progression from lowest job to the current one (or vice-versa, it really does not matter). Each position will entail greater responsibility, and the position for which you are applying will appear to be the next logical step. Furthermore, it is a decided asset if you are white, male (for good jobs), between 25 and 35 years old, married with two children, have written for the professional press, hold office in a library association, and belong to the Kiwanis or Jaycees.

If you are black or female or both or gay or divorced or an active SRR Tabler or in any other way controversial, things can be quite difficult. My slight involvement with the SRRT in its early days (and tacked on to the résumé for effect) cost me at least one interview that I know of in the South.

Solution? A résumé should emphasize professional and related activities and de-emphasize those activities that might raise hackles. If you plan nationwide coverage, it might be good to write regional editions of your résumé. In other words, tell them what they want to hear (manipulate) in simple concise language. Summarize. State that you are a member of various ALA committees rather than listing your involvement with the subcommittee on dental hygiene materials of the Committee on Dental Materials Resources of the Medical Studies Materials Section of the Human Anatomy Division of the Biological Sciences Consortium, etc. A résumé is for effect. It is the copy on the package of what you are selling--you.

Including referees (this British and Commonwealth expression immediately classes you among the drinkers of Grant's) on your résumé saves time and trouble and is appreciated by the prospective employer. Referees must be chosen with care. A poor referral, and the boss moves on to the well-referred candidate. If at all possible, include a well-known name or two. Library directors are very impressed by those who have made it. But it is wise to make absolutely sure your referees will write good references. And be sure that includes the inevitable phone call between referee and prospective employer. If you have had a bad experience with a possible referee, never, never, use that person, regardless of how well you think things were patched up or smoothed over.

Libraries and Librarians 61

Where does one find jobs? I should emphasize, find jobs. Sowing your résumés to the wind is largely wasted effort. The have-you-got-anything request invariably brings a nonresponse no. The same, I suspect (sorry LJ), goes for advertising your availability. It is expensive, and after nine years in library work, I have yet to see anyone find work that way. If someone has, I would be delighted to hear from him.

Ads in the literature and in the New York Times, placement office files, and word-of-mouth are traditional ways to find employment. But it still remains a constant that the best jobs are rarely advertised. And it is also discouragingly true that these days employers do not have to go looking for candidates. Furthermore, well advertised positions will be ones for which there is fierce competition: cat and dog type.

The best sources for jobs are the major professional journals (including some state publications and Canada's Feliciter), word-of-mouth from friends and contacts, and well-run library school placement offices. The New York Times library ads can generally be ignored these days. They either duplicate what is otherwise advertised or else want someone who can type, keep files, and show a lot of leg. Sometimes, buried in the teacher ads, there will appear notices of vacancies for "media utilization advisors" (reference librarian for those outside of Bergen County, New Jersey) or learning resources consultants or some such. Generally these seem to be ads placed by community colleges requiring, in addition to an M.L.S., an M.Ed. in media and an all-but-dissertation doctorate in curriculum development. Usually these are jobs reserved for minority group candidates under some kind of a quota system.

Once a decision is taken to apply for a certain position, it is good to remit with the résumé a cover letter indicating your desire for that job and that job only. (This assumes a well-copied résumé.) "I have long sought for a position where I may use my talent for the benefit of northern Maine potato farmers. As a pre-cataloging searcher in the Caribou Junior and Technical Institute, I know (that's important, never say think or believe) I can fulfill my dream of service to these hardy people ... etc." Employers are impressed if they suspect you are happily employed and looking for that just-right position.

Today, getting a job, as crass as it may seem, is a game. Very infrequently does one find and get appointed to "the" job. If you assume a potential employer is a bibliothecal Machiavelli and can anticipate his moves, your chances of getting the job are considerably improved. Mutual trust and respect rarely exist, and it's best to assume it does not, unless you have all the time in the world and are very fussy about what job you will take--a luxury the economy does not now encourage.

Responses to an application range from nothing to an invitation for an interview. With depressing regularity, they are the former. I had both time and the requisite experience to be selective, but out of 45 applications, I received only four interview invitations and discovered the job I now hold (one of those rare exactly-what-you-want-types) while being interviewed for another position. According to friends, colleagues, and card-carrying fellow-travellers, mine was an unusually productive experience. Ah, for the good ole days when they came after you, begging!

An invitation for an interview is a sign that someone thinks you might have what they want. Depending on the institution, diminishing recruitment-travel funds means fewer interviews. Accordingly, an interview must be well-orchestrated for full effect. It is, again, depressingly true that the boy-scout male-chauvinist syndrome afflicts many prospective employers. Top jobs seem to go to clean-cut dependable males. ("You will be pleased to know, Mr. McDonald, that you are one of three men being given serious consideration for this position.") Furthermore, discreetly sexy females (if my observations are correct) come off far better in interviews than any other type. By sexy I mean more than just visual impact. I also mean maintaining an appropriately you-are-desirable-but-look-at-my-good-manners rapport with the male interviewer. An honest, straightforward, clear-thinking, true-to-herself woman will be resented because she is neither male nor "feminine."

Most boards, deans, presidents, interviewing committees, and other sundry undesirables are notoriously inept at interviewing. This, if handled skillfully, can be turned to the interviewee's advantage. You must appear to be in command and convey the impression (subtly, of course) that you are conferring an honor on the interviewer by consenting to be questioned. After all, he is interested in you, and playing ever so slightly hard-to-get relieves the interviewer of his anxieties concerning the reasons you might have for wanting the job he is dangling in front of you.

Assuming you know your level (librarians do not normally go from Cataloger I to California State Librarian), have properly girded your loins, have respectable résumé (it does not really matter that <u>you</u> are not respectable, but your résumé must be), are clean-shaven if male (or female), don't care about geography, and have at least five years of experience, you should be able to land a job--some job--in approximately five months. Other factors reduce the time (big name, qualifying for racial or sexist quotas), and others increase it (little experience, wrong color, geographical preference, or wrong sex; both ways, eh, what, Goddard!?).

But in that great big final analysis in the sky, when all library employers are made to spill the beans, toilers in the vineyards of man's recorded experience will discover what they always suspected: it really pays to know your committeeman.

THE CHANGING ROLE OF DIRECTORS OF UNIVERSITY LIBRARIES*

Arthur M. McAnally
Robert B. Downs

Traditionally the directorship of a major university library has been a lifetime post. Once a librarian achieved such a position of honor and leadership in the profession, he usually stayed until he reached retirement age. In the 1960s, however, an increasing number of incidents occurred which indicated that all was not well in the library directors' world, resulting in a vague feeling of uneasiness. Then in one year, 1971-72, the seriousness of the situation became dramatically evident: seven of the directors of the Big Ten university libraries (plus the University of Chicago) left their posts, only one a normal retirement for age. These are major universities on the national scene whose directorships had been stable in the past.

To discover how widespread this condition might be, an investigation has been undertaken among the seventy-eight largest university libraries--members of the Association of Research Libraries. Exactly one-half of the directors were found to have changed within the past three years, four of them twice. This is an extraordinarily high rate of change. If such a rate were to continue, the average span of service for directors would be five to six years. Next, to find out if the development was related to size of the library, those university libraries holding more than 2,000,000 volumes were compared with the twenty smallest libraries in the association. Size apparently has some bearing, but does not appear to be a major factor: while 60 percent of the larger libraries had changed directors, 45 percent of the smaller

---

*Reprinted by permission from the March 1973 issue of College & Research Libraries, pages 103-125. Mr. McAnally died unexpectedly shortly after completing this article.

ones did, too. The authors are well aware that the directors of libraries in many small universities--as well as those in intermediate and large institutions--are in severe difficulty or under intense pressure. Oddly, the chief librarians of colleges and junior colleges do not appear to be affected. The problem seems to be limited to university librarians only.

Several explanations of the phenomenon have been offered. Edward G. Holley observed the trend during visits to a number of urban university libraries in 1971: "At the end of the sixties it has not been uncommon for chief librarians, who by any objective standards served their institutions well, to retire early from their directorships, some with sorrow, some with relief and a few with bitterness. Very few have retired with the glory and honor that used to accompany extraordinary accomplishments in building resources and expanding services."[1] Holley attributed the condition partly to changing attitudes of the library staffs. On the other hand, Raynard C. Swank questioned whether many directors really had retired in great favor in the past. He also suggested that the present high rate of change might be due partly to a large number of directors who were appointed some thirty years ago all nearing retirement age about the same time.[2] Others believe that the problem reflects a highly critical attitude towards the university library itself rather than just criticism of the directors. Still others conclude that an era is ending and old ways are having to give way to new: those who will not or cannot adapt are finished. The suggestion also was made that a few of the changes might be attributable to weaknesses among the directors. Though each of these explanations may have some validity, the full story is far more complicated.

Directors who have recently quit their jobs should be authoritative spokesmen on the subject. The authors corresponded or discussed the subject, therefore, with twenty-two directors or former directors whom they knew well personally.[3] Each was asked for his opinions about the causes of the extraordinary turnover in directorships and to suggest possible remedies. Every one replied, and many gave keen analyses of the causes as well as suggesting steps that should be taken.

BACKGROUND FACTORS

The numerous changes in directorships indicate that

some fundamental dissatisfactions have arisen within university libraries or their environment in recent years. The underlying causes may be deep-seated and varied. Thus the director might be under fire, as he unquestionably is, because he is the most visible representative of an agency that is under attack, the university library itself. Therefore, recent trends in society and the university were examined, as well as movements in university administration, the world of scholarship and research, and the publishing and information world, as well as the university library itself.

Growth of enrollment. The extraordinary growth in enrollments in higher education during the decade of the sixties forced the university itself to make many changes to attempt to cope with the flood of students. Total enrollments grew from almost four million to approximately eight million. The number of graduate students tripled, from 314,000 to more than 900,000. The tremendous increase produced changes in the university far beyond merely making it larger. It became a far more complicated institution.[4]

University expansion began long before the sixties, of course. Probable effects upon the university library were noted in 1958 by Donald Coney, and the title of his article is prophetic: "Where Did You Go? To the Library. What Did You Get? Nothing."[5] Except for the creation of undergraduate libraries in some of the larger universities beginning at Harvard in 1948, few changes were made to cope with the rising flood. Most universities remained oriented basically to the single-copy research concept.

Changes in the presidency. Growth in size of the institution placed great pressure upon the president, and other factors added to his problems: rising expectations, growing militancy of students and faculty, disillusionment and a newly critical attitude towards higher education on the part of the general public that developed as a result of student activism, political pressure from hostile legislators or governors, growing powers exerted by state boards of control, and, to cap it all, financial support that began to decline or at least levelled out. Harried from all sides, forced to act often on bases of emergency or expediency, and with little time left for academic affairs, the position of the president has become almost untenable.

It is not surprising that the average tenure of univer-

sity presidents in the United States is now a short five
years. Chancellor Murphy of UCLA stated that the office of
president or chancellor has become impossible, and suggested a maximum term of ten years. He observed that
"The chief executive of an institution makes his greatest
creative impacts in the first five to eight years. He may
need a few more years to follow through in the implementation of these creative impacts. Beyond that, however, the
housekeeping function inevitably becomes larger, and much
of the vitality, drive, and creativity declines."[6] President
Lyman of Stanford noted that directors of libraries appeared
to be in the same situation as presidents. Herman H. Fussler added that the tenure of all senior university administrators--not only presidents but also vice-presidents and deans--
had declined considerably in recent years. He asked, why
should librarians expect to be different?[7] Booz, Allen &
Hamilton predicted that term appointments for presidents
might become common, and that even peer election could
come in the late seventies.[8]

Proliferation in university management. To cope
with the greatly intensified pressures on the president, and
in the belief that universities were undermanaged, nearly
every university in the country has added substantially to its
central management staff. The most striking increase has
been in the number of vice-presidents.

The proliferation of vice-presidents was noted and
commented on by several directors: Lewis C. Branscomb,
Thomas R. Buckman, Richard N. Logsdon, Robert Miller,
and Edward B. Stanford. All observed that this movement
has had the effect of interposing a layer of administrative
officers between the chief librarian and the president. The
director no longer has direct access to the president; thus
the role of the library in the university and the power of
the library to present its case has been reduced. Logsdon
commented that unfortunately the presidents rarely have
utilized existing administrators, such as directors of libraries, who have a broad overview of the university, to
help with the growing burden of general administrative affairs.[9]

Changes in the world of learning and research. Several factors beyond the obvious one of expansion of existing
graduate programs and establishment of new programs have
affected the university and its library. A major instance is
the continued fragmentation of traditional academic disciplines.

New specializations continue to break off from older fields; each, of course, smaller than the original. One authority has referred to the trend as "the Balkanization" of learning.[10] Another movement of the sixties which is having a major impact on libraries is the emergence of interdisciplinary programs, including area studies. New social concerns and the demands for relevance also foster the growth of interdisciplinary institutes and other irregular patterns outside of established fields. Even engineering is moving towards a juncture with the sciences. To help cope with the flood of students, teaching methods have turned increasingly to larger classes, increased use of teaching assistants for regular classes, and, to a lesser degree, the newer media, such as closed-circuit TV.

These changes in the world of learning may presage a fundamental reorientation, according to Peter F. Drucker. "The emergence of knowledge as central to our society and the foundation of economy and social action drastically changes the position, the meaning, and the structure of knowledge.... Knowledge areas are in a state of flux. The existing faculties, departments, and disciplines will not be appropriate for long. Few are ancient to begin with, of course.... The most probable assumption is that every single one of the old demarcations, disciplines and faculties is going to become obsolete and a barrier to learning as well as to understanding. The fact that we are shifting rapidly from a Cartesian view of the universe, in which the accent has been on parts and elements, to a configuration view, with the emphasis on wholes and patterns, challenges every single dividing line between areas of study and knowledge."[11]

All the foregoing movements have implications for the libraries. As was remarked by Warren J. Haas, the rise of small new specializations tends to drive up the price of books and journals because the clienteles are small. Interdisciplinary studies tend to weaken the old system of departmental libraries. Spread-out departmental libraries do not serve the new needs well, and no university can afford to create the many new branch libraries presently being demanded. The multitudes of teaching assistants are not adept at utilizing the library in their teaching. Furthermore, the large numbers of students in single courses demand more copies of any title than the library is able to provide. Few libraries are equipped or staffed or budgeted to add the newer media to their services, and most are not oriented

Libraries and Librarians

in that direction. The effects of all these patterns of scholarship upon library resources have been ably summarized by Douglas W. Bryant.[12]

The information explosion. The constantly accelerating production of knowledge has been so widely publicized that it hardly calls for comment. When the knowledge produced by the world up to 1900 is doubled by 1950, and doubles again by 1965, as has been estimated, the term "explosion" seems applicable. As early as 1945, Vannevar Bush wrote that "Professionally our methods of transmitting and reviewing the results of research are generations old and by now totally inadequate for their purpose...."[13] No significant changes have occurred since Bush's statement. By 1970, a national Committee on Research in the Life Sciences concluded that "Investigators in the life sciences have not been able to cope with the waves of information since 15 years ago."[14] The rate of growth in science and technology seems fairly constant at 10 percent a year, which means a doubling every eight years.

University libraries quite obviously were going to be overwhelmed by this flood sooner or later; the velocity of change produces a faster expansion of knowledge than can be appraised, codified, or organized. Fremont Rider first called attention to the problem in 1944, pointing out that research libraries were doubling in size every sixteen years.[15] The annual studies at Purdue since 1965 indicate that the rates of growth discovered by Rider have continued unabated through 1971.[16]

So long as financial support of the university and its library grew steadily year after year, university libraries could hope at least to keep their heads above water. They clearly were in a very precarious position at best, however, and anyone could foresee that when hard times came, as they inevitably would, sooner or later, there would be serious difficulties. Those times have now arrived.

Hard times and inflation. The current financial problems of universities hardly need documentation. Earl F. Cheit in a study for the Carnegie Commission on Higher Education and the Ford Foundation calls it "the new depression."[17] Budgets have actually been cut, or the rate of increase slowed drastically.

Planning and budgeting. A static budget when coupled

with inflation spells real trouble for universities. All have begun to reassess goals and functions, and to try to improve their planning and budgeting processes. State boards of control appear strongly interested in program planning and budgeting systems, even though these devices have doubtful validity for colleges and universities. Clearly, long and short range planning and analytical budgeting are going to be a way of life in universities henceforth.

One of the budgets likely to be looked at hard with an eye to cutting is that of the university library, partly because it looms large. Certainly libraries can no longer count on steady increases to help them in their efforts to keep abreast of continuing increases in rate of publication. In addition, libraries are harder hit than most parts of the university, especially in regard to acquisitions, because the rate of inflation (or increases, if we accept the subject-fragmentation factor as one cause for increases in the price of materials) is higher than it is in other aspects of our economy. The declining status of the director of libraries in the administrative family also tends to reduce his effectiveness in presenting library needs.

Technology. Ever since Vannevar Bush proposed the Memex in 1945--the storage of all the information a research scholar needs in microform within the space of a desk, recallable at will--technology has been seen as a promising means of coping with the ever-growing flood of knowledge. Microtext has been adopted readily by university libraries, though it should be noted that government agencies do not allow the counting of materials in microtext in basic reports on resources. There have been many experiments with the computer, especially in computerized bibliography, the best examples being the National Library of Medicine's MEDLARS (now succeeded by MEDLINE), and Chemical Abstracts. Many experiments have been undertaken, numerous books have appeared on the subject, and the federal government has established a special agency on scientific information. One director declared in 1971 that "Computerization of information, long hoped by some to be the solution to library costs, is for that purpose substantially bankrupt."[18] This judgment may seem harsh, but it reflects general disappointment. Perhaps everyone, including librarians, had over-optimistic expectations. Time may change the situation, but it is now thirty-seven years since Vannevar Bush's proposal was first advanced.

Libraries and Librarians

Changing theories of management. Certain new theories of management emerged beginning in the early 1960s. Based on psychology and the study of human relations in an organization, the new ideas appeared first in business and industry and subsequently spread to governmental agencies. The new theories are characterized by the growing involvement of people in organizational decision-making, loosening of the traditional hierarchial structure, what might be called creative tensions, growing complexity, constant change, and open-endedness. Leadership is with a soft voice at a low key. Motivation and morale are stressed. Several excellent books on the new system have appeared.[19] One of the cycle theories, an aspect of the open-end concept, is that management is in constant change and that a successful organization evolves through five stages, the last of which is collaboration.[20]

The new theories seem especially suitable to an academic organization, because it is made up of intellectual and rational men, it is bureaucratic, and hardly compatible with the principles of hierarchy and obedience. One of the particular virtues of the new management plans for a university is that it tends to provide a defense in depth for the institution, when it comes under attack. It marshals all resources (administration, faculty, students, staff, and regents) against any onslaught. Predictions are that universities generally will adopt the new methods.[21] Ideas about participatory management in university administration are documented well by Henry L. Mason in a study promoted by AAUP.[22] Mason, in turn, reflects the ideas of Demerth, Millet, Carson, Kerr, and other authorities in academic management.

Unionization. Social conditions are changing, and therefore management needs to change. Factors promoting acceptance of the new theories of management include the growing educational level of workers, social disillusionment, activism including a demand for a share in the government of the enterprise, the need for more effective use of employee knowledge and spirit, the protection which they provide against outside attacks, and unionization. The unionization even of faculties, long regarded as unlikely, appears to be on the increase.[23] Participatory management may be an acceptable alternative. However, tight money and the over-supply of Ph.D.'s may speed the trend of college and university faculties to unionize "at a revolutionary pace."[24] Even the AAUP is moving away from its former cooperative attitude towards a position of being spokesman for the faculty as a defender of all faculty interests, including salaries, class size, and similar concerns. Unionization is one form of participation in management.

<u>Increasing control by state boards.</u> State boards of regents for higher education are becoming increasingly powerful and exerting more and more control over state-supported institutions. In part, this movement is a result of public disillusionment about higher education, especially universities where the student activist movement has been most evident, and partly it is a product of legislative wishes. Such boards, in some instances, are adding highly qualified specialists to their staffs, developing long-term master-plans to which the universities must conform, and emphasizing the budgeting process. Many already budget by formulas, and nearly all are strongly interested in program planning and budgeting systems. In a number of states they are creating new community and junior colleges which are less subject to public disfavor, and also are politically popular. The junior institutions draw heavily on both state building and state operating funds for higher education. Typical of the movement towards stronger control is the recent reorganization of the State Board of Governors in 1971 by the North Carolina Legislature, giving the board complete authority to determine functions, educational activities, academic programs, and degrees. Previous assignments of functions or responsibilities to designated institutions were cancelled.[25] The state boards appear to be using for overall research and planning the National Center for Higher Education Management Systems (NCHEMS) of the Western Interstate Commission for Higher Education, at Boulder, Colorado. The center's studies and recommendations therefore are of basic importance.

University libraries are becoming more and more subject to the state boards, especially in the budgeting process and in their demands for more effective cooperation among all state academic libraries. The coming pattern of state budgetary controls for university libraries was predicted ten years ago. McAnally found in a survey in 1962 that a majority of state boards were not yet using formulas for university library budgets (even though some already had formulas for college libraries), because of the complexity of the problem, but that many were interested in the subject.[26] Now there is a definite trend towards formulas for budgeting for university libraries, and many state boards also are considering PPBS.[27] The Washington "Evergreen" formula, developed by business officers, in cooperation with the state's college and university libraries, is typical of the newer, complex formulas. It has certain disadvantages for university libraries.[28] McAnally and Ellsworth had referred to the dangers of equalitarianism in formula budgeting for university libraries. If graduate programs and quality are not given adequate weight, this could be an end result. It remains to be seen what the effect of PPBS will be on university libraries, if this budgeting system is adopted widely.

No national system for information. The last of the background problems for libraries is the failure to achieve an effective national system for the sharing of information. The present uncoordinated system was reasonably satisfactory around the turn of the century when advances in knowledge were slow and leisurely. The information explosion is now producing an enormous wealth of knowledge, published and distributed according to the techniques of 1900, which is beyond control and a source of frustration, dismay, and continued irritation to scholars. Steps such as interlibrary loan, cooperative acquisitions plans, union lists and catalogs, and the Center for Research Libraries have been useful, but too little and ineffective, and hardly acknowledged by the community of scholars. Control is not necessarily a library problem, though librarians seem to catch the brunt of the blame. Instead, many agencies ought to be helping to solve the problem: the various professional associations in different subjects, publishers of books and journals, computer and information specialists, foundations, and last, but not least, the federal government. Information is a resource of national importance; certainly the center of an effective system will be enormous in size and complexity. The federal government has made some useful efforts toward the control of scientific information, but only in medicine has the work been supported adequately.

In any event, university libraries receive the principal blame for failure to solve the problems of access, with the result that the director of the library has lost stature and prestige within his institution. Buckman believes that some substantial progress must be made towards the solution of major national problems, such as this one, before the director of libraries can hope to regain his proper status within the university.[29]

INTERNAL PROBLEMS

Many of the newer problems facing directors of university libraries have their origins in changing social conditions or within the institution as it attempts to adjust to these social trends. Some of the problems, however, have developed within the university library itself. Few of the internal problems are new; mainly, they are expansions of existing or latent difficulties.

Greatly intensified pressures. The most obvious change in the director's job is the extraordinary increase in the pressures exerted upon him. Many of the directors with whom the authors corresponded wrote quite feelingly upon this point. A few key phrases describe the situation succinctly. Herman Fussler observed that "the pressures on the library and director have changed by one or two orders of magnitude in the past twenty years ... the librarian sits between the anvil of resources and the hammer of demands.... The strain is greater, just as it is for presidents of universities."

Louis Kaplan wrote, "Administration is never easy, and there were problems galore even when money was plentiful.... I had lived through the 'glory' years...." Louis Branscomb noted that "It has become a matter of running faster on the treadmill every year in order to stay where you were the year before." One director said that at his first interview the new president informed him that he did not believe in buying books, and later elaborated this statement. Another reported that the president had refused to see him for ten years. David Otis Kelley suggested that the university should have "a younger man to sit on this hot seat." Edward B. Stanford referred to the "present climate of creeping discontent that pervades the faculty, students and staff on so many large campuses." Ralph Parker observed that "I have found the life of a Dean on this campus to be much cosier than the life of a librarian." And the title of a talk by Warren B. Kuhn describes the situation vividly: "in the Director's office, it's 'High Noon' every day!"

Writers on management agree that to a certain degree stress stimulates executives to better performance. But they also agree that excessive stress is harmful. As the pressures on the director increase, he has a tendency to become more and more decisive in attempting to cope with the growing multitude of problems alone, until he ultimately offends too many people or else concludes that the rewards are no longer worth the cost.

<u>Pressure sources.</u> The growing pressures on the director are exerted by five different groups. They are, in probable order of magnitude, the president's office, the library staff, the faculty, students, and, in publicly supported universities, state boards of control. It may seem odd to list the library faculty as high as second, but in those cases in which the principal cause for the director's quitting his position can be identified, the library staff ranks second.

Unquestionably, the president's office, including not only the president but also the academic vice-president and particularly the financial vice-president, bring the strongest pressures to bear on the director. In part, this is because the president is the most powerful man in the university, in part because he reflects institutional opinion. The president's office is a source of many of the director's frustrations. Numerous directors commented on this problem, and on the deterioration of these relationships. As already pointed out, the proliferation of top-level administrators has severed the director from direct contact with the president, interposed a layer of officers between the two, and reduced the ability of the library to present its case. Directors also have realized, as Thomas R. Buckman remarked, that they have no power base on which to operate, and others noted that the director could not even get to the point of a showdown, much less win one. All presidents are harried, some are inexperienced, and others may come from nonlibrary oriented fields such as the sciences.

One of the major frustrations of the director may be with the financial vice-president. Robert Vosper calls attention to a prediction by a social scientist as early as 1961, of coming conflicts between the library and budgetary authorities.[30] The rate of growth of libraries observed by Rider and others obviously had to end eventually. The director sees clearly the financial needs produced by the ever-growing flood of publications, increased enrollment, expanding graduate programs, rising expectations and demands, and inflation, but may not be able to convince the budget officer of the acuteness of library needs. Besides, the financial vice-president may have no new money, is reluctant to make cuts elsewhere for the library, which he may regard as a "bottomless pit," or may have less money than previously.

Financial demands pressed hard are likely to see the director relieved of his post. A noteworthy example of this fact occurred in one of the great Ivy League schools--when the director wrote bluntly and bitterly about financial support, on the first page of his annual report (his only or last recourse?), he was immediately relieved and transferred to the School of Religion. The financial problems of the university library are not likely to decrease for the indefinite future.

Staff pressures. It may seem strange that the director should be under attack from his own staff, or fail to receive badly needed support in relations with the administration and faculty, but it is so in many cases. Robert Miller wrote: "In recent years there has been pressure exerted upon the library administrator by the library staff, the overt features including a strengthened organization, unionization, requests for participation in administrative decision-making, faculty status, etc. To me and to other benevolent and beloved administrators, this is an attack on the father image which I have long fancied. I know one man who felt this so keenly that he resigned."

Nowadays the library staff, both the academic or professional and the nonprofessional, are far better educated than in the past. Most librarians hold at least a master's degree, and many higher degrees. They also are more socially conscious, action-oriented, and impatient--in common with the rest of our society. They want and expect a share in policy decisions affecting themselves and the library.[31] The rise of library specialists in university libraries also is producing severe strains on the library's administrative structure, and represents a force for change in administrative practices, according to Eldred Smith.[32]

A particular problem that has not yet surfaced fully is that the director has two staffs, one academic or professional and one clerical or nonacademic. The latter is the larger of the two. Different administrative styles are needed for each. There is some danger that the two groups might end up in opposition to each other, especially if the nonacademic group unionizes and the academic group does not.

The old methods of organization may no longer be acceptable, but good alternatives are difficult to find. Booz, Allen & Hamilton identify the problem in their Columbia study.[33] In any event, new administrative styles are being called for, and those directors who will not or cannot adapt to the newer ways may be lost.

Faculty sources. The latent conflict of interests between librarians and the faculty were commented upon recently by Robert H. Blackburn and Richard H. Logsdon. Blackburn stated that librarians have the books, professors have the students.[34] Logsdon pointed out that the typical faculty member wants complete coverage in his subject and centralized service; the professor sees the size of the library budget and regards the library as an empire with all kinds of staff help when the professor cannot even have a secretary. As one director wrote, these and other frustrations lead to "a gradual building up of small things into big, lose a friend here and there every year, and there's bound to be a critic in almost every department."[35] A simple but cynical explanation of the growing problem in faculty relations may be financial--when there is not even money enough for any raises for the faculty, faculty support for other university functions inevitably declines. The growing militancy in society generally also may be a factor in bringing existing problems to the fore.

Student pressure. Students do not yet have the power in the university for which they are agitating, but their power is growing. They, too, are action oriented, and are demanding improvements in library service. "Under pressure from students and faculty there has been a forced change in academic library priorities," Robert A. Miller finds. "Service is more important, or holds more immediacy than collection building. More service is wanted and in more depth ... reference to limitations of funds, space, personnel is not accepted as a sound reply, but only as an alibi for non-performance."[36] When there is no new money, improved service must come at the cost of collections. A special problem is that most university libraries have overemphasized services to research, so that except in those institutions where there is an undergraduate library, the collections tend to be single-copy collections. Professors, when they select books, prefer to cover as much of the new literature in their fields as possible, and are reluctant to spend money on extra copies, even of important titles. Approval plans also produce only single copies. To cap the problem, changing emphases of human rights over property rights lead to losses--not nearly as great as faculty and students think, but certainly causing a very serious problem in public relations.

Declining ability of library to meet needs. Apparently the university library is becoming increasingly less able to meet the legitimate needs of its university community. The causes have already been outlined in background factors: the information explosion, inflation, more students, and continued fragmentation of the traditional disciplines, coupled with hard times. A recent study at Harvard concluded that with 8,000,000 volumes the library was less able to cope with the demands of scholars than it was when it had only 4,000,000 volumes. Ralph Ellsworth, in his 1971-72 annual report at Colorado, came to the same conclusion. David Kaser states plaintively: "The lugubrious fact is that our ability to supply the books and journals needed by Cornell teaching and research programs is rapidly diminishing, and no one seems to know what to do about it. Computerization of information, cooperation, and microminiaturization have not provided solutions.... The somber conclusion fast being arrived at by the library staff is that the only solutions likely to be effective are (1) more money, or (2) a substantially reduced academic program for the library to serve, neither of which appears imminent. The library needs, and would welcome, advice in this matter."[37] Another director observed that "when the library is unable to perform at the level of satisfaction to the faculty, the head of the library is held personally responsible and it is assumed that he is incapable of being Director."

Lack of goals and planning. Like the university itself, the library has rarely done a good job of planning, either long-range or short-range. One director remarked: "Many university librarians have rigid, pre-conceived notions about the proper objectives of their libraries. The traditional library objectives summarized cynically in such phrases as 'more of the same' and 'bottomless pit' are probably unrealistic, and yet little is offered in their place."[38] Now that higher education and all its parts are under critical review, the lack of realistic, practicable, and accepted goals, and of long-range planning, is a major handicap. There are some noteworthy exceptions, such as UCLA, Columbia, and Illinois. Several writers have discussed this problem.[39]

Inability to accommodate to educational changes quickly. The university library, like the university itself, is a bureaucracy which is difficult to change, even though the need may be recognized by nearly everyone concerned. In addition, the university library may have large collections, sometimes built up over centuries, research collections which cannot be changed quickly; the library is housed in a great building or buildings which would cost millions to replace; and its staff of specialists has been developed over a period of years. The two groups most impatient for new philosophies and new types of services are the students and the president's office. Inability to make changes rapidly, even though he tried, cost at least one director his job.

Decline in status of the director. This subject has been dealt with previously, but is so important to the welfare of the library, as well as to the director personally, that it should be noted again in a consideration of internal problems. The director no longer is in the upper level of university management and cannot participate in institutional policy decisions, including planning and budgeting. Partly the decline is due to lack of basic support. The director seldom has an opportunity to defend the library, or if he does, no one wishes to listen to him. And on him now falls the chief burden of asking for institutional book funds as well as staff money. Many directors commented on this aspect and asserted that it made real achievements impossible and reduced the attractiveness of the position.

Declining financial support. When financial support for the universities slows down, stands still, or decreases, the library must suffer too. A static or declining budget causes especially acute problems in the library, because of the continuing proliferation of publications and increases in the prices of print well above the national average. A number of directors, in discussing this problem, referred to "housekeeping" or "caretaker-level" funding. Booz, Allen & Hamilton warns that the president is inclined to look at the library budget as a place to economize. There is widespread evidence that the percentage of the total educational and general budget allotted to the university library has declined in recent years, including some of our most distinguished universities. The national situation cannot be determined readily; however, Statistics of Southern College and University Libraries, which reports percentages spent on the library, reveals that decreases slightly outnumber increases over the past five years, but decreases outnumber increases two to one over a ten-year period.

Renewed questioning of centralization. Every director

is probably aware of the declining efficiency of the general
library and the old departmental library system in meeting
new needs and rising expectations. Interdisciplinary studies
and fragmenting disciplines are not served well by the system, and libraries have no funds to expand. Peter Drucker
expects the entire university curriculum to be reorganized;[40]
if so, this problem may well increase. Every director also
is aware of the rise of many office collections, unofficial
institute libraries funded from grants, and departmental
reading rooms supplied personally by the faculty. All these
developments indicate growing dissatisfaction with centralized
controls. "Institutionalizing library resources inevitably
denies individual faculty members the degree of control they
would prefer.... Add to this the even stronger desire on
the part of professional schools to be autonomous within the
university and you have another set of frictions."[41]

<u>No effective sharing of resources, computerization, microminiaturization.</u> Failure to make substantial progress on these national problems is blamed on the library and its director, and some believe it an important factor in the decline of prestige of the director.

<u>Old-style management.</u> As noted above, the traditional hierarchical and authoritative style of management is increasingly unacceptable. As one director observed, it "no longer has any purchase in the market place." Many directors are unwilling or unable to adapt. In addition, the director's office now operates in a condition of constant change, intense pressures, and great complexity. These factors are of crucial importance to the director personally, demanding the highest administrative abilities as well as durability, flexibility, and determination.

SOLUTIONS AND CHANGES

It is far easier to identify the multitude of problems facing the university library and its director than it is to find solutions to these troubles. Nevertheless, there are answers to some problems and partial solutions to others. Perhaps the most important fact for the director to recognize is that the old ways are being questioned and that changes are evolving; he should be receptive to continuing change, both for his library and for himself personally, and try to see that the best possible choices are made among various alternatives. The university library obviously will survive, for it is a fundamental part of the university, but its nature will continue to be transformed. What happens to the individual director may not be important, heartless though this may seem. Either he adapts to new ways, or another person will be brought in who has the qualities needed in the new era. But what happens to the leadership of the library embodied in the position of director of libraries is exceedingly important.

Solutions to national problems. To restore the confidence of the university in the library and its director, there has to be "general acceptance and implementation of some significant national programs that really come to grips with fundamental problems of providing information and knowledge for people working in the universities.... They probably won't get it fully until he and his colleagues attack the national problems in such a way that the local university library becomes a manageable operation."42

Unfortunately, the problems are so vast that there seems to be little that the individual director can do. Instead, the solutions must come at the national level. No deus ex machina is likely to appear any time soon from the computer-information world, microminiaturization or other technologies; it is therefore the responsibility of librarians to develop answers, even though they may be only partial and prove temporary. However, the librarian can make his views known and speak out vigorously about the urgent need to national agencies which are in a stronger position to attack the problems. These include the Association of Research Libraries, agencies of the federal government, and the American Library Association. Efforts of the Association of Research Libraries to promote a national acquisitions program and to develop plans for more effective sharing of resources for research are constructive, but the organization is dependent upon the federal government and foundations for research funds, and is not funded to operate any continuing program. Nonetheless, its leadership is vitally important in the overall situation. Only the federal government can provide the sizeable funds needed for a proper national plan. There are four comprehensive federal agencies in the field--the National Commission on Libraries, the Library of Congress, the National Science Foundation, and the Department of Health, Education, and Welfare--none of which is funded properly for the task, nor has national responsibility for information been fully accepted by the government. The American Library Association can be helpful but has many diverse interests and at present has internal management problems.

Current developments of promise are the recently completed ARL interlibrary loan cost study, the same organization's current study of the feasibility of a computerized national referral center, and ongoing studies of national-regional periodicals resources centers or lending libraries by the National Commission on Libraries, ARL, and the Center for Research Libraries. Both the Association of Research Libraries and the Center for Research Libraries have broadened their membership considerably in recent years, thereby increasing their strength. ARL has adopted automatic membership criteria based on 50 percent of the ARL averages on certain factors. Some librarians see networks as an answer, but existing examples are uncoordinated and vary widely in scope and in value. It should be noted again that political pressures are strong for more and more effective cooperation, especially from state boards of higher education and from HEW.

Better planning. Failure to plan for the future has been one of the major weaknesses of university libraries in general, a condition which many authorities agree must be corrected in the seventies. "Planning is the orderly means used by an organization to establish effective control over its own future ... to be effective any plan ... must be logical, comprehensive, flexible, action-oriented, and formal. Furthermore, it must extend into the future and involve human resources."[43] In an era of change in the university and of static financial support, the allocation of resources becomes especially important. The components of comprehensive library planning include (1) university requirements and expectations for library services; (2) the library's own objectives and plans in support of academic programs and general learning needs; and (3) library resources (financial, personnel, collections, facilities, and equipment) needed to implement agreed-upon plans. There are four ways to accommodate change. (1) Appoint a new chief librarian. (2) Call in an outside consultant--so far as the director is concerned, results are the same as (1) four times out of five, especially if the university calls for the consultant. (3) Establish a committee within the library organizational structure as a research and planning group.[44] (4) Appoint a staff officer in the director's office for planning and research, to do some of the work and to assist the staff committee. Kaser points out that in the university "academic decision making ... is not accomplished through the organizational tree that we have come to associate with large organizations. Such a structure does exist in universities, but it exists for nonacademic decisions; academic decisions ... are rather initiated and made by faculty members as individuals and with practically no centralized control over them."[45] Implications for the library are obvious.

Improved budgeting. During this period of hard times for the university, the university library must improve its budgeting and control practices greatly if it is to receive its fair share of limited resources. The old add-on type budget is gone, at least for a while and perhaps forever. Librarians need to prove their value to the classroom faculty as well as to the university administration--libraries are indispensable, but how indispensable? Libraries now have to demonstrate their importance to the educational program of the institution. There also must be more accountability-- directors must provide better justifications for budget increases. Some steps that the director should take include adding a business-trained budget manager to the library staff for budget preparation; enlisting the support of instructional departments in preparing budgets; seeking faculty and administrative recognition of the fact that any new academic program requires money and that special financial aid should be given to the library for it; making productivity and cost benefit analyses regularly; participation in computerized networks and information-sharing systems; and having the director sit on the highest university policy board.[46] A discovery of considerable significance was made by Kenneth S. Allen, who found among thirteen sampled institutions that "the percentage of educational and general expense funds allocated to the library appears to be favorably influenced by having faculty status."[47] Further study is needed to see if this is true nationally.

State boards of higher education clearly are going to affect budgeting practices of state-supported university libraries, as previously observed, for their financial control is growing rapidly. The methods they adopt will govern library methods. Six types of budgets currently are in use: the traditional budget by objects of expenditure, program budget, performance budget, Planning, Programming and Budgetary Systems, formula budgeting and combinations.[48]

New organizational patterns. If present trends in the academic programs of the university continue--breakoff of new subjects from old disciplines, growth of interdisciplinary

studies and area studies, rise of programs oriented towards
current social problems, more independent study programs,
and more adult education work, or if indeed there will be
entirely different curricula by 1980 as suggested by some--
then the university library may have to make considerable
change in its organizational structure to accommodate to university needs. Some modifications are needed already, for
internal as well as external reasons; our present patterns
are over seventy-five years old.

At present, no one knows with any certainty exactly
what changes in organization may be needed. The most interesting suggestions to date, the Booz, Allen & Hamilton
proposals (limited to staff and service only) for Columbia
University libraries, appear unwieldy and cumbersome. The
experiment should be watched with interest. The company
reflects a business-industrial management firm's approach.
In any event, the director needs to be aware that organizational changes may be needed, and to remain open-minded
and flexible on the subject.

Services vs. collection-building. The director must
recognize that the emphasis in university libraries is shifting from collection-building to services, under growing pressures from students and faculty, and that the library must
conform. Library staffs also seem to be becoming more
service conscious and program oriented. When financial
support is static, there is no place to obtain the money for
improved services other than book and journal funds. Therefore, the percentage of the library budget allotted to acquisitions will decline, unfortunate as this is for the world of
scholarship in general and the university in particular. In
its most affluent days, no library was able to acquire more
than a portion of the world's published output.

Every director has been made increasingly aware of
the growing dissatisfactions with library service. Formerly
faculty members and students were reluctant to voice criticism and make suggestions; nowadays, neither seems to hesitate to make attacks. Failing to receive satisfaction, they
may go to the president or to the campus newspaper. Courteous hearings and boxes for complaints and suggestions are
useful. Another evidence that every director must be aware
of is the rapid growth in recent years of alternatives to
standard library service--office collections, unofficial institute libraries, faculty-supplied departmental reading rooms,
and the like. Dougherty suggests that a new attitude and

new types of service may be needed for the latter group.[49]

Undergraduate libraries (or learning resources centers as some state boards prefer to call them) seem successful and desirable, and are popular with students. They are possible, however, only in large university libraries. They help improve service, but there seems to be little or no correlation between the presence of such a unit and the tenure of the director.

Collecting policies. Several changes in collecting policies may be desirable. The first and most obvious change is that, with stable or declining funds, the library needs to be more selective in choosing from the world's output. Unless the library receives a book and journal budget that increases steadily at least 12 percent a year, the recent rate of inflation in the price of print, library intake will decline. There is a trend towards selection by library specialists. Blanket order and approval plans are becoming widespread. Both movements seem to be satisfactory and acceptable to the faculty. When book funds decline, many libraries tend to protect their periodical subscriptions first.

Institutional pride and rules of agencies for counting library statistics emphasize the codex book and the journal. Microprint is well used by libraries but is not acceptable for the basic count. Libraries need to widen their collecting net to include information in other forms, including the so-called newer media and information on computer tapes or discs. Douglas Bryant has pointed out the growing variety of forms that must be collected.[50]

Rare books. Some presidents, legislators, and state boards have long looked askance at the use of budgetary funds for the purchase of rare books per se. Now the attitude appears to be spreading to the faculty and to students. A little checking with faculty members in almost any department except history, English, and classics or other humanities is likely to prove startling. Neither scientists nor social scientists are likely to appreciate the need. Perhaps the attitude is a product of severe financial problems, or McLuhanism, or strong emphasis on the current problems of our society. The director may be well advised to use only gift funds for such purposes, and to publicize this policy among the faculty. "Friends of the Library" organizations can be quite helpful in providing funds for "frosting on the cake."

More copies of important books or current titles in heavy demand ought to be purchased. Most university libraries, with the exception of those with undergraduate units, are basically single-copy libraries. The most severe criticism of every university library in the country probably is the inability of students or faculty to secure a copy of a high-demand title when needed. Changes in acquisitions policies clearly are required.

Institutionalization of resources. Some loosening of centralized control over resources and services may be in order. This will seem downright heresy to some, and an encouragement of inefficiency and wastefulness by others. But the fact is that this is already occurring. Professional associations in medicine and law in concerted campaigns have gained a great deal of independence for their schools, including their libraries. Other professional associations are beginning to work on similar programs. The rise of many unofficial office collections, institute libraries, and departmental reading rooms has already been noted. The library itself cannot establish the needed new branches to serve interdisciplinary and similar new programs, due to the financial pinch. Actually, at least two great university libraries have always been federations of libraries--Harvard and Cornell. The financial and supportive aspects of allowing some degree of freedom were suggested by Donald Coney in the 1950s. When asked why he allowed so many independent branch libraries at Berkeley, he replied, "We get more money that way." Cooperation and a new kind of personalized service to meet new needs are suggested by Dougherty.[51] Holley suggests that coordinated decentralization as at Harvard should be looked at, as well as the view that after a certain size has been reached, some form of decentralization may be both necessary and desirable.[52]

Directors undoubtedly need all the help they can find nowadays, and by cooperation they can maintain some degree of coordination which might otherwise be lost. As the rate of acquisitions declines, libraries may have excess staff in their acquisitions and cataloging departments which could be utilized. Policies on these matters need to be reviewed, and either re-affirmed or modified.

Status of the director. Most directors commented on the decline in status of the office of director, reflected in the interposition of layers of vice-presidents between the president and the director. Some decline in general approval of the library itself also seems to be evident. This is unfortunate for the director, but very serious indeed for the university library itself. The library's representative usually no longer participates in institutional policy decision making processes, and cannot present the library's case at the top level.

Buckman believes that the four requirements to restoring confidence and credibility in the director, and by implication the library, are: (1) some effective attack on major national problems; (2) establishing an effective working relationship with the administrative officers of the university; (3) providing a framework in which the director can operate effectively within the university's power structure and (4) setting reasonable and widely understood goals for the library.[53] Branscomb suggests that this may be a problem to be worked out individually on each campus, rather than by a considered attack from research libraries as a group.[54] Booz, Allen & Hamilton propose that the director be made a vice-president.[55] The vice-president needs to adopt a university-wide viewpoint when this is done. The idea is attractive, and has been implemented at Columbia, Texas, and Utah, the two latter perhaps for different reasons. An important factor, for directors considering such a move, may be that the office should be a vice-president for information services for the entire campus, assuming responsibilities for the newer media, even closed-circuit TV and certain aspects of computerized information services. Separate budgeting for the latter units seems fundamental.

The status of the director is sometimes a negotiable matter which should be dealt with as one of the conditions of appointment. The rank of dean may be negotiable; the status of vice-president possibly not. The welfare of the library itself as well as the opportunity for achievement by the director of course are involved.

Term appointments. One of the solutions proposed by several directors is appointment for a fixed term, perhaps for ten years, perhaps for five years, with one renewal possible.[56] If Chancellor Murphy is correct, and if the post of director is comparable to that of a president, then his observation that an individual's major creative contributions are made within the first three to five years, with ten years the maximum time needed to complete programs, the idea should be considered carefully by the profession. Both the library and the individual are certain to suffer when the director remains in the position past his period of optimum contribution.

Several universities presently have term appointments for deans and other such administrators--with extensions possible--Cornell, Texas, and Illinois. The de facto tenure period for directors of ARL libraries over the past three years has averaged between five and six years. Vosper does note, however, that very short terms inhibit planning and focused concentration, such as the three year elective term in Japanese academic libraries.

If term appointments are adopted, some orderly plans or structure to facilitate wise change in administration must be formulated. So far there is none, though at West Virginia a president acquires retirement privileges after five years, and at Kentucky deans who return to teaching retain their salaries at the expense of the general administration. A majority of directors who have quit their posts have gone into teaching, but there are limitations to this concept--many universities have no library school, and the ability of schools to absorb a succession of directors may be limited. Others have become curators of special collections, taken early retirement, or moved to another university. If peer appointment should come for presidents, as has been suggested, it might also apply to directors. In such circumstances, moving to a lesser position in the library would become more practicable. In any event, the profession needs to give some thought to the problem of how to make such changes feasible rather than traumatic.

<u>Increase the percentage of nonprofessional staff.</u>
Some twenty-five years ago university libraries in the United States generally had a 1:1 ratio between professional librarians and supporting staff. Then following a series of articles by Archie McNeal and others in the middle 1950s, pointing out that perhaps two-thirds of the work in an academic library could be done successfully and more economically by nonprofessional people, libraries generally moved to a staff composition of two nonprofessionals to one professional. With few exceptions, this distribution is common among university libraries today.

Among Canadian university libraries the ratios are different: from three-to-one up to five-to-one. The movement began in the catalog department at the University of British Columbia; when catalogers complained about the amount of routine and clerical work they were doing, the library increased the size of the supporting staff to what they deemed proper. Canadian university libraries have close working relations, and the movement spread rapidly. The new ratios are reported to be acceptable and satisfactory.

This subject requires further examination on the part of directors and their staffs. The education of the entire population has improved greatly in the last fifteen to twenty years, from which it follows that nonprofessional personnel ought to be able to carry more and higher level duties. A careful survey of student opinion about the central library at the University of Oklahoma revealed that the four areas of greatest dissatisfaction fell within the province of the nonprofessional staff. Obviously the library needs more assistants.[57] Eldred Smith also had speculated that the university library may not need many more academic or professional staff, but better qualified and more specialized individuals.[58] Harold F. Wells suggests that the ratio of clerical to professional ought to be five-to-one; adding that all staff are better educated, one year is a short period of graduate education, the Army is very dependent on sergeants, and libraries ought to upgrade clericals and assign more duties to them.[59] A tentative inquiry about a research grant to establish the proper ratio was unsuccessful.

In relation to nonacademic staff members, there are three special problems for the director: they may fit a somewhat different administrative pattern, no one knows what are the proper relationships between the academic and the nonacademic staff, and clerical assistants appear to be more likely to join a union.[60] Booz, Allen & Hamilton proposals in the Columbia study attempt to come to grips with the problem, one of the first efforts to date. Other approaches need to be explored. In one major university library, the two groups have already come into conflict. The problems will grow in proportion to increases in size of the assistant group.

CHANGING PATTERNS OF MANAGEMENT

New management styles rapidly are replacing the old traditional techniques in the university library world. The trend has been observed and commented on by several librarians who have made surveys of university library management around the country during the last two years: Edward G. Holley, Maurice P. Marchant, Eldred Smith, and

Jane G. Flener.[61] Involving increased staff participation in the management of the library to one degree or another, they are called participatory management, collegial management, or democratic administration. The theory and principles have been drawn from two different sources, business and industry, and academia itself. The new styles are being adopted rapidly because the arguments in their favor are persuasive. They draw in to the solution of problems a diverse group of good minds with varied viewpoints, thereby improving the quality as well as the effectiveness of decision making. They are the answer to growing staff pressures, particularly from the academic or professional staff, for participation in planning and policy decisions, as well as administrative affairs affecting themselves. They tend to improve the morale and dedication of the staff. They marshal the entire staff in defense of the library against attacks from outside, thus relieving and supporting the director, a defense in depth, as it were. The director has to surrender some of his old authority, and becomes more of a leader. His influence may not be diminished, but it must be exerted in different ways.

There are three principal styles, two based on business and industry, the other on university academic practices. The three might be called the business management plan, the unionization method, and collegial management or academic plan. A director may not be free to choose among them. If his university has not, and probably will not, grant academic status to librarians, such as the Ivy League universities, he must choose one of the first two. If the professional staff already has faculty status, then he would be wise to accept that style. A show of hands recently in the Association of Research Libraries indicated that three-fourths of the directors already had academic status or were interested in seeking it for their staffs. If a staff is unionized already, a new director has no choice. All of the new styles are so new, comparatively speaking, that there are still wide variations in practice in all three groups. Each may be successful. The director who enters upon any one of the paths grudgingly and because he is forced to, and drags his heels all the way, however, is likely to find himself in trouble after a short time.

Business management plan. Examples of libraries experimenting with the professional but not academic approach (i.e., their staffs do not have faculty status nor are they unionized) are Cornell, Columbia, UCLA, and recently

Harvard. The method may give more options to the director, and allow him to make more decisions concerning the degree of staff participation. There are no firm outside models; therefore, the director and his staff have to make many basic and difficult decisions. A director who goes into this system determined to cede only what he has to treads a very difficult and possibly dangerous path. There is likely to be a latent restlessness in the staff which will burst forth if there is even slight provocation. Given hard work, good judgment, and cooperation from both sides the method should be successful.

It is interesting to note that Booz, Allen & Hamilton, Inc., in their original report of 1970 on <u>Problems in University Library Management</u>, make no mention of staff participation matters. Subsequent papers by Seashore and Bolton of the firm's staff, however, stressed the desirability of extensively involving the staff in management, and their recommendations in the Columbia study also emphasize this feature. A representative of the firm declined to commit himself about faculty status for librarians.

<u>Unionization</u>. Management by collective bargaining probably produces the most drastic changes in management of all the three methods. In some respects it is the newest and least-known of all. Chicago, California (Berkeley) to a certain extent, and the City University of New York are examples. A guide exists on the subject of unionization of library staff.[62] De Gennaro believes that unionism and participatory management are incompatible; which will emerge as the trend of the future is still uncertain.[63] One university library union, it should be noted, includes both professional and nonprofessional staff members.

Factors that might tend to lead to unionization are large size and unsatisfactory business management types of participative management. The larger the staff, the more difficult it is to develop participatory management plans that will effectively involve all of the staff. Academic, faculty, or collegial management seems less likely to lead to unionization of the professional staff, but if the classroom faculty is unionized, the library faculty undoubtedly will be included.

<u>Academic management</u>. The model for the third or academic style lies in the university itself--administration of a college. The director should be comparable to the dean of a college or perhaps a vice-president, and the pro-

fessional staff to a college faculty. Like the first method, however, it has both advantages and disadvantages. First, despite many libraries working in this direction for a number of years--Illinois, Minnesota, Oklahoma, Ohio State, Oregon, Penn State, Miami, and Kentucky, for example-- there are still about as many variations as there are in the first method. Excellent statements of principles under this system are those produced by Miami, Houston, Oregon, Minnesota, and Oklahoma. Numerous problems exist; the transition is neither simple nor easy. The director has less choice about the degree of participation in management which is to exist; he has more than many think, but the example of faculty-dean is close at hand, and there the respective roles are well-established and clear. To find out what the role of a director may be in such a plan, he has only to examine the role of the dean. A guide to the effects of academic status upon organization and management is that by McAnally.[64] It should be noted that a dean of a nondepartmentalized college tends to have considerably more power and influence than a dean of a college with many departments. The role of a dean of libraries in a large university library which has to be subdivided into both academic and administrative departments is quite different. Middle management tends to be much stronger in this case. Both types of colleges flourish in American universities. Another disadvantage of the system is that numerous time-consuming committees are required. The excesses to which committee operation could be carried were illustrated at the Library of Congress by a pioneer in participative management, Luther Evans.[65] Committees of classroom faculty members produce certain problems and this is an area the director needs to watch.

The advantages of academic management or operation as a college are substantial. It provides recognition of the library as an academic unit. The methods of management fit the standard university pattern, hence are accepted readily by administration, classroom faculty, and the library staff. It draws in to planning, solution of problems, and management generally a wide variety of backgrounds and knowledge, so that decision-making tends to be better and the decisions accepted more readily. It promotes continuing education and professional growth, and increased professionalization. Morale is higher. One study indicates that it tends to improve financial support of the library.[66] Another indicates that the classroom faculty tends to be better satisfied with the library when the library operates as a faculty-academic unit.[67]

Productivity. Productivity under participatory management has been questioned by Lynch.[68] Her comments would seem to apply to business-style participatory management, academic management, and the unionization method alike. Marchant, however, points out that "While group decision-making alone appears to be neither adequate nor necessary to assure high productivity, it has been found to be generally characteristic of high-production organizations."[69] In a highly professionalized staff, his observation would seem particularly applicable. Any director who is convinced that the traditional hierarchical and authoritarian approach should be retained because it is best for the university would be well-advised to start looking for a new job, or a series of them, in view of current management trends.

Uncertain place of the supporting staff. Currently in university libraries in the United States, as previously observed, the supporting staff outnumbers the professional or academic staff two to one. The proportion is likely to rise during the next five years to the three to one up to five to one common in Canadian university libraries. The place of the nonprofessional staff in the management system, however, is still generally uncertain. Only in unionism is its role clear. Obviously, there must be solutions found for the proper involvement of the supporting staff in the government and management of the university library. Its members are better educated and better qualified than they were twenty years ago, and they will perform two-thirds to four-fifths of all work done in libraries. Various plans should be tried to find the best. Currently most nonacademic staff members operate under rules set by the university personnel office.

QUALITIES OF A MODEL DIRECTOR

The qualities required of a director of libraries are the same as they have always been. Certain aspects, however, receive more emphasis nowadays than they did in the past. First, the director must be more flexible and adaptable; the old certainties are being questioned or are gone, and the university library will continue to undergo changes. He must be willing to accept change as a way of life, and be open-minded about alternatives. Any man (or woman) unwilling to operate in such a milieu, or unable to accept uncertainty as a way of life should not undertake the management of a university library for the years immediately ahead.

Second, he must possess a stable and equable temperament, and the ability to keep his emotional balance under the constant tensions that come at him from all directions. The tensions are unlikely to decrease. The apothegm of a former president seems appropriate: "If you can't stand the heat, stay out of the kitchen!" Third, he must have endurance. Luther Evans, who once described the qualities of a good library administrator, chose the term "endurance" instead of the term "vigor," which business and industry favored.[70] His choice seemed odd in the 1940s, but more apt now.

Finally, the director must be exceptionally persuasive. Ability to present library interests and needs effectively to the administration, classroom faculty, students, and state boards is essential. He must have facts derived from continuous planning and from continuing cost studies, including cost-benefit, but he also needs to have a personality that commands attention and respect. The new type of leadership within the library requires that he be a leader and not merely an authority. Sometimes it seems that a worker of miracles is wanted--a search committee for a new director of one of the major university libraries specified a mature and experienced man having at least ten years of professional career yet to go who would be able to persuade the university to increase financial support of the university library in an era of declining institutional income!

REFERENCES

1. Edward G. Holley. "Organization and Administration of Urban University Libraries." CRL, 33 (May 1972), 275-89.
2. Raynard C. Swank. Discussion with McAnally, Chicago, Jan. 1972.
3. Lewis C. Branscomb, Thomas R. Buckman, Robert Carmack, Herman H. Fussler, John A. Heussman, Edward G. Holley, Robert K. Johnson, Louis Kaplan, David Otis Kelley, Roy L. Kidman, Warren B. Kuhn, Frank A. Lundy, John P. McDonald, Stanley McElderry, Robert A. Miller, Ralph H. Parker, Benjamin B. Richards, Eldred R. Smith, Edward B. Stanford, Lewis F. Steig, Raynard C. Swank, and Robert Vosper.
4. For a brief survey of some of these changes, not only in size but in other areas, and their probable effects

on the university library, see President Richard Lyman (Stanford), "New Trends in Higher Education: The Impact on the University Library." Association of Research Libraries, Minutes of the Twenty-Eighth meeting, May 14-15, 1971. Washington, D.C.: A.R.L., 1971; 3-7. Also Booz, Allen & Hamilton, Inc. "Trends in Higher Education and Their Implications for University Libraries and University Library Management." In: their Problems in University Management. Washington, D.C.: Association of Research Libraries, 1970; 11-20.

5. Donald Coney. "Where Did You Go? To the Library. What Did You Get? Nothing." CRL, 19 (May 1958), 179-84.
6. Franklin D. Murphy. "Some Reflections on Structure." In: John Coffrey, ed., The Future Academic Community: Continuity and Change. Washington, D.C.: American Council on Education, 1969; 88-94.
7. Herman H. Fussler. Letter to McAnally, Mar. 8, 1972, p. 2.
8. Earl C. Bolton. "Response of University Library Management to Changing Modes of University Governance and Control." CRL, 33 (July 1972), 308.
9. Richard N. Logsdon. Letter to McAnally, Aug. 10, 1972.
10. Jean Mayer. "The College and University: A Program for Academic Renewal." Harvard Bulletin (Nov. 16, 1970), 21-27.
11. Peter F. Drucker. The Age of Discontinuity; Guidelines to Our Changing Society. New York: Harper & Row, 1969; 389-90.
12. Douglas W. Bryant. "Problem of Research Libraries: Development of Resources." A.C.L.S. Newsletter, 22:1 (Jan. 1971), 3-8.
13. Vannevar Bush. "As We May Think." Atlantic Monthly, 176:1 (July 1945), 101-08.
14. National Research Council. Committee on Research in the Life Sciences. The Life Sciences: Recent Progress and Application to Human Affairs, the World of Biological Research, Requirements for the Future. Washington, D.C.: The National Academy of Sciences, 1970; 406.
15. Fremont Rider. The Scholar and the Future of the Research Library; A Problem and Its Solution. New York: Hadham Press, 1944.
16. O. C. Dunn, et al. The Past and Likely Future of 58 Research Libraries, 1951-1980: A Statistical Study

of Growth and Change. Lafayette, Ind.: University Libraries and Audio-visual Center, 1965- .

17. Earl F. Cheit. The New Depression in Higher Education: A Study of Financial Conditions at 41 Colleges and Universities; A General Report for the Carnegie Commission on Higher Education and the Ford Foundation. New York: McGraw-Hill, 1971.

18. Cornell University Libraries. Report of the Director of University Libraries, 1970/71. Ithaca, N.Y.: Cornell University Libraries, 1971; 7.

19. Representative leaders include Chris Argyris, Understanding Organizational Behavior (Homewood, Ill.: Dorsey Press, 1960) and his Interpersonal Competence and Organizational Effectiveness (Homewood, Ill.: Dorsey Press, 1962); Rensis Likert, New Patterns of Management (New York: McGraw-Hill, 1961); Peter F. Drucker, The Effective Executive (New York: Harper & Row, 1967); Robert A. Sutermeister, People and Productivity, 2d ed. (New York: McGraw-Hill, 1969); Alfred J. Marrow et al., Management by Participation; Creating a Climate for Personal and Organizational Development (New York: Harper & Row, 1967); and Harlon Cleveland, The Future Executive (New York: Harper & Row, 1972). A good summary of the early movement is Timothy Hallimen, New Directions in Organization Theory (Santa Monica, Calif.: RAND Corp., Sept. 1968; P-3936).

20. Larry E. Greiner. "Evolution and Revolution as Organizations Grow." Harvard Business Review, 50:4 (July-Aug. 1972), 37-46.

21. See for example Earl C. Bolton. Response of University Management, 308.

22. Henry L. Mason. College and University Government: A Handbook of Principle and Practice. New Orleans: Tulane University, 1972.

23. See for example Myron Lieberman, "Professors, Unite!" Harper's Magazine, 243:1457 (Oct. 1971), 61-70; and Terence N. Tice, ed., Faculty Power: Collective Bargaining on Campus. Ann Arbor, Mich.: Institute of Continuing Legal Education, 1972.

24. "Unionization of Faculty Expected to Pick up Speed Because of Tight Money and Ph.D.s." College Management, 6 (Sept. 1971), 38.

25. "Analysis of an Act to Consolidate the Institutions of Higher Education in North Carolina, Session Laws of 1971, Proceedings, Chapter 1244, Ratified 30 October 1971."

26. Arthur M. McAnally. "Budgets by Formula." Library Quarterly, 33 (Apr. 1963), 159-171.
27. Kenneth S. Allen. Current and Emerging Budgeting Techniques in Academic Libraries, Including a Critique of the Model Budget Analysis Program of the State of Washington. Seattle, Apr. 1972.
28. Washington (State). Office of Interinstitutional Business Studies. A Model Budget Analysis System for Program 05 Libraries. Olympia: 1970.
29. Thomas R. Buckman. Letter to McAnally, June 8, 1972, p. 2.
30. Second U.S.-Japan Conference of University Library Directors, Oct. 17-20, 1972. Robert Vosper, "The Role of the University Library Director: Principal Issues of the Seventies," p. 7. The social scientist is Richard L. Meier. See "Information Input Overload: Features of Growth in the Communications-Oriented Institutions," LIBRI, 13:11 (1963).
31. See L. Carroll De Weese, "Status Concerns of Library Professionalism." CRL, 33 (Jan. 1972), 31-38. Also Edward G. Holley, "Organization and Management." Also Maurice P. Marchant, "Participative Management as Related to Personnel Development." Library Trends, 20 (July 1971), 48-59. Directors who commented on this point, besides Robert Miller, included Edward B. Stanford, Lewis C. Branscomb, David Kaser, and Richard H. Logsdon.
32. Eldred R. Smith. The Specialist in the Academic Research Library: A Report to the Council on Library Resources. [Berkeley, Calif.] May 1971.
33. Booz, Allen & Hamilton, Inc. Organization and Staffing of the Libraries of Columbia University: A Summary of a Case Study. Washington, D.C.: Association of Research Libraries, 1972. (The full study will be published in two volumes.)
34. Robert T. Blackburn. "College Libraries: Paradoxical Failures; Some Reasons and a Possible Remedy." CRL, 29 (May 1968), 171-77.
35. Richard H. Logsdon. "Librarian and the Scholar: Eternal Enemies." Library Journal, 95 (Sept. 15, 1970), 2871-74.
36. Robert A. Miller, letter to Arthur McAnally, dated Mar. 17, 1972. Also, see Hendrik Edelman, "Motherhood, the Growth of Library Collections, Freedom of Access and Other Issues." Cornell University Libraries Bulletin, no. 176 (Apr. 1972), 5-6. See also Eldred R. Smith, "The Specialist in

the Academic Research," p. 34.
37. Cornell University Libraries. Annual Report of the Director, 1970/71. Ithaca, N.Y.: The Libraries, 1971; 7.
38. Thomas R. Buckman. Letter to McAnally, June 8, 1972.
39. See Booz, Allen & Hamilton, Inc., Problems in University Library Management. Also David Kaser, "Planning in University Libraries; Context and Processes." Southeastern Librarian, 21 (Winter 1971), 207-13. For a pioneering effort in long-range planning, see Marion Milczewski, "Cloak and Dagger in University Library Administration." CRL, 13 (Apr. 1952), 117-21.
40. Peter F. Drucker. The Age of Discontinuity; Guidelines to Our Changing Society. New York: Harper & Row, 1969.
41. Richard H. Logsdon. Letter to Arthur McAnally, Aug. 8, 1972.
42. Thomas R. Buckman. Letter to McAnally, June 8, 1972.
43. Earl C. Bolton, Response of University Management, 309. See also Booz, Allen & Hamilton, Inc., Problems in University Library Management, 5-6 et passim.
44. Robert P. Haro. "Change in Academic Libraries," CRL, 33 (Mar. 1972), 97-103.
45. David Kaser. "Planning in University Libraries," 288.
46. These and other excellent suggestions are made by Kenneth S. Allen, Current and Emerging Budgeting, 37-46. See also Booz, Allen & Hamilton, Inc., Problems in University Library Management.
47. Kenneth S. Allen. Current and Emerging Budgeting, 40.
48. Ibid., 18.
49. Richard M. Dougherty. "The Unserved--Academic Library Style." American Libraries, 2 (Nov. 1971), 1055-58.
50. Douglas Bryant. "Problems of University Libraries: Development of Resources." ACLS Newsletter, 22:1 (Jan. 1971), 3-8.
51. Richard M. Dougherty. "The Unserved."
52. Edward G. Holley. "Organization and Administration," 186-87.
53. Thomas R. Buckman. Letter to McAnally, June 8, 1972.
54. Lewis C. Branscomb. Letter to McAnally, Apr. 3,

1972.
55. Booz, Allen & Hamilton, Inc. Organization and Staffing of the Columbia University Library: A Summary of the Case Study. Also their Problems in University Library Management, op. cit.
56. Herman H. Fussler and Robert Vosper, op. cit. Larry Powell made a similar observation to Vosper.
57. University of Oklahoma Library Ad Hoc Committee on Library Service. Final Report of a User Survey of the Bizzell Memorial Library with Special Reference to Problems. Norman: July 1972.
58. Eldred Smith. Page 11 of "Academic Status for College and University Librarians--Problems and Prospects." CRL, 31 (Jan. 1970), 7-13.
59. Harold F. Wells. Telephone conversation with McAnally, July 8, 1972.
60. Edward G. Holley. "Organization and Administration," 182.
61. All have been cited already except Jane G. Flener: "Staff Participation in Management in Large University Libraries." Indiana University Library News Letter, 8:1 (Oct. 1972), 1-3.
62. Melvin S. Goldstein. Collective Bargaining in the Field of Librarianship. Brooklyn: 1968.
63. Richard De Gennaro. "Participative Management or Unionization." CRL, 33 (May 1972), 173-74.
64. Arthur M. McAnally. "Status of the University Librarian in the Academic Community." In: Research Librarianship: Essays in Honor of Robert B. Downs, ed. by Jerrold Orne. New York: Bowker, 1971; 19-50. Administrative operation is p. 31-46.
65. Luther H. Evans. "The Administration of a Federal Government Agency." L.C. Information Bulletin, Sept. 20-26, 1949, Appendix, p. 1-9. See also his annual reports of the period.
66. Kenneth S. Allen. Current and Emerging Budgeting. Thirteen institutions.
67. Maurice P. Marchant. Participative Management, 54. Also Lewis C. Branscomb, letter to McAnally, Apr. 3, 1972.
68. Beverly Lynch. "Participatory Management in Relation to Library Productivity." CRL 33 (Sept. 1972), 382-90.
69. Maurice P. Marchant. Participative Management, 48.
70. Luther H. Evans. "The Administration of a Federal...."

INFORMATION SCIENCE AS AN EMERGENT DISCIPLINE:
EDUCATIONAL IMPLICATIONS*

D. J. Foskett

Listening to a discussion on the radio recently, concerning the social implications of computers, I was struck by the expression, "Education is always in arrears of technology." It was spoken, of course, by a computer specialist, and typifies the pragmatic and often superficial view of those who have been most loudly vocal in their advocacy of these machines. Particularly today, we have to beware of allowing technology to rule society, of proclaiming that if a thing can be done, it must be done, and that all who question the necessity of this or that technological marvel are fuddled reactionaries who wish to hold up progress for the sake of preserving their own positions. But the antithesis of the "technology or slavery" school of thought has lately become manifest in the outcry, on the world scale, against the destruction of the environment by ruthless exploitation of natural resources on the one hand, and its pollution by industrial waste on the other.

I began my paper with this diatribe for two reasons. Firstly, information science as an emergent discipline cannot escape the charge of evading some of its responsibilities for serving the mind of Man; second, it is only through improved educational systems that we stand any chance of seeing our planet safely into the twenty-first century, and it follows from this that education must not be allowed to go stumbling along in the wake of technology. All of us engaged in education, whether as planners, administrators,

---

*Reprinted by permission of the Library Association from the July 1973 issue of Journal of Librarianship, pages 161-174. "A paper read to the FID Seminar on Information Science as an Emergent Discipline at Vezprem, Hungary, in September 1972."

teachers or students, must be well aware of the nature and results of technology, must be able to forecast the future as well as describe the present, and must, above all, aim at ensuring that those whom we are educating are also alive to all these things, having contemplated them philosophically in the light of real social needs. The pragmatic approach alone is not good enough: anyone can sit down and describe what could be done with a given technology. J. C. R. Licklider[1] has already prophesied that libraries will soon be replaced by "precognitive systems," in which the clash of human minds, the sharpening of wits in reflection and consideration, will be replaced by the characteristic behaviourist heaven of the total reduction of all enquiry to a question and answer situation; not, as in Socratic dialogues, between a learner and a great teacher, but between a learner and a mechanical moron. As we all know, this kind of approach, in which the technology dictates the objectives--"we must do it because we can do it"--has led to a trail of disasters unparalleled in the long history of library and information services. We know this, even though we do not usually read of such disasters in our literature; but, as we know just as well, the chat at the bar may, in due course, prove to be more revealing than the pages of even the most reputable journals with the most devoted of gate-keepers.

Obviously, I am not saying that we ought to deprive ourselves of the benefits of the new technology. What I mean is that the students of today must be so prepared, in their professional studies, that they are able to understand, not merely what the technology can do, but what we ought to require it to do. It is of the first importance that information scientists and librarians should appreciate the capabilities of computers, but it is no less important, though far less often recognized, that computer specialists should, in their turn, pay heed to our opinions because in this discussion we are likely to have a far deeper understanding of the real needs of users, since we deal directly with them. A profession may, indeed it should, change its views on the nature and scope of its activities from time to time; as a profession, it should be alert to the significance of new ideas, and be ready and willing to incorporate them into its education programme. But, as a profession, it has also the duty to preserve its integrity, not for its own sake, but because the integrity of a profession is the highest form of safeguard for those whom the profession serves. If we believe in the social value of information science, it is for us to maintain and demonstrate the unity of professional activities and standards amid the diversity of readers' needs. It may seem a far cry from the small public library to the information services of great corporations, but fundamentally these all serve the same social purpose: they all help to achieve the transfer of organized thought from one human mind to another.

THE NATURE OF THE PROFESSION

Education for information science must be designed as education for a profession, and what characterizes a profession supremely is that it does not exist for its own sake. A profession comes into being when a group of individuals, recognizing the existence of a genuine social need, join together to find means of meeting that need through the elaboration of certain techniques. It is the need, not the techniques, that is primary; a professional person does not seek to create an unnecessary want, nor could the service one profession offers be provided just as well by another; professions are not competing with one another in the marketplace. The social need for information is far removed from the artificial creations of advertisers, and can hardly be met by accountants or dentists, valuable and necessary though their services are, any more than an information scientist, qua information scientist, is himself a dentist, or chemist, or accountant.

I have introduced the public library into this discussion deliberately, so before I go any further, I ought to make clear my position on the nature of "information science" itself. I speak as one committed to the view of a unified profession which includes librarians of all kinds as well as information specialists. I know that this view is not held in some parts of the world, where the backwardness of the authorities has produced backward public libraries staffed by ill-trained technicians who do not understand the meaning of information science. But in my country, as in many others, public and university libraries have demonstrated in practice that they are able and willing to offer information service, and that their methods in so doing are of the same order as those of the most advanced information system in the largest industry. I maintained this position in my book, Information Service in Libraries, after ten years' experience in industry, and my fifteen years in a university since then have only served to confirm me in it.

To those who claim that the public library or the university library are not involved, my reply is the corollary of what I have already said in my criticism of technology. It is that, because an institution does not do domething, this does not necessarily mean that it cannot or should not. In concrete terms, the backwardness of some librarians is no justification for preventing others from developing into information officers. As I have said before, librarians do not suffer from some biological handicap which makes them incapable of continuing to learn. Similarly, by "information science," I do not wish to restrict myself, as some have, by going to the opposite extreme and meaning no more than the basic theory of information flow, whether this be mathematical, psychological or even philosophical.

A CURRICULUM FOR INFORMATION SCIENCE

When I speak of "information science," therefore, I mean the discipline that is emerging from a cross-fertilization of ideas involving the ancient art of librarianship, the new art of computing, the arts of the new media of communication, and those sciences such as psychology and linguistics, which in their modern forms bear directly on all problems of communication--the transfer of organized thought. I do not now wish to lose myself in a discussion of nomenclature, but we must also bear in mind that the word "Informatics," introduced by our Soviet colleagues to describe such a new discipline, is already current in some countries to signify only "computer science." The conference in Rome last November [i.e., 1971] nearly came to grief on several occasions through this confusion.[2] As presented by Professor A. I. Mikhailov and his colleagues in their paper, "Informatics: Its Scope and Methods," the new discipline is an independent discipline within the complex of the social sciences and, they say, "is in a way a continuation of bibliography and library science, but the experience inherited by informatics from these branches of science is being subjected to complete re-appraisal and appears in a new quality."[3] Their original outline of the discipline was as follows:

Informatics and laws of sciences development
Interrelation of Informatics with other fields of knowledge
General concept of information
Theory of information retrieval systems
Linguistics problems of Informatics
Information languages and classification problems
Psychological problems of Informatics
Study of information needs and inquiries

Efficiency of scientific information activity, its criteria
and indices
Theoretical basis for reasonable presentation of scientific information
The role of hardware in science information activity

This admirable table emphasizes the need for drawing in several subjects hitherto thought to be outside the curriculum in schools of library and information science, but the necessity for much further thought is shown by the subsequent <u>Guide for an Introductory Course in Informatics/Documentation,</u> prepared by Professor Mikhailov and R. S. Giljarevskij for Unesco, which is in fact somewhat more traditional in its range of contents.[4] For example, it includes very little material on the psychological, linguistic and sociological foundations; on the other hand, it also neglects management and comparative studies, which have lately received considerable attention in the UK and USA.

I would like to outline at this point some ideas of my own on the nature of a curriculum, and then go on to relate it to the social situation that now faces us as information scientists and educators:

The universe of knowledge.
  Study of the nature, forms and disciplines of knowledge, the inner structure of subjects and their interrelationships.
Production and publication of knowledge.
  The processes of research and communication, including psycholinguistics; publishing, formal and informal systems. Social and technical facets of the book trade. Primary and secondary classes of documents. Reprography.
Acquisition and arrangement of materials.
  Bibliography: sources of documents and information about documents.
  Classification and indexing languages and their structure, information retrieval systems, retrospective searching.
Dissemination and use of knowledge.
  Techniques of dissemination: current awareness services. Psychology and sociology of users and user groups and their reading habits.
Library and information service technology.
  The use (not the manufacture) of all types of hardware, including audio-visual equipment and comput-

ers. Basic sciences (e.g., logic, mathematics) only in sufficient detail to acquire understanding of how these influence performance in the context of Informatics.
Planning and management.
Techniques required to plan and carry out these technical services, including General System Theory, Output Budgeting, statistical and other techniques of scientific administration.
Comparative and historical studies.
Study of national and international systems. Comparative study, interpreted as scientific method in the social sciences, and applied to all facets of information service operation.

It will be evident that such a course is very wide-ranging, and I would expect any school to draw up a series of options so that students might choose to follow a measure of specialization. Nonetheless, after allowing for such limited depth studies, I would regard it as essential that all students should have at least a basic grounding over the whole field.

I have discussed elsewhere three major factors that influence education for a professional role,[5] but perhaps I may briefly repeat them here:

1. The needs of the student.
2. The needs of the employer.
3. The needs of the profession.

The student, who has probably begun his course with a minimum of practical experience, requires a thorough grounding in all those areas of professional activity in which he will be operating and taking decisions. Since he intends to be a "professional," he will probably reach a position with a certain amount of managerial responsibility fairly soon after his initial training has been completed. His teachers therefore have to give him a convincing account of what is done in the name of professional activity, why they are done as they are, and what principles of organization have to be called upon in order to see that they are done. This means that he must be given a reasonable account; it is not sufficient for him merely to be told that such and such is the case, and for him to have to memorize these facts. He has to go beyond the description of the present situation, and assimilate a whole structure of rational discourse about these principles so that he may reach a satisfactory level of professional judgement as well as competence. This is particularly true of the present age, when information services are going through a period of rapid transition, and methods popular even five years ago may be quite obsolete when the new student reaches his first position of authority.

The needs of employers conflict with these aspirations. All employers would naturally prefer to recruit young would-be professionals who are mentally alert and vigorous, full of knowledge about the very latest advances in techniques, but at the same time amenable to instruction in the practical wisdom of those who are already in positions of authority in the system. And employers actually want more even than this: they want to recruit new employees who can be immediately posted to a particular job, having already the ability to do that job with very little extra practical instruction, thus causing a minimum of wasted time. These two requirements are somewhat in conflict with each other, and many arguments for both views often appear in our professional literature.

It is however, the needs of the profession that determine the basic requirements of the other two categories. The management of an information service is not an end in itself, and this last category might well have been called instead "the needs of the users," to emphasize that the needs of a profession derive, in fact, from the needs of those served by the profession. These are that it should, as a corporate body--an association of professional people--have a full awareness of what its corporate role should be in relation to the various institutions of society. It should have the social responsibility for ensuring that its members are thoroughly motivated by the desire to provide services for these institutions at the highest level of technical competence. The profession is the guardian of the professional conscience. It follows that it should also assume the responsibility for maintaining the standards of performance of its members and, as a corporate body, keep a continuous watch on the development of practical methods for implementing professional aims. The identification and public discussion of these aims is a matter for professional educators, and we should expect younger members to bring a critical eye to current formulations of aims and to the possibilities of having to modify them in the light of changing circumstances and beliefs. A school for educating information scientists, therefore, has a responsibility not only to the student who is being taught and to the employer who is the cash customer for the product, but also to a generalized body of professionally accepted knowledge and wisdom.

THEORY AND PRACTICE

When we speak of such a notion as a "generalized body of knowledge," we immediately come face to face with the age-old problem of any professional course carried out at an institution of higher learning: what should be the relation between theory and practice? Is it the function of an educational course to instruct the student in practical skills, so that he has reached a high standard of execution before he receives his qualification? I do not think it is; I believe that excellence in practical skills can only be acquired by practice in a real-life situation. Of course, we must not divorce theory from practice altogether, and I would certainly insist on the inclusion of a practical element in every course. But this would be to illuminate the theoretical foundations, not to bring the student to a peak of excellence. For if it is true that theory without practice is sterile, it is equally true that practice without theory is blind, and the task of an educational institution, to my mind, is to enable a student to learn in depth the body of generalized theoretical knowledge, by means of which he will be able not only to interpret the practical situation in which he finds himself at work, but also to formulate for himself his own role, his duties and responsibilities, in the light of a professional consensus. Such an intellectual approach will surely bring with it the desire to perform well, and will thus lead quickly, in practice, to the attainment of excellence in the practical skills. Whereas the mere instruction in practical skills, on an initial education course, however devotedly and expertly carried out, does, as we all know, often lead to frustration and even consternation when the newly-fledged professional finds that what he has just learned has to be unlearned because things are done differently in the system he has just joined.

If, on the other hand, we were to insist, as some critics of schools of library and information science do, that practical training is of the essence, and that theoretical understanding can only come with depth of practical experience, we should, in my judgement, be in danger of reducing our practice to a craft, and we could then no longer claim either the title of information <u>science</u> or the right to be educated at universities. The essential difference lies in this:

that the craftsman sees his product from beginning to end, and it is therefore his own individual work. He does not have to conform to any particular public consensus or standards, for he is not representing a profession by his work, only himself. A professional, by contrast, may have to subordinate his own personal inclinations from time to time, for the sake of the public good as represented by his professional standards and ethics. A university-based education aims at providing knowledge of the consensus, how it has been reached and what it signifies, and where lies the justification for the subordination of personal interest for the public good. Similarly, what characterizes a science, above all, is that it consists of a body of truths abstracted from the observation of phenomena. A body of knowledge cannot claim to be a science if it consists merely of descriptions, whether these be of natural phenomena or of specialist technical operations.

The history of the art of librarianship throws light on the situation. The traditional role of the librarian, since antiquity, has been that of a curator of records, of one sort or another, from the astronomical and meteorological data of Ancient Egypt to the sacred books of many different civilizations. The curators did not only look after the records, they also prevented them from falling into the wrong hands. Since they served a ruling élite, they in fact made it possible for civilization to progress, because the élite no longer needed to rely solely on their memories in order to appear wise. Knowledge could be cumulated, and the techniques of librarianship were originally evolved to identify and retrieve documents for their information--a function analogous to that of the human memory. The human mind carries out the same sort of operations of classifying and retrieving, and the techniques of the curator were designed to imitate the structure of the intellect. This meant systems for identifying and describing documents, that is, cataloguing and bibliography in all its forms; the arrangement or classification of the documents in ways that made sense to the users of the collection; staffing and managing the collection. Such were, and still are in many schools, the basic elements of the initial courses.

The inheritance of this emphasis on the techniques or methods rather than on analysis of social role and purpose is that two main factors have influenced the controversies that have occurred over the content of curricula for information scientists. Firstly, the differentiation of specialist knowledge through the great increase in research and discovery, made very obvious by the corresponding increase in publications, and establishing a need for specialist information officers playing an active role in organizing and disseminating information. Second, the invention of new machines for data processing, which makes it possible to handle these publications and the data they contain more cheaply and expeditiously than with traditional manual methods. We now have many more writers, many more subjects, more libraries, more users. These have cumulated to the extent of producing a qualitative change in the part to be played by the information officer who cannot remain a curator, but must act in a more positive way to promote the communication of ideas. New techniques and new forms of secondary publication such as indexes, abstracts, surveys, combine with new forms of social organization of users and of their information needs to make it necessary for us to re-think our educational programmes, not simply in the light of understanding the mechanisms of techniques, but in relation to new social situations--the real needs of users in our contemporary civilization.

A PROPER ROLE FOR COMPUTERS

The solution does not lie in the wholesale application of computers to every possible process, even though the computer has acted as the catalyst in bringing about the birth of this new professional role. Many of those who write about computers in information science seem to take the behaviourist view that every transaction in an intellectual milieu can be reduced to a question and answer, that information services need only fit themselves to supply discrete pieces of data. Information has been reified into a commodity, and all the enthusiasm and skill devoted to production drives now goes into its manufacture. Dr. Bentley Glass, whose important series of John Dewey Lectures has been published in a book significantly entitled <u>The Timely and the Timeless</u>, [6] has again emphasized the danger:

> The data and the facts alone do not constitute knowledge, in the sense of understanding. Information is needful, but the observations must be fitted into concepts and conceptual schemes, or paradigms, that determine one's outlook and direct one's processes of investigation and enquiry ... the study of a science must penetrate beyond its data and its laws and embrace also its method of

enquiry and its historical process.

In our present situation, where the single research worker who recorded and published his results when he considered that his project was complete has been replaced by the research team, whose programme is continuous and whose publications record, not a finished work, but every step, no matter how trivial, along a never-ending road, the specialist literature is in grave danger of becoming clogged with work of no value to anyone.

Much of the so-called research in mechanized methods of documentation is based likewise on "models" that imitate the industrial mass production line, and are so remote from the real life information retrieval circumstances as to make their results unusable except in similarly remote laboratory situations. We must never forget, moreover, that when a production process is based solely on the least effort for the producer, as it usually is, the interests of the users are very liable to suffer; for while a "simple" input operation may indeed make it possible to use unskilled clerical labour at input, the output is likely to prove just as "simple," that is, it will be so primitive in use that it will either give unsatisfactory results or demand an exorbitant effort on the part of the hapless user.

The key to the educational implications of information science as an emergent discipline, therefore, is that we must cease regarding our discipline as not more than a collection of techniques worthy of study and operation for their own sakes; they must be subjected to critical scrutiny in the light of the social function they perform. Certainly we need to produce specialists who have studied and mastered individual techniques in depth, like the British Classification Research Group, and similar groups throughout the world, who have been meeting for many years, and have made important contributions to the advancement of that part of our science. We have a particular need for specialists who understand the mysteries of the computer sufficiently well to resist the blandishments of computer salesmen, without at the same time sacrificing the chance to improve our technical processes. The successful development of bibliographical systems by VINITI in the USSR, by the Chemical Abstracts Service in the USA, and by INSPEC at the British Institution of Electrical Engineers, to name only a few of the most famous, bears witness to the potential value of the machines when handled with practical insight. Many other organizations, such as UVTEI in Czechoslovakia and the IBBD in Brazil, both known to me personally, have established equally successful systems on a more modest but no less significant scale.

Not the least aspect of their significance, however, is that most of the most successful operations are clearly developments from previous systems, for what they amount to is the mechanization of publication. In other words, they have improved existing techniques and made possible their application in fields hitherto uncultivated. The same advances have not been so evident in the newer aspects of information science--the active role of retrieval and dissemination of information. The KWIC index is doubtless an extremely clever thing for a computer to do. Many titles, in the exact sciences at least, are expressive of the subjects of their articles; but even the most cursory inspection suggests that many are not, and this has been confirmed by the analyses made by R. T. Bottle in several fields. Even in chemistry, where one might expect a high rate of success, the actual findings are only mediocre. But authors must be free to choose what they consider to be words significant for readers who will be scanning titles to see whether they indicate potential interest. These words may, or may not, coincide with what a skilled indexer or information scientist would choose as a search term, because searching is a different operation from scanning.

The other faults of KWIC indexes are well-known: lack of synonym control, failure to provide cross-references, inordinate duplication of entry, confusion of homonyms, and so on. Now all of these would be regarded as mistakes, and corrected, if practised by a human indexer. What justification can there be for excusing such malpractices simply because they come from a machine? The only possible answer can be that they are justified precisely because they come from a machine. The technology has dictated the objective.

Fortunately, one can now point to cases where good sense has prevailed and the use of KWIC indexing has been quietly dropped, or modified to the extent that it is no longer KWIC indexing. But I use it as a case study because it illustrates very clearly the responsibility we, as professionals, must accept on behalf of those we serve. When H. P. Luhn first suggested this technique, he had in mind a product which would be used in a manner similar to the end product of most computer operations, namely calculations for which the computer provides the answer. Much of the time, the research worker feeds in his problem, notes the answer and throws away the printout, which he does not need to carry about with him. Similarly, Luhn's idea of a KWIC index was that titles would be scanned and fed in by clerks within one organization for the printout to be used by others in the same organization to see if there were any items in their library's current acquisitions which they ought to read. They would then have no further use for the printout itself. They would recognize significant words because they were part of the organization and knew the context in which they were working. Above all, since this was a current awareness service with a limited purpose, it would not be too much to expect the users to scan the whole list, as they would if they were scanning the collection of journals from which the titles were listed.

The KWIC indexing technique itself merely provides a case study--evidence for my thesis that education for information science must look beyond the concept of information processing, which is merely moving marks from one place to another, and begin to ask more pertinent questions, such as "Who needs information, and why?" "In what form?" "Who provides it?" "Where can it be found?" It is the answers to questions like these that will point the way ahead. They should result in a re-orientation of our views of professional education, so that we change from an inward-looking attitude inspecting and describing techniques as if for their own sake, to an outward-looking attitude studying which techniques are required to achieve the objectives we have previously determined as socially desirable contributions for our profession to make. If we let the objectives define the technology, instead of the other way about, then we shall also be in a position to offer useful comments to the technologists themselves, since they, too, ought to be directing their own progress towards socially desirable objectives.

SOCIAL OBJECTIVES

We have now reached the crux of the whole matter: what are "socially desirable objectives" for information scientists? I have not been able to find a great deal of pertinent examination of this question in our literature. All too often, it seems, we do not go to the proper starting point, but instead we take for granted that, because all this mass of data, information and documentation is there, we have to process it; and the more there is, the bigger machines we shall have to have. With some systems, my impression is not one of helpfulness to the user; it is rather that a vast quantity of rubbish has been processed merely in order to demonstrate that we can process vast quantities of rubbish. The obvious but neglected conclusion is that this is not a matter for us to decide for ourselves and by ourselves. If we are to reach any consensus on our objectives, it is vital that we should consult with both the producers and the users of information and documentation. In the days when the output of specialist literature was small enough to be manageable by the individual scholar or student, the free play of the marketplace meant that a reasonable feed-back occurred from user to producer in the form of sales, and this acted as a regulator on the quantity of production. Now, when the State intervenes to provide stores of documents in the national library collection, this direct relationship has disappeared, and there can be no doubt that libraries are now buying a good deal of material that adds nothing to the public store of knowledge. The once-proud boast of a fine library, that it tried to collect everything in its own field, has become degraded into a confession of irresponsibility in selection.

It follows from this that one objective must be to meet the real needs of users economically and effectively. There is no point in our piling more and more computerized bibliographical masterpieces on the desks of people who are crying out for help precisely because they cannot cope with what is there already. More attention must be paid to the question of how people use new information, how they assimilate it into their existing conceptual schemes, and how these schemes may be modified in the light of the new knowledge. In my paper to the Rome Conference, I tried to describe some of the implications for us of recent work in the psychology of the learning process, such as that of Piaget, Guilford, Vygotsky and Luria. Unless what we provide as information has meaning for the recipient, he will regard it as a nuisance, not a blessing; and it acquires meaning from two aspects. One is its relation to the paradigm of which it is part, that is, its subject connotation. The other is its relation to the user's own context of thought. These two factors justify the inclusion in our curricula of study of the patterns in the universe of knowledge, and of the psychological processes involved in production, communication and assimilation of new knowlege.

If we are to provide this service of intrinsic value, then we must first ensure that the right materials are available to us. We must become fully acquainted with the formal and informal systems of publication and distribution; this explains the importance of the work of, for example, Professor da Solla Price, and of the studies of Diana Crane on the role of scientific "gatekeepers."7 All too rarely have information scientists become involved in these fields to the point of acquiring enough authority to exert an influence on the course of events. Where they have, the results have been outstandingly successful. But once again it is necessary to look further than the outward manifestations in the form of the published literature. We need to discover and analyse the significance of Emile Durkheim, Karl Mannheim, Talcott Parsons, and the other sociologists who have investigated the sociology of knowledge itself. As in so many other matters of vital concern to us today, one of the pioneers in this field was Francis Bacon, whose Novum Organum and New Atlantis charted the course of modern science, and who called his information officers "Messengers of Light." Another pioneer was Karl Marx, whose deeply penetrating insights into the social nature of consciousness are only now receiving their due attention in the Western countries.

All this adds up to a greater integration of library and information services into the wider society of which we are part, and in this respect I find the elaboration by Ludwig von Bertalanffy of his General System Theory of high importance. 8 It first came to the attention of the British Classification Research Group some years ago when we began to turn our attention from the construction of specialized indexing languages or classification schemes to the theory of a general scheme. Our search was for a theoretical foundation for the selection of Main Classes, or better starting points for facet analysis, and the attraction of the General System Theory is that it recognizes the inevitable interconnections between all realms of natural phenomena, but utterly opposes reductionism in all its forms. The relevance of this for the classification of knowledge is clear, but the theory also helps to illuminate the management process, because it reminds us that no library and information service should be considered as an entity by itself, any more than any technical process; that all our services are parts of wider systems, of many different kinds. We have systems of libraries themselves, with their schemes of inter-lending and of co-operation in acquisition and processing of documents. We have our international networks, fostered by the FID, by IFLA, by Unesco. Each library is part of its system of users, whether it be an industrial firm, a government research organization, a university, or a local community. Each set of users is also part of a still wider system: a professional association, a scientific group engaged in one subject field, a nation.

Only by acknowledging the reality of these wider horizons shall we succeed in bringing our educational systems to the point where they cease to be vocational training in technical skills, no matter how advanced, and become "educational" in the true sense: the cultivation of a human mind so that it can form sound judgements on the basis of a correct understanding of all facets of our work. When this is the sort of education we give our students, they will be enabled to arrive at an understanding of users such that they will be able to eliminate the distinction between user and information scientist, because they, too, will have become users, acting on behalf of other users. Education will then have ceased to be in arrears of technology, and will provide the light of truth which guides technology along those paths that are of most benefit to humanity.

REFERENCES

1. Licklider, J. C. R. Libraries of the Future. Cambridge, Mass.: MIT Press, 1965.
2. Italian National Information Institute and FID. "The Training of Information Workers." Conference held in Rome, Nov. 1971.
3. Mikhailov, A. I., et al., eds. On Theoretical Problems of Informatics. FID 435. Moscow: VINITI, 1969.
4. Mikhailov, A. I., and Giljarevskij, R. S. Guide for an Introductory Course on Informatics/Documentation. Paris: Unesco, 1970.
5. Foskett, D. J. "The Education of Librarians." In: The Metropolitan Library. Ed. by R. W. Conant and Kathleen Molz. Cambridge, Mass.: MIT Press, 1972.
6. Glass, Bentley. The Timely and the Timeless: The Interrelationships of Science, Education and Society. New York: Basic Books, 1970.
7. Crane, Diana. "The Gatekeepers of Science: Some Factors Affecting the Selection of Articles in Scientific Journals." In: The Sociology of Knowledge: A

Reader. Ed. by J. E. Curtis and J. W. Petras. London: Duckworth, 1970. (This volume also contains many other papers of interest to information scientists.)
8. Bertalanffy, Ludwig von. General System Theory: Foundations, Development, Applications. London: Allen Lane, The Penguin Press, 1971.

THREE PEAS IN A POD: A HERO
AND TWO HEROINES*

Caroline E. Werkley

Andrew Carnegie would have liked my mother, who for many years presided over one of his public libraries, but I am not sure he would have cottoned to me. Mother, after all, had many of the traits of his mother, whom he adored, and she also shared some of his own qualities. The only things Mr. Carnegie and I would have had in common were strong-minded mothers--Margaret Carnegie was said to be the one person whose will was never bent in surrender to her son--and the fact that we both at one time took elocution lessons. Also, each of us had our earlier literary work published in Sunday School papers.

I have an unpleasant feeling that Mr. Carnegie would have thought me feckless, and certainly, since I was rated as inferior minus in my class in college economics, I would never have made a fortune. Although Mother did not make a fortune either, I do not doubt that had she been a man and moved in Mr. Carnegie's circle, she could have done so. Her financial notebooks, begun early in her married life and kept for over a period of thirty years, were proof of that. They recorded every penny made and spent, even the expenditure, on 16 May 1904, of ".01 to Ada" and ".25 duster from a blind man," and revealed a pattern of saving that was characteristic of her throughout her life.

The meticulous records show her to have had the same good business sense that Mr. Carnegie loved to acknowledge publicly he had inherited from his mother. Every entry reveals my mother to be as thrifty, as good a manager of a meagre income, as was Margaret Carnegie, and

---

*Reprinted by permission from the Spring 1973 issue of Library Review, pages 11-16.

as willing to work hard to give her children the better things of life.

Margaret Carnegie assumed the role of her family's breadwinner in the terrible period of poverty of her son's boyhood when the change from handloom to steam-loom deprived her husband of his living as a weaver. She not only opened a shop for selling vetegables in her own home but she even added further to the family income by binding shoes for her brother Tom in order to provide food for her family and keep Andrew in school.

"It became necessary for that power which never failed in any emergency--my mother--to step forward and endeavour to repair the family fortune," recalled Andrew Carnegie. "I do not know to what lengths of privation my mother would not have gone that she might see her two boys wearing large white collars, and trimly dressed." With my mother, the important thing was that my sisters and I should have smocking or hand embroidery on our dresses.

My mother entered the working world as a librarian after the death of my father had left her with three young daughters to provide for. She allowed herself only a momentary anguished protest in her diary entry of 9 May 1918 --"Luther died, and there's no more home or need for accounts. It's all over." As early as July, however, the accounts had begun again, the homely entries of bacon, 10 cents; eggs, 28 cents; potatoes, 25 cents. She had pulled herself together bravely as she had back in June of 1905 when she entered: "Bank broke with our $275 and have not a thing"--although by November 21 of that year she and my father had "Paid Dr. Rubey $81 on note on home and finally have home all paid for."

Now, in that same spirit, refusing to be broken by sorrow, she settled her little family in the town of her girlhood, and her notebooks show that she even made her peace with the world to the extent of purchasing twenty-five cents' worth of watercolour paper in order to continue her painting. Nor would her children be culturally deprived. "Took $55 out of bank for piano," noted her diary. Her world may have fallen apart, and she, who had been used to facing the public only at such pleasant social functions as meetings of the Shakespeare and Tourist Clubs or missionary society groups, would have to go out and make a living, but her family would still pursue the finer things of life. Margaret Carnegie would have understood this resolution.

Mrs. Carnegie did not hesitate to uproot herself and her family to come to America in order to give her boys a chance in the world. In Scotland, she felt they could never make a decent living. My mother, too, was determined that her three daughters should prepare for respectable professions. "Wise men are always looking out for clever boys," Mr. Carnegie himself once wrote. And girls too, Mother reminded us. From the time when she was left alone to bring us up, she planned for our college educations, early settling on teaching as the ideal position of respectability, or, as Mr. Carnegie would say, that life which would be the most elevating in its character. My sisters obliged my mother by securing their college degrees in education and promptly becoming school teachers. I dutifully studied teacher's training in my first two years of college, but when I went on to the University of Missouri I enrolled, in unexpected rebellion, in the School of Journalism.

After wondering, in the pages of an agonized letter to me, what would become of me for my defection from the study of a profession that would have ensured me security and respectability--"You will never make a living as a newspaper reporter"--Mother consoled herself with the thought that journalists were not actually looked down upon professionally, and I might even end up teaching journalism. The fact that I read and wrote poetry and drama showed that I was a person of sensitivity, and hopefully this would bring me safely through the perils of association with what she was sure were the more casual standards and ideals of journalists. She had read somewhere that by the nature of their work they were inclined to a certain amount of carousing, which to her meant staying up till all hours, doing heaven-knows-what. She protested to the bitter end, however, the fact that I was taking a course in religious journalism, in which only one other person besides myself was enrolled.

"It surely can't be of much importance or more would take it," she observed desperately. "Oh, why did you not take something of more value?"

Although she might disapprove of some of my shortcomings herself--she even endured a period when I vowed I would be an actress and nothing else--she would allow no one else to do so, any more than Margaret Carnegie would have listened to complaints about her boy, such as Mr. Morgan's statement to another big money maker, Mr. Schwab, that "Carnegie is going to demoralize railroads just as he has demoralized steel." In the early days of my marriage I wrote plaintively to my mother that my landlady did not think I was a good housekeeper.

"The idea of that woman saying you were not a born housekeeper," Mother responded indignantly. "I did not born you for that, but for higher things. But you ought to be a good housekeeper," she added sensibly, "I feel it is a reflection on me, so do try to improve in that line for I know you can."

Although Mother was such a great admirer of Mr. Carnegie, I do not think she realized how much alike they both were in many ways, even to extremely small hands and feet, physical traits Mr. Carnegie had inherited from his mother. Both my mother and Mr. Carnegie were short of stature. Mother was only four feet ten, and Mr. Carnegie was just five inches taller, not a great height as masculine standards are usually considered. Certainly, however, he could have looked down on Mother in comfort, which should have been balm to his masculinity. Both were effervescent, talkative, liked to argue, and did not hesitate to express their opinions. Andrew himself admitted to his "argumentativeness, or perhaps combativeness, which has always remained with me." He once even remarked that public libraries should look aggressive.

Both Mr. Carnegie and Mother liked to get the best of a bargain, although for different reasons; Mother because every penny saved was important to her restricted budget, Mr. Carnegie because a bargain delighted his canny Scotch nature. It did him good, he once admitted gleefully after concluding a business deal with John D. Rockefeller, to think he had got ahead of his fellow millionaire in a bargain--no easy thing to do, since John D. was also a bargain hunter.

Mr. Carnegie was "at times rough shod in his treatment of such companions as presumed to take opposing views," wrote one of his biographers. Well, this was certainly my mother when I was determined to do something she did not think was best for me. Carnegie's eyes had a steely glint in moments of severity, continued the biographer.

My sisters and I did not like the steely glint in my mother's eyes when we had provoked her to anger, either. Nor did any tradesmen whom she felt had overcharged her, thinking that she, as a woman, would not notice.

It was said of Carnegie that no man ever suffered fools less patiently. Three girls can be three fools a great deal of the time, and it was probably not easy for Mother to suffer us. Certainly she deserved better. Since she had no son to be her right hand and to regard her as a heroine, as Andrew did his mother--the dedication of his first book was "To My Favourite Heroine, My Mother"--surely at least one of her daughters should have had more "get-up-and-go." We were all, as a matter of fact, timid, spendthrifts, and inclined to let opportunities slip by us, a failing she found particularly hard to accept and understand, as would Andrew Carnegie, who was described as having an "instantaneous appreciation of opportunity, an ever present audacity in taking a chance."

"You know opportunity does not knock at your door always," Mother wrote to me in college. "Don't let even one little opportunity pass," she begged. No one, of course, ever had to beg or remind Andrew of this. He was ready to grab opportunity almost before the knock came announcing it. When he was twenty-five years of age he was receiving, in addition to other income, an annual dividend of over five thousand dollars because he had seized the opportunity to invest in a sleeping-car company. By the time I was twenty-five, I realized my mother knew what she was talking about when she said I would not make a living as a newspaper reporter, but for once I showed some common sense--I married a former classmate who was making a living as one. He had not been led astray by religious journalism.

Mother and Mr. Carnegie and his mother all shared an admiration for Robert Burns. Mother was forever quoting to us girls a motto from the Scotch poet, "Thy own reproach alone dost fear," that Mr. Carnegie had adopted early in his life, and that he remarked had been more to him than all the sermons he ever heard. All it did to me was make me worry. I would rather have heard a hellfire-and-devils sermon by one of the visiting evangelists who came to the Methodist Church from time to time than have to live with my own reproaches. I could always find plenty of things to castigate myself about without having such a handy phrase to remind me, and I would have thought An-

drew would have had similar worries. It certainly was not
very nice of him to refuse to aid the man who had first got
him started on the road to his fortune. True, he did reproach himself for this. He said it gave him a great deal
of pain not to come to his friend's financial rescue, although
the gold clanking in his own coffers probably deadened the
pain somewhat.

Another literary tie that Mother and Mr. Carnegie
shared was Shakespeare. Mother, an ardent Shakespeare
admirer, read <u>Coriolanus</u> in 1916, a few years before she
became just as ardent an admirer of Andrew Carnegie. Interestingly enough, she underlined in this volume a critical
comment in the introduction: "He [Coriolanus] is prouder of
his mother than of himself; cares more to please her than
himself ... in brief, he looks up to her as a superior being
whose benediction is the best grace of his life ... we have
the sublimity of filial reverence...."

This was Coriolanus and Volumnia? It might have
been Andrew Carnegie and his beloved mother, Margaret.
Mr. Carnegie once expressed his belief that an expurgated
edition of the New Testament, as well as the Old, was
needed to correct the passage about Jesus asking a man to
forsake his father and mother in order to be His disciple.
"I do not think Jesus could have said that." His companions
to whom he spoke of this said they felt Andrew's statement
was prompted by his well-known affection and reverence for
his own mother. "She was the guardian angel of his life--
his 'saint,' as he always called her," wrote one of his biographers.

Both Mother and Mrs. Carnegie believed in the importance of their children doing what was right, but the
phrase did not grate on Mr. Carnegie as, I fear, it did on
me. Mr. Carnegie recalled lovingly that his mother told
him and his brother they could be useful men, honoured and
respected, if they always did what was right. As long as I
can remember, Mother similarly admonished my sisters and
me in all situations. When I would ask her what she wanted
for a Christmas present, hoping she would long for some
treasure I could buy, such as a painted tray from Woolworths,
or a gaudy brooch from Kresges, she never seemed to want
<u>things</u>, as I did, and as was natural.

"All I want is for you to be a good girl and do
right," she would tell me. This was maddening and it was

no answer. I already was a good girl and did right most of the time--who would dare do wrong with a mother like ours? I was too young to understand concepts as gifts, and wanted a glittering, marvellous purchase to show affection, as other children did.

I could always in my mind see Mr. Carnegie doing right--what a laugh this would have given his competitors in the iron and steel business--and smiling as he did so, because Mother often reminded us of Mr. Carnegie's quotation that "a sunny disposition is worth more than fortune." If I protested that I did not feel happy and sunny natured, Mother would reply that Mr. Carnegie said a happy disposition could be cultivated, that "the mind like the body can be moved from the shade into sunshine." ("He prefers optimism's blue skies to pessimism's dark caverns," wrote one of his admirers.)

It was all very well for Mother and Mr. Carnegie to like laughing their troubles away, as Mr. Carnegie further advised, and move from the shade into the sunshine, but there were times when I positively enjoyed being gloomy and miserable, and the thought of the eternally laughing Andrew Carnegie only made me gloomier. Although Mr. Carnegie asserted that "no man would whine and give up--he would die first," since I was only a girl surely I was entitled to an occasional whimper.

It was not just physical characteristics, personalities, and literary interests that Mother and Mr. Carnegie shared. Perhaps the most important idea they had in common was their attitude toward sharing their wealth with those less fortunate. Mr. Carnegie, in his thirty-third year, wrote a memorandum outlining his views on this subject, a draft that later was to emerge in his famous Gospel of Wealth.

"The fundamental idea of the gospel of wealth," said he in later years, "is that surplus wealth should be considered as a sacred trust to be administered by those into whose hands it falls, during their lives, for the good of the community."

Mother did not, like Mr. Carnegie, have wealth in the form of cold cash to distribute, but thanks to him she had at her disposal, as librarian, wealth in a different form, all the great literature, the priceless information that even a small library has accumulated over the years.

The Moberly library said what Mr. Carnegie believed every free library should say: "Welcome to my treasures that are within."

With these treasures of which she was the guardian, Mother was lavish. Gold was to be had for the asking, the gold of great thoughts lying like a Sultan's fortune--or the 311 million dollars that Mr. Carnegie gave away--there on the library shelves and in her clipping folders and boxes. One did not even have to <u>ask</u>--she was forever bringing forth pictures of such marvels as the Taj Mahal, the golden, dragon-winged Cellini Cup, the Grand Canyon, and the Bayeux Tapestry, and featuring them on a bulletin board. Mother constantly brought to the service of the public, as Mr. Carnegie advised, her "superior wisdom, experience, and ability to administer, doing for them better than they would or could do for themselves." She had, after all, majored in philosophy in college, and had always been an eager student of literature.

Mother was in agreement with Mr. Carnegie "that the parent who leaves his son enormous wealth generally deadens the talents and energies of the son, and tempts him to lead a less useful and less worthy life than he otherwise would." Since Mother had very little in the way of worldly goods to leave us, it comforted her greatly to remind herself that Mr. Carnegie was confident that "the greatest and the best of our race have necessarily been nurtured in the bracing school of poverty--the only school capable of producing the supremely great, the genius." She might, however, have argued a bit about Mr. Carnegie's going on and on about how wonderful it was to be a poor child so that his mother could be to him a "nurse, seamstress, teacher, inspirer, saint, his all in all." It may be a fine heritage for the child, all right, but it was mighty hard on the nurse-seamstress-teacher-inspirer-saint and all-in-all.

The nearest Mother ever got to setting down on paper her own Gospel of Wealth was a little document that she must have composed soon after I was graduated from college and that I found not long ago in one of her notebooks:

> I was left with one great trust to carry on alone. The goal to be reached was that each of our three daughters obtain a University degree. This June, as I saw our baby graduate with honors, I knew the profits on my many years 'in-

vestments' had weathered the storm; not only without loss, but with an inestimable increase in the credit side that would still continue to increase for them as the years go by. I also knew that my investments of the money for which I have labored unceasingly, and planned its use so carefully, have returned to me one hundred thousand fold, as I see the three girls happy in the work that the careful application of their education, obtained through my investments, has made possible for them. And when friends inquire how much I lost during the depression, they look at me at first in astonishment as I reply: 'My investments were so safely placed and have proved so very profitable, and therefore accumulated in the years, all because I invested only in the brain trust of my three daughters, which proved a safe and sound venture.'

It is true that none of her daughters was supremely great or a genius, but then we had not actually lived in poverty, as Mr. Carnegie recommended, only genteel straitened circumstances. And if we were sometimes a little inconsiderate in our demands for money from Mother, perhaps it was because we, as well as Andrew, knew that our mothers would never let us down.

"I felt sure the money could be raised somehow or other by my mother," Andrew remembered affectionately of the occasion in his youth when his mother had provided the money for his first investment. We were just as certain that in the little chamois bag filled with money that she wore about her neck, or in the black metal box where she stored her valuable papers and more money--or even in the bank--Mother could always find the means to pay for some special object that we deemed necessary to our happiness.

I myself have always secretly thought Mr. Carnegie went a little too far when he wrote in a rich lady's album, "I should as soon leave to my son a curse as the almighty dollar." Mr. Carnegie might have taken into consideration the fact that people who get inferior minus in college economics are not known to be as sharp with money, and as able to save, as was he and Margaret Carnegie and my mother. And if money was such a dreadful thing, so to be scorned, why did Mr. Carnegie have sterling silver plumbing fixtures in his Fifth Avenue mansion, as well as five crystal chandeliers in his waiting room, and rose brocade covering the walls of his music and drawing room? And why did he tell a friend who asked him how he was getting on, "Oh I'm rich, I'm rich!" if it wasn't fun? Nevertheless he was not common and piggy about money. To want more than forty or fifty million profit in a year, he once wrote to his associates, seemed wicked. Sometimes his millions even seemed to embarrass him. "Ashamed to tell you profits these days. Prodigious!"

I had never made a penny by myself even at the age of nineteen. Thus, unhardened by life's knocks, my attitude towards money and my appreciation of its value was so casual that once, when I was in college, Mother threatened that I would simply have to stop school if I could not take better care of my clothes and be more thrifty. "I cannot buy you eight pairs of hose every two months and wouldn't if I had plenty of money, because it is not the way to teach you to live--that sounds like poor common people. You never see well-to-do people as careless as that. You will have to cut out perfume and rhinestones and have hose for Christmas."

She did not have to remind me that Mr. Carnegie had once remarked that rich and costly dress and jewelry were barbarous. I had been told that before I went away to college, when I begged for a fur coat, assuring Mother piteously that I would be the only girl at the university without one. I could not take Mr. Carnegie's remarks about fancy clothes too seriously, however, because I had once read that his wife wore a white satin and lace gown at a reception for her husband in St. Andrews, Scotland. All the ladies present had, indeed, worn "sumptuous evening gowns." The Dowager Countess of Limerick was magnificent in a black lace robe with applications of silver embroidery, and Lady Griselda Cheape was just as elegant in grey satin with touches of sable. Lady Florence Pery's white satin frock was painted with pink roses, with garlands of tiny button roses taking the place of sleeves. Was I truly so barbarous in my desire for adornment, if these eminent ladies also liked rich and costly dresses?

Ah, what a trio they were, Margaret, Andrew and my mother! All with their energy, ambition, iron wills, determination and fearlessness--and scorn of such frivolities as perfume and rhinestones. The wolf of poverty would never <u>dare</u> howl at <u>their</u> doors. Mr. Carnegie said of his mother that her blood contained a considerable Norse infusion, and her strength, her fearlessness, traced back to the

distant Vikings. My mother's blood might have flowed from
the Norsemen, too, for all I know, but certainly it contained
the fierce Scotch-Irish infusion from early colonial scourgers
of Indians only a few generations back. Some of her Hutton
ancestors were ambushed by redskins as they travelled in
their covered wagons from North Carolina to what is now
Washington County, Virginia. Naturally Mother's direct ancestors got away and continued to their destination. If they
were as fearless as Mother, no Indian would have been so
foolish as to try to stand up to them. The Huttons would
have taken their scalps.

By the time I had grown up, I realized, as I think
my Mother would never have acknowledged, any more than
Mrs. Carnegie would have, that there were really two Andrew Carnegies. (One of his biographers recounts that in
Carnegie's maturity it was a common remark that there
were a half-dozen Andrew Carnegies--the various personalities reflected in his rapidly changing eyes.) There was
Our Mr. Carnegie, the lover of culture, who shared his
wealth with us in the form of libraries, and then there was
The Other Mr. Carnegie, a stranger to us but the man his
business colleagues and enemies and workmen and labour
unions knew. Our Mr. Carnegie had eyes that were kindly,
innocent, and true blue, like my mother's. The Other Mr.
Carnegie had mean, hard, terrible eyes, as though his own
had been removed and chunks of blue steel from one of his
foundries had been stuffed into the sockets.

Our Mr. Carnegie was sentimental and spoke lovingly
of the historic and sacred objects in his home town that had
influenced him. For him, in the town of his birth, Dunfermline, Scotland, foremost was the Abbey, the Westminster of
Scotland, founded in the eleventh century by Malcolm Can-
more and his Queen, Margaret, who was canonized in 1250.
Mr. Carnegie as a child could see Edinburgh to the south,
and to the north the peaks of the Ochils.

"The child privileged to develop amid such surround-
ings absorbs poetry and romance with the air he breathes,
assimilates history and tradition as he gazes around," he
wrote nostalgically.

And could anyone who thus absorbed poetry and romance and loved an Abbey be bad? The Carnegie libraries
were proof that he was not, even if his steel company in
Pittsburgh was accused of such things as hiring immigrants

because of their willingness to work long hours and overtime without a murmur.

Dunfermline was sacred and historic to Mother and me, too, since the ancestor, the very first of all the Carnegie libraries, had been established by Mr. Carnegie in his own home town. But Moberly was sacred and important historically to us as well. It had no romantic Norman towers, and Kansas City and St. Louis were too far away to be seen from our highest hill, but my own grandfather Hutton had been one of the pioneers of the town and had established its first grocery store. The area where Grandpa's store had once stood seemed somehow almost as romantic as any of Mr. Carnegie's towers and ancient churchyards, even it was proscribed territory for us as children. There had been saloons there in more recent years, although Prohibition and the W.C.T.U. had taken care of that. Forbidden and thus delightful, and also historic because of Grandpa's long vanished store, this was the block I always longed, but did not dare, to enter.

Mother was greatly attached to the memory of her father, and thus there was one vital issue on which she and Mr. Carnegie were not peas in a pod. Andrew Carnegie was a Union sympathizer in the Civil War, and Mother's father, Joseph Campbell Hutton, had been a Confederate soldier. Mother was smart enough, however, to know that geography had a lot to do with this--"We don't know what we would have done if we'd been in Mr. Carnegie's shoes." Mr. Carnegie was a Northern railroader when the Civil War broke out, and he served as an assistant in charge of the military railroads and telegraph system for the government. My grandfather at this time was only a country lad living in the part of Missouri that held with the South. He had fought with the Confederates and had been captured and suffered in a prison camp. Mother was a member of the United Daughters of Confederacy, but as a good librarian she felt she was above prejudice when it came to presenting historical materials in the library: Abraham Lincoln got as much attention as General Robert E. Lee. Scratch the surface, however, and if anyone asked whether she was for the South or the North, she would have remembered her father in that prison camp, and Mr. Carnegie or no Mr. Carnegie she would have made no secret of the fact that she was for the South.

There is one other point, also, where Mr. Carnegie

and Mother would not have seen eye to eye. One's mother, thought Mr. Carnegie, was too special ever to be made copy of, no matter how affectionately. "I feel her to be sacred to myself and not for others to know." When Margaret Carnegie died he would not for many years allow her name to be mentioned to him nor any of her pictures shown. Because James M. Barrie had written of his mother in one of his books (Margaret Ogilvy), Mr. Carnegie had a distinct aversion to all of Barrie's work.

Mother would not have gone along with this at all, of that I am sure. "No need to hide one's light under a bushel," I can imagine her telling Mr. Carnegie spiritedly. After all, Mr. Carnegie was fully aware that people would write about him after his death. If Mother's attitude seems a little disrespectful, one must remember that Mr. Carnegie himself had once been cheeky to the Prince of Wales. When the Prince asked him at a dinner party why America did not adopt the monarchial system and have a king, Mr. Carnegie, as outspoken as my mother, replied that America was entirely satisfied with its presidents. "Many of your English kings," he said triumphantly, "you will admit, have been rascals."

And as the future King only laughed and forgave Andrew for this heresy, I think Mr. Carnegie would have forgiven Mother for her lack of proper respect for his opinions about the sacredness of mothers. His own mother, he knew, would have been just as outspoken.

All this did not mean, however, that Mr. Carnegie would have changed his mind about me. I am sure that privately he would have thought I could not hold a candle to my mother. He might have been willing to pay off the mortgage for Mother if she had had one--this he did for an absolutely strange, unknown woman who requested it of him, simply because she bore a strong resemblance to his mother. But if I had asked him for a quarter, I think he would only have looked up from his Burns or Shakespeare, eyed me smilingly, and remarked righteously that the almighty dollar was a curse, and a sunny disposition is worth more than a fortune.

WHO RUNS THE LIBRARY?*

Edward G. Holley

In my presidential address to the Texas Library Association, in 1971,[1] I took as my text two suggestions from John Hersey's Letter to the Alumni. Some of you may recall that Hersey advised the Yale alumni that society needed two things in its search for a viable future: (1) a restoration of a sense of trust, and (2) decentralization of power. In my introductory remarks, before we get to the real discussion section of our program, I want to go back to that text to provide a backdrop for our subsequent conversations on "Who Really Runs Libraries?"

Few would doubt that there has been a steady erosion of trust in all areas of life during the sixties: in government, in the courts, in the schools, in higher education, and in librarianship. This rising distrust applies especially to those who exercise leadership roles in libraries, whether they are trustees, or mayors, or college presidents, or head librarians, or library department heads. Suspicion, discord, and distrust have been an increasingly difficult element with which anyone has to deal if he assumes responsibility for a supervisory role, whatever his position may be, and this applies to supervisory clerical personnel as well as professionals. The supervisor had better be prepared to deal with it in terms of whatever options are available to him, even though those options may sometimes appear somewhat limited and may seem to offer little in the way of long-term solutions.

One of the most serious criticisms of libraries is that most employees, whether professional or clerical, are

---

*Reprinted by permission from the spring 1973 issue of Texas Libraries, pages 35-44; originally presented as a paper at the Texas Library Association Conference in 1972.

not involved in or do not participate directly in decisions that affect their life styles, their day-to-day performance, and their "life, liberty, and pursuit of happiness," to use Mr. Jefferson's famous phrase. On the other side the citizen finds government and libraries unresponsive, public service virtually non-existent, and, to quote one of my interviewees of last spring, that "nobody really gives a damn."

Under these circumstances it is not surprising that many a supervisor who may have occupied a position of power and influence over a long period of time, e.g., a director of libraries, who may have held a leadership role for fifteen or twenty years, finds it increasingly difficult to continue to fulfill such roles. Many are retiring early. Some with bitterness, but most with relief, others are actually being moved aside, some are moving into library school teaching (with what may turn out to be surprising results if they haven't been in the classroom for a while), and I know of at least one public library director who chucked it all for the presumed less demanding task of running a branch library.

What I'm saying is that any individual who has been in a given position for a fairly long period of time is likely to be in trouble. This applies no less to other supervisory positions in libraries than it does to directors. Directors are merely the most visible and most convenient symbol on which to focus one's unhappiness. Boards of trustees, whether of public libraries, or schools, or colleges, have often been astounded at the open contempt in which they are held, not just by the general public but by the people who must ultimately implement the policy decisions they have decided upon for the operation of libraries, even though many of those same critics may have had substantial input to the working papers which provide the framework for those decisions. Down the pyramidal ladder, meanwhile, department heads frequently have trouble integrating new staff into their departments, especially if there is a significant age differential, or if the department is understaffed, or if the physical space is cramped and unsatisfactory.

Indicative of the depth of feeling about personnel problems in libraries was the comment of one elderly reference librarian I met on my Council on Library Resources Fellowship trip last spring. Reference Librarian X was head of a large departmental library in a new separate library building at a major Midwestern university. I'm afraid

my first impression was that he was the typical fuddy duddy
librarian, so I expected to spend little time with him and
certainly didn't expect to learn much. Moreover, it was
five o'clock--the end of a long, tiring day of interviewing.
"What," he asked, "are you really looking for?" In my
most urbane and professionally polished manner I suggested
to him that I was trying to find out how urban university libraries were organized, whether or not they were developing
different patterns of management, and whether or not I could
apply any emerging patterns to the University of Houston.
In unexpectedly harsh tones that really made me sit up and
take notice Mr. X replied, "Nothing is going to change the
way libraries are managed until head librarians cease having
contempt for their staffs. You can have any kind of organization you want, you can draw nice charts, but until head
librarians respect their staffs, it won't make any difference."
As he proceeded to warm up to his subject, I learned that
faculty disrespect merely reflected disrespect from the director, that there was no staff participation in the management of that library, that the director never listened to the
staff, that departmental meetings were a farce, and that the
director always controlled staff meetings by presiding, preparing the agenda, and writing the minutes. This was pretty
heady stuff for five o'clock in the afternoon. Mr. X did
grudgingly admit there were occasionally some reference librarians who were incompetent, but he thought they paled
into insignificance when one compared them with directors
of libraries. As far as he was concerned, "lines on paper
don't mean a thing."

  Although I tried to argue with Mr. X and suggested
that he was much too harsh on directors (after all, I was
one), I remembered that there were a number of my di-
rector-colleagues who fit his description fairly well. Some
of them had suggested to me that they thought none of the
staff, except them, of course, deserved faculty status, and
they rarely encouraged professional staff development in any
real sense. Certainly one thing that my trip brought forcefully to my attention was that interpersonal relations between
chief librarians and staff have suffered much in this past
decade of tremendous expansion. As my friend Anna Hall
of the Carnegie Library of Pittsburgh remarked, "One of
our biggest hurdles is the remoteness and depersonalization
of administration from other staff. These are some of the
attendant disadvantages of growth." Certainly contempt from
the director has been repaid by the staff and whatever may
be the reasons for "the summer of our discontent" there is

little doubt that this resentment for directors has affected seriously and will continue to affect seriously the operations of all libraries, big and little, school, public, college and university. Usually the cry goes up "lack of communication," and while that is a serious problem, it by no means is the only problem nor does it get to the root of the problem.

In this particular Midwestern university it seemed to me that the library staff was longing for some really dynamic leadership with strong staff participation in the academic enterprise. At the same time, hardcore dissidents on the staff are also realists; most of them don't expect a charismatic leader to arise and save them. Rather, they are looking quite hard at unionization to save them. However, in this situation, I wonder if unionization will not further polarize the staff with consequences which may last a long, long time. While unionization may be good for the staff in terms of salaries and fringe benefits, the effects of the battle on service to the public may well be disastrous. That would, I suggest, lead to further disenchantment with the library on the part of the students and faculty and mean ever less sympathy for the library's rapidly mounting financial problems. Can one really say, under the circumstances, that unionization would ultimately benefit that particular library?

Later, at another distinguished university, the director confessed to me that in the pressures of raising money for a new building, planning its construction, working on its equipment, and finally moving into the building, the top library administrators had lost contact with the rest of the staff with more serious consequences than they had ever envisioned. In this particular library situation the library administration had taken a calculated risk. They realized that staff morale would likely deteriorate in the two or three year period when administrative energies of necessity had to be directed into other channels. What they had underestimated, and underestimated very seriously, was the extent of the strain this would place upon the rest of the staff. As a result there had been staff caucuses, an attempt at unionization, and a scurrilous newsletter with language that made future communication difficult if not impossible. Somehow it is not easy to sit down across the table from colleagues and discuss controversial personnel matters in amicable fashion with people who have just called your veracity in question, and have further undermined your leadership by broadcasting this to the total campus community. Perhaps this is like the old joke about hitting the mule in the head with a two-by-four to get his attention, but rather than moving the mule sometimes it may only make him more stubborn.

I cite these two large universities as indicative of the breakdown in trust that is occurring in many libraries, with its concomitant effect on total staff performance. In both cases there are, or soon will be, new directors, so no one can predict how either situation will ultimately be resolved, or if it will be resolved. I would merely venture the opinion that new directors in such situations had either better be prepared to spend enormous quantities of time listening to and working with the staff (with probably serious consequences for their relationship with faculty and administration) or they had better set up machinery for good arbitration and bargaining procedures.

This leads me to my second point: decentralization of power. I suspect as librarians we have pushed too hard on the virtues of centralization for economy and efficiency these past two decades. If we had worked harder on decentralized service, we might well have more public support in this time of financial crisis for libraries. But libraries have long been organized along hierarchical lines and that pattern served fairly well when staffs were smaller and most of them saw each other, including the director, every day. It has served less well in recent years as staffs have grown larger and in some libraries has been the cause of endless friction. Part of the difficulty has been the lack of perception on the part of the chief administrators that their leadership role was changing. If one were to write a job description of the director of the Houston Public Library, the Houston Independent School District Library Supervisor, or the Librarian of Rice University today, and then compare it with an equivalent description which might have been written ten years ago, you would be greatly surprised at the differences. For one thing, directors used to stay home more. Travel funds were smaller, there were fewer professional associations, librarians were less involved in the political process, massive grants from the federal government, at least for libraries, were non-existent, and librarians were not expected to be money raisers. If the mayor, or the superintendent, or the president said "no" to a library request, that ended the matter. He controlled all of the money likely to be available for any of his units and determined, with advice of his lieutenants to be sure, how much of the total pie went to library purposes. That simple and uncomplicated relationship now appears quaint to most library directors. A really aggressive director will have been consorting (I use the word advisedly) with federal, state, or foundation officials to see if he can work up additional support for one of his projects, often before he even sees the president. Thus his role as an external agent for the library has changed drastically. If it hasn't, then you probably ought to be worried about how well your director perceives his task.

Let me cite a concrete example of administrative behavior that affects all staff members from the janitor to the director: the matter of salaries. All of us recognize that librarians' salaries are less than we would like. The second Cameron study from the Council on Library Resources,[2] which appeared in 1971, contains conclusions that demonstrate some academic librarians continue to be greatly disturbed (as well they might) by the disparity between their salaries and those of professors. On the other hand most of us recognize that our salaries have increased substantially during the past decade. That, dear friends, did not happen accidentally. Even in an affluent society somebody has to convince the powers that be--whether school officials, state officials, donors, or presidents--that money spent for excellent staff may well be the best money they ever spend. To secure money for increased salaries, or books, or buildings, or whatever, legislatures have to appropriate enough dollars or foundations and private donors have to give enough dollars so that all of this becomes possible. Chief administrators, for the most part, are well aware of this. That's why they spend so much time in Austin and Washington. What they have failed to do, and often failed miserably at doing, is to explain to the staff, most of whom are woefully ignorant of the budgeting process, how library objectives and purposes are ultimately funded. Unfortunately, in most cases the only time many staff members learn about the budgeting process, even at the departmental level, is when they sit down with the chief administrators once a year to decide whether or not Suzie Jones gets a $200 or $300 raise this year.

Some people believe that the new process of program/performance budgeting or other new management techniques will change all of this.

The summary of the Booz, Allen & Hamilton case study of the Columbia University Libraries,[3] released last year, makes much of the restructuring of the Columbia li-

brary system and management-by-objectives technique.
Whether this approach will actually result in a greatly
changed structure is not yet clear. Permit a skeptic to
opine that a good deal of it sounds all too familiar but the
language seems a little different.

Another case in point is the UCLA Library Administrative Network, which also involves the application of the newer behavioral science methods to library management. Both UCLA and Columbia make much ado about use of staff committees, Columbia having some 80 professional staff members out of 150 currently serving on committees and UCLA having an involved committee structure of advisory committee, random groups, and staff resource committees[4] the like of which you wouldn't believe. Sometimes it sounds like the Biblical story of Ezekiel's wheels within wheels, or in other words, bizarre. Both systems, however, do come down strongly on the source of ultimate authority: the chief librarian, who continues to make the final decisions. I suspect that element is much in line with the traditional American approach of strong managers and may make more sense than another development, library governance, to which I shall shortly return.

Incidentally, if you want to pursue either of these matters in more detail, I refer you to my lecture, "American University Libraries: Organization and Management," which Texas A&M University Library published recently as its Miscellaneous Publication No. 3 and will sell you for $1.00, and my expanded version of this "Organization and Administration of Urban University Libraries," which appears in the May, 1972, issue of College and Research Libraries.

Whether management-oriented or faculty-oriented, university libraries are groping toward a method of decentralizing the power structure. It may very well be true, as one of my correspondents wrote, that participatory democracy in management, or "off with the heads of heads," is one of the shortest lived phenomena we are likely to encounter. Though I suspect he's wrong, one thing librarians should clearly keep in mind: most librarians, like most citizens generally, like strong leadership. For instance, see E. J. Josey's study of academic status in the March 15 [1972] issue of Library Journal[5] where two-thirds of the reference librarians in New York academic libraries took a dim view of rotating chief librarians though they had, by a little more than 50 percent, supported the concept of library governance. As my correspondent noted concerning presidents, on three campuses where the faculties were marching against authoritarian leadership a few years ago, those same faculties can now be heard muttering that the new president isn't leading them.

My gratuitous remarks aside, let me proceed to a further example of decentralization of power by discussing briefly the movement for faculty status, particularly as it applies to library governance. Faculty status for academic librarians is largely a post World War II development. The first major university to have equivalent salaries and ranks for librarians was the University of Illinois, and all of us who ever served in that great library system are dedicated to its faculty rank concept for librarians. Under the leadership of Robert B. Downs, 6 for whom faculty rank for librarians was an article of faith, many other institutions in the intervening twenty-five years have followed the Illinois lead. Some institutions didn't go all the way with this, and stopped short of faculty titles and salaries, with a sort of halfway house called "academic status." On the other hand, even where librarians became assistant professors, associate professors, and full professors, they did not proceed to organize themselves as a faculty body with committees on promotion, tenure, grievances, etc., and certainly not with the election of chairmen, as often happens in other academic departments. Professional staffs even played relatively minor roles in selecting new directors, that function being considered too important to be left to mere librarians, however faculty oriented they might be.

By the sixties, however, a few libraries began moving in the direction of library governance. Two of the most notable are the libraries of the City University of New York, whose faculty status is clearly spelled out in their forty-page union contract, and the University of Miami at Coral Gables. The latter, to my way of thinking, has one of the most outstanding examples of library governance I have encountered. Within the faculty government charter, librarians are given responsibility for their own organization and for participation in the appointment and retention of professional staff members and administrative officers. Certainly libraries planning to organize as a faculty should have a close look at the relevant portions of the Miami Faculty Manual. 7

As a result of the ACRL Membership Meeting in

Dallas in 1971, any academic library which takes seriously the new ACRL Standards will have to come to terms with library governance, since paragraph two reads:

> College and university libraries should adopt an academic form of governance. The librarians should form as a library faculty whose role and authority is similar to that of the faculties of a college, or the faculty of a school or department. 8

Perhaps it is unnecessary to remark that the role of the chief librarian will undoubtedly undergo a decided change if the faculty governance model is followed. The chief librarian may become a dean, and thus primarily an administrative official, or he may become a department head, possibly elected by or at least confirmed by the staff. The normal academic procedures would then come into play: regular meetings of the total faculty, selection of faculty committees, more formal standards for professional development, as well as the endless arguing, professional jealousies, and cumbersome decision-making that follow in its train. The California State College system wants to move into a situation where at least the library department heads are elected by the library staff, while some City University of New York librarians want to go further and elect the chief librarian.

If one believes that faculty governance, under serious attack in some quarters, is the adequate model for libraries, that still leaves the clerical staff. What do you do about them? If one assumes as a general principle that individuals in a democracy have a right to participate in decisions that directly affect them, can he ignore the clerical staff who constitute anywhere from 50 to 70 percent of most library staffs? "They have their union to protect them," intoned one library director, but that position assumes that clerical personnel in libraries are interested only in benefits and working conditions while professional librarians are the only ones interested in policy matters. Are librarians really interested in policy matters or are they chiefly interested in their own benefits and working conditions? I strongly suspect the latter, but I do so with disappointment, for I think the truly dedicated professional ought to be interested in policies of the library in which he serves. Moreover, one has to ask himself seriously if the advent of library governance really does improve the problem of communications. The evidence on this point is by no means clear, but there is fairly good reason for skepticism. Despite its enormous and time-consuming effort the Library Administrative Network at UCLA, which did indeed improve communications, is still regarded by many of the staff as being peripheral to their major concerns.

Meanwhile, back at the ranch, what does the client think of all this? Is he really likely to be better served if we provide a different system of library governance and better status for librarians? To that question I would like to venture a tentative "yes," for I cannot conceive that a good librarian is either undeserving of faculty perquisites or unable to measure up fully to their standards. Yet I must admit that the evidence is not all that clear. In some cases service has definitely not benefitted from new forms of organization and governance. Indeed, it has deteriorated. In other cases it has not necessarily improved but at the very least it has resulted in improved morale for a dedicated group of professionals who have served their universities well over a long period of time.

The question to which we really need to address ourselves, and which I hope this discussion will open up, is how do we want to participate in library management? Do we want to have participatory democracy or representative democracy? Do we want strong or weak leaders? Do we want unions, faculty organization, or some as yet undetermined organization? If we restructure, how shall we see that the normal work load is distributed evenly? Can all this be done with benefit to ourselves and without harm to our patrons? And, finally, what influences, both internal and external, keep us from personal development and professional service at a high degree of excellence? These are all questions that I hope we'll think about and discuss together, for they will assume increasing importance in the next few years.

REFERENCES

1. Edward G. Holley. "Whither the Texas Library Association?" Texas Library Journal, 47 (Summer 1971), 49-51, 85-87.
2. Donald F. Cameron and Peggy Heim. How Well Are They Paid? Compensation Structures of Professional Librarians in College and University Libraries, 1970-71; The Second Survey. Washington, D.C.: Council on Library Resources, 1972.

3. Booz, Allen and Hamilton, Inc., Organization and Staffing of the Libraries of Columbia University: A Summary of the Case Study. Washington, D.C.: Association of Research Libraries, 1972.
4. The best description of the UCLA program now available is Joanna E. Tallman, "The New Library Management Network at the University of California, Los Angeles," ibid.
5. E. J. Josey. "Full Faculty Status This Century." Library Journal, 97 (Mar. 15, 1972), 984-989.
6. Downs has written often on this topic. His first article, "Academic Status for University Librarians: A New Approach," appeared in College and Research Libraries, 7 (Jan. 1946), 6-9. He edited an ACRL Monograph, The Status of American College and University Librarians, in 1958 and his article, "Status of Academic Librarians in Retrospect," in: Lewis Branscomb, ed., The Case for Faculty Status for Academic Librarians (ACRL Monograph no. 33), Chicago: American Library Association, 1970; 111-118, is a good summary.
7. "Faculty Government." Faculty Manual 1971-72. Coral Gables, Fla.: University of Miami, 1971; 33-38, 45-46, 50-56.
8. "Standards for Faculty Status for College and University Librarians." College and Research Library News (June 1971), 171.

LIBRARIES, LOVE, AND THE PURSUIT OF HAPPINESS*

Arnold P. Sable

Part I: Libraries I Have Loved

There are probably hundreds of libraries I could have fallen in love with had I only the opportunity of knowing them. As it is, my knowledge of libraries is limited to where I have worked or visited. As there are many States I have not set foot in, so there are enchanting, tucked-away libraries which I have never seen. Among those I have seen and used, here are some of my favorites. Admittedly they are only a rare handful. However, they are libraries which have given me a particular pleasure at a particular time. How good it is to have known these libraries.

GEORGETOWN, South Carolina. To take a summer job that paid no money was something short of foolhardiness. I was going to college then, and when the offer came, I seized it without consulting my parents who now would have to bear more of my college expenses for the coming year. The job was in a region I had never been to: the Middle South. My biology professor liked the way I mooned over the sense of order in plant kingdom taxonomy and the way I defended mechanism--the philosophy that one day man will create life in the laboratory--against my God-seeking fellow students, the vitalists. He proposed I accompany him in some field work he was going to be doing. I would help him collect frogs in the marshes of South Carolina. It was so romantic and irrelevant that I jumped at the chance.

We drove all night in a battered truck filled with plant presses, scoop nets, sleeping bags, and kitchen utensils. The truck banged and clattered because of its latticed

---

*Reprinted by permission from the December 1972 issue of the Wilson Library Bulletin, pages 343-352. Copyright © 1972 by the H. W. Wilson Company.

sides which were loose and shook with every imperfection in the road. I stayed awake in the front seat, watching dawn peer through the sheets of morning haze on Maryland cornfields. We stopped for breakfast in Virginia in a highway diner William Inge would have loved, down to the sopping rag used by the disheveled, sleepily moving waitress as she wiped our table. It was then that, for the first time, I heard about me the soft liquid sounds of the Southern accent.

The house we were staying at, a wood frame bungalow with an attic, belonged to the professor's parents. They used it occasionally and planned to retire there. It stood facing a one-lane dirt road that wriggled out toward the marshes, stopping at the cove where the rowboats docked and where, on the brown mud banks, fiddler crabs hobbled in and out of holes like grotesque creations in a monster movie. We unpacked the truck in a rising summer heat, tortured by swarms of mosquitoes which suddenly, in seemingly still air, swooped down upon us and bit us without mercy. The mosquitoes never left us. They were in the air day and night. The bungalow was carefully screened, but unless we rubbed a greasy, nauseating repellent over every exposed part of our skin, we could not go out during the day. I used to stand at the window in the attic and lay my palm against the screen. In seconds, numerous mosquitoes, attracted by the body odor, would be hovering outside, moaning to get in. I played at teasing them until I tired of the game.

But it was not only the mosquitoes which kept us indoors. The spring had been dry, with little rain, one of the driest on record, said our drawling, weathered neighbor down the road. The lack of rain meant there was little water for the frogs to spawn. Without a goodly crop of frogs, there could be no research. Without the research, there was nothing to do. We collected some plants in the plant press. But most of the day, while the professor painted the house or fixed the fence enclosing what was to become a garden after someone cut the waist-high weeds, I sat in the attic systematically reading through piles of ancient <u>Life</u> magazines, reading about smalltown drum majorettes and unusual gorillas in zoos and USO Service Club hostesses until I thought I would go out of my mind. The isolation, the boredom, and the unreality of the South Carolina marshes pressed heavily upon my nerves.

Finally, I could stand it no more. I had to get out.

I decided to hitchhike to the nearest town, Georgetown, and try to get a card at the public library so I could have some honest reading to fill the endless hours. The walk to the main road, accompanied by heat and mosquitoes, was anguishing. But when I got a ride and was zooming down the highway, the heat and the mosquitoes fell back, and I was free once more.

The library was where I expected it, on the main street, Carnegie-ish, dimly lit, without the fluorescent light and pastel paint which had slowly begun to penetrate American libraries. It was one of those Miss-Hudsill-gets-the-job-because-she's-an-unmarried-worthy-lady kind of library. The atmosphere was unmistakeably Confederate: Robert E. Lee under glass looking down at the librarian's back, two real crossed swords above the history section, wood panelling and jacketless books in nearly the same dark, respectable color. I chose a novel by Dickens out of a long green set, plus something on philosophy by Will Durant.

The Southern hospitality. What a cliché the term is, yet how true it can be. I remember the kind, gracious librarian, how easily she gave me a card although I did not live in town and was a temporary visitor to the region on top of that. She had heard of the professor's parents, and that helped. It was a world of respectability, like an Ellen Glasgow novel. I liked being part of the easy-moving atmosphere. During the remainder of the summer, the excursions to the library became my Going to Town days. Like a young boy about to buy his first shotgun, I looked forward to going to the Georgetown library with an excited anticipation that heightened the summer's adventure. Society was a firm, eternal thing in the South. I imagined myself part of the world where everything was in place, and the Victorian novels and the solid biographies that I tried to read confirmed the sensation. For me, the whole summer might have been a fantasy world soon to collapse. But the sweetness of the smiles and the unchanging, delicious "backwardness" of the library lingered in my mind long after I had returned North and discovered that science was no longer my cup of tea.

MATUNUCK BEACH, Rhode Island. The library sat on a rise overlooking a four-lane super-highway that ripped through the rolling coastal plain. The building had once been someone's comfortable summer house. Now, with gardens intact and walls torn out to make room for shelving and circulation desk, the house still maintained the beach-like airiness. To get to the library from the beach, we had to drive east almost to the Wakefield cutoff, quickly cross the highway, and drive back west almost to where we had been before. Children came on bicycles; there were shirtwaist dress ladies, too, and retired men who read seriously. The library seemed run by volunteers. There was the bustle and the informal scurrying around which library volunteers make when they are enjoying their work. The first time I entered--my wife and children all came, because going to a library, any library, was a family-centered obligation--some of the women had opened a bridge table in the open mending room, had spread a tablecloth, and were beginning to lay out their lunch. Everything was close by in this friendly, crowded library, and the fact that they were eating and chatting around the corner from the circulation desk seemed to bother no one.

We were spending our summer vacation at the seashore. The air had a smell of berries and cutgrass lawns. At night the stars came out all over the sky and we sat in the living room of our rented cottage curled up on the sofa, reading until drowsiness dimmed our eyes and we became aware of the distant, endlessly falling surf. The children slept in separate rooms, with visions of <u>Little Ping</u> and <u>The Man Who Wouldn't Wash His Dishes</u> dancing in their heads. My wife sank herself deep within <u>The Fellowship of the Ring</u>. But I, in my first library visit, had discovered the Rhode Island section, and now I devoured local history.

What strange, homespun tales. People living alone on the sea-encircling salt marshes, Indians remaining throughout the white settlement to fish and to intermarry with separate blacks who came wandering into the region in the mid-nineteenth century. The smell of sea, hollyhocks, and salt grass came up from the mimeographed and privately printed pages. It was the one area which seemed to resemble the Cornwall moors. Once had lived real Characters in this place, where isolation bred eccentricity, and eccentricity bred family feuds, spying on one's neighbors, and murder. Now lawnmowing machines, the summer theater, and the supermarket had superseded the fish net and the bow and arrow, but some of the homespun country atmosphere remained in country fairs and church bake sales and at the Matunuck library, and we were grateful.

LaGRANGE BRANCH LIBRARY, Town of LaGrange,

New York. Perhaps it is not fair to end the list with one's own library. But it also happens to be one of my favorite libraries. I used to drive a half hour out into the country of an evening and use the branch like a regular patron. I liked working there in the summer when the librarian went on vacation and we at the central library had to take turns subbing for her. LaGrange had once been a sparsely settled farm community. But new suburbanites working for IBM and DeLaval Separator Company had moved to the country to split-level ranches and joined the old families who were now planning new schools and roads and other public services.

The library branch had been one of their endeavors also. When a suggestion was made to establish a library facility in the town of LaGrange, a farseeing councilor on the Town Board proposed partnership with the city of Poughkeepsie. LaGrange would provide the building and utilities, and the city library would stock it and administer it. The costs seemed moderate and the prestige for the city library high. After various negotiations, the proposal was accepted and a contract drawn up between the two governmental bodies. It was the start of a pleasant, satisfying relationship.

Rounding out the happy fusion of bygone country life with modern city appointments was the building itself. The same town councilor saw possibilities in an old building the LaGrange Historical Society now owned and used--but only once a month for meetings--and he dared suggest that it be converted into a library. It was situated on a knoll off the main highway, partly hidden from view by sentinel trees, standing with its clapboard front and frame doorway as it had stood for one hundred and thirty years. An authentic little red schoolhouse. What a romance it was putting order into its interior, filling its cozy, associations-full spaces with new lighting, shelving and carpeting, respecting the integrity of its old architecture so that, in the end, we had made no structural changes. An old, slant-topped teacher's desk in the corner served as a focus for a local history display. Two authentic, scarred, ponderous pupils' desks-- what they could evoke if they could speak!--we placed back-to-back and used as picture book tables. The old pot belly stove, repainted jet black and moved to an out-of-the-way corner, now, instead of a wood fire, sported a vaseful of flowers. The two blackboards remained on the wall, filled from time to time with large gay chalk drawings: Easter rabbits, or grinning witches, or maybe Santa Claus before his fireplace.

The LaGrange Branch was a great success from the beginning. The middle-class suburbanites, who are a natural pushover for libraries, relieved at no longer needing to drive to the city library, heavily patronized the branch. The collection was attractive, the librarian very capable and sympathetic, and the building such a gem of American rural architecture that no one could help but come. What I enjoyed, too, was something that few modern libraries could offer: the intimate spatial relationships. It was a gentle yet sturdy building, built at a time when people drew into themselves for comfort and amusement. When snow had whirled and blinded the landscape, the pot belly stove inside and the flushed, upturned faces were all there had been, or need be, in the world.

Part II: Antisocial Behavior in Libraries

No librarian lacks stories on the lunatic fringe of the public. There is something about a library (What could that possibly be? It is so kind and harmless) that brings out the worst in some people. Something about groups of girls, bare arms bent over Collier's Encyclopedia and the Readers' Guide, studying at reference tables, that stirs the blood in some men. And for others, crowded, closely spaced book stacks are the sexiest thing since Brigitte Bardot.

Unfortunately, it is never the contents of books which inflames this thankfully minute minority. The socially disturbed, the psychologically maimed are drawn to the library like May flies to a lamp. The library never did anything to them. But somehow they have to strike out at the poor library. Book mutilations and property defacement are no longer discussed by librarians, so common are their appearances into library life. The angry ones exercise their spleen on library books, filling them with dirty words, obscene drawings, swastikas. There are others who never touch the books but who lie in wait for the nubile, deodorant smelling, hair-tossing young girls.

Especially girls from Catholic high schools. Because these girls wear skirts. What a joy it is, if you are disturbed, to be able to steal a glimpse under a girl's dress. The Adriance Memorial Library was plagued by a structural device which made looking up girls' dresses very easy: the

old glass-floored and steel shelving tiered stacks. In these
stacks, the shelf uprights go from the building floor up to the
ceiling and, between, there rest the layers of glass floors
which divide the uprights into levels. On each glass floor,
underneath the bottom shelf, an open space was provided
which, in 1890 or 1910, permitted light and air circulation.
But in 1960, the open spaces were a boon for skirt-watchers.
They could stand on a downstairs stack level and, pretending
to be searching for books on the topmost shelf, they could
look right through the open spaces up to the legs of busy,
intent schoolgirls.

One of the janitors suggested blocking off the spaces.
Girls were becoming aware of the stacks' dangers and complained to the librarians. We could not police them at all
hours and besides, the women librarians were reluctant to
do so themselves. After a while, I could spot a skirt-
watcher: the way he lounged about aimlessly, flitting from
bridal books to Japanese literature to books in Russian.
But if he was not harming anyone at that point, how could
I ask him to leave? The janitor went ahead with placing
pressboard covers over each space. For two weeks he
drilled holes in the cast iron struts, breaking drill bits frequently. But within a week after completion, every board--
the janitor facetiously dubbed them "Peek-a-boo Boards"--
had been kicked in and the spaces re-exposed. Our busy
men were at it again. We tried recovering the spaces with
sheets of steel bolted into place. Our desperate friends
must have responded with pliers, because on nearly every
board the ends were twisted back in frantic attempts to open
the spaces. But we had won.

I like the story one librarian told me about the time
she was working in the Widener Library stacks. She was a
stocky, mannishly speaking woman who worked while her
husband went to college. One day, in the cavernous, never-
ending stacks, in the deep quiet of miles of bookshelves, a
shudder went through her as she stood searching for a particular volume. Something was wrong. She could feel it
down to her bones. She looked downwards, down to the
glass floor. There, through the similar open space, on the
stack level beneath her, a pair of eyes watched her. A
beam of light from a flashlight was focused upward.

The librarian screamed. "Why you dirty--." She
spun around and dashed to the nearest stairway. But when
she finally reached the spot above which she had once stood,

the caller was gone and the stack level empty as far as she could see.

Part III: Two Crises

    I am not putting on record these experiences just for a pat on the back. Situation well handled, old boy. Nor do I intend to compete with the case study approach to library problems with its lady-or-the-tiger endings: now what would you have done in this case. I am interested in the varieties of library experiences. There is nothing static about being a librarian. The range of individuals who compose the profession and the public is an ever-interacting one. He who calls working in a library dull, has no eyes to observe and no feeling for people.

    WITH AN ADMINISTRATOR. When I first became a librarian, I was all gung-ho. I wanted to follow all the ideals, do everything that the manuals recommended. When the call went out for more book reviewers for Library Journal, I volunteered. I liked the surprise of not knowing which book might arrive in the mail. Condensing the review into twenty-one lines of type became an exercise in precision and conciseness. Most of the time, the books sent to this novice reviewer were unimportant junk. The veterans got Mailer and Henry Miller. It gave me a chance to be snidely nasty, like Dorothy Parker reviewing Katherine Hepburn. Sometimes the new book came in galley, and as I finished each page, I dropped it to the floor, so that, by the end of a reading, my chair was swimming in a sea of yellowish papers. Loose, they were difficult to stuff into the garbage pail. But how do you read a book composed of unattached, slippery sheets that are nine inches wide and about a yard long? One novel I reviewed, which I found refreshingly funny, I labeled in my review "the funniest book since The Egg and I." Lo and behold, when the book was displayed with other new books of the publisher in a two-page ad in the New York Times Book Review, the printed blurb under my book read: "The funniest book since The Egg and I, Arnold P. Sable." What a way to reach fame through the pages of the Times Book Review. Though my enthusiasm might have been a kiss of death. I never heard of it again.

    When my first review appeared in print, I burst into the director's office excitedly clutching the magazine. "Look what I'm doing now," I said proudly, displaying my first effort. He looked at it, mumbled something, and asked me to leave the issue with him. I was on a bright cloud when I left. But next morning, as he was dashing up the stairs to his office, he paused and between the banisters he called down, "Come to my office. I want to speak to you." I had no hint of what would come under discussion. So I climbed up to his office expecting no surprises. When I sat down beside his desk, he looked at me with a face caked with a smile, but it was not really a smile but how he looked when he was stern.

"I want you to guess what you did that was wrong," he said.

My jaw fell. That was wrong? I could not believe my ears. Did I hear correctly? I thought I was doing a decent enough job in this out-of-the-way town. I got a bank to put a library display in the window. I joined the Chamber of Commerce. I was helping to streamline the cataloging of new books. I went to bed early and I was not having affairs with anyone's wife.

He passed over my not responding. "Okay, I'll tell you what you did wrong," he said finally. The voice was sharp and the smile grew on his face. "You're reviewing books for Library Journal under our library's name. I don't want anything bad to be associated with this library, do you hear? You're a staff member and what you say reflects upon the library. You had no permission to do book reviewing. I'd like to see beforehand what you write, before you submit it."

He went on and on. I felt as if I was shrinking to the size of a paper clip, like Alice in Wonderland. I wanted to do such a good job in his library, and here I was being stepped upon. His anger left me with an answer.

After he had spoken long enough, after the black pall of depression had completely enveloped me, he said, "Well, that's it," and I left his office. He gave me back my copy of Library Journal--the one I had received personally because it had my review. I somehow blurted out, "Thank you." In the end, I was glad he had not forgotten to return it. I knew now what was my answer. When I went downstairs to the cellar where books were processed, finding the room empty, I opened the magazine to the classified section and began looking for a new position elsewhere.

THE BOOK WEEDING FIASCO. The W. Library should not have been referred to as a public library. It was run by and for a select group of old families in the town. A token sum came from city hall. But the greater part of its scrawny budget was raised each year through volunteer donations, like a sick person needing a rare operation. When I surveyed its chaotic interior--books on makeshift shelves on the radiators, books on the fireplace mantle, not inviting books, but patched with streaks of masking tape, battling the ever-mounting, threatening pile of gift magazines and oil company reports and printed prophecies from a seer in Texas--I felt a hunger to set everything in place, to make open spaces and let in light. I was mad for weeding. Books to the right of me. Books to the left of me. Out, out, out. The old, unwanted books flew. With a deranged excitement, I attacked to get the place clean.

Forty-five copies of Grace Livingston Hill. I threw out thirty, and then five more. "But," shrieked one of my pensioners on the staff, "people come in to get them." Let them come, I said. Thirty copies of Joseph C. Lincoln. I discarded twenty-five. "There are men coming in here all the time to read Lincoln," she gasped. I continued weeding. I weeded early in the morning when she had not yet come to work. I weeded in the evening when she had already gone home. Like someone out of Theodore Dreiser, she resented my taking over the library where she had reigned so long. I tried being kind at first, but the embarrassing, tactless comments she dropped before the public made me impatient. Her first loyalty was to herself and her status.

As the weeded books piled up in mounds in the basement, I searched about for a way of disposing of them. The State library did not want them. They were too shabby and out-of-date to give to a new library. Then quietly, stealthily, I chose to throw them out. Get rid of them fast. Flush them out of sight and be rid of the oppressiveness of books waiting to fall on your head as soon as you opened the front door. Behind the library stood six barrels. I instructed the janitor to begin filling the barrels with the discarded books.

But also behind the library was the high school. One thousand spirited, all-American kids ready to explode with energy when they were released from school. The school day ended, and as they ran down the hill and saw the barrels overflowing with books--the janitor had made thrifty use of their capacity--they recognized a carnival when they saw one. Hey, take a look at this. What are they doing in there? Hey, it's free books! Soon a hundred students were tearing into the barrels. The air was full of flying books like flak on a firing line. Loose pages and torn covers fell on the parking lot and the school driveway. Paper blew onto the straggling rosebushes in the neighbor's house. Teachers were beginning to stop their cars on the hill to get a better look at the insurrection.

When some helpful students came into the library carrying armfuls of discarded books, thinking they were salvaging them so they could be returned to us, we knew something was going wrong. I ran to the rear window. What a frenzy of grabbing arms and flying papers. Walpurgisnacht had come to Apple Valley. I called to the janitor and together we hastened outdoors. My dignity fell aside as I pushed into the circle. "That's all," I shouted. "You can all go home now." I think I was a little surprised that they listened to me. I stood by the barrels, arms outstretched, fingers waving, and the students slowly began to leave. As best we could, we gathered up the nearby book fragments. Then, side by side, we grunted and heaved and shoved until the barrels were inside the delivery room.

But the book storm had only begun. In the radio editorial on the local evening news there was mentioned something about the library "throwing out books." The president of the board phoned me. Could I give him an explanation? I did my best, quoting Bessie Graham and Helen Haines. But he called again an hour later, his voice more terse and correct. The telephone lines had been busy all over. He was calling a special board meeting tomorrow night to discuss this latest incident.

We sat around the table after the library was closed, twelve from the old families and me. I was on the firing line. I tried to be polite, unaffected, giving my professional opinion. They were not convinced. Somehow I had attacked the holiness of the very concept of Book itself. A book with print lives on until eternity. It is not made to be thrown out, not like old shoes and bent wire hangers. We talked about library goals--or rather, I tried to be lofty. But they were unmoved. They condemned my weeding, appointed a member of the board to oversee the discarding, and decided that, in the future, if it was absolutely, absolutely necessary to get rid of books from the library, they would recommend they be placed in storage in the basement. It was the beginning of a reign of mistrust between the board and the administrator.

Part IV: My Library Crimes Confessed

Before I knew you could find books by subject headings and what was a Dewey Decimal System, I was climbing up the inside marble stairs of the Boston Public Library to the top floor and the Music Room. I was not living in Boston, so I could not qualify for a borrower's card. I was using the massive, awesome library for reference purposes, although even then I did not know that is what you call it. The building, its marble and frescoed halls, was like the downtown Boston movie palaces on Washington Street. In the Music Room, amidst the commemorative displays of the Boston Symphony Orchestra about Beethoven or Wagner, amidst the screened-off shelving that continued upwards for two stories, amidst the busts of the Masters and the serious cello professors from the New England Conservatory of Music, I sat at the card catalog with a tray in front of me, and I copied out on printed forms the classification numbers of all the piano music I found listed under "Boogie Woogie."

I was studying the piano then with a tall, gaunt music teacher who taught "popular." He showed me how to play boogie woogie from the shoulders, not from the wrists, so that my fingers would not tire easily when I had to roll out the bass pattern in the left hand over and over again. Some left hand figurations he had written down for me in a little blue book of music staves. From these examples I practiced daily. My passion for boogie woogie and my interest in expanding my little blue book repertoire led me somehow to the Boston Public Library Music Room. Here I was, under the fixed, green-shaded reading lamps, doing "research" of my own.

One day I went down to the second floor to see if, by lying, I could get a library card. In a huge waiting room where people sat and waited to receive word on books they had requested from the closed stacks, I approached the New Cards window. A matronly, unsmiling woman sat behind the desk filing cards in a box. I waited to get her attention. Finally she looked up at me with traces of annoyance in the corners of her mouth. "Yes?" she snapped. "I--I'd like to get a library card," I said. I was beginning to be frightened of the stare of the imposingly cold eyes.

"What's your address?" she asked. Then I lied. I gave her the address of my grandmother in East Boston.

She spun around in her chair and began to run her finger down the pages of a huge book behind her. After an unbearably long time, she turned around slowly and confronted me, her pinched face drawn into steely hardness.

"There's no one by that name living at the address," she said coldly.

There was a pause. I was about to explain that I was a poor little orphan boy living with my grandmother. Or anything that would come into my head. But I panicked. I opened my mouth. The words were jumbled on the tip of my tongue. But no sound came. I looked at her expectant body poised for an explanation. She kept staring at me. My heart beat wildly. I was a madman confronted.

I fled. Like Mr. Hyde escaping through the streets of London, I dashed away, out of the waiting room, down the central stairs and outside to the traffic of Copley Square. No one had followed me. I sat on the library steps until my breath returned.

I did not go back to the second floor waiting room for a long time. But the Boston Public Library was where I committed another crime, though it was not related to the first and had nothing to do with revenge, with paying back the library for the first humiliation. The Boston Public Library was where I once stole a library book.

Several years later, after a summer spent in Paris, I returned to the States fired by a course I had taken at the Sorbonne. The course was in modern French literature. I was eager to read further of the authors I had studied. In the newly renovated General Collections Room of the Boston Public Library, I found a book that suddenly seemed important to me and I had to have it immediately. The book was the journal of Julien Green, a minor French novelist, and why he loomed so large in my French literature scheme of things I cannot remember. By that time, I lived in a room in the Back Bay, so I had a library card. But the urge to possess this book was a private one. I wanted it in a personal way. I wanted it for my own. I would steal it from the library.

I picked it up casually and walked out of the room. The photo-charging machines were located in the lobby. The approach to the exit led through the photo-chargers. I walked steadily, looking neither to the right nor left. The book rested lightly in my hand, as though it belonged to me. At the charging machines the clerks were drowsily pressing buttons and tucking cards into book pockets. Eyes straight ahead, I walked by them. I had escaped. When I reached home, I ripped off the plastic-and-wallpaper jacket, tore out the book pocket, and tried to erase the stamps.

I remember one quotation from Green's journal because I copied it down and kept it with me for years. The quotation went something like: "To allow a day to escape without writing it down is to allow a bit of Life to be lost." I thought it was one of the profoundest quotations I had ever read. But I was one-and-twenty.

A few weeks later, when I noticed the book resting on the bookshelf, I wondered why I had been so enamored of it. My admiration had fizzled. It was now a book like any other book. I wondered why I had smudged my honor in stealing it. I did not want it any more. Remembering all the procedures in crime movies, I put on a pair of gloves and wrapped the forlorn book up in a package. I could not take it to the post office to be weighed, because I was mailing it anonymously, and I did not want to make a pathetic, suspicious figure in the post office. I bought stamps and, in my room, affixed them to the parcel. I think I pasted on the brown wrapping paper enough stamps to mail the unabridged <u>Oxford English Dictionary</u>.

Thus the book was returned to the Boston Public Library.

SELLING THE PRESIDENT, ARCHITECTURALLY*

Ada Louise Huxtable

Architectural footnote on current political events: the Nixon Library is not dead, only dormant. It is "on the back burner," according to Leonard K. Firestone, head of the foundation that will build it. But he gave an important tidbit of design information. It will be in "early California Mission" style. That does not really represent any giant leap backward for the Administration's building record, because there has never been any giant leap forward. Although there has been a good deal of impressive talk about architecture and "the design necessity" in this year's Administration-backed First Design Assembly, it obviously hasn't filtered up.

The announcement perpetuates an almost unbroken tradition of architectural-know-nothingness-at-the-top, or how to ignore great buildings of the present and the fact that the late 20th century--it is later than you think--has its own superlative style. President Johnson alone tried to embrace it, but more of that later. Style is not exactly something that has marked the Nixon Administration. Its style, values and standards have been mostly advertising and expediency, a redundancy of terms, and that leads to a lot of cultural and other confusion.

"Mission Impossible," the professional publication, Architecture Plus, calls the Nixon Library design proposal, but it offers a few suggestions to the architects that might help.

"A large section of the building should be white-

---

*Reprinted by permission from the September 30, 1973 issue of the New York Times. Copyright © 1973 by The New York Times Company.

washed," the editors write. "At least one area should be
perfectly clear. All electronic outlets should be exposed.
The area dealing with Mr. Nixon's replies on Watergate
should be in the form of a rotunda, perhaps engagingly to
be called "the Nixon run-around." The area dealing with
the relationship between Mr. Nixon and some of his appointees
should be in the form of a double cross (this is a recurring
political motif, rarely an architectural one.)" It might be
a little difficult, the editors remark, to fit all this into "early California Mission" style, "but the architects of the world
are surely up to the task."

In case you haven't thought about it, there is a link
between what's wrong at the White House, what's wrong with
the world, and what's wrong with Presidential libraries. In
fact, it is hard to think of anything that has gone quite as
monumentally wrong as the whole idea of Presidential libraries, and it is tempting to speculate on why and how it
happened.

One thing that is conspicuously wrong with the world
is the fact that its economic well-being rests largely on the
creation of false and unnecessary needs and their so-called
satisfaction through unsatisfactory and unnecessary products.
That rests, in turn, on the promotion of those needs and
products at extraordinary expense to suggest values that
neither exist nor would be desirable if they did.

All this supports multibillion dollar industries that,
generally, people should be ashamed to be part of. The
standards are despicable. The goods are shoddy. The perversion of values is insidious and universal. This is a fairly wretched way to guarantee a civilization's viability, and
it is also a fairly certain way to corruption in large and
small things. But nobody cries on the way to the bank.
And too many of the people and practices have found their
way to the top levels of government and public affairs. It
is salesmanship, not statesmanship, that runs things now.

Presidential libraries have not been immune to the
process. The provision of archives has turned into the promotional manufacture of questionable Presidential monuments.
What started out as a rational, scholarly depository for documents has grown into a public-relations monster. Propaganda has replaced appropriate purpose. Scholarship has
taken a back seat to masterful image-selling.

This is all fairly clearcut; where the moral quicksand comes in is at the point where scholars and architects capable of giving the stamp of credibility and taste to these increasingly peculiar enterprises lend their names to them, affected, perhaps, by equal dreams of glory. They package the dubious product with high expertise. Then it is handed over to tourism and head counts. A whole false thing has grown up, icon-conscious and publicity-wise, supersold, with a skillfull eye cocked at the masses. At what moment, one wonders, did American Presidents get into the competitive pantheon business?

These ostensibly above-politics buildings are highly political and partisan. Set up as foundations manned by a President's friends and political associates, they are funded largely by his supporters, aided by a general patriotic appeal. Once built by private funds, the increasingly enormous and elaborate structures are then paid for in maintenance and operation by the General Services Administration of the Federal government. The expenses have gotten bigger with the buildings, and they are, of course, open-ended for the duration of the Republic.

So now you have a library, a museum, a monument and a memorial, with each element inflated for maximum impressiveness, and with each President being his own image-maker and all of them playing can-you-top-this. It has evolved into architectural hard sell. Place it at a university, add a school of government or public affairs, and size and status increase immeasurably. It doesn't matter that researchers, usually people with limited funds, have to hop across the country from monument to monument for Presidential papers. It is not important that this extravagant exercise in ego-gratification becomes ludicrous, redundant and gross.

There may be some poetic or philosophical justice in the fact that the Johnson Library is cracking up shortly after it was built, suggesting both the vulnerability of an overblown concept and the morality of contractors, which is no better or worse than anyone else's today. Here is a building whose joints we personally admired, notable for a Pharaonic air of permanance, falling apart at the seams. No one seems sure who should sue whom. Can you sue an American value system?

One of the most interesting things about the Johnson

Library is that the architect, Gordon Bunshaft, has translated that value system into a truly effective edifice, a paradoxical achievement, if there ever was one. That great travertine hall and stairs, the soaring sweep of scarlet-boxed papers behind glass, holding what the shredder didn't get (one assumes that there were shredders and bugs before the Nixon Administration) is great architectural drama and calculated symbolism. Nagging doubts keep raising their heads as to the purpose and meaning of the drama. Who is glorifying what and whom for what purpose? Researchers will just want to know where they keep the tapes.

The trend is toward something that is part Hollywood, part hokum and part Grand Old Flag. How far to the Taj Mahal and Forest Lawn? No one has come up with a "Presidentland" yet, because it is all being done on a very high plane, but there are links. At what point did the archive become instant memorial and did instant memorial become consummate ballyhoo? The ball is rolling, and it obviously will not be stopped.

It is rolling right now in Cambridge, Mass., where plans for the Kennedy Library--and museum--and school of public affairs--are in process. Part of the complex was unveiled this spring. There was hesitancy about discussing the full dimensions of the scheme because the community is already passionately protesting its location and scale.

We do not propose a design critique here, since the plans have not been fully revealed, and the architects, I. M. Pei and Partners, deserve that courtesy. Mr. Pei is one of the country's best practitioners, and he admits to considerable soul-searching about the impact and implications of the job. He has even used the word "anguish."

What has come out of that anguish thus far is an 85-foot high truncated glass pyramid for the public museum and memorabilia, connected by an open plaza to a long, wraparound, five-story building for an Institute of Politics for Study in Government and Public Affairs, part of Harvard's renamed JFK School of Government. It has a Harvard Square site, adjacent to the university.

The project started as something much simpler, but it soon became clear that it would attract many more tourists than scholars, and the program changed to emphasize "imagery" and memorial functions. "Library" has become a thorough misnomer.

   Twelve thousand people a day are expected to visit the museum-monument, with 1500 people at one time in the glass pyramid in summer months. Members of the Cambridge community are quite correctly asking whether the revised concept belongs here in its totality, in terms of urban disruption and appropriate location of functions. They have a right to be alarmed. Someone has to ask these questions, and to answer them.

   As a nation, we are creating a most curious set of Presidential shrines. If they don't fall apart, historians and archeologists are going to have a wonderful time.

Part II

TECHNICAL SERVICES / READERS' SERVICES

CATALOGUING IN PUBLICATION*

Verner W. Clapp

From June 1958 to February 1959, the Library of Congress in Washington (LC) conducted an experiment in what Dr. Ranganathan called "pre-natal cataloguing" which was regarded as of great importance in the United States. In this experiment, known as Cataloging in Source (CIS), LC (in collaboration with the Library of the United States Department of Agriculture, now the National Agricultural Library) catalogued 1203 books prior to publication, using the page proofs of the book for the purpose, and making it possible for the resulting catalogue entries (the CIS entries) to be printed in the books as published, usually on the reverse of their title-pages.

On 1 July 1971, after the lapse of more than a decade, LC commenced a new pre-publication cataloguing programme, this time called Cataloging in Publication (CIP). (The term was selected in order to distinguish the project from the earlier experiment and at the same time to comprehend all forms of publication--motion pictures and even maps, as well as books.) The new programme is intended not to be experimental but continuing. The purpose of the present article is to explain what has happened since 1959 when the CIS experiment ended.

The first major occurrence thereafter (in the United States) was the publication in 1960 of LC's report of the CIS

---

*Reprinted by permission from the January-February 1973 issue of Unesco Bulletin for Libraries (XXVII:1), pages 2-11. Copyright © 1973 by Unesco. "Mr. Clapp submitted this article shortly before he died on 15 June 1972."

experiment.[1] This was a scrupulously exact document which described in detail the manner in which the project had been conducted and provided elaborate statistics regarding its accomplishment. It reported on the post-experiment conferences held by LC with the participating publishers in order to learn their reactions, and on the extensive consumers' survey conducted in order to learn the desires of librarians. Finally, it evaluated the total experience in the light of all the various factors.

The report acknowledged that in number of titles catalogued and in speed of cataloguing, the experiment had exceeded its target. (The aim had been to catalogue 1000 titles in a "turn-around"[2] not to exceed twenty-four hours. The accomplishment was 1203 works catalogued, yielding 1236 CIS entries in the amazing average time of 7 hours 10 minutes--amazing because the cataloguing process required handling by some twenty pairs of hands and--in addition--the typesetting, proofing and printing of a catalogue entry to be returned to the publisher.) The report acknowledged the readiness of a majority of the participating publishers to go forward in a continuing programme, and it reported the all-but-unanimous desire of librarians for continuance. In spite of all this, it concluded that CIS should neither be continued, nor even tried again. Why?

The reasons given by the report for its puzzling conclusions were numerous. They included the cost of the experiment to the publishers and the disruption caused to their schedules; the prospective of great cost of continuance to LC itself; the excessive pressure caused for LC's cataloguing staff in attempting to meet urgent deadlines; the objections of authors and publishers to the form of some of the CIS entries (e.g., the inclusion of authors' birth dates, the substitution of real names for pseudonyms, and the use of certain subject-headings such as "juvenile literature" to characterize books for young people); the excessive number of errors in the CIS entries resulting from discrepancies between the books as catalogued and the same books as published (for example, the page proof might have consisted of 258 pages and have had a 1958 imprint, while the published book might have been reduced to 256 pages and displayed a 1959 imprint); and, finally, the shortly expected availability of two commercial bibliographical services which would make it possible for librarians to procure LC cataloguing information for new books very rapidly after publication.

The report--or rather, its conclusions--fell heavily upon the expectations of the American library world. The conclusions seemed to be at variance with the facts of the experiment which it reported and librarians felt that there was something here that they could not understand. Nevertheless, they were willing to attempt to make use of the commercial services which were held out to them with such promise.

A decade passed. Instead of getting better, the situation with respect to the availability of LC cataloguing information grew worse. The basic reasons for this were two: on the one hand, there was an enormous increase in the number of books that LC was cataloguing, with a correspondingly enormous increase in its production of printed catalogue cards; on the other hand, there was an even greater rate of increase in the demand for these cards. To be specific, the number of printed catalogue card titles produced by LC increased from 111,000 in 1959 to 244,000 in 1969, an increase of 120 percent, while in the same period the number of cards which it distributed rose 160 percent, from 35 million to 101 million. (That's a lot of cards! If set on edge--the normal position--in a catalogue tray, this number of cards would require a tray sixteen miles long; if laid end to end they would stretch for 11,803 miles!)

In fact, LC had reached--or even exceeded--the limit at which its card distribution service could be operated efficiently by manual methods, and although it had already for some time been planning the installation of automatic methods, these were not as yet developed. And, meanwhile, the same circumstances that delayed the availability to libraries of LC's cards simultaneously delayed the release of the cataloguing information contained in them through the commercial services that, in 1960, were expected to provide a superior alternative to CIS.

Under these conditions, it was not surprising that the suggestion for "pre-natal cataloguing" should have a new birth.

At the annual conference of the American Library Association in Atlantic City in June 1969, the Joint Committee of the Association's Resources and Technical Services Division and of the American Book Publishers' Council (now the Association of American Publishers) co-sponsored a preconference programme on acquisitions. Following the completion of this programme, the Joint Committee met to discuss its results and the problems in acquisitions procedure which it had identified. It was agreed that the principal problem resulted from the delay in the availability of LC cataloguing data. Because of this lag the processing of new acquisitions was retarded and their availability to the libraries' users was unduly postponed. When calculated on a national basis, the total resulting loss of usefulness of new books in many thousands of libraries throughout the country, at a critical moment in their careers, was staggering. In addition, for want of LC cards, libraries were being compelled to perform much unnecessary original cataloguing themselves, thus diverting to unprofitable uses money which should be used more profitably.

In seeking a way to ameliorate this situation, the Joint Committee was impressed by the suggestion that a new look be given to ascertain whether improvements could be effected by a new pre-publication cataloguing programme.

Just as the Joint Committee was girding its loins to act on this suggestion, the proposal received unexpected but important support from an article by Dr. Joseph L. Wheeler, the distinguished former librarian of the Enoch Pratt Free Library and one of America's great librarians. His article, calling for top priority to be given to a new pre-publication cataloguing programme, and making suggestions for obviating the principal obstacles to renewal posed by the 1960 report, immediately became a rallying cry.[3]

Shortly thereafter, the Joint Committee arranged for its "new look" at the feasibility of a new pre-publication cataloguing programme. For this it secured the willingness of LC, which--for the reasons mentioned above--embraced the opportunity for simultaneously lightening the enormous burden of its printed catalogue card distribution and for reducing the culpability which was being imputed to it for delaying the processing of books in other libraries. The Joint Committee also sought assistance from the Council on Library Resources which had funded the 1958-59 experiment, and which now lent to the study a member of its staff as consultant. The Association of American Publishers gave staff and other support to the project as it developed, and the Joint Committee designated an advisory subcommittee to channel its assistance.

The first task undertaken in the study was to ascertain, from the records of the CIS experiment, just what was the real cause of its non-continuance--which among the numerous reasons given by the report[4] were those that were controlling.

It was soon discovered that the principal reason for discontinuance was caused by a vicious circle of interrelated circumstances: (a) because of the desirability of basing the CIS entry upon the nearest approximation to the final form of the book, the cataloguing was conducted from page proofs; (b) but the page-proof stage is almost at the end of the publishing cycle, and any delay resulting from the use of the proofs for other than intended purposes could easily upset the publishers' schedules; (c) to minimize this interruption, and to retain the good graces of the publishers consequently required that the cataloguing should be accomplished in the least possible time, and the twenty-four-hour "turn-around" and the "non-stop rush" hand-to-hand cataloguing cycle were established; (d) the resultant pressure upon the cataloguing staff became insupportable on a permanent basis.

Next only in importance as a controlling factor for the non-continuance of the CIS experiment was the number of errors in the CIS entries, resulting principally from discrepancies between the page proofs and the books as printed. These were found in no fewer than 50 per cent of all entries. They necessarily caused acute anguish to LC's passion for accuracy. But upon closer scrutiny, the necessity for this factor dwindled. It was observed that nearly two-thirds (65 per cent) of the errors were in elements of description for which pre-publication cataloguing was quite unneeded, namely in the imprint and the collation. With respect to these two elements it could properly be assumed that the possessor of a copy of the book would be able to serve himself.

The picture began to become clearer. If the pre-publication cataloguing entry would no longer be required to include imprint or collation, could it be created without dependence upon page proofs? Could the remaining necessary information be satisfactorily obtained from galley proofs? If so, could the danger of disruption to publishers' schedules be obviated? If so, could the twenty-four-hour "turn-around" be avoided? Much depended upon the answer to the initial question; but there were others, of course.

By February 1970 the study had progressed to the point at which it was possible for the consultant to submit to

the Librarian of Congress (L. Quincy Mumford) a series of
eleven questions requiring satisfactory answers if a new pre-
publication cataloguing programme were to be considered
feasible.[5]

1. How should a pre-publication cataloguing cycle be modified in the light of the 1958-59 experiment?
2. How should the pre-publication cataloguing entry be modified in the light of the 1958-59 experiment?
3. Would a new pre-publication cataloguing programme, so modified, be acceptable to librarians?
4. To publishers?
5. To the cataloguing staff involved?
6. What benefits would a modified programme confer?
7. What adjustments would need to be made between a modified programme and LC's normal cataloguing and catalogue card distribution programmes?
8. What adjustments would need to be made between a modified programme and MARC (the computer-tape edition of the LC catalogue)?
9. How much would such a programme cost?
10. How might a permanent programme be funded?
11. What effect might a permanent programme have on LC's economy?

To seek answers to these questions, a steering committee was organized at LC. In its discussions and investigations during the following spring and summer the solutions were gradually worked out. It was early agreed that the purpose of pre-publication cataloguing (given at this time the designation of Cataloging in Publication or CIP) is to provide the recipient with standardized and professionally prepared cataloguing information that he cannot generate himself, but not to supply data which are readily available to him in the book which he holds. It was agreed, in consequence, that the subtitle, imprint and collation can be omitted from the CIP entry, but that all other elements usually found in an LC printed catalogue card should be retained. The CIP entry would consequently include the following elements: main (author) entry; brief identifying title; series statement; bibliographical notes; subject entries; added entries; LC call number (class number plus author number); Dewey Decimal Classification class number; LC card number; ISBNs (international standard book numbers for each format of the edition, e.g., trade edition, paperback, etc.).

It was agreed that the CIP entry should best be

placed on the reverse of the title-page (known in the United States as the copyright page) under the heading "Library of Congress Cataloging in Publication Data," but that the publisher should have freedom with respect to the typographic design of the entry. Accordingly, a CIP entry might appear as follows:[6]

> Library of Congress Cataloging in Publication Data
> Sloan, Irving J.
>   Blacks in America, 1492-1970.
>   (Ethnic chronology series)
>   First-2d ed. published under title: The American Negro: a chronology and fact book.
>   Bibliography: p.
>   "Discography: Afro-American folk music in the United States." p.
>   I. Negroes--History--Chronology. I. Title.
> II. Series.
> E185.S57   1971   973'.04'96073   76-170977
> ISBN 0-379-00262-0

At this point in the steering committee's discussions the question was whether even this reduced number of elements could be derived with adequate reliability from any form of the book earlier than page proof. (For the steering committee was adamant that there should be no more twenty-four-hour "non-stop rush" pre-publication cataloguing.) It was found by experiment that only late galley proofs (but especially if supplemented by copy for the book jacket and other informative material) would be adequate. But new questions arose: Have not galley proofs been rendered obsolete by modern printing technology? (The answer was, yes for a minority of books, but by no means so for the majority, either now or foreseeably.) Would the use of late galley proofs permit sufficient time for deliberate cataloguing, yet not unduly interrupt publishers' schedules? (The answer was, ordinarily yes.) Armed with these responses the steering committee could now be confident that the duration of a new "turn-around" could be set so as to assure avoidance of staff strain (in the event, it was set at a maximum of ten days).

To ascertain the reactions of librarians and publishers, two questionnaires were administered by mail: the first to a random sampling of 391 librarians in eighteen categories; the second to 273 heads of publishing houses and 471 other publishing-house officials, based on lists provided by

the Association of American Publishers. As for MARC (the
acronym of Machine Readable Catalog, the computer tape
form of the LC catalogue) it was immediately clear that it
and CIP were made for each other; MARC could make the
CIP entries available to subscribers in some cases months
before the publication of the books described, and update the
same entries with little delay following publication. As for
costs, it was estimated that though these would be considerable, they would be fully justified by the savings to the beneficiaries (not the least of whom would be LC itself), quite
apart from the value of improved services. As for sources
of funds, it was agreed that LC should seek foundation support for a pilot project, and request Congressional funding
only when that should prove successful.

Even before these studies were concluded, it became
necessary to report their progress at the annual conference
of the American Library Association in Detroit in June-July
1970. At that time the results of the survey of librarian
opinion were reported: 65 per cent of respondents had
stated that they would welcome CIP "with enthusiasm, " 32
per cent "with interest, " 2 per cent "with indifference" and
1 per cent "with disfavour." To the question whether financial saving from CIP could be estimated, responses ranged
from $750 a year for small public libraries to $50,000 a
year for the school library agency of a state; but many benefits were foreseen other than through savings of money.
Among the most important of these was the diversion of
funds from cataloguing to the purchase of additional books. [7]
At the same meeting, William J. Welsh, the director of
LC's Processing Department, sketched the arrangements
planned for a permanent CIP programme. [8]

The questionnaire to publishers was mailed in late
August 1970. Two weeks thereafter, the Association of
American Publishers sponsored a meeting in New York City
for publishing-house representatives, at which the details of
the planned programme were aired and questions answered. [9]
Replies were consequently soon in hand from nearly a hundred publishing houses, expressing in-principle willingness
to collaborate in a new pre-publication cataloguing programme.

Accordingly, by early October 1970 it was possible
for the consultant to report once more to Mumford that the
questions formulated in February had now all been satisfactorily answered, and that it only remained to launch a

Technical/Readers' Services

pilot project.10 At about the same time, the president of the Association of American Publishers, Sanford Cobb, informed Mumford that the publishing world was prepared to collaborate with the library world in a new pre-publication cataloguing programme.

And so, eight months later, on 20 June 1971, Mumford was able to announce that a pilot CIP programme had been assured as the result of a grant of funds made jointly by the Council on Library Resources and the National Endowment for the Humanities, with the National Science Foundation and the United States Office of Education on record as intending to contribute at a later date.11 As a result, on 1 July 1971, LC initiated a project whose objective was to be able, by the end of the initial phase in 1973, to provide CIP entries for most of the books published in the American book trade, estimated at 30,000 to 36,000 titles a year. The project is executed under the general direction of William J. Welsh by Glen A. Zimmerman of the Descriptive Cataloging Division and William A. Gosling as project manager.

By the end of its first six months the CIP project had developed its procedures not only for the typical new book which goes from manuscript through galley proof to final printing, but also for books which skip the galley stage, including especially scholarly reprints which are currently numerous. It had arranged with ninety-nine publishers to commence submission of galleys for their new books, and with fifty-eight others to start early in 1972. It had catalogued 1350 titles in a "turn-around" of from one to five working days, leaving the goal of a ten-day "turn-around" still reasonable to expect for the time when the 30,000 titles a year rate is reached.12

It is still too early to measure the response of the libraries to the new service. The number of books that have been catalogued is still comparatively few, and of these an even smaller number has been actually published. But use of the MARC edition of the CIP entries is already being reported[13] and it may be expected that use of the service will grow with increasing rapidity during the course of the present year (1972).

It must be remembered that the usefulness of cataloguing information to an individual library, when the information is in other than card form, is dependent upon the

ease with which the library can reproduce its own cards.
In the United States, equipment for this purpose is all but
universally available.

It is still too early, too, to ascertain whether the
new service will be found useful by other than libraries--for
example, by booksellers for arranging their stock in accordance with one or the other of the two classification
schemes reflected in the CIP entries; by individual owners
of collections of books for the same purpose; or for providing a standard form of citation. But all these forms of usefulness, and possibly others also, may be expected.

Other Programmes for Pre-Publication Cataloguing

While the above-described developments were taking
place in the United States, the "pre-natal cataloguing" idea
was gaining or had already gained acceptance elsewhere.
At the time of the CIS experiment, interest was expressed
in several other countries, notably Brazil and the U.S.S.R.
At that time the Instituto Brasileiro de Bibliografia e Documentação of Rio de Janeiro began to insert pre-publication
cataloguing entries into its publications, but this did not develop into national practice. But on the very day that LC
commenced its new CIP project, the Câmera Brasileira do
Livro of São Paulo established a Centro de Catalogação-na-
Fonte, intended to provide CIS entries for all books published in the state of São Paulo, which constitute approximately half of the entire book-production of Brazil. These
CIS entries are based upon the final proofs of the books.
The head of the centre is Professor Regina Carneiro, a
principal instigator of this project.14

In the U.S.S.R., matters took a much earlier and
quite different turn. Just when LC was reaching the decision
not to extend or repeat the CIS experiment, the U.S.S.R.
authorities were reaching a quite opposite conclusion. On
22 September 1959 the Central Committee of the Communist
Party of the U.S.S.R., in a directive entitled, "Conditions
and Measures for Improving Library Services Throughout
the Country," instructed the ministries of culture of the
Union and of the several republics, and all publishing houses,
to "organize a centralized system of classification and cataloguing of books."15

Centralized cataloguing services were of course no

novelty in the U.S.S.R. at this time; they had been rendered for many decades by the book chambers of the Union and of the republics, by the Lenin State Library, the All-Union Library of Foreign Literature and other principal libraries.[16] What seems to have been new about the directive was the introduction of the publishing houses into the picture. It was apparently expected by the Central Committee that by harnessing publishers with libraries, the supply of cataloguing information could be made simultaneous with the supply of books.

Now, while there were several ways of achieving the Central Committee's objective, they all required that the books be catalogued before distribution. In practical terms, this was equivalent to requiring that they be catalogued before publication. Regulations for effecting this, through collaboration between the publishing houses and the central libraries, were issued by the Ministry of Culture of the U.S.S.R. in an order dated 10 October 1959 bearing a title almost identical with that used by the Central Committee.[17]

But a mechanism for conveying the cataloguing information to libraries, in a form suitable for use, was also needed. Several methods offered themselves. The most effective, from the point of view of a recipient library, was the insertion in the book of a set of catalogue cards, ready for filing. Another method, somewhat short of this, was the insertion of a single card only, leaving it to the recipient library, or to the book collector (distributing centre) on its behalf, to reproduce the single card in the quantities required. Still another method was to print the cataloguing information in the book, again leaving it to the book collector or the recipient to reproduce it in card form. The last method would obviously be the simplest from the point of view of the publishing house, which would thus be enabled to avoid the trouble and expense of printing catalogue cards and inserting them in the books--a hazardous operation at best, since the cards are only too likely either to be omitted or to be lost in transit. Indeed, the regulations currently allow the publishing houses this alternative.

As the system evolved over the decade following the issuance of the Central Committee's directive, all of these methods were tried. By 1969, practice had become sufficiently stabilized so that it was possible to incorporate its principal features into a government standard entitled, "The Imprint in Publications."[18] In the same year, the situation was described by R. S. Giljarevskij of the All-Union Library of Foreign Literature in a report prepared for Unesco under the sponsorship of the International Federation of Library Associations.[19] In 1970 it was again described, in greater detail, by Eleanor Buist of the Columbia University Library.[20]

As prescribed by the government standard, the pre-publication cataloguing arrangements apply primarily to books intended for public libraries; and principal responsibility for executing these arrangements rests on the publishers. However, they are expected to look for help to the great central libraries; those in Moscow and Leningrad to the Lenin and the Saltykov-Ščedrin State Libraries in those cities, while publishers in the republics and regions may send their books for cataloguing to the republic or regional book chambers or central libraries. Uniformity in cataloguing is provided through the use of published standards or manuals--for descriptive cataloguing, subject classification and assignment of author ("Cutter") numbers.

Thus, a book intended for public libraries is required to bear in the upper left corner of the reverse of the title-page a call number consisting of a class number taken from the classification for public libraries (a simplified form of the Universal Decimal Classification--UDC) and a two-digit author number. It must also include, either on the reverse of the title-page or at the end of the book, a model of a catalogue card. (In lieu thereof, a copy of the card itself or set of cards may be laid in the book.) If the book is a scientific work, it must show the full UDC number following the public-library call number and should also include an abstract of the book, also on the reverse of the title-page. If, on the other hand, the publication is a children's book, the class number must be taken from the published classification for children's books. If the work is intended for book-trade distribution, the appropriate number from the book-trade subject classification must be placed in the lower left corner of the reverse of the title-page, as well as the number given to the book in the publisher's announcements.

The catalogue card, whether laid or printed in the book, must be in standard form, containing the descriptive entry for the book and an annotation, with the author number in the upper left hand corner, the library class number below to the right, and the book trade numbers below to the left.

Technical/Readers' Services

In 1971, T. Borisenko of the Lenin State Library, in an article entitled, "The Government Standard Must Be Implemented,"[21] reviewed the extent to which compliance with the standard had been achieved. He found that 161 publishing houses (41 central and 120 in the republics) out of a total of 228 were providing annotated model catalogue cards, or descriptive dataloguing entries with call numbers, in their books. He estimated that savings in local library processing costs derivable from complete adherence to the standard would be no less than 5 million roubles and could be made even greater. In order to assure full implementation of the standard the author recommended that the Ministry of Culture of the U.S.S.R. and the Lenin State Library be given joint responsibility for co-ordinating the work and maintaining the quality of the product.

In his 1969 pamphlet for Unesco, Giljarevskij argues strongly that the idea of printing a catalogue card in the book must be abandoned and that a single catalogue entry, prepared (on paper) by a central library from an advance copy of the book, after printing but before general distribution, be inserted in each copy.

This was exactly the original plan suggested by Justin Winsor (at that time librarian of the Boston Public Library) in 1876, namely, that publishers should insert into their books slips of stiff paper of uniform size, bearing cataloguing information prepared by the Boston Public Library and the Boston Athenaeum, principal American libraries at the time. But when the suggestion was tried out, it was not found feasible to bring the books and the slips together, and the catalogue entries were in consequence published separately. But the essential intent of the suggestion, namely, to make the cataloguing information available simultaneously with the books, was thereby aborted, the service was not used, and the experiment failed.[22]

More recently, for the past quarter century, LC again attempted--through a programme called "cards with books"--to put Justin Winsor's suggestion into effect. It laboured long and hard with publishers, and later with the library suppliers (jobbers) to this end. But, with the exception of an occasional publisher with a market directed to libraries, this effort has been without effect. Two principal obstacles interpose. In the first place, distribution of a trade publication in the United States usually commences immediately after completion of manufacture, and it is not feasible to persuade publishers--for other than commercial reasons--to delay distribution while a copy is being catalogued. In the second place, neither publishers nor suppliers have been found willing--for other than commercial reasons--to accept the expense of inserting the catalogue cards into their books.

It was because it had not been found possible, in attempts spanning more than eighty years, to arrange for the insertion into new publications of catalogue cards resulting from post-publication cataloguing, that the suggestion for pre-publication cataloguing rose in the United States in the 1950's. The first attempt to implement it there in 1958-59 failed, and the lessons learned at that time are now being applied in a second attempt. In the U.S.S.R., trial and error has followed a somewhat different course, and it is interesting to observe that while in the United States the effort is centralized (in the Library of Congress), in the U.S.S.R. it is decentralized (among the publishing houses). But in both cases the result of the effort is taking the form of a model catalogue entry printed in the book, rather than of a slip or card laid in the book.

In any case pre-publication cataloguing may be viewed as the latest stage in the gradual development of what has been called "Autobibliography"--the technique by which a book announces its identity.[23] Each stage in this development, from the mediaeval incipit/explicit through the interesting but transitional colophon to the inexhaustible variations of the title-page, has made it possible for the book to announce itself with increasing accuracy and completeness to the reader, the bookseller, the librarian and the bibliographer. But at no stage did the announcement contain enough information, or information in that form which would satisfy the legitimate needs for the bibliographic detail which would correctly characterize the book. It is this situation that pre-publication cataloguing hopes to correct, and in so doing to make books even more useful than ever.

REFERENCES

1. The Cataloging-in-Source Experiment: A Report to the Librarian of Congress by the Director of the Processing Department [John W. Cronin]. Washington, D.C.: Library of Congress, 1960.
2. That is, the elapsed time from the receipt from the publisher of the page proofs (on which the cataloguing

was based) to the return to him of a printed catalogue entry.
3. Joseph L. Wheeler. "Top Priority for Cataloguing-in-Source." Library Journal, 94 (Sept. 15, 1969), 3007-12.
4. Op. cit.
5. "Renewal of Prepublication Cataloging ... A First Report." Memorandum from the present author to the Librarian of Congress, Feb. 27, 1970.
6. "Library of Congress Cataloging in Publication Program." Cataloging Service (Washington, Processing Department, Library of Congress), Bulletin 101, Nov. 1971.
7. V. W. Clapp. "CIP in Mid-1970." Library Resources and Technical Services, 15 (Winter 1971), 12-23.
8. William J. Welsh. "Report on Library of Congress Plans for Cataloging in Publication." Library Resources and Technical Services, 15 (Winter 1971), 23-7.
9. Publishers Weekly, 198:14 (Oct. 5, 1970), 35.
10. Cataloging in Publication (CIP). Letter from the present author to the Librarian of Congress, Oct. 9, 1970.
11. "Library of Congress Receives Grant...." United States Library of Congress, "Press Release 71-34," for release Sunday, 20 June 1971.
12. United States Library of Congress, Processing Department. CIP--Cataloging in Publication; Progress Report, 1 (July-Dec. 1971). See also: Glen A. Zimmerman, "Bibliographical Communication Between the Library of Congress and American Publishers for the Library Community." International Cataloguing (IFLA), 1:2 (Apr.-June 1972), 3-5.
13. H. D. Avram. "Library Automation: A Balanced View." Library Resources and Technical Services, 16 (Winter 1972), 11-18 (see p. 15).
14. Regina Carneiro. "Catalogação-na-fonte." Boletim Bibliográfico (Biblioteca Municipal Mario de Andrade, São Paulo), 28 (Oct.-Dec. 1971), [77]-93.
15. "O Sostojanii i Merah Uluč̌šenija Bibliotečnogo Dela v Strane [Postanovlenie TsK KPSS ot 22 sentjabrja 1959 g.]." Partijnaja Žizn' (Moscow), 20 (Oct. 1959), 25-9. Reprinted in: Ministerstvo Kultury SSSR, Glavnaja Bibliotečnaia Inspektsija, Sbornik Rukovodjaščih Materialov po Bibliotečnoi Rabote (Moscow: Izdatel'stvo Vsesojuznoj Knižnoi Palaty, 1963), 26-[32]. Also in: Rukovodiaščie Materialy po Bibliotečnomu Delu: Spravočnik (Moscow: Izdatel'stvo "Kniga," 1968), 11-16. Translated in: Victor Fediai, "Expansion of Library Service

in the U.S.S.R., "ALA Bulletin, 54 (May 1960), 379-81. Also as: "Uber den Stand und die Massnahmen zur Verbesserund des Bibliothekswesens im Lande. Beschluss des ZK der KPdSU vom 22, September 1959," Ministerium für Kultur der UdSSR, Hauptbibliotheksinspektion, Sammlung richtungsweisender Materialen zur Bibliotheksarbeit ([Berlin:] Deutscher Bibliotheksverband [1963?]), 14-20.

16. G. G. Firsov. "Centralized Cataloguing and Its Importance." Unesco Bulletin for Libraries, 21:4 (July-Aug. 1967), 200-6.
17. "O Sostojanii i Merah Ulučšenija Bibliotečnogo Dela." Prikaz Ministra Kultury SSSR, no. 593. Reprinted in Sbornik, 1963, p. 45-50, and Spravočnik, 1968, p. 18-25, cited in footnote 3, p. 11; translated in Sammlung, 1963?, p. 29-40, also cited there.
18. Gosudarstvennyj Standart Sojuza SSSR ... Vyhodnye Svedenija v Izdatel'skoj Produktsii. GOST 7.4-69. Moscow: 1969.
19. R. S. Giljarevskij. "Cataloguing at Source," International Distribution of Catalogue Cards. [Paris:] Unesco, 1969; 31-40.
20. Eleanor Buist. "Steps Toward Cataloging at Source in the U.S.S.R.," Wilson Library Bulletin, 10 (June 1970), 1033-9. I am greatly indebted to Miss Buist for assistance in preparing this article.
21. T. Borisenko. "GOST Dolzhen Vypolnjat'sja." Bibliotekar', Sept. 1971, 59-60.
22. The Cataloging-in-Source Experiment, footnote 2, p. xii-xvii. Max Müller is also often credited with suggesting (1876) an approximation of cataloguing at source. But he made authors the sources of the cataloguing information (ibid.).
23. V. W. Clapp. "The Greatest Invention Since the Title-page? Autobibliography from Incipit to Cataloging-in-Publication." Wilson Library Bulletin, 46 (Dec. 1971), 348-59.

PROTECTION OF LIBRARIES*

Oscar M. Trelles

    The 1972 fire at the Temple University Law Library[1] aroused considerable interest among law librarians throughout the world, especially in the United States. This fire did not destroy the entire collection, but it made obvious to the library profession that, even when a library's collection is not entirely lost, it is still subject to prohibitively expensive salvage processes.

    Out of a total figure of 400,000 books and pamphlets damaged, over 100,000 volumes, damaged by water and smoke, were restored by the General Traffic Service Company, the recovery and salvage subsidiary of the Insurance Company of North America. In order to avoid mold and mildew, the volumes were chemically treated, individually wrapped in waterproof paper, and dried in an air-conditioned warehouse for several months. Another 60,000 volumes that were heavily watersoaked were submitted to a restoration process that involved a freeze-drying process, as a result of advice received from Library of Congress representatives. INA, who is the insurer for all of Temple University, had initially claimed that the loss might have exceeded the total count of documents damaged in Italy during the 1966 flood.[2]

    Many librarians do not realize the unlimited value of their collections as records of our civilization, and generally act on the theory that "the possible occasional loss of a building would cost less than the amount that would have to be spent annually if all buildings were insured."[3] This theory is followed by the Federal government, and thus no insurance is carried, for example, on the Library of Congress.

---

*Reprinted by permission from the August 1973 issue of Law Library Journal, pages 241-258.

In a 1946 work, The Insurance of Libraries, which
was considered at that time to be a classic manual and
which is still an important book on the subject, its author,
Dorothea M. Singer, recorded some opinions expressed to
her by other librarians, which reflect not only yesterday's
opinions but today's as well: "Nothing much ever happens
to libraries...." "Books do not burn easily; even if a fire
should start, it would spread very slowly...." "Library
buildings are well kept, and liability or other claims seldom
arise."[4]

However, in 1963, in the introduction to the important
study, Protecting the Library and Its Resources,[5] published
by the American Library Association, it was established that
"on the average, fifteen fires can be expected to occur in
North American libraries every year, with a total loss of
one million dollars."[6] It added that "when one considers
the current rapid expansion of library facilities and services,
it may fairly be assumed that this annual loss will probably
increase." This report also states that "library assets in
the United States--the buildings, the books, and other property--represent values in excess of five billion dollars."[7]

A 1968 ALA report also pointed out that libraries in
the United States are so "little insured that widespread public knowledge of this inadequacy would result in a nationwide
scandal. Librarians and library administrators are so
shockingly ignorant of the insurance needs of their institutions, and so derelict in educating themselves in this area,
that it is hard not to think of them as verging on incompetence. If only three of over one hundred major libraries
which could be named had a serious fire in 1968, the uninsured loss would exceed fifty million dollars. What is
worse is that proper solutions have been available for some
time."[8]

However, the author is especially worried about the
many libraries that are insured, either separately or as
part of a parent organization, but are blatantly underinsured,
as their insurance policies have not been reevaluated periodically. One could cite the case of a major university library, which, although its building, collection, and other
materials were valued at $23 million several years ago,
has not reevaluated its old insurance policy, valued at only
$1 to $3 million.

The author contacted a large number of law libraries

--bar association, county, State, Federal, law firms, corporate, and academic--and the answers received regarding measures taken against disaster have been generally so vague, and have revealed so little knowledge of the topic, that the idea of a national survey covering the subject of insurance was dropped immediately, as it would have resulted in a complete waste of effort and time. It seemed abundantly clear that such a survey would again have revealed almost total ignorance of the topic, as well as a complete lack of interest.

The insurance factor has been positioned at the foot of the list of library administrative priorities for too long. Most of the concern to be found among librarians is limited to the insurance of the rare book collections, not the entire holdings. In too many cases, insurance is bought in a careless manner, without understanding its importance to the library administration as well as the future consequences that could result from this lack of interest. Many librarians also mistakenly think that, if in many instances they can purchase insurance on the contents of a library building without presenting an inventory of the holdings or without having any data to support their evaluation, they could still receive a full refund in case of loss. The truth, however, is that insurance companies can, and often do, raise what they call "proof of loss." This problem comes up in the settlement of claims involving less than total loss, in which case (assuming there are no up-to-date inventories and information on the collection and other building contents) the insurance company might have grounds for refusing reimbursement to the claimant.[9] It could be said now, as it was in 1941 by the ALA Fire Insurance Committee, that "then too, there are very few in our profession who are either interested in or qualified to pass on this problem which has both professional library and business aspects."[10]

Theft, Vandalism, and Other Types of Damage to Library Materials

Undoubtedly every librarian is acquainted with the theft, mutilation, and vandalism taking place daily in the nation's libraries. It is doubtful, however, that all librarians know specifically how much money is involved in these losses. For some reason, many librarians do not take physical inventories of their holdings periodically. It would, therefore, be unlikely that one could find an accurate general figure for losses by theft or mutilation. This author will restrict himself to mentioning the outdated but indicative figures of the 1963 ALA work, <u>Protecting the Library and Its Resources</u>. This book indicates that, at that time, an estimated $5 million worth of books was disappearing from library shelves each year. The same book cites several reported cases of vandalism, one of which mentioned that "through vandalism of building and grounds, mutilation of books, and theft of the same, it was losing roughly $40,000 a year."[11] This author also knows of a great variety of incidents in which libraries have been subject to vandalism; for example, all the drawers of the card catalog of the main library of the University of Detroit were emptied on the floor in 1970 or 1971 by rioting students. In another instance, a drawer from the card catalog of the University of Michigan Law Library was stolen several years ago and was never found. It is obvious that, in libraries where some evidence of theft, mutilation, or vandalism appears, appropriate security measures should be taken. For example, all books, briefcases, and handbags of persons leaving the premises could be searched; or some form of electronic surveillance could be instituted to protect library holdings. In cases where the disappearance of rare or valuable items occurs, insurance might be recommended to alleviate the situation. In short, libraries can be protected against elements that can destroy, damage, or injure both property and lives through (a) preventive and (b) corrective measures.

Preventive Measures

Although it is true that all libraries should be insured, it is also true that there are sections or specific contents within them that no amount of money could replace. Even if these items were replaceable, such a procedure would be very costly in both labor and time. The insurance premium is also reduced whenever preventive measures against disaster are taken, either before or after the construction of the building in which the library holdings are maintained.

Succinctly stated,[12] it could be said that, in order to fulfill the administrative obligation of preserving and protecting the contents of a library, its administrators must acknowledge such responsibility, recognize the need for positive protective measures, carefully examine the loss possibilities in that situation, and take appropriate action. The librarian is often working under the supervision of others (the director of libraries, deans, trustees, senior law partners, etc.) and, in these cases, it is the librarian's responsibility to see that the people at that level are properly informed and convinced of the need for effective measures of protection.[13]

Library administrators should consider the following factors in formulating a means of preventing losses in their libraries:

(1) Location of the library. The geographical area as well as the proximity of other buildings, and the common features of the neighborhood as related to possible fire hazards, should be known to library administrators.

The building code in effect for the area will probably contain provisions regarding construction methods, such as those aimed at reducing the probabilities of earthquake damage in areas known to have a high incidence of earthquakes.[14] The librarian should be acquainted with the capability and quality of the fire department personnel and equipment available in the community. He should also acquaint the local fire and police department with the library itself, so they may know in advance of the peculiarities of the building, the location of personnel, the possible presence of any unusual conditions or fire hazards, etc. A periodic inspection visit could also be arranged with members of the fire department, either annually or semiannually, and immediately after any large rearrangements or alterations.[15] An inspection by the fire department would also make them aware of the extensive damages that would result from the excessive use of water.[16]

(2) Usage of the library building. The library building could be occupied only by the library, or jointly with the department it serves. In some cases, the library shares the building with a great many other types of departments, businesses, or operations. Some of these joint occupancies might be a threat to the library, due to the direct exposure to fire and smoke damage.[17]

The size of fire areas should be minimized through the use of fire resistant materials. The use in construction of unprotected steel structural elements should definitely be avoided. The best stack arrangement would be the free-standing type of ranges on concrete floors, and the floors should be structural parts of the building. Open, multi-tier stacks, especially, should be avoided. Fire walls and self-closing fire doors would help to break up open spaces that generally allow the fire to spread rapidly. The enclosure, with fire resistant construction, of vertical draft openings (i.e., vertical openings in the floors of multi-tier stacks, open stairways, elevator shafts, etc.) is a must in preventing fire hazards. Exit facilities should be provided, with enough distance between to provide hazardless mass exit. Automatic sprinkler systems, fire detection equipment, and alarm apparatus should be installed and checked regularly for operational readiness.

(3) Materials used to furnish the library. Metal furniture is preferable to wooden furniture, and metal cases are preferable to wooden or plastic ones; steel carts are preferred to wooden ones.

(4) Location of service area. The bindery, carpenter shop, gardener's storage room, heating plant, kitchen, paint shop, print shop, receiving and shipping room, as well as any other areas that might be considered hazardous, should not be close to the areas where the library collection is located. In addition, if any of these operations are located in the same building, they should be segregated from one another by concrete floors, fire walls, and the enclosure of vertical draft openings.[18]

(5) Air conditioning, electrical, heating, and plumbing systems. The librarian should be sure that the air circulation system can be shut down quickly in an emergency to avoid the spread of smoke and fire. All fluorescent ballasts should be individually fused to avoid operational failure and the quick ignition of nearby combustible materials, dripping pitch, or explosions of the ballast case. Sufficient capacity for the addition of new circuits should be provided for electrical services, and circuit breakers should be present to avoid circuit overloading. There are even times in which emergency power arrangements should be available through batteries or a standby generator for exit lighting, fire detection, and alarm purposes. Drain, steam, and water pipes should be placed in such a manner that, if defective, they cannot damage the collection.

(6) Library inspection, emergency procedures, and evacuation programs. If a library building is being planned, representatives of insurance companies and fire protection

engineers should be consulted, and advice should be requested from the usual sources--the architect, engineering specialists (structural, mechanical, and electrical), officials of the municipal building department, and the contractor. In this way, the librarian will be taking full advantage of the flexibility of modern construction, fire prevention, and electrical codes, as well as securing lower insurance premiums.[19]

If the building is already in existence, there should be a general detailed inspection of the entire structure, including the internal structural arrangement and the contents, being alert to any potential fire hazards. This general inspection would ideally be performed by competent (and expensive) fire protection engineers. Representatives from insurance companies, however, can in many instances carry out the same type of inspection at little or no cost. It sometimes occurs that insurance companies employ qualified engineers to make periodic inspections, at no cost to the insured party, of property they have insured.

Another means of securing no-cost appraisal of the library's security is to contact local building, electrical, and fire inspectors and have them determine whether the library fulfills the requirements of the building code, electrical code, and fire code. The local police department can also be asked to examine the library to ascertain how safe it is against burglary, vandalism, and other threats from the criminal element. The librarian should have the staff perform daily inspections at closing time to insure that no conditions exist that might constitute fire hazards.[20]

The Card Catalog and the Shelflist

Both of these catalogs should be heavily protected against hazards. Regardless of the amount of money for which they could be insured, they must never be exposed to total destruction, as their reconstruction would involve an extremely lengthy process and certainly a very costly one. The most complicated process, however, would *not* be the result of having lost the card catalog, the shelflist, and the collection, as all newly acquired items could be cataloged from scratch. Losing part of the collection would not be such a catastrophe if the card catalog and shelflist were not damaged, since the shelflist could be used to identify missing items, which could then be purchased. The cards for these items would already be in the card catalog, thus eliminating much of the clerical work necessary in cataloging an item, typing tracings, and filing cards in the catalog. The most frightening prospect would be losing the card catalog and/or the shelflist, or a significant part thereof, while incurring little or no damage to the collection. If the damaged portion of the catalog were very large, it would be more efficient to rebuild the catalog in its entirety than attempt to salvage what remained.[21]

Many libraries still follow the custom of using the shelflist only as a record of the holdings, not as a copy of the main entry card with a listing of all the tracings. In these cases, both the card catalog and the shelflist must be equally protected. However, if libraries were to use an exact replica of the main entry card for the shelflist, this would be the only catalog that would need to be protected.

The card catalog and the shelflist can be protected as follows:

(1) Duplication of the card catalog and shelflist. Some public libraries keep a copy of their card catalog at branch libraries as well as at the main library. This is a good way to protect the card catalog if: (a) the duplicate card catalog is up to date; (b) the card catalog and its duplicate are sufficiently separated; and (c) both are protected from any hazard.[22] One of the problems with this system is that of keeping the records current, as the card catalog is continually changing. The other is its exhorbitant cost. For law libraries specifically, one of the major drawbacks would be that it could only be applicable in departmentalized university libraries and in some large county law libraries with branches. Other types of libraries without branches could always arrange to have a duplicate of their card catalog, or preferably their shelflist (only if it contains exact copies of their main entry cards), kept in either the local public library or the local high school or university library. This method is too expensive and troublesome to be recommended.

(2) Microfilming card catalog or shelflist. This is the most popular method of protecting either the card catalog (for those libraries that keep all the tracings of their catalog cards on the main entry card) or the shelflist (for those who use a copy of their main entry cards for the shelflist). If the card catalog is microfilmed, this method could become quite expensive to update and too troublesome

to maintain after a few years, as there would be hundreds
or thousands of separate alphabets, which, in the case of
reproducing them into cards, could present an enormous
problem of editing and filing.

There are two ways of microfilming the catalog. The
least expensive and maybe the best solution, in a modern,
fire-resistant building where the risk may be considered
small, is to microfilm the cards by the cheapest means
available. This would provide a duplicate catalog from
which the main catalog could be reconstituted in case of
disaster. The other way is more expensive. It would require a careful process of microfilming so the film could
be used later to reproduce the cards directly by the use of
equipment such as the Xerox Copyflo. With the former
method, money and time are saved, as the microfilming
process does not require such detailed care, and automatic
equipment can be used. In the latter method, more time
is spent in the microfilming process in which planetary
equipment is generally recommended. The first method was
the one recommended in 1963 by the Library Technology
Project of the American Library Association. Such a recommendation was based on the theory that (a) cards eventually reproduced by Xerography cannot be better than the
film from which they are made, (b) the quality of the film
depends on the operator's care, and (c) the quality of the
reproduction depends on whether or not the material on the
card is clear.

In the same source, a better alternative is given,
that of filming the entire catalog at intervals of, for example, five years, and providing for the intervening additions and changes in some other manner, say, a "catalog"
of main entry cards, kept up to date in a separate location.
This supplementary "catalog" is then discarded at the next
complete filming time, and so on.

Catalog cards may be reproduced from microfilm at
a low cost, but it is recommended that the insured value of
the card catalog (or the shelflist) include provision for the
considerable labor costs involved in reproducing catalog
cards, filing them, and the almost certain need for editing
the reproduced cards. The microfilm itself should definitely
be physically protected from all hazards, as this is the only
way this method could be considered a form of partial insurance.[23] Another benefit of microfilming the catalog is
the lower premiums paid on microfilmed catalogs, as this

process makes possible a lower valuation on the catalogs.[24]

(3) Book catalogs. Another method of protecting the library catalog is computerizing it and printing a book catalog every so often. A book catalog can be made of all or part of the card catalog via regular means, but this is not advisable due to the cost and the excessive amount of time required.

The only way the book catalog would be recommended by this author would be through the storage of catalog information in a computer. The computer, if so programmed and if needed, can create a complete new catalog, in either book or card form, more efficiently than any other known method.

(4) Fire resistant vaults. Placing the entire card catalog (and probably the shelflist) in a fire resistant vault has been recommended as a way to physically protect the catalogs and to obtain some savings in insurance premiums. In order to use this protective method, the equipment used could vary from individual safes for a catalog, cabinets for several such safes, or to an entire insulated room where space would be provided not only for the catalog but also for the patrons and staff who must consult it. This method would be ideal if it were not for the inconvenience of the thick walls of the cabinets, the enormous weight on the floors, the cost, and the fact that these vaults are not entirely fireproof.[25]

Prevention of Fire by Use of Halon 1301 Systems

Some forms of heat-actuated devices--like carbon dioxide systems--have been successfully used by libraries to prevent fires, but have been discontinued due to the potential hazard to human life. However, a system that has been in use in industry for many years is now being used with greater frequency by libraries to protect their valuables from fire. This system is called Halon (also known as Freon) 1301 (Bromotrifluoromethane: $CBrF_3$).[26]

The National Fire Protection Association defines this system in its standards as "a colorless, odorless, electrically nonconductive gas that is an effective medium for extinguishing fires."[27] The fire suppression action of Halon 1301 is not clearly understood. It is thought to be a chemical effect rather than a physical one. Unlike water, which puts out a fire by cooling, or carbon dioxide, which smothers flames, Halon 1301 does its work chemically, as it interferes with the combustion cycle, stopping it immediately. The halogen compound reacts with the transient combustion products that are responsible for rapid and violent flame propagation. This reaction terminates the combustion chain reaction and thereby stops the spread of the flame. Halon 1301 is the first fire extinguishing Halon to have a boiling point below 0°C.[28] This gas is able to reach places inaccessible to other agents; it is considered a "clean" agent; it leaves no residue, as it is a vaporizing agent; and it does not attack or react with any materials normally used in construction or equipment. It is particularly advantageous for use against fires involving delicate electrical, mechanical, or electronic equipment, high-value storage areas, museums and places such as libraries, where water could cause as much damage as fire. Halon 1301 can be successfully applied to the three main classes of fires: Class A (cellulosic materials such as wood and paper), Class B (flammable liquid), and Class C (involving the live electronic circuits) fires.[29]

Halon 1301 was introduced to fire extinguishing work with its testing at the Fort Belvoir military test facility in 1950. By 1954 this material had been tested for toxicity and found to be much less toxic than other extinguishing gas systems; and, in 1962, nationally-recognized testing laboratories gave their approval to the Halon 1301 system. In 1968 it was the only halogenized fire extinguishing agent officially recognized by Underwriters' Laboratories, Inc., the institution sponsored by stock fire insurance companies of the United States.

In 1970 the National Fire Protection Association published the first standards for its use. As of this date, Halon 1301 is used to extinguish small fires, as well as for total flooding of hazard spaces.[30] This system comes in units as small as one-half pound for outboard marine engines to 3-1/2 ton systems to protect 300,000 cubic feet in oil processing buildings. Halon 1301 is used to protect racing car drivers, the crews in armored carriers used by the United States Army and Marine Corps, and commercial airliners (aircraft engines, cargo compartments, and passenger cabins). It is being used increasingly to protect computer rooms and telephone exchanges, libraries, museums, historical buildings, kitchen hoods and ducts, file rooms, radioactive "caves" and hot cells, as well as for many other industrial applications.[31] Like sprinkler systems, Halon 1301 extinguishing equipment operates in connection with fire detection units or heat actuated devices. It can also be manually activated. "The system consists of a container of agent arranged to discharge through nozzles to release an adequate quantity of agent to extinguish the fire. A suitable detector may be connected to the release valve to operate the system automatically." There are many small portable extinguishers and even local application systems; however, most systems currently are of the total flooding type. The latter system is designed to provide fire protection within containers, enclosed machines, ovens, rooms, vaults, etc.--wherever fixed enclosures are used. A factor that makes this system very easy to install is that no complicated piping is necessary; it can be placed anywhere without the extra cost of remodeling existing buildings and as easily as if the building were still on the planning board. Savings can thus be realized in hardware requirements and space used for the system.

The activation of the system produces a two-stage response: first, an alarm is sounded, which warns occupants that the area should be evacuated. Shortly thereafter, the required amount of the agent is released into the affected area. The amount of agent required is based upon the size of the enclosure and the concentration needed to extinguish or inert the specific fuel or fuels involved.[32] The "National Fire Protection Association Standard 12-A specifies an average concentration of less than 5 percent by volume of Halon 1301, as opposed to 35 percent by volume of carbon dioxide gas required for extinguishment of fires involving various hydrocarbons and commercial solvents. The system is electrically operated--with a battery standby also--and has a normal design discharge time of less than five seconds. Agent storage containers are strategically placed throughout the zone to be protected, eliminating the need for expensive piping in all but a few special installations. The resultant high-speed suppression of a fire reduces property damage and thermal products of de-composition to the lowest possible level."[33] Total flooding is achieved within 10 seconds.

Halon 1301 has an extremely low toxicity, and it is considered one of the safest of the halogenated fire extinguishing agents. Underwriters Laboratories classifies this agent in Group 6, their least toxic classification.[34] The problem encountered with carbon dioxide, that of reducing the amount of oxygen to such a level that life can not be sustained, is not the case with Halon 1301. In humans, Halon 1301 in concentrations below 7 percent produces no effects for brief (4 to 5 minutes) exposures. At concentrations above 7 percent, an anesthetic effect is noticeable, becoming increasingly sharper up to about 15 percent, at which point there is a feeling not unlike a mild intoxication or dizziness. No tests have been conducted on exposures over 17 percent, but it is supposed that such a condition might cause unconsciousness or even death.[35] However, as was mentioned before, only approximately 5 percent of this agent is needed to extinguish most fires, whether they are surface or deep-seated. Once this fire extinguishing agent comes in contact with fire, it decomposes. The main effect of the decomposition products is irritation; their odor is acrid, even in very low concentrations. This aspect of Halon 1301 is advantageous, as it serves as a built-in warning system for the agent. However, this sensation will disappear completely once the agent is no longer inhaled. The safest post-extinguishment atmosphere will be a result of prompt detection and quick extinguishment of the fire, as the amount of Halon 1301 that will decompose in any fire depends on the size of the fire and the type of the fuel, the size of enclosure, and the agent discharge time.[36]

An instance of a library that has recently installed a Halon fire suppression system is the Bentley Historical Library of the University of Michigan in Ann Arbor. This library has its three floors (a total of 57,330 cubic feet) protected by Halon 1301, with provision for a 6 percent concentration by volume as suppressant. The design concentration level of 6 percent will be achieved in less than 10 seconds after agent release. System actuation will occur, causing immediate agent release, when appropriate Ionization Smoke Detection Panel contacts close. This early detection method is utilized in order that the fire may be extinguished while it is still a surface type fire, thus causing a minimum of damage to the library contents. The Ionization Smoke Detection system is a three-zone system where one zone is utilized for detention of products of combustion in the return air ducts and to sound an alarm if products of combustion are present. The "Cross Zone Detection" method is employed so that an alarm condition on at least one detector in each zone is required to interlock ventilation equipment and dampers and to start a short time delay after which time the agent is discharged. The Cross Zone Detection method is utilized for protection against an unwanted alarm

causing discharge of agent, and yet affords rapid response
to products of combustion when needed.

The Halon fire extinguishing system can be considered a capital investment, and it would definitely lower the insurance premiums of any library having such a system. However, to this date, costs still stand in the way of automated fire protection for many libraries, as it costs approximately 30 cents to 50 cents per cubic foot of space protected by a Halon 1301 system. This is a system that is obviously intended for rooms or buildings with extremely valuable or irreplaceable contents, where the use of water or other extinguishing agents could cause extensive damage. It is ideal for rare book rooms, card catalog locations, and places where the shelflist is located. It is recommended in general for the entire library, if it can be afforded.

Insurance

A theory followed by many librarians or their supervisor-administrators was mentioned at the beginning of this paper. This theory justifies the practice of not insuring libraries, in the belief that payment of insurance premiums would cost more than the "possible occasional loss of a building." This type of decision, of course, can be reached only by those in charge of administering the destinies of any given library. No general statement can be made either in favor of or against such a theory. However, in order to reach that decision, a very careful study of the individual assets of the given institution should be undertaken. Such a study would clearly reveal whether or not that institution could stand a loss of a given substantial amount of money without being insured. This writer will leave that topic for a later date and will discuss here some of the different types of insurance available to librarians, and some general comments and recommendations.

In 1937 the Fire Insurance Committee of the American Library Association published its report in the <u>American Library Association Bulletin.</u>[37] Some of its recommendations regarding fire insurance still apply:

> The library should select as its adviser a high-grade, service-giving insurance agency, and place with it the largest share of its insurance, to give the agency prestige in settlement when loss occurs.

Policies should be written only with companies having an "A" rating. Companies are organized under somewhat different methods, such as stock companies, mutual companies, reciprocals, etc. Before placing insurance, it would be well to investigate these different types of organizations.

Policies should be written, whenever possible, on a three-year basis, the price for which is two and one-half times the one-year rate. (Five year policies may be secured, but the slight extra saving is not considered sufficient to warrant the additional outlay.) Policies should expire so that the annual expenditure is evenly distributed; that is, about one-third of the total each year.

The replacement valuation of the building above the foundation footings should be determined by a competent builder. The need for full insurance on fire resistant buildings, if the flat rate is used, is not so important as on other types of construction.

If full insurance is carried, or a definite percentage of it, the library has the advantage of the co-insurance clause, the price for which is considerably less than the flat rate.

If full insurance is not carried, then such as is carried should be placed at the flat rate.

Libraries having a number of branches may find it advantageous to carry group insurance under a blanket form.

Policies should cover books, exhibitions, and other property lent to the library (provided such property is not otherwise specifically insured), wearing apparel of the staff members, etc.

Book rarities, valuable art objects, or unusual items should be included in separate policies or on special memoranda.

A book and/or other content inventory by location, and interior photographs taken in various locations, are very desirable. They should be placed in a safety deposit box.

The shelflist is perhaps the most important and valuable tool in the library. It should be well protected. If a steel case is not used, the shelflist case should be enclosed in a fire resistant cabinet having a shutter front, to be closed when each day's work is done. To determine shelflist values, multiply the total number of its cards by the cost per card, adding for labor.

The number of cards in the card catalog may be determined by multiplying the number of titles in the library (shown by the total number of shelf-list cards as above) by the average number of cards for each book (which may be obtained by examining the tracings on all the author cards in a selected number of catalog drawers) and adding an estimate of the number of cross-reference cards.

Furniture and other contents should be carried at cost less depreciation.

Liability insurance should be carried for employees, and public liability as well, unless the city government takes care of this by group or other insurance.

Steam boiler, wind storm, tornado, airplane damage, and other insurance may be carried at discretion.

Fire extinguishers, of approved and standard makes, properly distributed about the building, will reduce fire insurance rates.

The installation of the sprinkler system will radically reduce the rates; but, if used, insurance must be carried to offset any loss caused when no fire occurs.

In addition to the above recommendations the following should also be considered:

(1) The valuation of books may be determined quite accurately by a study of average book costs, by sections or subjects, over a period of several years. (For further information on the subject, see "Evaluation of Library Facilities and Collections," p. 256.)

(2) It is of the utmost importance that the library building and its contents be insured in the proper amount (actual cash value) and that these valuations be kept up to date every year. If the librarian underestimates the value of the library, the money received in the event of a catastrophe would not be sufficient. However, if the librarian overestimates the value of the library, he is creating the possibility of litigation over adjustment grants. It also means the payment of inflated premiums while the policy is in force.[38]

In Globe & Rutgers Ins. Co. v. Prairie Oil and Gas Co.,[39] the "actual cash value" was defined as the "value at the time of the loss or damage." It is the replacement cost at the time of loss, less depreciation, or obsolescence. If the amounts of insurance are individually listed by specific articles, it is essential to ascertain whether these were figures accepted by the insurance company, or were assigned only because they are the limits of the liability of the company. If the policy does not clearly state that the specified amount is the agreed cost of the item, the "actual cash value" will have to be established after the loss occurs,[40] in which case the insurer requests a detailed proof of loss upon which reimbursement will be based. This might mean a delay of many months, or longer, or even the very distinct possibility of litigation.

(3) The date of insurance policies should be checked to ascertain if there have been any changes in bringing them up to date.

(4) Try to keep in one specific area parts of the collection that are being kept only because of the existing extra space. The insurance coverage should be ascertained, basing that decision on the need for replacement of the material if it were lost.

(5) A binder for an estimated amount should be obtained until an accurate figure is given, "if there is no coverage or the community or parent institution has a self-insurance plan that provides only partial coverage, or if coverage has not been updated for years. An approximate estimate can be reached by checking expenditure files for library materials for a given length of time, adding a standard processing fee"[41] and an estimated increase on the replacement cost, which would bring the price up to the actual cash value. Deductions should be made for whatever withdrawals have been made in the collection.

(6) If the library is a government depository and the documents have a specific function in the library, insure them for replacement value.

(7) Gift processing should take place in a specific location, and those selected to be added to the collection should be insured the same as the regularly purchased titles, at replacement value plus processing cost.

(8) All microforms and audiovisual material should be insured at replacement value. Insure the microform alone, if it is being considered as the master set and the

originals of the microforms are also available in the library.

(9) The periodical collection should be surveyed to ascertain that all items are valuable. Estimate the value of periodicals at replacement cost plus processing cost and an added percentage for binding.

(10) Keep a library plan, including the stack arrangement. Capacity, dimensions, and nature of the collection should be estimated as closely as possible.

(11) Acquisitions records should be kept consistently, and the price paid should be entered.

(12) The shelflist should also be kept up to date, showing additions and withdrawals as they occur.

(13) Keep the insurance coverage on the contents up to date. Notify the proper department of any important changes, if the insurance coverage is handled in that way.

(14) Obtain specific insurance coverage for off-premises loss. Circulation percentages should be checked to reduce cost of fire protection.

(15) Fire insurance is the principal coverage that should be obtained to protect the collection.[42]

(16) In calculating the value of the collection, the replacement value should include borrowed items; i.e., interlibrary loan materials.

(17) The background experience of the insurance company agent should be examined as to how many policies this agent has written for other libraries.

(18) The policy should contain a self-inflation rate. The inflation rate should be comparable to the Bowker Annual rate increase. If this rate cannot be written into the policy, it should be reviewed on a three-year interim basis.

(19) In case of severe damage, the policy should cover the removal of debris, plus the cost of attempting to salvage damaged items.

(20) One should consider the amount of time necessary to prepare all new material for the shelves; i.e., bookkeeping, opening boxes, stamping, making entries on the shelflist, kardex, circulation pockets, etc.

The insurance coverage should be arranged in such a manner that the library would be insured in the time between the moment the loss occurs and the time the claim is settled.

Besides the above, library administrators should be

aware of the fact that the insurance policy could become void if any misrepresentation or fraud regarding the insurance were to be discovered, either before or after a loss. The librarian should try to obtain coverage under which, in the case of loss by fire of all or part of the holdings, funds would be adequately provided for the replacement of the lost items at, or close to, the current purchase cost plus the cost of labor involved in replacing them. The inventory and appraisal of the contents of the library should be made by the librarian and any other expert assistance that can be recruited for that purpose. The inventory is of the utmost importance in preparing a claim in case of loss; lacking it, the insurance company will ask for one as soon as the loss occurs. It is also important to decide the proper amount of insurance to be carried. The inventory and appraisal is also necessary if an "all-risk" broader form of coverage on a valued form may be purchased.

It is the intention of this author not to discuss rates and premium costs, as it is almost impossible to refer to this subject in a general way. These costs vary according to the State in which the library is located and the hazards present, as well as the type of construction. The following, however, are two principles that can almost certainly be applied everywhere: (1) the greater the protection against the start and spread of fire, the lower the rate; and (2) the more extensively the policy can be written, the lower the average annual cost of the insurance.[43]

Types of Insurance

The amounts and types of insurance available for each different library are virtually limitless. Insurance will vary in form according to whether or not a library occupies its own building or a rented structure, whether or not it occupies a building alone or jointly with other tenants, whether or not it is located in a major metropolitan area or a rural section of the country, etc. In short, every library administrator will have to consider a host of variables in determining what kind of insurance he needs and the amount of coverage necessary to the requirements, and the budget, of the institution in question.

For a more detailed explanation of some of the types of insurance available to libraries, their property and contents, one can turn to Coverage Applicable, by Roy C.

McCormick.[44] This work could almost be described as the
abridged bible of the insurance world in the area of coverage.
For the purposes of this article, however, only the most important and the most common types of coverage will be
described in any detail. Others will receive only passing
mention.

If one is interested in insuring the property and operations of the library, a full Institutional Program package
policy may be drawn up. Such plans can be made subject
to a package credit for eligible risks. In addition, special
rating treatment can be used in cases in which risks qualify
for public and institutional property coverage under fire insurance rules.

One must ascertain at what point a new building becomes the property of the insured. If the building belongs
to the insured party from the inception of construction, complete Builder's Risk Insurance would be desirable. This
would include Property coverage, Time Element coverage,
and Liability coverage. When the building is completed,
this type of insurance can be replaced by permanent insurance coverage. In addition, one should be sure that
Property coverage under these types of policies is written
in such a manner as to avoid overlapping or gapping in protection, both for buildings and for their contents. All Risks
coverage is available on a blanket basis for buildings and
personal property.

The term Automatic Increase in Insurance Endorsement is used to describe that type of insurance that increases the limit of liability under Building coverage by a
certain percentage (e.g., 1 percent, 1.5 percent, or 2 percent) at the end of each three-month period. The purpose
of this insurance is to keep the total coverage abreast of
construction cost increases. Thus, as construction costs
rise, so does the cost of replacing a building, and the
coverage rises to meet the need.

Fire insurance is obviously one of the most important
types of coverage in the case of public buildings. For an
administrator who is truly interested in seeing that his library is adequately covered, the following forms should be
used along with the standard fire policy:

The Public and Institutional Property form is one
that protects not only against the perils of fire, but also can

Technical/Reader's Services

(at the option of the insured party) be extended to cover vandalism, malicious mischief, and sprinkler leakage. Other types of damage for which provision can be made under the Extended Coverage Endorsement are direct loss or damage caused by windstorm, hail, explosion, riot, civil commotion, aircraft, vehicles, and smoke. This coverage may vary slightly from State to State, but it usually includes the more hazardous perils.

The Building and Contents form covers not only the buildings described in the policy, but also all permanent fixtures belonging to and constituting a part of the insured buildings. Thus, the following types of fixtures are covered: machinery used in building service, air-conditioning units, boilers, elevators, etc.

In addition, as the operation of such fixtures as boilers, hot water heaters, and elevators involves a hazard to property and persons, serious consideration should be given to this aspect of insurance. The first concern should be to reduce the hazard; however, insurance would probably be desirable to cover damage caused to the building and its contents, injuries sustained by employees, as well as damage to property of third parties or injuries caused to the person of third parties.

The Deductible Fire Insurance Plan is similar to the above; however, in case of disaster, the insured party bears a certain specified amount of any loss in consideration for a credit applicable to published premium rates. In this way, the insured party carries the risk of smaller losses, while the insurer pays for the catastrophes (less the deduction, of course). Full reimbursement for the actual cost of repair or replacement of an insured building can be arranged under the Replacement Cost Endorsement. In this case, there is no deduction for depreciation; however, a building must be in sound condition to be eligible for this type of coverage.

In dealing with the protection of buildings, another form to keep in mind is the Glass Insurance form. This type insures the replacement of plate glass that may be broken either accidentally or maliciously. It also covers glass that may have been damaged by acid or chemicals, and it may also include coverage for supporting frames and bars, as well as cost of lettering and ornamentation.

Sprinkler leakage insurance, mentioned briefly above, includes all direct loss to building and contents as a result of leakage, freezing, or breaking of sprinkler installations, or any form of accidental discharge. Damages caused by flood, mudslides, and earthquakes are additional elements for which coverage should be considered.

So far, this article has concentrated to a large extent on damage to buildings and to permanent fixtures; however, there are other elements that have been mentioned briefly and will be discussed in somewhat more detail at this point.

The contents of libraries are often just as valuable, if not more valuable, than the buildings themselves. It is recommended that the contents be insured under the same policy or policies that apply to the building. This has the effect of reducing the number of policies for which the responsible officials must account. A separate policy should, of course, be used to insure the contents of nonowned buildings.

The Standard Fire Policy is the basic contract. The more common books and other items of no special value can be insured under a regular fire insurance policy, with added coverage such as that for earthquake, explosion, water, and windstorm damages. In the case of loss of the card catalog, for example, this policy would cover only the cost of replacing the card stock, plus the cost of putting the catalog information on the cards. It would not cover the substantial costs involved in cataloging, cataloging research, or supervision and instruction of catalog department personnel.

The Public and Institutional Property form provides not only building coverage, as described above, but also covers, on a blanket basis, all personal property owned by the insured, personal property of others for which the insured assumed liability prior to loss, the liability of the insured party as imposed by law for the loss of personal property of others, and the insured's interest in personal property belonging in whole or in part to others. Other forms used in this area are the Building and Contents form, the Office Personal Property form, the Extended Coverage Endorsement, the Vandalism and Malicious Mischief Endorsement, and the Replacement Cost Endorsement--all of which were discussed above or whose purpose is obvious through their titles.

In addition, there are certain types of property that call for the broad protection provided only by Inland Marine insurance. Two of these classes of protection are the (1) Valuable Papers and Records Policy, and (2) the Fine Arts Policy. The former will reimburse the insured party for loss, destruction, or damage to valuable papers or records while they are on the described premises. It can also cover the same property while it is being conveyed outside the premises or within the premises of others, but not while in storage. This type of policy insures on an all-risk basis, which includes misplacement as well as mysterious or unexplained disappearance.

Libraries, of course, house manuscripts, rare books, and other records of great historical value. The best coverage on contents, it would seem, is that of insuring the rare and more valuable books and holdings under a Valuable Papers and Records Policy. This form of insurance policy has two sections that can be used either alone or in conjunction with each other. One section is intended for the insurance of specific rarities, which must be listed and valued individually. A second or "blank" section is one in which a lump sum is provided for the great majority of a library's holdings, the non-rarities. The Valuable Papers Policy also provides reimbursement, depending on the amount of insurance carried, for cost of the research needed to reconstitute card catalogs, shelflists, payroll records, and any other library operating records. It may also cover the actual cost of replacing or reproducing the books lost.

This type of policy carries no co-insurance clause, but it does provide off-premises coverage for materials any place in the United States or Canada, as long as the material is not in regular storage.

The Fine Arts Policy is similar to the Valuable Papers and Records Policy in the form of valuables that are to be insured. This is an all-risk form used for paintings, valuable rugs, statuary, etchings, pictures, and tapestries, and for other bona fide works of art or rarity having historical value or artistic merit. It too requires a complete listing of the articles insured, with their individual values. Protection is afforded against loss or damage stemming from water and fire, burglary or theft, and other hazards.

Next, we reach the problems involved in General Liability Insurance. Assuming that sovereign immunity is not available as a defense to an action for third party bodily injury and property damage claims, what are the forms of insurance that a library should carry to be protected against such claims?

The most effective form of insurance is the Comprehensive General Liability form. This type of policy insures against all specified existing liability hazards and, in addition, any liability hazards that may arise during the policy terms. These hazards may arise from buildings, premises, or operations. Of particular concern are hazards involved in escalator or elevator maintenance, as well as the condition of floors and stairways. It is even conceivable that this coverage might extend to liability arising from situations in which reference librarians went beyond reference requirements and actually engaged in the "practice of law" by giving erroneous legal counsel.

However, important contractual agreements, such as construction contracts, are not automatically covered. The policy must be endorsed to include them. The term Contractual Liability policy is applied to those that cover the insured's liability assumed under specifically described contracts, as distinguished from liability imposed by law. For example, liability assumed under a contract for the lease of a building or under a contract for elevator or escalator maintenance is covered under the basic Premises-Operations insurance.

Other forms of insurance that should be considered, whose purpose and function are fairly obvious from their names, are Workman's Compensation Insurance; Automobile Liability (for damages and injuries caused by library cars or cars rented by the library, as well as by employee-owned vehicles used for library business); Collision; Medical Payments; Surety Bonds (where library staff acts as notaries to the public); Welfare and Pension Plan Bonds; Comprehensive Dishonesty, Destruction, and Disappearance Policies; Data Processing Equipment Policies; Blanket Crime Policies; Fidelity Bonds; and Travel Accident Insurance. Each administrator must determine which of the various types of insurance are needed and which can be justified in terms of benefits and cost. These policies can specify in minute detail the risks to be insured against, or they may take a form similar to the Umbrella Liability Insurance policy.

Technical/Readers' Services

Fire insurance companies also offer reduced rate clauses for their policies. These are generally known as "co-insurance." Co-insurance was created to balance the premiums between those who insure for a small portion of the value and those who insure for full or nearly full value.

These reduced rated clauses have been used in Europe since almost the beginning of fire insurance. In the United States, the principle of co-insurance was acknowledged by underwriters, but no orderly effort to use it was made until the early 1880's.

Co-insurance as commonly used is based on the agreement that the insurance will be kept at a specific percentage--80, 90, and even 100 percent--of the value of the property; and large reductions from the basic, or "flat," rate are given. In any type of insurance contract--flat rate or co-insurance--the loss paid would be equal if the requirements had been fulfilled, provided that the same amount of insurance were kept under both co-insurance and non-co-insurance policies. If the insurer applies a given co-insurance clause, he agrees to keep that proportion of the insurance to sound value. The librarian will buy the insurance at a much lower price than the flat rate, in some cases at 30 or 35 percent reduction. In some areas, for a fire-resistant building, the rate would be lowered from 80 to 90 percent. If the librarian has kept the required proportion of insurance, he would receive the full amount of a loss up to the amount of insurance carried. If the insurer had not maintained the required proportion of insurance to value, he would become a co-insurer with the companies and would collect only a partial insurance in proportion to his under-insurance.[45]

Special Library Insurance Policy

This policy was developed by the Insurance Committee of the American Library Association and published as a chapter in Protecting the Library and Its Resources, a manual published in 1963 by the Library Technology Project of the ALA. To date, this policy has been adopted with minor changes only by the Hartford Fire Insurance Company. It has been approved by the insurance departments of 42 States and the District of Columbia. The States that have not yet approved it are: Alaska, Hawaii, Massachusetts, Mississippi, New Jersey, North Carolina, Oregon, Texas, and the

Commonwealth of Puerto Rico. Local insurance regulations currently preclude the sale of this particular package form of insurance in these States.

The ALA designed this policy to serve library insurance needs as part of a major study of techniques and equipment for the protection of libraries against fire and other types of losses. This policy protects libraries against all risks of physical loss or damage to insured property from any external cause (except those excluded by name). The policy will not pay for loss or damage due to "insurrection, war or war-like action; nuclear reaction, radiation or radioactive contamination (except loss by resulting fire); errors or omissions in processing or copying (unless fire or explosion ensues causing loss); wear and tear, gradual deterioration, insects, vermin or inherent vice; dishonesty of any officer, director or trustee; electrical or magnetic injury, disturbance or erasure of electronic recordings"; nor will it pay for either loss or damage to "property which cannot be replaced (unless specifically declared); furniture, fixtures, tools, supplies, improvements or personal property caused by industrial or agricultural smoke or smog, rust, rot, atmospheric conditions, temperature changes or mechanical breakdown (unless loss ensues from sudden and faulty operation of heating or cooling equipment)."

This special library policy covers all property owned or in the care of the library, whether on premises or off, anywhere in the world, including (a) general collections of books, periodicals, documents, recordings, microforms, sheet music, etc.; (b) administrative records such as shelf-lists, card catalogs, registration and withdrawal cards, microfilmed data; (c) special collections of manuscripts, rare books, etc.; (d) fine arts such as paintings, pictures or sculpture; (e) furniture, fixtures, tools, equipment, supplies; (f) personal property up to 10 percent of the total amount of insurance purchased, but not exceeding $500 for articles owned by the library; (g) personal property up to $500 for articles owned by any officer or employee of the insured while located on the library premises; (h) improvements or betterments to buildings occupied but not owned by the insured. This policy also has a special impairment of services feature that provides for payment of the excess cost of continuing operations after loss has occurred, while repairs are being made. "Excess" cost is defined as total expense above and beyond the normal operating expenses if no loss had occurred.

Property not covered by the library policy are money, securities, notes, deeds, accounts, bills, evidence of debt, aircraft, motor vehicles, or trailers.

To assure adequate coverage at lowest possible premiums, a $250 deductible has been included in the Special Library Policy in most States. The deductible is applied to each claim.

In conclusion, some difficulties in settling library claims may arise if:[46]

1. An inventory of the library holdings has never been taken or has not been updated.
2. The collection and shelf lists have never been weeded.
3. The coverage of the insurance has not been changed with the changing of the collection or with the appreciation or depreciation of that collection.
4. The collection has been arbitrarily swollen with gifts and other miscellany to occupy space or to push up the volume count.
5. Large amounts of periodicals and other materials have been accumulated for the same reason.
6. The same general areas are shared by used and unused books.
7. The shelflists include miscellaneous information and the price data has not always been recorded.
8. A large portion of the collection and the stacks have been totally destroyed.
9. The policy in question contains a co-insurance feature, which, in case of fire, leads to the conclusion that the collection is underinsured.
10. It is questionable that the books and other library materials are really part of the contents of the library as covered by the insurance policy.

This author recommends that, if insurance is contemplated, the model ALA library policy be chosen. However, if the latter cannot be applied in a given State or if the librarian decides not to use it, then a combination of the Public and Institutional Property form with a Valuable Paper Policy and a Fine Arts Policy should be chosen, as these would provide equivalent protection at a more economical cost. "Insurance gives a twenty-four-hour-a-day coverage, 365 days a year. The cost is relatively low for the protection it affords."

Exclusions

This author will mention here only the exclusions that are generally part of most insurance forms, which would have to be covered by specific endorsements if coverage were desired. Most insurance policies state clearly that their companies are not liable for loss caused by, resulting from, contributed to, or aggravated by any of the following:

1. Flood, surface water, waves, tidal water or tidal wave, overflow of streams or other bodies of water, or spray from any of the foregoing, whether driven by wind or not;
2. Water that backs up through sewers or drains;
3. Water below the surface of the ground, including that which exerts pressure on, or flows, seeps, or leaks through sidewalks, driveways, foundations, walls, basement or other floors, or through doors, windows, or any other openings in such sidewalks, driveways, foundations, walls or floors;
4. Earth movement, including but not limited to earthquake, landslide, mudflow, earth sinking, earth rising or shifting;
5. Power, heating, or cooling failure, unless such failure results from physical damage to power, heating, or cooling equipment situated on premises where the covered property is located, caused by the peril(s) insured against;
6. Riot, riot attending a strike, civil commotion, or vandalism and malicious mischief;
7. Electrical injury or disturbance to electrical appliances, devices, fixtures, or wiring caused by electrical currents artificially generated, unless fire ensues, and, if fire does ensue, the company will be liable only for its proportion of loss caused by such fire;
8. Loss, including debris removal expense, occasioned directly or indirectly by enforcement of any local or State ordinance or law regulating the construction, repair, or demolition of building(s) or structure(s);
9. Hostile or warlike action in time of peace or war, including action in hindering, combating, or de-

fending against an actual, impending, or expected attack, (a) by any government or sovereign power (de jure or de facto), or by any authority maintaining or using military, naval, or air forces; or (b) by military, naval, or air forces; or (c) by government, power, authority, or forces, it being understood that any discharge, explosion, or use of any weapon of war employing nuclear fission or fusion shall be exclusively presumed to be such a hostile or warlike action by such a government, power, authority, or forces.

10. Insurrection, rebellion, revolution, civil war, usurped power, or action taken by governmental authority in hindering, combating, or defending against such an occurrence.
11. Loss by nuclear reaction or nuclear radiation or radioactive contamination, whether controlled or uncontrolled, or due to any act or condition incident to any of the preceding.

Evaluation of Library Facilities and Collection for Insurance Purposes

To arrive at an approximately correct valuation of the library's building and contents, one must have a detailed knowledge of the collection and of the monies invested on: (1) books, documents, periodicals, rare books, etc.; (2) furniture and fixtures, book stacks, etc.; and (3) the catalog and card records.[47] The problem of valuation is not restricted to the consideration of specific items owned on a specific date, but also includes a realistic evaluation scheme for maintaining insurance on those items acquired between reevaluations.

Buildings, supplies, equipment, etc., should be insured for full replacement cost. Physical depreciation on buildings is very small if they have proper maintenance; it should be within the range of 1 to 1-1/2 percent per year. In any event, total depreciation should not exceed 40 percent in the majority of cases, since maintenance will compensate for any further depreciation at about that point. Building valuation by a professional appraiser is preferred in establishing the required amount of coverage.

The values for personal property should be based on

the cost of buying the same property new at the time it is lost. A regular rate of depreciation based on the estimated life of this type of property should be applied. However, if used property of the same age and quality is readily available, its price could be used as the replacement value.[48] In the case of office machinery, such as typewriters, photocopying machines, etc., one must ascertain if they have been purchased or rented. In both cases, the librarian should investigate whether they have been insured by the parent organization or by the company renting them out, as they should be insured against fire, and possibly against earthquake, flood, riot, and storm. A co-insurance clause could be applied to real or personal property, in which case a rate reduction is given by the insurer, as it is as advantageous to the insurance underwriters as it is for the insured party to have the property insured as close to its full valuation as possible.

The evaluation of library books requires knowledgeable personnel, who can be found among respected book dealers, professional appraisal companies (insurance agents are supposedly acquainted with appraisal firms, and might be able to make a recommendation), and qualified library administrators.

In evaluating rare books, it is suggested that they be separately listed and individually evaluated. They can then be covered by specific insurance.[49] The value for most of the books and periodicals can be established by assigning average amounts per volume; this is called the "unit" method. In this method the evaluation of book material is done through the shelflist, counting the number of volumes in each "class." Then, with the help of the records of orders filled, the average cost per volume of books in this "class" is determined. For the evaluation of periodicals, the librarian must go to the shelves or to the periodicals records to count each bound volume. The average cost per volume of periodicals can be obtained through the use of serials order records. The next step is to ascertain the average cost of binding per volume per periodical. In many instances, librarians overlook this factor. In a law library, this omission could mount to a very large figure, which would not be covered in case of loss. With these two averages combined, the librarian will have the average cost per bound periodical volume. The same method applies to unbound periodicals, with the exception of binding costs. This author believes that no percentage of depreciation should be allowed when evaluating the periodical collection of a law library, as the books in this collection are of permanent value as research tools in this type of library.

The valuation of the holdings of a law library should be done by location, if not in the law library area (i.e., faculty library, lawyers' room, storage, etc.) and by groups of classification, if in the area of the law library (i.e., digests and citators, bar association and society publications, looseleaf services, government documents, reports, statutes, session laws, etc.).

There are items that cannot be replaced, due to their nature or lack of availability. However, the librarian will wish to insure some of them. Their value could be ascertained through auction catalogs, treasurer's books, library records, and prices listed in the catalogs and lists of publishers and dealers. There will be items that, although the librarian will not be able to purchase exact copies of them, other equivalent representative material could be obtained to serve patrons' needs.[50]

Librarians should insure their valuable records for the amount put into them, plus the amount needed to replace them. Some of these valuable records are: (1) the shelf list, (2) the public card catalog, (3) the catalogs in any branch or departmental collections, (4) acquisition records, (5) serials records, and (6) director's office records.[51] An extremely safe way of preserving all these records would be microfilm them and store the film in a safe. The ALA has recommended a procedure to determine the value of the shelflist records, which, due to its simplicity, is reproduced here:

1. Count the number of cards in an inch of space.
2. Count the number of inches in each catalog drawer.
3. Multiply to determine the number of cards per drawer.
4. Multiply the total number of cards in all drawers by the replacement value (including cost of cards, plus processing, salary of catalogers, etc.) to obtain the approximate insurance value of the shelflist records.[52]

When insuring the card catalog, the labor cost involved in its creation and the replacement cost of its card content should be considered. The previously cited book, Protecting the Library and Its Resources, recommends the following formulae to determine the cost of replacing the card catalog:

A. Situation
1. Catalog and shelflist completely destroyed.
Formula: The number of different titles not destroyed (including those out on circulation) multiplied by the cost of cataloging a single title (including the cost of card reproduction).
Notes:
(a) The number of titles not destroyed in a "total loss" will vary from library to library. However, this number can be estimated by adding the average number of books out on circulation to the number of titles housed in other locations (branches, etc.).
(b) The cost of cataloging a title varies among libraries and depends on the type of library (public, college, research, etc.), size of library, and procedures. Each library would have to calculate its own cost of cataloging a single title.

2. Catalog and shelflist damaged, but all information on cards remains intact.
Formula: The number of different titles not destroyed (including those out on circulation) multiplied by the average cost of reproducing a single card.
Notes:
(a) Although the cost of pulling a set of catalog cards will vary between libraries, it can readily be calculated by each library. The average number of cards per title cataloged will also vary from library to library.
(b) The cost of reproducing a single card will depend on the method (photography, Xerography, etc.) used.

The above-mentioned report ends:
It should be remembered:
a. Since we are actually dealing with variables, there is no way that a firm figure applicable to all libraries can be established.
b. The above formulae should be used only by those libraries that have not taken the precaution of microfilming their catalogs and shelflists.
c. In addition to having microfilms of its catalog and shelflist, some libraries store extra copies of their catalog cards in a vault outside the library.
d. Smaller libraries with less complicated cataloging problems and fewer cards per set will probably have a smaller unit cataloging cost.... 53

Conclusions

In reviewing all the above considerations, one might summarize by stating that, for card catalogs, shelflists, and other valuable records, an insulated room, equipped with a heat and smoke detection system, is recommended; and the latter alone if the former is unfeasible. However, there are conditions such as flood, earthquake, etc., that cannot be fully prevented and for which insurance is the only "consolation," if self-insurance is not considered. The fireproof vault and the smoke and heat detecting systems are specifically recommended for rare books or materials considered irreplaceable, rather than establishing an insurance coverage on some supposed basis.

The lack of interest of some librarians regarding the security of their libraries is shocking. It is distressing to see how responsible librarians, with the qualifications and desire needed for such an endeavor, cannot, due to lack of authority over the destinies of their own libraries, enforce either preventive or correctional measures in their institutions, but must follow the whims of their nonlibrarian superiors, who generally lack knowledge of and interest in libraries. However, it is the responsibility of the head librarians to inform their superiors of the measures needed to protect their libraries, as well as to request the specific measures from them. Librarians should be aware of the items in existence to protect their libraries, even though the particular action taken may be limited to instructions to contractors or discussion of such problems with fire protection engineers, other consultants, or with the librarian's superiors.

Thomas F. Dougherty and Paul W. Kearney point out in Fire (page 220):

> The cue for tomorrow is Fire Resistance: that twin practice of building in a manner that will retard fire, and protecting the building with sufficient automatic control. It has frightened many because it is a method that commences with a check book. But it should reassure them to know that it has the redeeming feature of ending with a bank balance!

It should be stressed, however, that in order for the library to attain a condition of safety, not all the protective measures, devices, or equipment available should be introduced, but that the different corrective actions taken in a given library must be related to each other.

Perhaps the American Association of Law Libraries could consider the establishment of a new committee, the Insurance for Libraries Committee--similar to that of the ALA--which would publish on an annual basis a revised list of book values, by class, as well as values for periodicals, microforms, and audiovisual materials, by unit within each class.

Should we take some action now to prevent future disasters, or should we wait for another library to burn and learn a bit more from that experience?

REFERENCES

1. For more information on this fire, see Library Journal, 97 (Sept. 15, 1972), 2756-57.
2. "Temple University Books Restored by Salvage Firm." Library Journal, 97 (Nov. 15, 1972), 3667.
3. "Insurance for Libraries." Library Journal, 52 (1927), 828.
4. Singer, Dorothea M. The Insurance of Libraries: A Manual for Librarians. Chicago: American Library Association, 1946; 3.
5. For a very thorough study of the subject of protection of library resources from fire and other disasters, see: American Library Association. Library Technology Project. Protecting the Library and Its Resources; A Guide to Physical Protection and Its Insurance. Chicago [1963].
6. Ibid., xiv.
7. Ibid., xv.
8. American Library Association. Library Administration Division. Insurance for Libraries Committee. "Making of a Nationwide Scandal; A Report." ALA Bulletin, 62 (Apr. 1968), 384.
9. Roth, Harold L. "Check Your Fire Insurance." ALA Bulletin, 55 (Jan. 1961), 54.
10. American Library Association. Insurance for Libraries Committee. "Annual Report," ALA Bulletin, 35 (Oct. 15, 1941), 620.
11. See note 5, p. 21.
12. For a detailed explanation on prevention of losses, see

note 5, pp. 22-41 and 98-120.
13. Ibid., 23.
14. Ibid., 101.
15. Ibid., 35.
16. Ibid., 36.
17. Ibid., 33.
18. Ibid., 111.
19. Ibid., 98-99.
20. Ibid., 24-25.
21. Ibid., 37.
22. Ibid., 38.
23. Ibid., 39-40.
24. Mixer, Charles W. "Columbia Insures Its Main Card Catalog." Library Journal, 82 (Oct. 1, 1957), 2308.
25. See note 5, p. 37-38.
26. "Halon" is a contraction of the words "halogenated hydrocarbon." The U.S. Army Corps of Engineers created a numbering system intended to simplify references to these chemicals, and in this system Halon 1301 represents, in order, the number of carbon, fluoride, chlorine, bromine and iodine atoms present in the molecule. In the above system, terminal zeros (as in the case of Halon 13010) are dropped and atoms not accounted for are assumed to be hydrogen. Therefore, the Halon 1301 molecule consists of one carbon, three fluorine, no chlorine, one bromine, and no iodine atoms: $CBrF_3$.
27. National Fire Protection Association. Standard on Halogenated Fire Extinguishing Agent Systems--Halon 1301 (1972), 7.
28. National Academy of Sciences. An Appraisal of Halogenated Fire Extinguishing Agents (1972), 10.
29. Ford, Charles L. "Where and Why to Use Halon 1301 Systems." Actual Specifying Engineer (Jan. 1972), 74.
30. See note 28, p. 10-11.
31. See note 29, p. 74.
32. E. I. du Pont de Nemours & Co. Dupont Halon 1301 Fire Extinguishant (1972), 3.
33. Fenwal Incorporated. Protection Systems Division. "Fenwal Halon 1301, Fire Supression System; Installation, Operation and Maintenance Manual" (1972), 3.
34. Ibid.
35. Ibid.
36. See note 32, p. 9.
37. American Library Association. Insurance for Libraries Committee. "Annual Report," ALA Bulletin, 31

(Sept. 1937), 562-64.
38. Schmchl, Lawrence H. "Insuring Your Law Library." Law Library Journal, 39 (1946), 45.
39. Globe & Rutgers Ins. Co. v. Prairie Oil and Gas Co., 160 C.C.A. 462, 248 Fed. 452 (1917), 269 Fed. 771 (1921), 16 F.2d 776 (1927), 49 F.2d 716 (1931), 31 A.M.C. 1389, 50 F.2d 805 (1931), 77 F.2d 833 (1935), 131 F. Supp. 678 (1955), 229 Ala. 356, 157 So. 63 (1934), 300 Mass. 473, 15 N.E.2d 807 (1938), 194 Minn. 326, 260 N.W. 354 (1935), 214 Wis. 14, 252 N.W. 166 (1934), 423 S.W.2d (1967), 22 A.L.R. 408, 56 A.L.R. 1155, 56 A.L.R. 1156, 105 A.L.R. 107, 49 A.L.R.2d 94, 49 A.L.R.2d 138, 61 A.L.R.2d 715.
40. See note 5, p. 130.
41. See note 9, p. 55.
42. Ibid., 55.
43. Page, James R. "Planning a Library Insurance Program." ALA Bulletin, 36 (Aug. 1942), 573.
44. McCormick, Roy C. Coverage Applicable. Indianapolis: Rough Notes Co., 1972; 78-82.
45. American Library Association. Insurance for Libraries Committee. "Annual Report," ALA Bulletin, 30 (May 1936), 383.
46. See note 9, p. 54.
47. See note 38, p. 46.
48. See note 5, p. 130.
49. In specific insurance, a specified amount of insurance is allocated to each item by either numerating each one with a specific amount of insurance on the policy form or by writing separate policies for each one of the items so insured. The opposite to this type of insurance is the blanket insurance, in which several items are covered under a single amount of insurance.
50. Handover, R. A. "Valuation of Libraries." Unesco Bulletin for Libraries, 21 (July-Aug. 1967), 172.
51. Deale, H. Vail. "Insurance Re-evaluation." Library Journal, 80 (1955), 2818.
52. Ibid., 2817.
53. See note 5, p. 63-64.

DISTRIBUTING BOOKS*

Dick Higgins

     A long time ago I promised myself I wouldn't write about business. But the corruption in my "industry" is so total that I figured I'd better do so, as part of my promise to spend '73 talking about Literature. Because books are part of literature. So I must break one promise to myself to keep another to other people.

     The book industry is the most stupid and the most corrupt of all in the country. What should be part of an information flow is part of a very possessive information monopoly. For reasons I'll shortly explain, publishers don't make money on books. They make them on rights, reprints, movie permissions, magazine serializations. And every time an independent publisher gets bought up by an information conglomerate, even if the Big Corp leaves the publisher alone pretty much and doesn't really interfere with it editorially, the motivation is removed to do important work or, in fact, to do anything besides turn a profit. That isn't very good for work that isn't likely to be serialized, or that would be hard to "do" in French or Spanish or German or Japanese.

     Start the analysis. You read this [The Something Else Newsletter], so you probably like books. You can buy as an individual or you can borrow from a library. Individual first. You read about things from time to time. Friends tell you about our books and other things they've been reading. Mostly they tell you about the who. This isn't McLuhanish, really. You don't set out to buy a book, usually. You're interested in the particular person's ideas

---

*Reprinted by permission from the April 1973 issue of The Something Else Newsletter, pages 1-4. Copyright © 1973 by Something Else Press, Inc. Written January 30, 1973.

(or in a field). One sits down for an evening of TV, but
one reads "Fuller," "ecology," or "feminism" whenever and
however one can fit it in. One writes literature fairly often,
but reads it less so. You read a literary book only when
you can't help it. Really that's the result of the corruption,
but I'll address myself more to that later.

So you go to a library and you take out the thisses
and thats which you've been thinking about. If you live in
the country--or if you want to have for working with--the
books you need, you buy them. You don't trust the mails
(who'd dare?), so you go to a bookstore. This brings us to
the second link.

A bookstore. The people who work in it have to be
fairly literate. That costs. The store has to be fairly
central, if it's to handle any off-the-street traffic (of course
some stores specialize in mail order, but they're special
nowadays). And to get a good place they have to compete
with hamburger joints, hi fi shops, etc. That costs. A
grocery gets a 60% discount on some items, and others
come in on consignment. A bookstore gets around 40% a
little more if they can take on enough books. And it has
to carry a very large inventory if it's to satisfy your request when you come in the door. Maybe 8,000 different
titles if it's a little store. And these probably come from
500 different publishers, at least--which means keeping up
500 accounts. And the books have to be paid for after 30
days, ideally, though in practice it usually works out to 60
days. And often the store simply can't pay for a book it
knows it might need but doesn't happen to have an immediate
customer for, so the store has to pay part of its bills by
returning the books. Just for the record, here's the discount schedule and return policy that Something Else Press
offers to stores:

Discount Schedule to the Trade:
(Single or Assorted Titles)

1- 4 books, 20%	200-299 books, 44%
5- 24 books, 40%	300-399 books, 45%
25- 49 books, 41%	400-499 books, 46%
50- 99 books, 42%	500-749 books, 47%
100-199 books, 43%	750-up books, 48%

Return Policy: Books in resaleable condition
may be returned for full credit in not less than

Technical/Readers' Services

90 days nor more than 12 months from the date of invoice. Requests to return must be made in advance. If the invoice number and date are supplied at the time of return, 100% of the invoice price will be credited. Otherwise it will be assumed that the original discount was 42% and a handling charge of 10% will be deducted.

So you go into the store. You want a book that is important. Naturally they don't have it. So you ask them to get it. They phone a wholesaler, perhaps one of the best, like Dimondstein's or Bookazine. Most likely the wholesaler doesn't have it either. So they tell you the book is "out of print," and you go home thinking it was. Even if the wholesaler had it, a single book order would probably come in giving them only a 20% discount--how could the wholesaler offer more?--and if the book's a paperback, the bookseller would be lucky if he broke even on the transaction, considering his overhead costs, the cost of the phone call, postage, etc. Recommendation to the industry: book stores should not special order but should refer this kind of thing to the publishers--very few publishers can or should refuse a prepaid order.

Well what does the wholesaler do? Actually he isn't a warehouse for huge titles. He's a common stocker of well-selling titles. He gets his profit from the perhaps 50% and sometimes more that he gets from the publisher. But he has a huge warehouse to support. He can't do it from 50% of a 35 cent magazine--and he won't. He does it by ordering and returning to the publisher (if they don't sell, and both publisher and wholesaler lose money on this) on a large volume basis. Say, now, you're a small publisher. You were lucky: a big metropolitan newspaper reviewed you. You have no sales force. You put out feelers, the wholesaler picks you up. But by the time the books get to the wholesaler, the people who were in the stores asking for your book aren't going in asking for it any more. So the books come back to you. In the meantime maybe you've had to go back to the printer and get him to do a few thousand more books, because they're all out at the wholesalers'. Then when they come back--financial disaster for all.

You're the publisher. You do a thousand books. They cost $2.25 each to produce. That's a $2250 printing, binding, typesetting and paper bill. If you had done 5000 copies, it would have cost perhaps $3600. This would be

72 cents each. But it's still a lot more money for you to invest. (And this would be a very small book.) So you just stop doing books that would only be done in a thousand copies--poetry, first novels and (even more) second or third novels, literary essays, etc.

That's why bigger publishers are often more able to take a chance than smaller publishers. Or why they can afford to do a better production job, give better royalties.

But let's look what this means. It cost $2.25 to produce our book, we've said. To get a proper retail price, we multiply by four and by five and make a compromise between them for best selling price. That would mean this book should cost between $9.00 and $11.25, if production is to be between 20% and 25% of the price of the book. For comparison, it costs about 16 cents each to manufacture a typical phonograph record edition of 4000, apart from editing --it is then sold for $4.95. Rather a more favorable situation, isn't it? Back to the book: let's assume you've decided on $10 as a price. Well, the store will get upwards of 40% if it orders a few copies. If you have a salesman, he'll get another 15%. If he sold to a wholesaler, the discount would be 50% + 15% = 65% total. If you go sort of half in half, the average amount the publisher receives is about 45% (including mail orders). And if our manufacturing cost was 23% for production, then the publisher and author must split 22%. Suppose the author gets 10%, a usual arrangement. On the edition he'd then get 10% of $10,000 or $1000. The publisher would then have $1200 to pay the (not-yet-mentioned) designer, any editor involved, and all promotion. He'd be lucky if he were left with a penny. But we're talking about a literary book, remember. People don't pay $10.00 for books like that. They wait for the publisher to go out of business and buy them at remainder (that doesn't stop them from trying to get the publisher to publish their things). Or they growl. Or they simply can't afford them, because they're buying so many phonograph records, which are ever so much more elegant and party-oriented. Like I said, people think they can write, but they simply won't read, so as not to disillusion themselves.

So the publisher has a book which, theoretically, would give him a little profit. But not at $10.00. So he makes the price $2.95. The salesman, then, gets 44 cents commission on the book. But he'd rather sell silly Admiral Nohow's Exposé of the Vietnam War (Private Seaman Nudnik

being dead) for $10 and get $1.50 a copy. He has to, even.
The biography is easier to sell, and he has a living to make,
not to mention travelling expenses. He can dream at night
of the $2.95 book being another Ginsberg Howl, but it
doesn't happen every week. In the meantime, at $2.95, the
publisher isn't necessarily selling any more books than he
would have at $10--maybe a few, but not enough, really, to
make up the difference, so he's in a sweat. So the salesman lives on dreams, and the publisher gradually grows
broker and broker. He's forced to offer insultingly low advances to the authors he publishes--$400 is average at this
writing, because it has to be, but it really is an insult to
give a person so little for a year of concentrated effort.

 Recommended to the industry: a program via the National Endowment, which could double the amount of advance
royalty, given as an advance, upon publication of any literary
work as such (over yea many pages or some such qualification). As it now stands, the publisher has to do it all, and
what this means is he won't publish serious literature.
Fewer do each year. And what gets done is of an increasingly low quality, with only a few token things standing out
to reap in the appropriate prizes.

 This publisher discussion has pretty much included
the author. But just to summarize, it is pretty discouraging to be an author. A person has something to say, he
works a year to say it, and he gets about $400--from a big,
commercial publisher maybe $1000. His cousin is a painter,
maybe, and receives about $2000 on the sale of a $4000
canvas (or does even the most iconoclastic art, e.g. Acconci,
and is well supported by galleries and media and, by no
means, treated as the interesting but derivative semi-this-
and-that which he is). This is amiss. A collaboration between Daniel Spoerri and Robert Filliou: Spoerri, the artist,
got the cheese, Filliou, the writer, got the toast. There
was a lot of money afoot on that exhibition, but the writer
didn't see it. Artists live in villas, writers live in very
small apartments. You can decide for yourself which you'd
rather support morally.

 The printer. What's his role? Well, he's paid
about $8.00 an hour around the country, for doing books he
often doesn't understand or like, and if he were paid less,
he'd probably quit his job and join the army. You can't
blame the unions for this, except maybe for their rather
myopic policies about bringing poor people and minority

people into their programs. The various book unions have not been too outrageous. After all the book printer charges $20 an hour for typesetting and the like, because he has a tremendous capital investment. His labor being so high, he has to make do with a level of equipment and technology that would give a German or a Dutchman the giggles. When I was in a shop in Turkey in 1963 I saw more modern presses than I had ever seen in any single shop in the USA.

If he, this USA printer, can't get any additional write-offs on his taxes or credits to buy new machines, there's very little he can do. You can't really blame the union, though it could help. You can't blame the printer-- he has to work on a 5% profit margin at best, with brutal hours for management. You can't blame the author--maybe he's already earning so little--I say this ironically and as an author--he should donate all his royalties to a Central Foundation to support appropriate projects (and make his own living from people who appreciate him like Writer-in- Residence programs, readings circuits, lectures and, well, Real people). You can't blame the public (they have their habits), the book store people (they're in a horrid crunch), or the wholesalers (their role isn't really understood). And the publishers make the least money of all, normally, yet we are called on to take the most responsibility. (A small publisher's dream is always to get a bigger publisher to do the selling and coordinating--but the big publisher can't do that without a 65% discount, which would mean the small publisher could only do sure-thing bestsellers in minimum editions of 11,000.)

So much for my outline draft. Now let me give my own experience. In 1967-68 I began to work on a coöp ar- rangement of a number of small publishers. We could pool sales force, perhaps pay less than 10% commission (justified by volume), share ads, and so on. (Sometimes I think the major media, such as the New York Times and the Village Voice, via their advertising--and the shortage of advertising outlets--are the only ones that make money on books, and it's they, not printers, publishers, wholesalers, salesmen or booksellers, who are ripping off the entire literary world.) It was a fine dream. So the editor of a fine photo magazine (the pictures, not the captions which remain ridiculous, but that's apparently the editor's taste) put together such a group. He rented an office in New York, and our orders were sent through there on a basis that was essentially a shared over- head. We had just introduced concrete poetry--on the heels

Technical/Readers' Services 219

of happenings, and just before we introduced cumulative prose and chance poetry. So our sales were at a peak, about $65,000 a year, not bad for a little press. (A little press is one which does its own thing, including its own business--but all the employees can share a taxicab after hours: if you need two cabs, you're big business.)

Well, I believe in collectivism, but that coöp didn't turn out to be collective, really. What it meant was that the photo fellow was getting our money towards an office pool without any real need (only a spiritual commitment) to sell our books. Well, let me make one thing clear: he was no crook. No rip-off. He was and is a good person. But he wanted to do $15 photography books, and I wanted to do $6-$7 Something Else books. So our books fell to a low in 1972 of about $22,000--still not bad for a small press, but much less than before and nowhere near enough to meet our obligations. In 1970, when we were working closely with this distributor, I figured it was okay to move to California, to "Mickey Mouse University," Cal Arts, but I later learned that was unwise. At that time at the Press there was only myself on payroll regularly, plus Emmett Williams, occasionally but welcome whenever possible. It turned out not to be a saving. The Cal Arts institute was kind of a dud too (they're still using the names of those of us who have since left to advertise the place), so I returned to Vermont.

It took a while to really get into the Press situation again. And what I found was this: the <u>more</u> books we sold through a collective, the <u>less</u> money we got. And there lay the problem, because I came back with a lot of really valuable books. We did various Steins, we started our new natural history program, and began to develop towards what was now obvious, doing our own distribution again. We hired people, opened new lines of credit, etc. And when the time came, gave word. Then to find that--a) our old distributor wouldn't let us go (why should he? we were paying much more than our share of his office expenses). b) he has used us to get a mailing subsidized by the National Foundation and the New York State Council on the Arts, an incredible and overpriced catalog for which we were assessed way over the proportion of our inclusion in the thing: we didn't even have any say over what things of ours were included (and a few were left out)--I saw rough proofs at 7:30 AM at our distributor's New York City apartment, but that was all. I doubt he would have gotten his grants to do

the mailing, even, if we had not been included to make it a
bit more catholic than his collection of publishers doing Benjamin Franklin and other ultramodern authors. The few
pennies that governments give to modern literature really
ought not go to dear old Ben Franklin, no matter how much
one may honor his memory. That's what I meant when I
said "corruption" at the beginning of this article. They use
the living to support the safely dead: for me, that's hard
to live with.

Recommendation: those with funds to support literature should try hard to support the risky and the vital, not
just what's safely past (few people kill each other any more
about attitudes concerning Alexander Hamilton)--and where
they have a choice, they should support the who that need--
any author or publisher (on a small scale) especially for
risky projects, not the what that needs (white-led study
groups on non-white projects, etc.). Safe, safe, safe!
After all, it's not the Eternity-Watchers, the This-is-good-
and-that-isn't crowd, that are hurting. It's the authors
and their publishers. Anything can safely be studied. But
the best literature cannot safely be published (economically).
It is to this need that funds should be addressed, not to
Ben Franklin, not to the safe.

So our distributor took our books on consignment,
and, as I've said we contributed every month towards his
office overhead. In principle this was fine, but in fact he
had no incentive to originate sales--we still had to do most
of that: his goal was to get a lot of people into his coöp
so the overhead would be well paid for and he could draw a
substantial salary. Result: we would plan a book. He'd
be enthusiastic. Then, once it was ready, he would go
through a mysterious disillusionment. And the books
wouldn't be sold. This was the fate of our Fantastic Architecture anthology, for instance, one of the most important
books we ever did--dreams of non-architects about space,
environment and buildings.

Or, as with our Stein reprints, he would "sell them
all out," sending us back to press. But the sales would
have disappeared by the time the sales report came through.
So we'd get colossal printing bills, which we couldn't pay.
And what with postage charged to our account, salesmen's
commissions, all that kind of thing, it became true that the
more of our books our distributor sold, the more in debt to
him (they called it "overpayment") we came to be. I don't

know on what terms our books were sold--perhaps I never will. But as of now, we haven't received moneys from our distributor for months, but because he had an exclusive, neither would he sell nor could we sell our books, which everybody agreed were salable.

Then, with the complications of pulling out from him, not only will we now have insane freight bills to pay, getting our stock to our warehouse (it took our distributor nearly a month to pack and ship to us), but his bookkeeping is such a mess that we have to sacrifice all the back orders he wrote up on our forthcoming reprints--so as not to have to pay him another 15% commission on those orders. Insane? Of course. I doubt we'll see our money he owes us till the end of March--which hurts our authors, among other things. And how much of it will really materialize is hard to say. All in all it was a supremely bad scene. Working with him left us thousands and thousands of dollars in the hole, not even including lost sales because his organization was not equipped to sell large numbers of our titles. His very sales force was only set up to handle the same kinds of deluxe art books he did himself, not the more lively kind of writing and science that we are interested in--which is almost inherently geared away from the coffee table and into the work room.

So simply to find a distributor isn't the answer. Especially not a coöp distributor. It may work for Italian wine growers, but it doesn't work for a large number of heterodox little publishers of big books. The best kind of coöp would have to be a sort of salesman who kept stock, who took in "members" that he liked, sold only to "his" list of stores, worked on a consignment/55% basis, had an exclusive in his area--a sort of limited, regional jobber. That would guarantee pretty much that the right kind of books would get to the stores that could sell them (that needed them and would therefore pay for them). Such a person could build a fabulous organization, probably employee operated, without a great deal of capital needed. And as long as he moved slowly and with a good deal of caution, he could come out in a fairly healthy way. That would be a real coöp, in the long run.

But today's ferocious, competitive jobbers are probably on the way out. They're too big. They should wholesale what they know about--then the other things wouldn't get lost along the way. Dinosaurs may get a little benefit from mass production, but when they start bleeding, who can dam the blood? At least they're sensible enough not to merge with other kinds of wholesalers.

And the stores? Well, the whole scene would be helped by this recommendation: stores should be allowed to deduct unsold books at the end of their fiscal years as an uncollectable expense in an amount not exceeding the amount of inventory paid for in the previous year. This would be tremendously advantageous in allowing them to take chances on new titles, to carry serious works. It would reduce the pressure to return anything that didn't sell right off and it would have a culturally uplifting effect. Some modification would be needed, to prevent unfair advantage being taken of such a rule--but the unsalable book should be a deductible cost, even if, later, it was, in fact, sold. Perhaps it should even be allowed that it be deducted twice (after all, books need space and space costs a lot) or even more. If, in effect, a book-store could deduct its inventory, within reason, from its income (much more than depreciation would allow), this would do more for literature of all kinds than a thousand grants to the Documenters of Yack-Yack and the propagators of the same.

Now, on to libraries. What are libraries? Well, they're places that information is stored in, and they're organizations where information (often books) is stored and retrieved according to a person's need. Nowadays they spend a very large part of their funds on postage. If the government can get free franking to try to sell us its Pan American magazines, and congressmen to try to get us to vote which one of them is to raise our taxes and misuse our money, why can't libraries get free postage? This would allow them to circulate information much more effectively, and it would mean that the people whom, as an author, one wants to reach, could never say "I can't afford...." Which is usually a put-on, in any case. Take a 52-page book and mark it down to $4.95 from $10.00 and people will buy it: try to sell it for $3.47 without saying it's marked down and they won't. I know, I did that once. Illogical? Yes. Any cloth book is automatically too expensive, no matter what is the price, while the buyer seldom looks at the price of a paperback. But if only you could get the books you really want at the library! That's always cheap. And it would lead to increased demands for the books we care about.

Some publishers offer libraries discounts to keep the libraries from ordering through library wholesalers. I think

this is kind of silly--the library wholesalers consolidate
orders, and may take forty books from the publisher, to be
paid for in thirty days. They're earned their discount.
The individual libraries if they "order direct" from the publisher will get a 10% discount only, maybe, but good heavens
what a lot of bookkeeping. And the forms--required by the
states of New York or California, for instance--are quite a
proverbial pain to fill out. Besides, the wholesalers are
sellers first and foremost--they issue newsletters to the libraries, and they let libraries know what will be needed.
Better to work with them, then, so long as it doesn't mean
your weekly order of one copy.

   What this means is you've got two structures, serving the same public. You've got library reader, library
wholesaler, distributor, publisher, author. Also book buyer,
bookstore, commercial wholesaler (jobber), distributor, publisher, author. Two chains. The only ones that ever get
grants to make work more available are: author, publisher
(for special projects) and library. This is one reason why
the field is in such a bad way. Millions are given to support ballet companies, and maybe 2% as much for all literary
projects altogether, in all the USA, the rich country where
the writers starve. The other links of the chain shouldn't
have to fight with authors, publishers and libraries for existing funds. But tax advantages should be created to help the
weak links--the libraries and the bookstores. (Unless the
whole system could be changed altogether.) For the individual author, he is best off eliminating one or another link
in the chain. Often he should self-publish (do his own books),
and sell when and where he finds it profitable. Looking for
a publisher may be a guarantee of poverty. Looking for a
distributor except on the special basis I outlined may be no
saving at all--he may never see his money again. But publicizing his special production (seeing to it that reviews appear in appropriate places) and then seeing to it that the
"goods"--his works--are available when the reviews appear
(and sharing energies with like-minded souls), this may allow a reasonable living. Or at least a reasonable return
on his work.

   Ultimately there's one more thing that has to be done,
though, that will make all this academic. The world has to
learn to read, if mind-art (words) is to be as important as
see-art or hear-art. Literature is a poor cousin. Where's
the sense in that? It used to be otherwise. And it's silly
to blame labor unions or publishers or some such. The art

got ingrown: its prestige was sick. Concrete poetry and other related developments cleared the air. Now we are free to use words again. But we should create an economic basis for something besides frustration.

WHO INVENTED DEWEY'S CLASSIFICATION?*

John Maass

In 1976, American librarians will mark three anniversaries:

The Bicentennial of the United States of America, commemorating the Declaration of Independence, proclaimed in July 1776 at Philadelphia.
The 100th Birthday of the American Library Association, founded by 156 librarians who met in October 1876, also at Philadelphia.
The Centennial of the Dewey Decimal Classification.

Librarians--just like the members of all other professions--have a flattering view of their own public image. You may resent it when I tell you that non-librarians are generally not very much aware of your professional activities. Try asking the first hundred people you meet to give you a brief account of "library science"--without looking it up at the library. You will probably get blank looks, but some people may respond: "Oh, you mean the Dewey Decimal system, don't you!" Decimal classification is the only aspect of library science which is familiar to many people outside your own field.

DC made Melvil Dewey the most famous librarian in the world. Again, I may gravely offend you by asserting that Dewey is the only librarian whose name is widely known to the public at large. Many distinguished persons have been librarians, but celebrities like Giacomo Casanova, the Brothers Grimm, and Archibald MacLeish are not primarily remembered for their librarianship. Again, I suggest that

---

*Reprinted by permission from the December 1972 issue of the Wilson Library Bulletin, pages 335-341. Copyright © 1972 by the H. W. Wilson Company.

you can test my assertion by asking one hundred random people to name librarians they have heard of; I do not know how many answers you might get, but I am reasonably certain that Dewey's name would lead all the rest. Melvil Dewey's fame has already surpassed that of his distant cousin Admiral George Dewey, the winner of a half-forgotten battle in a shoddy war. His renown will outlast that of Thomas E. Dewey, who is best remembered as a two-time loser. Outside the circles of educationists and professional philosophers, Melvil Dewey is now probably better known than John Dewey; as a matter of fact, students and laymen frequently mistake the latter for the inventor of "Dewey Decimal."

I am not a librarian. I am a lifelong reader and lover of books, a collector of books, and a writer of books. Early in 1972, I was completing a book on the Centennial Exhibition of 1876 (John Maass, The Glorious Enterprise, University of Victoria, Victoria, Canada, 1973). The Centennial in Philadelphia was America's first World's Fair and an event of international significance and impact. Before 1876, Europeans generally regarded the United States as a second-rate country at the outer fringe of civilization; at Philadelphia in 1876, America emerged as a major power which would eventually become the economic, political, and even cultural, superpower. In my study of the Exhibition I was struck by the fact that the 30,864 exhibits were classified and cataloged by a decimal system like Dewey's. I was familiar with the Dewey Decimal Classification, but I did not know when it had been introduced. Checking at the library (DC 25.4), I found that it was in 1876--a suggestive date.

The Centennial Exhibition opened on May 10th, 1876. Dewey's Preface to A Classification and Subject Index for Cataloguing and Arranging the Books and Pamphlets of a Library was dated June 10th, 1876. The format of this historic publication was an octavo pamphlet of 42 pages.

I then read the biographies of Melvil Dewey (DC 923.72). I learned that Dewey had devised his Classification early in 1873 when he was a 21-year-old student and library assistant at Amherst College. Dewey submitted an outline of the Decimal Classification to the Library Committee of Amherst College on May 8th, 1873. It is most remarkable that the idea of a 21-year-old student swept the world within a few years. It is also uncommon to be able to date the birth of a great idea with such precision. How was this idea conceived?

In the nineteenth century, "classification" was a subject of considerable interest and discussion not only among librarians but also in another field: international expositions. Classification meant the logical arrangement of objects in an exhibition building so that they could be conveniently examined, compared, judged, and listed in a catalog. The first such event was the Great Exhibition of 1851 in London. For this famous show in the Crystal Palace, the classification was worked out by a young English chemist, Lyon Playfair (later Lord Playfair). The French proposed a different scheme. Playfair suggested a fair play between the rival systems: to pick an object at random and to see who could locate it first in his classification. The walking stick of a French Commissioner was chosen. It took the French a long time to find it in the Sub-Section <u>Machines for the Propagation of Direct Motion</u>. Playfair spotted the cane instantly: it belonged under <u>Miscellaneous Objects,</u> Sub-Section <u>Objects for Personal Use.</u> The English Classification of 30 categories was adopted. At succeeding international expositions two types of classification were developed: "systematic" and "geographic." Under the first, all objects of the same kind were grouped together, so that, for instance, French, English, and American printing presses could be compared. Under the second system, all products from one country were displayed in one section: American printing presses would be near American lathes and sewing machines, to demonstrate the progress of American machinery. Frédéric Le Play, commissioner-general of the 1867 Paris Exposition, devised a "dual classification." All objects of the same kind were placed in galleries around the oval exhibition building; all products of a country were grouped along radial aisles. Thus, each exhibit was located at the intersection of the "systematic" and "geographic" coordinates in the hall. It is evident that this inflexible scheme works only if every nation exhibits approximately the same share of objects in every class. It was not used again after 1867.

The U.S. Centennial Commission entrusted the classification of the coming Philadelphia Exhibition to the best qualified man, Professor William Phipps Blake of Connecticut. Blake was a type of man characteristic of the nineteenth century, and virtually extinct now: he was a scholar and a man of action. He was born in 1826, the son of a dentist who was a nephew of the inventor Eli Whitney. He graduated as a chemist from the Sheffield Scientific School at Yale Uni-

versity, and soon displayed dazzling versatility and vigor.
Blake was tall, handsome, and captivating. He was at home
in laboratory and lecture hall, camp and canoe. He moved
on three continents and was at ease in every circle--with
Presidents and Secretaries of State in Washington, with
princes and archdukes at the imperial courts of Paris and
Vienna, with Japanese samurais and Chinese mandarins,
with Western prospectors and miners, with Russian sailors
and Indian guides. He made geological surveys in New
Jersey, North Carolina, Georgia, and Santo Domingo. He
explored plains, deserts, forests, mountains, rivers, and
glaciers in Texas, Arizona, California, Nevada, Utah, Montana, Idaho, Japan, China, Alaska, and British Columbia.
He discovered ancient Aztec mines in New Mexico. In 1861,
he established the first school of science in Japan. He was
a brilliant teacher and distinguished educator. He was a
successful engineer and inventor. He was an author on
many subjects. He had the gift of writing readably on technical topics. He was a capable artist with great skill at the
blackboard. He was a noted collector of ceramic art. He
was an efficient organizer who planned the Centennial Exhibition as an unpaid executive commissioner before the appointment of a paid director-general. He had also made
special studies of classification, and he was the able editor
of the official U.S. Reports on the Paris Exposition of 1867.

At a meeting of the Centennial Commission in Philadelphia on May 25th, 1872, Blake submitted an outline of his
Classification, and it was adopted after some discussion:

> We propose ten comprehensive divisions, to be
> named Departments.... We propose to subdivide
> each of these Departments into ten Groups, and
> each Group into ten Classes.... The notation will
> be better understood upon examining the annexed
> table.

Blake compared this system to the numbering of the streets
and houses in the City of Philadelphia. For example, the
office of the Centennial Commission was at 904 Walnut Street,
indicating its location between Ninth Street and Tenth Street,
on the south side of Walnut, in the third building from the
corner. This now seems commonplace, but it was unusual
in the eighteen-seventies. The north-south streets of Philadelphia bore numbers, rather than names, since the seventeenth century; consecutive numbering of the houses within
each block was introduced in 1854.

Table showing the notation of the Departments, Groups, and Classes.

Depts.	Groups.	Classes.
I.	1-10.	1-100.
II.	11-20.	101-200.
III.	21-30.	201-300.
IV.	31-40.	301-400.
V.	41-50.	401-500.
VI.	51-60.	501-600.
VII.	61-70.	601-700.
VIII.	71-80.	701-800.
IX.	81-90.	801-900.
X.	91-100.	901-1000.

It will be seen that Dewey's Decimal Classification is virtually identical with Blake's. But how could young Dewey at Amherst know of this classification, adopted at a closed meeting in Philadelphia?

At the Centennial Commission's meeting on December 5th, 1872, Blake presented printed proof-sheets of the Classification; the commission took action to publicize it throughout America. In February 1873, a special leaflet describing the decimal classification was sent "To the Officers and Teachers in the Universities, Colleges, and Schools of the United States." At the same time, another special circular was addressed to the clergy. Copies were certainly sent to Amherst College. The president of Amherst may have received several, as William A. Stearns was a college officer, a professor, and a clergyman. A leaflet addressed to the librarian would have been delivered to William Lewis Montague, professor of Romanic Languages. According to the standard history of Amherst College, Montague was noted for his "ineptitudes and inefficiency," and young Dewey performed most of his duties at the library.

In March 1873, the Classification was "printed in large editions" and mailed to professional men throughout the U.S. The format of this publication was an octavo pamphlet of 42 pages (DC 606. Ph 1876). It is certain beyond the shadow of a doubt that Melvil Dewey studied this pamphlet by Blake (dated February 27th, 1873) and derived from it the draft of his Decimal Classification (dated May 8th, 1873).

Dewey changed the names of Blake's divisions from
<u>Departments</u>-<u>Groups</u>-<u>Classes</u> to <u>Classes</u>-<u>Divisions</u>-<u>Sections</u>.
Here is a key feature of the Decimal Classification as
described by Blake and by Dewey. Blake (February 27th,
1873):

> If we can properly put all that belongs in each Department into five, or six, or eight Groups, it is proposed to do so, leaving the other numbers blank.... But as the work progresses and new inventions are made ... we may, under the plan suggested, institute a new Class, or a new Group, without changing the title or place of those already established.

Dewey (May 8th, 1873):

> It is desirable to fill out the scheme fully when an additional class is made.... If convenient nine subheads will be desirable because of symmetry-- but the system is not all affected if only a part of the nine figures is employed, e.g., if seven classes were made, 478 and 479 would not appear in the scheme.

It is psychologically interesting to see how Dewey avoided
Blake's "<u>five</u>, or <u>six</u>, or <u>eight</u> groups," and used "<u>seven</u>
classes" as his example.

Blake's and Dewey's Classes were, of course, not
the same. The former classified the products at one temporary exhibition; the latter tried to encompass all human
knowledge in a permanent library classification. But in a
few instances Dewey even took over Blake's categories.
For example--Blake (published 1873):

107	<u>Cooperative Associations</u>
1070	Political Societies
1071	Working Men's Unions
1072	Industrial Organizations
1073	International Congresses
1074	Secret Societies
1075	Miscellaneous Organizations for Promoting Well Being
1076	Banking
1077	Insurance

Technical/Readers' Services   231

Dewey (published 1876):

> 360 <u>Associations and Institutions</u>
> 361 Charitable
> 362 Religious
> 363 Political
> 364 Reformatory and Sanitary
> 365 Prisons
> 366 Secret Societies
> 367 Trades Unions
> 368 Insurance
> 369 Other

Note the peculiar grouping of Secret Societies with Labor Unions and Insurance Companies in both schemes.

Another example of Dewey's close study of Blake's Classification:

> 94 <u>Photography</u> [Blake]
> 940 Landscape
> 941 Architectural
> 942 Portrait
> 943 Albertype, Woodburytypes, Heliotypes, etc.
> 944 Reproductions
> 945 Bas-Relief
> 946 Photo-Lithographic
> 947 On Porcelain, etc.
> 948 For Stereoscopes, etc.

> 770 <u>Photography</u> [Dewey]
> 771 Materials
> 772 Ambrotype and Daguerreotype
> 773 Photograph
> 774 Heliotype, Albertype, etc.
> 775 Photolithography
> 776 Stereoscopic
> 777 Portrait
> 778 Landscape
> 779 Collections

Note the inconsistent mingling of photographic <u>processes</u> and <u>subjects</u> in both schemes.

Blake's 1873 pamphlet was mailed to professional men "with the request that they should indicate errors and suggest amendments and improvements." Dewey also copied this procedure. He mailed out his 1876 pamphlet with a request to "mark any corrections or suggestions."

Dewey's Classes were not at all original. Ernest Cushing Richardson's Classification (New York, 1901), enumerates no fewer than 131 "Theoretical Systems" and 122 "Practical Systems" before Dewey. It has long been known that Dewey copied his Classes from W. T. Harris, Catalogue of the St. Louis Public School Library, published in 1870.

Every librarian knows that the Dewey Classes are awkward in some respects. The overwhelming triumph of DC was not due to its classification but to its notation. The wonderfully simple and flexible decimal notation has proved so adaptable that DC remains a worldwide success after a century. Dewey copied that decimal notation from Blake and cunningly covered his tracks. The historians of library science failed to find this principal source of DC because they looked for Dewey's models only among other library systems. Few ideas are entirely original. Dewey deserves great credit for his "leap of imagination" in adapting Blake's system for a six-month exhibition to the wider and permanent use in libraries. Dewey's deliberate failure to ever acknowledge his large debt to William Phipps Blake is another matter. I leave it to the American librarians to make their own moral judgment on Dewey's conduct in this case.

In his original DC pamphlet, Dewey was curiously evasive but suitable modest:

> The author has no desire to claim original invention for any part of the system where another has been before him, and would most gladly make specific acknowledgment were it in his power to do so.

In later editions of DC, published when Dewey was the most prominent librarian in America, he used quite a different tone:

> The decimal form and many nemonic features hav not been found in erlier use, tho since their invention in 1873 these ... hav been very frequently copid, often with, but oftener without acknowlejment of their source.

Dewey acknowledged as "fruitful sources of ideas" the systems of W. T. Harris of St. Louis, J. Schwartz of New York, and Natale Battezzati of Milan. In his Introduction to Library Classification (London, 1918), W. C. Berwick Sayers stated that DC does not resemble the systems by Schwartz and Battezzati. Dewey may have deliberately cited them as "red herrings" to divert attention from his real source.

As the scale of the Centennial Exhibition and the number of its buildings grew, Blake's Classification was modified in 1875. The scheme eventually comprised seven Departments instead of ten, but the decimal divisions and sub-divisions were consistently maintained throughout. Thus, the Exhibition Catalog listed, for instance, Class 411--Water color pictures under Group 40--Painting in Department IV--Art.

In October 1876, 146 male and 10 female librarians met in Philadelphia. The time and place of this Library Conference was chosen so that they could also visit the Centennial Exhibition. At this Conference, the American Library Association was founded, and Dewey, age 25, was elected secretary. Dewey was asked to explain his Decimal Classification which had already been alluded to as "the discovery of the age in library management." Dewey replied:

> While I acknowledge the compliment ... I must beg to be excused from presenting its claims before this meeting ... the prominent part which I have had in calling this Conference makes me unwilling to use any of its time for a matter in which I have so much personal interest.

Dewey was wise to be so modest on this occasion. Catalogs and guidebooks of the Centennial Exhibition were for sale throughout Philadelphia. After such a presentation of his Classification, a colleague might well have raised his hand and said: "Why, Mr. Dewey, your system is just like the one at this Exhibition!"

Dewey would have been a successful librarian even if he had not invented DC. Dewey's driving energy would have assured success in any career he chose to enter. His official biography by Grosvenor Dawe, Melvil Dewey, Seer--Inspirer--Doer (Lake Placid, 1932), is a most valuable book for its vast amount of first-hand information. It is also a very odd book. The title suggests its "personality cult" flavor; the volume is stuffed with fawning tributes and bootlicking messages from Dewey's disciples and lieutenants. It may be compared with the eulogies of Stalin which were being published in the Soviet Union at that time. Fremont Rider's <u>Melvil Dewey</u> (Chicago, 1944), is also a respectful laudatory biography, but it does allow that Dewey was a man rather than a god. It is clear that Dewey had extraordinary abilities and determination. It is also evident that he was sometimes a ruthless politician and always a shrewd operator.

Forty-seven years after the event (in the <u>Library Journal</u> of February 15th, 1920), Dewey described how he discovered DC:

> ... One Sunday during a long sermon by Pres. Stearns, while I lookt stedfastly at him without hearing a word, my mind absorbed in the vital problem, the solution flasht over me so that I jumpt in my seat and came near shouting 'Eureka'! It was to get absolute simplicity by using the simplest known symbols, the arabic numerals as decimals ... to number a classification....

This reminiscence of a famous old man must be regarded with the utmost suspicion. Dewey here compared himself to Archimedes. He also patterned his story after the legend of Galileo, who was said to have discovered the law of the pendulum while listening--or rather not listening--to a sermon in the Cathedral of Pisa.

Dewey did, in fact, discover DC while studying Blake's pamphlet in the Amherst Library. It may have happened on March 7th, 1873, when Dewey wrote in his diary:

> My heart s open to anything ts either decimal or about libraries. In fact I hardly think I cd h entered life w any comfort xcept on e 10th of e month f my interest in 'decimals' s unlimited.

Dewey was born on December 10th. So was I. What became of Blake? He continued his many-sided career which inevitably brings to mind the somewhat hackneyed term "Renaissance Man." He was again active at the Paris Exposition of 1878 and the Chicago Exposition of 1893. In 1895 he moved to Tucson for the health of two of his children. Though he was 70, he became the first director of the

Technical/Readers' Services

University of Arizona School of Mines. He retired from the University at the age of 80 but remained active as a geologist. In 1910, after an exhausting field trip, he went to Berkeley to receive an honorary doctorate from the University of California. Four days later, he died of pneumonia at the age of 84. Rossiter W. Raymond, a noted scientist, closed a biographical sketch of Blake with these words:

> Out of our earthly life he has departed--stalwart, versatile, tireless, brave, and gentle to the last-- but from my soul, at least, his splendid presence and his serene yet eager spirit will never depart.

Blake published books, pamphlets and articles for fifty-nine years (1851-1910); his bibliography numbers over two hundred titles. He was certainly no stranger to libraries. What did William Phipps Blake say about the Dewey Decimal Classification? I do not know.

Part III

COMMUNICATION AND EDUCATION

SUCH GOOD FRIENDS*

Richard Kluger

... on the delicate relationship between publishers and reviewers

On a wet weekday morning last fall, I found myself at one end of a long table, pontificating before a group of creative writing students at Sarah Lawrence College on some of the more sobering aspects of trade-book publishing in America. As a recent arrival in the ranks of management, I was perhaps preoccupied just then by the fiscal aspects of the book world and, indeed, had to catch myself from dwelling on the materialistic before so callow a gathering. But my listeners (admittedly a captive crew) not only did not pelt me with dog-eared copies of Magister Ludi but even grilled me on sectors of the realpolitik of publishing that I failed to cover. The one question that pulled me up short was the one that, in theory anyway, I should have been admirably equipped to handle: "How would you describe the relationship between publishers and reviewers?"

I offered something profound in reply, like: "Important"--followed by five minutes of open-field jabbering that never really got to the core of the question. With the benefit of premeditation, I would have offered my young interrogator a multiple-choice answer: (a) symbiotic; (b) largely honorable; (c) occasionally treacherous; (d) conducive to

---

*Reprinted by permission from the January 1973 issue of American Libraries, pages 20-25. Comments herein on Life and Saturday Review magazines are, of course, no longer accurate.

paranoia among publishers; (e) conducive to overeating by reviewers; (f) essential in view of the chaos of the marketplace.

And of course the right answer is: (g) all of the above. For it is hard to think of another business enterprise in the great American system of mass marketing that is anything remotely like trade-book publishing--a business in which the zealous manufacturer is separated from his would-be consumers by a phalanx of men and women who are paid by presumably disinterested employers to pass judgment on the quality of what is being purveyed. Having been a book-review editor, I do not suggest for a moment that this intermediary function is anything but honorable and vital. But without a doubt it adds another thorny obstacle to the publisher's already formidable task of peddling his wares in a vastly overcrowded market, through a severely limited number of sales outlets within a brutally brief timespan, before a whole new crop of competing products clamors for display space on the retailers' inelastic shelves.

Reviewing is a sword that, of course, cuts two ways. For the publishers are also the beneficiaries of a good deal of free space in the nation's print media, and it is hard to think of any other product that receives this kind of gratis attention without the specter of payola being raised. Books, in short, are quite special products, and if trade-book publishing is highly hazardous and not very profitable as most American businesses go, it is at least not one that is scorned by inattention.

This is not to say that, from the perspective of a trade-book publisher, books receive anything like the attention they deserve, either in absolute terms or in comparison to other cultural activities. Most daily newspapers across the country give the shortest shrift imaginable to book reviewing. Only a couple of dozen papers pay a living wage to reasonably astute men and women whose principal task is the evaluation of books; most papers settle for "canned" or syndicated reviews or ignore books entirely (though most of the better dailies pay lip-service to the muse of literature by throwing in a book page to break up the glut of ads in their bloated Sunday editions). The same staff situation exists in the television reviewing field, but consider that space given over daily to the TV program listings. Ditto the sports page and the comics, which are readily justified as entertainment features of far more universal appeal than

Communication and Education   239

books, which, after all, have been known to require real effort by consumers.

Still, the reviewing ranks are robust enough for most publishers to view them as adversaries and necessary evils (when they pan a perfectly lovely new book) as well as collaborators and enlightened oracles (when they love that same lovely new book) in the ongoing task of bringing written works of lasting or fleeting value to the American reader. Perceptive or cloddish, sensitive or peevish, reviewers wield enormous power by virtue of the hard facts of the trade-book marketplace: too many titles are contesting for their day in the sun. Without receiving reviewers' scrutiny (friendly or hostile) and barring a heavy outlay of advertising or promotional money by the publisher (usually impossible except in the case of titles for which the publisher has high sales hopes), any given title is likely to pass over the face of the earth like a shadow, unheard of, unlamented, and with a life expectancy comparable to that of a fruit fly in a blizzard.

Thus, a publisher's evaluation of the reviewing profession, for public consumption at any rate, is likely to be benign and bland. One does not flay out loud the daily book reviewer of the New York Times for entirely missing the point of the lead novel on one's spring list. Next week the same reviewer may have glowing words for a solid but ungainly nonfiction title you had pegged for sales of four thousand copies. Besides, if you antagonize the fellow unduly you may prod him into doing the one thing no publisher can afford: he may henceforth ignore your list entirely.

One may thus begin to gather the value of a few operating principles that can be said to guide publishers in their crucial relationship with the critics. Rule 1 may be codified as follows: Ask not what reviewers can do for you; ask what you can do for reviewers.

What the publisher can "do" for a reviewer has little to do with tangibles. Certainly, it would seem in questionable taste to send a complimentary Porsche to one's favorite and/or the most pliable (not to mention powerful) reviewer in sight. And the opposite tack--trying to have the cad fired for penning unfavorable notices or bringing economic pressure on the publication for which he writes (presumably in the form of boycotting its advertising columns-- a step reportedly urged a few seasons back by some publishers who disapproved of the new team running the New York Times Book Review)--would seem equally imprudent and, more likely, counterproductive. What conscientious publishers "do" for reviewers (and themselves, in the process) is try to be friendly and informative so that the reviewing fraternity will at least be attentive when your glittering new list of titles is unfurled twice a year.

This friendship and informativeness ("Our author is widely regarded as the hottest novelist to come out of Patagonia in fifty years") are usually expressed over a mid-Manhattan lunch that costs the publisher somewhere between fifteen and thirty dollars for two. If the publisher is represented by the house publicity director, the luncheon may be timed to the twice-a-year issue of the catalog for the coming season--and the lunch is likely to be a working session at which, depending on the lighting, the reviewer will actually flip through the catalog and note which titles the house is particularly keen on. This exchange is, of course, not a guarantee of anything, and no one in Manhattan publishing believes these sessions can make or break a book. But they are an important part of the winnowing out process that is essential if the more important titles are to be separated from the chaff. For, although no publisher likes to admit that any of his house's titles is a "list-filler," not all books are created equal, and the publisher is constantly making qualitative and quantitative judgments about which books the house will push hardest. Thus, if a reviewer, scanning a list with the house's chief publicist, does not pick up excited vibrations about, let us say, a novel by a writer he has never heard of, he has probably (consciously or unconsciously) relegated the title to the also-rans list and may never happen to think about it again.

While publicity people are paid by their houses to publicize, some of the most vital missionary work is done at other levels and in other settings. Many of the more effective top editors carve out their own circle of friends and acquaintances among the reviewing fraternity and entertain them at home on a regular or random basis. Under these circumstances, the sell is distinctly softer--and perhaps more effective. And since there is a definable community of interest between reviewer and editor, the social intercourse may be freer and more candid here. It is perhaps a mark of the successful higher-up editor that he or she combines his or her professional and private life in such settings, to the point that it is no longer easy to say when, if ever, the work-week ends.

Then there is wining-and-dining summitry, a practice whereby the head of a house has the reviewers to his home --on a rotating basis, to be sure--when the other guests are almost certain to include some of the publisher's most eminent authors. It is a disarming technique and often an engaging way to pass an evening, and while it is a flattering device, it is also transparently a means of ingratiating the house to the reviewers. Being, to my knowledge, men and women of unassailable integrity, most reviewers accept this hospitality for what it is and enjoy themselves without feeling in any way compromised. In recent years, furthermore, the reviewers have started reciprocating by picking up the check when the arena of exchange is a public dining place and not the publisher's digs.

These ample opportunities (as well as occasional or perhaps regular telephone contact) for pressing warm words upon the reviewers, most of whom are cordial and accessible if sometimes a bit irritable at being the quarry of so many eager glad-handers, gives rise to Rule 2: <u>Do not try to make a silk purse out of a sow's ear or else the quick brown fox will consume the lazy dog.</u>

Reviewers will listen to any reasonably modulated and not over-lengthy sales pitch, especially if it is disguised with a bit of hollandaise sauce; after all, it makes their job a bit easier. If a publisher is excited about a title and singles it out from the batch, there is probably a reason for it. This does not mean it is a good book, necessarily, but it probably is better than most of the other titles on the list. With rare exceptions, reviewers are not misanthropes; they do not prefer to write hostile notices. Most major reviews are more favorable than not, and the last thing a reviewer or the periodical he or she writes for wants is a hostile notice about a book nobody cares about by an author nobody has heard of. Reviewers have a lot of books to read and a lot of titles to choose from, and so the prudent publisher takes pains not to sing halleluiahs for books of only modest virtue.

Beyond the feverish pursuit of reviewers is something more than publisher's hopes for glowing words about their new books in the review columns. The reviews themselves are merely the tip of the iceberg, since most publishers do not know (or do not want to know) how carefully or often the

reviews themselves are perused by newspaper and magazine
writers; it is apparent that they are not the most carefully
or frequently read sectors of the publication in which they
appear. What the publishers really want as the major by-
product of reviewers' attention is that quotable phrase or
sentence that can be set in large type at the top of bold advertisements that will make the acclaimed title seem like
the biggest thing to come along since sliced Tolstoy. Many
publishers find themselves reading reviews backwards since
that key quotable phrase is more often than not found (when
it is there at all) at the bottom of the review. Thus, book
reviewers serve the additional, if indirect, function of being
the main advertising copywriters of the book trade. Some
reviewers rather like seeing their names in lights in this
fashion--unless the publisher has distorted the overall thrust
of the review by selecting only the few words of praise and
skipping the dissapproving balance. This latter practice,
which seems to be on the decline, is simply unethical. But
often a given review can be in the gray territory between a
plus and a minus and many publishers do not hesitate, in
that situation, to do a bit of distorting.

But if you give a reviewer a bum steer--or a series
of bum steers--you rapidly produce a yawning credibility
gap and have lost an important link in the publishing process.
The reviewer naturally reserves the option to ignore the
publisher's advice regarding any single title, but at least
the lines of communication should be left open: tomorrow
is another day and the next book you ballyhoo may receive
inordinate attention.

This care and feeding of the reviewing community is
a necessarily calculated undertaking--a fact that produces
Rule 3 in the publisher-reviewer code of conduct: <u>Some reviewers are more equal than others.</u> (Here, as elsewhere
in this article, the term "reviewer" naturally includes book-
page or book-section editors who have the responsibility of
selecting which titles will be reviewed.)

It is an indisputable fact of life that the most important book reviewing medium in the United States is the
<u>New York Times</u>. There may be room for debate as to
whether the daily book page or the Sunday <u>Times Book Re-
view</u> is the more influential; one school holds that New York,
by far the number one book market in the country, pays
more attention to the daily book page, while the other school
holds that the <u>Times Book Review</u> (hereafter TBR) is the

truly national magazine devoted to serious books and therefore incomparably more important than the daily. Either way, the daily and Sunday book columns in the Times rank numbers one and two. And because most of the people in the initiating end of the book business read the Times, its influence is compounded. Publishers advertise their wares in the Times more heavily, I suspect, than in all other media put together, and so it is not surprising that you will find something approaching a consensus in New York publishing circles that the Times reviews count more heavily than all other reviews rolled into one.

This is hardly to say that the other media are not of concern to publishers, but there is a prevalent feeling that if your star book has not been reviewed in either the daily or Sunday Times, it has not been reviewed, period. And so perhaps the two most influential men in American book-reviewing circles at the moment are named John Leonard, now rounding out his second year as editor of the Times Book Review, and Christopher Lehmann-Haupt, now in his fourth year as the Times' senior daily book critic. In their thirties, both are highly sophisticated in their literary taste and their awareness of the nuances of literary politics. Leonard, himself a novelist, wrote highly charged reviews for several years as Lehmann-Haupt's colleague on the daily book page before taking the helm at the TBR. His reviews won him high praise among publishers because when he liked a book, he made his pleasure known in no uncertain terms --a priceless gift to the author and publisher beneficiaries as well as to readers seeking consumer guidance. Lehmann-Haupt is a man who deeply resents the publishing practice of yanking a couple of laudatory phrases out of context and bannering them in big type to imply that a moderately friendly notice was an iridescent rave, and so he takes pains to measure his words which seem to say, in effect, that books are subtle creations and grossly simplified judgments of them may serve commerce but not the cultural life of the nation. But if Lehmann-Haupt is less useful to publishers than they would like, he has demonstrated a keen knack for knowing what books are worth being given serious attention-- and he attends to them with a seriousness and dedication unmatched among the nation's regular reviewers.

Leonard, for his part, has been criticized for turning the TBR into "too literary" a magazine, too often featuring reviews and essays about books of comparatively little mass interest. By contrast with his predecessor, Francis

Brown, this is certainly true. Brown, a conscientious editor who staffed the TBR with a lineup of extremely gifted younger editors, was a trained historian whose preference for nonfiction was well known in New York publishing circles; he was, moreover, laboring under a regime that was far more interested in the timeliness and news value of books than in literary content. Invited to reshape the TBR, Leonard has done just that, and if some publishers feel he has not helped book sales in the process, Leonard can quite properly say that this is not his function in life and that the advertising columns of his magazine are open to one and all to sell their wares.

Leonard and Lehmann-Haupt are no one-man shows, and publishers have come to know the other Times reviewers and editors as equally dedicated and astute men of letters. Leonard's successor on the daily side, Anatole Broyard, writes quite literate and engaged reviews on books of serious social or literary content, and veteran daily reviewer Thomas Lask, dealing with perhaps somewhat less momentous titles, ranges widely over the literary landscape. From time to time, the daily reviewers are spelled by any of a number of editors on the TBR, who when they are not sifting through publishers' lists deciding which titles deserve space in the Sunday section, fashion perceptive reviews of their own: Roger Jellinek, Richard Lingeman and Richard Locke, all strong writers. The other TBR veteran editors, including Charles Simmons, Nona Balakian, Raymond Walters, Jr. and Mel Watkins, are all writers of varying skill and production as well as editors. The point here is simply that it is not for nothing that the Times book people hold their preeminent position among the nation's book reviewers.

If, by virtue of the quality, quantity, and visibility of its attention to books, the Times is by a long shot the number one force among reviewing media in impact on sales and especially on the minds of the moving forces within the trade, including book club personnel and the paperback houses as well as the publishers and chief buyers, the second echelon of influence may be said to be held by three weekly magazines printed on slick paper and read collectively by many millions: Time, Newsweek and Life.

It may be ventured that since the recent adoption by both Time and Newsweek of the policy of signing each review, the seriousness of the reviews has increased. Previously it was possible--if not the practice--for anonymous reviewers to huddle invisibly behind their typewriters turning out witty and sometimes savage pieces that often enough scored what current usage calls "cheap shots" at the expense of the books. Now the reviewers are above-board, card-carrying members of the reviewing clan who derive their standing not merely from their institutional affiliation but from their known (and signed) performance in the tightly packed columns of their magazines. Despite almost impossible space limitations, superior criticism is being turned out these days by R. Z. Sheppard, Timothy Foote, and Martha Duffy (to my knowledge one of the very few women in America, and easily the most prominent, who plies the reviewing trade) on Time and Peter Prescott, Walter Clemons (an ex-Times hand), and, on too infrequent occasion, Jack Kroll of Newsweek.

Both magazines, but more often Time, will use books as the take-off point or the focus of an article in another department of the magazine (e.g., "Modern Living" or "Science"). While these pieces tend to be more like book reports than critical evaluations, they are particularly cherished by publishers because they call the book's attention to that portion of the magazine's readership with the keenest interest in the book's subject. Both magazines, which derive virtually no book advertising (because their rates are prohibitively high for most books' advertising budgets) for their troubles, have not flinched from maintaining their coverage of the field. And except for Life, no other publication even approximates the two news weeklies in the size and range of their readership. Still, each magazine can cover only a handful of titles a week, and so they must stand far to the rear of TBR, the only publication in America that makes any real effort to supply regular comprehensive coverage of the new books.

Life, with its still enormous circulation, is nevertheless an almost special case in reviewland. The magazine covers only one or two titles a week on a national basis, so that it is a rare distinction to be designated, in effect, Life's book of the week. A rave on its pages is of course a special prize, particularly so if the beneficiary title happens to be a "sleeper," a not-so-well-known title that for one reason or another appeals to Life's book editor David Scherman. Perhaps the classic ease of a Life send-off was the review there of the late Eric Berne's Games People Play, which soared to the top of bestsellerdom in ensuing months though its sales had been minor to that point.

The third echelon of reviewing impact may be said to
be divided into two categories--a short list of prestigious
magazines and the book pages of certain newspapers that, in
marked contrast to most papers across the country, feel
books are worth spotlighting.

      Among the magazines, three are preeminent in their
value to publishers. The New Yorker, word for word still
the best-written magazine in America, runs some of the
finest essay-reviews to appear anywhere in the English-
speaking world, but its coverage is highly quixotic: books
are often reviewed many months after they appear, and very
few individual titles receive extensive treatment. But attention, either extensive or token, as in the useful if unexciting
"Briefly Noted" column, is highly valued because of the
literary standing of the magazine and the presumptively high
book-buying habits of the magazine's subscribers. The New
York Review of Books was designed for and deals with the
interests of the intellectual elite of the nation, and while its
reviews are extensive (and too often endless) and at a very
high level indeed, the editors seem to pay little heed to publication dates of books and to be downright hostile to reviewing fiction. But no other magazine deals as extensively
and at as high a level with serious and specialized (which is
not to say technical) books as the Review. Its readership,
clearly dedicated to the life of the mind, is nevertheless
comparatively small (circulation is about 92,000) and its impact on book-buying habits is correspondingly assumed to be
limited except in academe. But since its readers are re-
putedly among the intellectual leaders of the country, a good
notice in the Review is highly coveted. Saturday Review is
the third in the triumvirate of magazines that publishers
care most about. Under new direction and manned by new
personnel from top to bottom, SR is in a transition stage,
but it is already evident that the magazine is undergoing a
renaissance. For years, its coverage of books had been
extensive but stodgy, and while New York publishers were
relatively indifferent to its corps of obscure reviewers, the
magazine was recognized to be popular in middlebrow America. The new owners have installed Eliot Fremont-Smith,
well regarded when he was the Times lead daily book reviewer and most recently the editor in chief at Little, Brown,
as SR's literary editor, and an immediate pickup in the live-
liness of the book coverage has resulted. A generous allot-
ment of space has been made to the book section, and publishers, eager for an advertising medium of national scope
charging rates that are not exorbitant in light of the avail-

able budgets, could turn to SR in increasing numbers.

Three monthly magazines also offer serious review coverage and are prized by publishers--Harper's, Atlantic, and Commentary. Each is a magazine of high social and literary content, and a notice in any of them is keenly welcomed, but because they appear only once a month and can treat at length only a few titles per issue, their importance is relatively peripheral to the vending of trade books across the country.

Perhaps half a dozen other general magazines of varying frequency of publication give meaningful review coverage, and their relatively lower standing on the impact scale has more to do with the size of their circulations than the quality or quantity of their review columns. Included would be the New Republic, the New Leader, Commonweal, National Review, and the Progressive. Each has a somewhat special readership in mind, and the books selected for review reflect that editorial predisposition. Two other magazines with considerable circulation are hard to guage: Playboy, with its enormous monthly press run, does cover books but more as a service feature than as a serious effort to assess the new titles, and its impact on book-buyers is judged to be limited. One somehow assumes that most Playboy readers, whatever their level of affluence, would prefer to wait until the book reviewed appears in paperback. And Norman Cousins' new magazine, World, has allotted a good deal of space to book coverage and named Midge Decter, a literary and social critic of high standing, to run the book section--two encouraging signs. But it is simply too soon to know if World is here to stay and if its arrival signals the availability of another valuable, national forum for extensive and engaging discussion of books.

On the newspaper side, once one moves beyond the New York Times, the bag is very mixed indeed. Generally speaking, publishers care most about those cities that are the best "book towns"--where most books are sold either in absolute numbers or relative to the population: Chicago, Los Angeles, Washington, Boston, and San Francisco. The Washington Post is probably the most prized among the papers in these cities as a newspaper committed to sustained book coverage. Its Sunday book section, Book World, for several years a joint venture with the Chicago Tribune but now on its own (as is the Trib's section), is the closest thing outside New York to a real book section. Under editor

William McPherson, it has shown early vigor. The Post's daily reviews, though uneven, are among the best to appear in any daily in the entire country. Herman Kogan's Chicago Sun-Times Sunday section has been useful and solid if not particularly exciting, and the Trib's section has only recently acquired a new editor bent on reshaping it into a potent literary voice in the Midwest. At the moment, no individual reviewer in Chicagoland has anything like the influence that Robert Cromie used to have when he was writing regularly for the Tribune--an eminence he has now transferred to the TV screen, where his show, "Book Beat," is the best (and only) TV program about books in all America, to my knowledge.

In Los Angeles, now a vast booming book market that publishers are eager to exploit, things have been looking up in recent years as a result of the effort of Robert Kirsch and more recently Digby Diehl. This pair of alert and savvy critic-editors for the Los Angeles Times, have been behind the steady improvement of its book coverage in the weekend-entertainment and arts section and its relatively new monthly Book Review, a modest section for so rich a newspaper. Still, the paper itself has not seen fit, for all its owners' interest in the arts, to make a major allocation of space and resources to book coverage.

In fact, only a relatively small number of newspapers, regardless of size or cultural ferment in other communities, offer adequate book coverage, and those that do tend to focus their efforts either entirely or largely on their Sunday editions. Among the papers that turn out strong Sunday pages, taking pains to enlist competent local reviewers and not relying on syndicated material, are the Milwaukee Journal, consistently superior under the direction of Leslie Cross; the Providence Journal under Maurice Dolbier; the Boston Globe under Herbert A. Kenney; the Kansas City Star under Thorpe Menn; the Dallas News under Lon Tinkle; and the Greensboro (North Carolina) Daily News-Record under Jonathan Yardley. Others that stand considerably above the average performance are the Christian Science Monitor, the Nashville Banner, the Louisville Courier-Journal, the National Observer, the Worcester (Massachusetts) Telegram and Evening Gazette, the San Francisco Chronicle, the Denver Post, the Fort Worth Star-Telegram, the Raleigh (N.C.) News and Observer, the St. Louis Post-Dispatch, and, recently under new book editor Leslie Hanscom, the powerful Long Island daily, Newsday.

What is astonishing and somewhat shocking is how few papers see fit to offer daily coverage of books or even thrice-weekly coverage. By far the most influential daily critic outside of the New York Times' trio is John Barkham, the veteran whose pieces appear in the New York Post and thirty-five other papers around the country. Miles Smith of the Associated Press appears in many more papers, but his reviews are more in the form of book reports than reviews with critical bite. Among dailies that do a reasonably good job in terms of quantity as well as quality are the Washington Post (as cited), Newsday (Hal Burton), the Boston Globe, and probably most important when it carries a book review, the Wall Street Journal.

All these magazines and newspapers are directed toward the general book-buying reader, but the publishers are by no means indifferent to the prepublication reviews within the trade. Except for books destined for bestseller lists from the start--most of them by well-established authors--the early trade reviews are often seen as a bellwether by publishers trying to determine which titles to take a bigger risk on in terms of printings and promotional activities. These distant-early-warnings, combined with prepublication endorsements they have been able to wangle from well-known authors or personalities, fuel the in-house enthusiasm that is essential if any book is going to exceed the rather dreary sales figures posted by most titles, regardless of their literary or social distinction.

The three review media all publishers keep an eagle eye on before pushing the button on first printings are Publishers Weekly, Library Journal, and the Kirkus Reviews. Each in recent years has significantly improved the quality of their short notices, averaging perhaps 150 words per title, and it is hard and perhaps pointless to distinguish among them in terms of impact on publishing policies. PW is probably the best read by the book trade and of most importance to book-sellers across the country. (Of special importance in the prepublication period are the fiction reviews of PW's senior editor Barbara A. Bannon, whose friendly nod can fan life into the sales expectations of any novel.) LJ clearly dominates in the institutional field, and more and more publishers, understanding the vital part of their business that comes from the library market, understand the value of LJ attention and praise. The Kirkus Reviews are stylistically the most ambitious of the lot and their impact among key buyers is recognized as very direct.

Trade publishers are less aware of the impact of the concise reviews appearing each month in Choice, issued by the Association of College and Research Libraries, and The Booklist, with its selected short notices, put out by the American Library Association. Neither can be said to have a weighty effect on publishers' plans, though each adds a useful voice tuned toward the burgeoning institutional market.

What matters most to publishers, hoping for attention in as many of the foregoing places as possible, is the quantitative aggregate, not the critical acumen, of the reviews. Certainly, one cherishes sensitive and/or glowing words from the budding Edmund Wilsons across the land, but their ranks are not legion. While it is true that a luminous notice in an important place--the Times most of all--can have a great influence on the sale of any single title (provided that the publisher is willing to broadcast that rave with a steady and costly advertising campaign), what publishers seek most is review attention for its own sake. This is especially true of nonfiction, where the literary performance is of less importance and the very existence of a review calls a title to the attention of many readers interested in that particular field, whether or not the reviewer waxes ecstatic about it. Thus, the publisher is likely to evaluate the merits of any given review of any (and all) of his titles in accordance with the following scale:

1. Was the book reviewed at all? (If so, five points.)
2. Did the reviewer like it? (If so, five more points.)
3. Can we quote from it? (I.e., are there golden phrases that can be lifted and economically reproduced in ads? If so, twenty-five points.)
4. Is it a perceptive, well-written and stimulating review, regardless of the verdict of the book? (If so, swell.)

As a result of the foregoing Cook's Tour (or rogue's gallery, depending on one's perspective) of the reviewing media, we may deduce the fourth and final rule in the publisher's handbook on the care and feeding of reviewers: Don't put all your eggs in one basket--unless the basket has a television antenna on it.

Some publishers believe that advertising doesn't sell books and that ads are for the authors' egos. Some publishers believe that favorable reviews don't sell books,

Communication and Education

either, except to that coterie of eggheads that can distinguish a good review from a bad one. Some publishers believe that neither book salesmen nor bookstores nor anything nor anybody else sells books, other than word of mouth (if the mouths are big enough). But everyone in publishing today agrees that television talk shows and quasinews shows help sell books. No one has ever been able to measure how many books it sells, but it is widely believed that with works of nonfiction, and specifically books that have a how-to or the inside-story slant that can be fed to the electronic machine in amusing or provocative tidbits, a TV tour to a dozen cities is an invaluable sales tool. And it costs the publisher only the author's travel and lodgings (which do mount up, but are minimal compared to advertising space costs) to reach millions of potential book readers.

The only fly in the TV ointment is the glaring fact that all those people watching the TV talk shows are obviously, at the moment and perhaps forevermore, not reading books. Books are harder to consume than TV, with the mindless lassitude it invites. But on sheer percentages, the millions watching the Today Show, by far the most important of the daytime talk shows, are sure to include vastly more real book readers than any other medium, print or electronic, can reach, and so publishers more and more direct their publicity efforts to TV and radio. In some good book cities, like Cleveland, the TV exposure is regarded as more important to a book's chances there than the reviewing attention.

By definition television rarely puts authors under harsh scrutiny. They and their books have been selected on the assumption that they will provide a stimulating few moments of air time. On the rarest of occasions, a TV person like Edwin Newman of NBC in New York will engage in a lively exchange, taking occasional issue with an author. William F. Buckley, Jr., relishes the taking of issue when an author is his guest on "Firing Line" but then he is rather glaringly the exception in this regard (more's the pity). For the most part, TV attention of a title can only benefit the author--unless he or she happens to show up at the studio semi-polluted to stave off the anxiety of show-biz.

Thus, art and commerce mingle inextricably in the publisher's mind as he evaluates the reviewing world. He is, in the last measure, dependent on the collective judgment of all the media and all the commentators who are likely to have the final say on whether any book's claim to posterity or at least its day in the sun is justified. But the publisher who sits back and waits for the wand of critical approval to descend gracefully upon his wares is no publisher at all but merely a manufacturer of bound pages. Successful publishing occurs when the delivered manuscript produces a spirited response within the house that will publish it and that understands it has to marshall all its sales, packaging, and promotional skills in the book's behalf.

The reviewing community can neither be charged with destroying a book's chances (by panning or ignoring it) or be credited with making it. But it plays a central part in the publishing act that defies all the known laws of the marketplace, except one: the bad drives out the good--or at least makes it mighty hard for the good to survive the incubator.

HUMANIZATION OF CARTOGRAPHY*

Denis Wood

Needless to say, maps have always been among the most distinctively human of things, if only because only man seems to make maps, and yet the claim for the humanity of maps has far deeper roots than this. It is platitudinous to say that all artifacts speak loudly of their maker, but it is less so to assert that there are those artifacts more redolent of their maker than others.

Buttons, for example, smell strongly of humanity, and the size, shape, color, materials of manufacture, design and use say a great deal about the button maker and user. But buttons are not a human constant. An artifact more widely employed by men of all persuasions is crockery, from the earliest and simplest primordial pot to the elegant and sophisticated Coke bottle. Crockery would seem to be a very human artifact, indeed, and yet one must ask to what in man crockery speaks? To his need to contain, perhaps, and to his ability to manufacture excessive amounts of a given entity demanding storage. Certainly this is very much a part of our fiber, and still it lacks that excitement that can make the blood run hot and cold with interest. As the two examples I have suggested must make clear, there are any number of artifacts that reek of man, and some reek more than others. For my money, no artifact is more enbued with the essence of man than maps.

There are a few reasons that I might advance in explanation of this unique position occupied by maps in the starry sky of human artifact. For one thing, a map can make the sort of difference in a life-and-death situation that a button never could. With a decent map, a man, or a

---

*Reprinted by permission from the March 1973 issue of the Bulletin--Geography and Map Division, SLA, pages 2-10.

tribe, or any army, can make it safely to the next water hole before all perish from dehydration. Only in the wildest fancy could a button ever do something like this, and even there only if a map were engraved in itaglio on the underside of the button. And while a cold Coke replaces the waterhole in this day of automotive interstate travel, it is still the map dispensed at every gas station that guides us from city to city, from road to road. Such human artifacts as crockery and buttons and books and paintings are all most greatly admired when we know where we are. When we're lost, getting found is uppermost in our minds and in these cases our minds are apt to turn to thoughts of maps. A map tells us where we are and how to get where we want to go--and only a map can do this. There are no cheap artificial substitutes that will do. A pair of cupped hands can replace a cup, and in a pinch a knot will do for a button. Nothing can replace the map.

To fulfill the demands made on maps they must be peculiar. While the choice of crockery to be used at dinner and the choice of buttons to be worn with a certain suit can be a matter of whim, whim will never do in the construction of a map. A map must be able to communicate a complex environment meaningfully to a very wide audience, and if it fails in this, it fails to be a map. Moreover, this communication process answers a constantly reiterated demand, sometimes silently posed, but at other times shouted to the skies: TELL ME WHERE I AM. All maps answer some form or other of this demand, and it is the centrality of the need to answer this demand for human beings that makes the map such a human--and humane--artifact, perhaps, of all the artifacts, the most humane of all.

Beyond this, maps have magic, an air, a charm about them, which, for all that it is ineffable, is nonetheless real. Maps belong to that class of artifacts that, like playing cards and toys and stamps and coins, is forever prompting fanatic worshippers at its shrine to write the Romance of Maps and to collect and hoard and treasure whatever examples can be acquired. In the grip of this collecting mania, even theft becomes condoned, for such theft is not for paltry gain, but rather astonishingly for love--and few loves are stronger. Yesterday's map, like last year's stamp, and yesteryear's coin, has the marvelous virtue of being useless, of being pretty to look upon, easy to store, and susceptible of purchase in that wonderful junk shop run by that nice, but ever so naive, old lady. She is never loath to part with a 1954 Mobil map of Pennsylvania for the ridiculous sum of only $10. After all, how could she know that was all you needed to complete your collection! This is all part of the lure of maps.

Finally--beyond the magic, the air, the charm--maps have mystery shrouding every line. On old maps it is the mystery of places vanished, ghost towns, rubble, puffs of desert air and sunk Atlantises, roads once thriving, now dimly shadowed paths through forests, scratches on the plains, or parts of interurban tracks poking through the turf. On maps as up to date as tomorrow, there is the mystery of places not yet seen, the mystery of the unmarked white space, the mystery of beyond the borders of the known. And the known is the map. Only the sight of a narrow road cresting a distant ridge in the sun of a late afternoon going who knows where has the same beguiling power. And as we shall see, the map also has the mystery of places found solely in the minds of other people.

And so behold the map: quintessential finder of man, irreplaceable, magical, mysterious, provoking, certainly beyond a doubt an artifact of, for and by man: a human artifact. As is the case with all such delectable things, the love of maps begins at an early age:

> I knew every page in that Atlas by heart. How many days and nights I had lingered over its old faded maps, following the blue rivers from the mountains to the sea; wondering what the little towers looked like, and how wide were the sprawling lakes! I had a lot of fun with that atlas, traveling in my mind, all over the world. I can see it now; the first page had no map; it just told you that it was printed in Edinburgh in 1808, and a whole lot more about the book. The next page was the Solar System, showing the sun and planets, the stars and the moon. The third page was the chart of the North and South Poles. Then came the hemispheres, the oceans, the continents and the countries.

Two people began an _affaire_ with maps with these words. The first of these was Tommy Stubbins, the narrator of the passage, and the other was me, who read the words. Tommy Stubbins and Dr. Dolittle used to play a game with this Atlas whenever they wanted to travel and couldn't decide

where to go. They would close their eyes and hold a pencil
over whatever Atlas page they opened and then stab the
world. Wherever the pencil landed they would have to go,
unless, of course, they'd already been there. Reading these
passages over and over woke a burning desire to own an
Atlas, which was satisfied when Santa Claus brought me the
Rand McNally Centennial Atlas for Christmas.

But this Atlas was not salve to the wounds of map
love acquired by reading still another more magical references to maps. It was said of Bilbo Baggins, most beloved
of all hobbits, that: "He loved maps, and in his hall there
hung a large one of the Country Round with all his favorite
walks marked on it in red ink." There were many things
about these passages that awoke nerve cells of wonder and
delight. First of all, it meant that maps needn't be of
states and countries and enormous cities, but could be of
the Country Round, the neighborhood, my place, my turf,
my world. And then it spoke of a large map, and as large
as were the atlas plates in my Atlas, I would never have
termed them large. Clearly, Bilbo had something out of
the ordinary. And finally and most importantly, he had
marked his favorite walks on this large map, in red ink.
I don't know which was more meaningful and bewitching to
me, the fact that he had entirely personalized his map, or
the fact that he had done so in red ink. For me it was a
powerful combination, like a right to the jaw followed by a
right to the jaw. I succumbed. But perhaps even more
delectable than the words about Bilbo were the maps themselves that decorated the endpapers of the Hobbit. They
were in red and brown inks and showed a world filled with
dragons and giant spiders and dangerous and adventurous
paths. These maps did not hint at mystery and magic.
They were, themselves, mysterious and magical.

Bilbo's nephew, Frodo, is also involved with maps:
"Frodo began to feel restless and the old paths seemed too
well-trodden. He looked at maps, and wondered what lay
beyond their edges: maps made in the Shire showed mostly
white beyond its borders." The Ring, which chronicles
Frodo's adventures in Middle-earth, contains some of the
most romantic maps in existence. There is the small map
of the Shire itself, a map of Gondor and Mordor, and the
sine qua non of imaginary maps, the now famous fold-out
map of Middle-earth. Some of the power of this map comes
clearly from the antiquarian symbolization, the use of drawings of trees for the trees rather than a green tint, the ac-

tual drawing of a tower instead of an abstract point symbol, but the balance of the force of this map comes from the way the world trails off into white at the edges. Faced with a map like this you know that the world remains still to be discovered, and comfortably ensconced in bed it is possible to imagine seeing unseen places and doing unheard of things. Like Tolkien I began to draw my own worlds and people them with my own beings, but like J. K. Wright I faltered in the attempt. The examples before me were overpowering, at once enticing and smothering.

I didn't actually start collecting maps until I read <u>Big Tiger and Christian</u>. This brought me more into the realm of the possible, into the world of earth in which I lived. Dr. Dolittle made it clear that once upon a time the world was fresh, and Tolkien made it clear that in our minds the world could be fresh forever, but Big Tiger and Christian made it obvious that these things still happened in our own day in the world of eating and sleeping. Big Tiger and Christian are two thirteen-year-old boys who make the first motor crossing of the Gobi Desert. A few prefatory words ensure us of the veracity of the tale, and research has shown that the author, Fritz Mulhenweg, did indeed travel through the Gobi with the Sven Hedin expeditions. The truth of the story is important, because it demands that we approach the map of the Gobi that prefaces the book in a different way than we approached the maps of Tolkien and Lofting. The adventures of Big Tiger and Christian and their relationships with maps--and the map itself--are real. That is, with a little luck, we too could enter their world.

> Big Tiger had never had a map in his hand before, but he pretended to know all about maps and remarked airily: 'I can't read the names on this one because they're in English.' Christian realized he would have to show his friend how to read a map. 'The top is north,' he said. 'The little circles are towns and villages. Blue means rivers and lakes. The thin lines are roads and the thick ones railways.' 'There's nothing at all here,' said Big Tiger, pointing to one of the many white patches.' 'That means it's just desert,' Christian explained. 'You have to go into the desert to know what it looks like.'

Which is a valuable and instructive remark. A map, after all is said and done, can't tell you what the world looks like. But then, it is not the role of the map to say such things. Big Tiger knows what the role of the map is:

> 'That's a fine map,' said Big Tiger. 'It's useful to be able to look up beforehand the places we reach later.' ... 'Are there really bandits about here?' asked Christian. 'Perhaps it's written on the map,' Big Tiger ventured. 'Look and see.'

The ability to use a map in this way is predicated on an unchanging world. Bandits can only show up on a map when bandits stay in one place and don't move about with great frequency. On the other hand, we find maps today that show even more transient things, like speed traps. In this case, the world changes rapidly, but so do the maps. But there are world views in which maps can never play a role. Good Fortune has such a view:

> 'Maps are no good,' asserted Good Fortune. 'You'd best throw it away. You look for a well, for instance, and there it is in big letters on the paper. But you don't find the well--it no longer exists, because it is filled up with sand. There you are in the desert with no water, all because of the map which was no good. If you see on the map Encampment of a Mongol Prince, he's moved away by the time you get there.'
> 'But the mountains don't change,' Christian objected.
> 'The mountains collapse and the hills are easily moved. These Mongol magicians do that every day at breakfast. You must be very careful.'

But even Good Fortune changes his mind:

> He looked on the map for the Lonely Tree, but did not find it.
> 'That map is absolutely useless,' said Good Fortune emphatically.
> 'Perhaps it's only a matter of looking long enough,' Christian suggested. 'Yesterday I found Durben Mot, and there's a lot of sand here ... we must be here, and the place is called Gatsen Mot, and there's a well near.'
> 'That's wonderful!' cried Good Fortune, and those who say a man should be sparing of his words are right. Gatsen Mot is Mongolian for

Lonely Tree, and I beg your pardon for my hasty speech.'

'Pray don't mention it,' said Christian, but he was very pleased.

These passages say a great deal in their not so innocent way about maps and a lot about people. Here they are, an American and two Chinese in the Gobi Desert trying to read an American map in English using Mongolian place names. Basically, Good Fortune has no need for maps because he knows intimately where he is, and has no time for maps because their static character but poorly reflects the dynamic world. Yet he must admire them when they show an awareness as keen as his. Christian, a foreigner at sea, needs the map (as well as the compass which Good Fortune also spurns) not only to orient himself, but also to help him come to terms with his environment.

There is a great wealth of maps and map talk in children's literature and all of it is very human. The maps are there for orientation purposes certainly, but they are also there for other reasons: to lend authority and magic and charm and good old bazzazz. Who will tell me how many hardnosed professional cartographers did not first find their love of maps in the endpapers of <u>The House of Pooh Corner</u> or <u>Mistres Masham's Repose</u> or in any other of that multitude of books so enticingly decorated. Somehow, if the answer were that not one of them had, I would be none too surprised. Maps of late have taken on an unimaginative aura. For all their crisp beauty and praiseworthy accuracy, I mourn the lack of a <u>hic dracones</u> here or there, or a brace of cannibals disporting across the empty heart of a continent. The old compelling white space of the unknown world has been replaced by precise graphs indicating the degree of trustworthiness or the date of the last ground control survey. Where in contemporary cartography is there space to imagine?

All over the place, it turns out.

* * * * *

But then, what is a map, after all? As far as I'm concerned, it's nothing more than the codification in some way or another of something too big to handle in any other way. Traditionally maps have been thought of as graphic expressions of selected aspects of the earth's surface. Now

they obviously include the moon's surface and the sun's and
all the planets', but nonetheless there is still a certain
rigidity in the air when it comes to calling etiquette a map.
Etiquette is a map. Like any other map it codifies some
phenomenon and then accrobatically becomes a guide to that
selfsame phenomenon. Outside of you there is this great
big frightening and exciting environment, on the one hand
peopled with mountains and rivers and cities and valleys,
and on the other hand landscaped with strange people daily
new in almost endless number. Some explorer, intrepid as
ever, has wandered in these worlds, the one as the other,
and has codified his knowledge of how one goes about navi-
gating these streams, aqueous and human. We, following
our guide, make a right-hand turn or shake a hand, head
north or use our best silver. As one maps a utopia, so
the ritual associated with kings and queens embodies our
ideals of manners; as new cities are freshly mapped, so new
social situations demand still newer rules; and as the great
streams erode both worlds, and mountains rise and earthquakes shake, so maps and rules alike are thrown away and
replaced.

      The Arunta tribes of Australia have merged the two
completely. One code covers all phenomena. The myths of
their gods provide the examples for behavior as they are inextricably linked to the land. "Every detail of the country-
side is a cue for some myth, and each scene prompts the
recollection of their common culture." Etiquette and map
are one here, nor here alone. The Tzotzil of southern
Mexico make common cause, their world view embracing
behavior, time and space--from the most ordinary family
mean to the all encompassing universe. The eldest male's
position at table is at once socially and geographically determined.

      If etiquette is a map, what is not? In fact, the
class of maps is not all that large. A map codifies to guide.
Remove that guiding function and the map has disappeared.
A thing that does not let you know where you are in relation
to something else is not a map. Language, for example, is
not a map, though maps may comprise a language. Music
is not a map, although sheet music as it guides the musician
or auditor is. A lamp is not a map, though the blueprints
it was made from are. A television is not a map, although
the circuit diagram inside the back is. A game is not a
map, but the rules are. A house is not necessarily a map
(some, among the Dogon, for instance, are), but the frontal

Communication and Education

views, plans and perspectives are. The old adage that you cannot tell a book by its cover may or may not be true, but it does prove that for many, a book's cover and a person's face are maps. In fact, one still occasionally comes across references to a person's "map" meaning his face. Will Shakespeare thought the body the world and mapped with metaphor on simile. Thus sometimes even poetry and map are one.

All a map need not of necessity be is some hunk of paper covered with signs representing some portion of this our globe, abstracted and condensed and rotated and static. Charles Ives, the greatest of American composers, wrote songs that could never be sung, demanding to know why the existence of a song had to be predicated on the limitations of the human voice. So I must know why a map must be limited to graphic pictures of earth. Of course, not only need they not, but the vast majority of maps have no corporal existence whatsoever, for in our minds are maps, not one or two, but endless reams of maps, atlas piled on atlas, folio after folio, sufficient to daunt even the resources of the most resourceful and indomitable of librarians, and yet even every librarian files away the same enormous number of maps--in the mind. Here is room to imagine, room to wander for a million lifetimes. Here is white space merged into more white space. Here is the unknown, the unexplored, the untrodden. Hic dracones is here no quaint souvenir, but the living reality of feared and foreign space. Cannibals live here devouring bodies--and worse if the truth be told: souls to be stolen and purity to be sullied and honor lost. Show me the man whose mental map lacks horrifying space and I'll show you the Angel Gabriel in disguise, for the maps in our heads are compendiums of distortion and ignorance, filled with demons and monsters to make old Munster blush for shame. And not the less distorted are the Edens in our minds, those gardens of wondrous space overflowing with flowers heavy with perfume and fields of waving grain, those mental nights in Tahiti, those postcard sunsets of our minds, those paradises, sometimes in the center of our imagined worlds, often beyond the known world's end that fill our heady maps.

No one moves an inch in life without reference to one of the multitude of mental maps. The alarm clock rings and you throw your feet over the edge of the bed. Where do you go from there? Straight ahead? To the right? To the left? Your mind shuffles through the Home

Atlas and turns to the Bedroom Plate. There it finds where
to go. You leave the house. How do you get to work?
Without the atlas called memory each day would be as the
first. But the atlas in your head sets your feet in the right
direction. Someone asks you about moving into a certain
neighborhood. You tell them that it's a dangerous one.
How did you know? The thematic mental map on neighborhood
quality told you. I don't know what these maps in our
minds look like. Likely they're a bunch of brain cells connected
in complex and unknown ways. But it doesn't matter
what they look like. These mental devices do what a map
is supposed to do: they let you know <u>where</u> you are in relation
to something else. They act like <u>maps</u>. They are
maps.

   Life is endless geography, endless exploring as moving
through life we correct our maps. That stretch of
street, that neighborhood so long avoided is finally walked
and lo! no demons spitting fire rush forth to give battle,
nor even pickpockets loiter. At long last that tricky freeway
entrance like a flash comes clear. After much scrimping
and saving the visions of Eden give way to neon lighted
hotel entrances and greasy Mexican bands playing last year's
tango and grass no greener than that around the house back
home, the agony oh so cruel of disappointment of voyagers
to Eden who must ignore the mental anguish and correct
their mental maps.

"For some reason I always get lost in this part of the city"
 "All my life I never figured out where the sun rises"
 "I never saw such crazy streets every whichway!"
 "Hey, could you tell me how I find my way?"
  "I imagined it was greener and wetter"
   "It is exactly what I expected"
    "It's so confusing to me"
    "Much more beautiful"
     "Uglier than ..."
      "WOW!"

     * * * * *

   The study of mental maps is not all that new. It
goes back at least to the extant Greek philosophers and probably
a lot farther back than that. But I'll not trace its history.
Suffice it to say that in our time the study of mental
maps is going on in a new way. A lot of people want to

Communication and Education

trace the origin of what's going on now back to early behavioral psychology. Others lay our current interest at the door of J. K. Wright, and still others at the door of Kevin Lynch. Psychology, geography, planning--it's a good cross section of the people that are interested. In the past interest waxed, and then it waned and now a new moon is upon us and our lunacy is strong, and mental maps or environmental images or cognitive representations or call it what you will, is all the rage in certain small, highly circumscribed and very rarefied atmospheres. We must not get carried away in our enthusiasm and imagine, in our maps, or cups, that hoards are with us, or for that matter even behind us. We are very much alone as yet in the insanity and apparent triviality of our concern. But wait till the moon is full.

And while we're waiting I will say once and for all that I, soon to be sore beset, will call what we are looking into: mental maps. You'd have to be a mental case in the first place to really care what it's called, I suppose, but there is a pleasant earthy simple strong vital character to the words "mental maps"--mean what they supposedly may or exclude what they possibly (only slightly possibly) do-- that is definitely lacking with "cognitive representation" (which likely means nothing at all) or "environmental image" (which reeks of pretentious grantsmanship). Furthermore, mental maps says it all. I mean, they are maps, after all, and they're stored in the mind, and I can see talking to somebody on the street about his mental map (in fact I frequently do) but think how silly you'd feel saying, "Now about that cognitive representation of yours...." It sounds like a dread disease. "Upon hearing these fatal words, the S clutches his heart and keels over in a dead faint, to revive but retain a lingering suspicion that something is really wrong." Besides, typing "cognitive representation" over and over again all day could get to be a serious drag.

There is a real reason for this terminological squabble and it is because there are so many kinds of mental maps and so many ways of collecting them and so many ways of analyzing them and so many different things to be learned from them. There are a couple of truly significant distinctions that should be made, the making of which should clearly mark out the various basic interests coagulated in the mental map movement. First of all there is the fundamental distinction to be made between the map in one's mind and the representation of that map that one makes manifest.

Sometimes the mental map is manifested by drawing on a
piece of paper, but far more frequently the mental map is
manifested in any other manner of action, such as moving
from place to place, taking one route instead of another,
shopping here instead of there, and so on. Thus there is
the mental mental map and the manifested mental map, these
manifestations being behavioral and including as a special
case the drawing of a map on paper. Some, of course, do
not even allow this distinction between mental mental map
and manifested mental map, vowing that they are one and
the same and without true knowledge about the real connections between the body and the brain, who can gainsay them.
But valid or not, the distinction between the map in the mind
and the map on the paper is useful and the distinction is retained here. Obviously, an Atlas can display only manifested
mental maps, and mostly those drawn on paper.

In and of themselves these manifested mental maps
have only the value of curiosity, and sometimes charm, but
little more, and the ordinary run-of-the-mill map has little
enough of the latter quality. Actually, your average mental
map is an object dull beyond caring, usually unimaginative,
poorly executed, and entirely insipid. Though occasionally
my day is made joyous by a map exciting in itself, the great
adventure lies normally in comparing and contrasting maps
with each other and with map sets collected from varying
groups of people. For ease of comparison, sets of maps
are compiled onto a single composite map. This adjective
has been verbalized and so we find ourselves "compositing"
maps. Often a map is composited from purely verbal material, from content analysis of descriptions or rankings of
preferences. These composites seem to be very powerful
in their ability to instantly portray otherwise complex and
incomprehensible information. There are also composites
of verbal information, and composites of information graphically overlaid on old-fashioned cartographic maps. The
composites are used by some to explain or demonstrate attributes of environments drawn or described. By others,
they are used to describe characteristics of the people who
drew them or talked about them. In the first class we find
planners, architects and geographers. In the second class
are psychologists interested in orientation, development,
personal styles, learning as well as more traditional psychologic interests. Often there is overlap between the two
classes of interests and things tend to become thoroughly
confused.

This confusion seems to me to be a healthy sign. It indicates that academicians are tending to forget their old castles and domains and realize that man is not some conglomerate of bits and pieces but a unitary whole, and that this whole extends beyond any single person's skin to embrace all of existence. There is, in truth, but a glimmer of this, but that glimmer is more than we have seen in a long time and is heartening. We are witnessing in these new maps the long overdue democratization of map making, returning the map from whence it sprang, from people and their needs and desires. The final humanization of cartography cannot be long in the offing.

PERSPECTIVES ON MEDIA*

Peggy Sullivan

Within the past few weeks, I have had two conversations which have confirmed a conviction that librarians have not been successful enough in identifying for themselves and for others what their real areas of expertise and distinctive usefulness are. In a telephone conversation with the staff member of a large information clearinghouse, I asked what the size of their professional staff was, and was told there were nine. Recognizing that some might be administrators or in special fields, I then asked how many were librarians. The answer: "Oh, only one. You see, our work is mostly related to abstracting, indexing, and using information. There really isn't much for a librarian to do." Later, in the same search for information, I talked with the director of a network which specializes in getting media for some specialists in education, and asked what information about their program they might want library school students to have. This time, the answer was: "Well, we're not really interested in reaching librarians. We want to get to the people who need the information." And to my further question, "But wouldn't librarians be helpful in making them aware of your service?" the answer was, "Well, how could they? This isn't library information." The meaning, of course, was that it wasn't necessarily books or periodicals or the more traditional media of information.

At the very time that the tightening job market is forcing those who are concerned with recruitment, education, and placement of librarians to think in terms of expanding the kinds of places where librarians may work successfully, using their hard-won expertise, it is discouraging to realize that some earlier gains and expansions of what librarians'

---

*Reprinted by permission from the January 1973 issue of
PLA Bulletin, pages 5-8.

roles and responsibilities may be are far from universally recognized. And if some of the limitations are in the eye of the beholder, some, it must be admitted, are in our own view of ourselves.

Terminology Hassle

Determinedly since World War II, the leadership of American school librarians has insisted on the concept of school libraries being, or at least becoming, centers for all of a school's media. Certainly, the terms have changed; instructional materials, a term which once seemed all-encompassing, may seem limiting to those who associate instruction with the work of a teacher, so they have gone to terms like learning resources. There is some hope that the simpler term, media, defined to include print, nonprint, and the necessary accompanying technology, may solve the terminology hassle. Frankly, I don't care. It is the concept of inclusiveness that is important. The real pity is that in the course of this hassle, we may have lost sight of what the purposes, functions, and day-to-day activities of a school media center should be. Too many librarians (learning resourcarians, media specialists, or instructional materials specialists) have reacted as though they could broaden the focus of their collections without broadening their own knowledge of the contents of those collections, while at the same time they have apparently cheerfully surrendered their links with books as basic tools of their trade.

An example illustrates the attitude I deplore. At the conclusion of an in-service meeting, a high school librarian, who had just participated in a long session about how to organize nonprint media in the library media center, commented to her supervisor: "You know, I've just about given up reading. How can I, where there's so much to do?" But it was his response that was really discouraging. Sympathetically, he said, "Oh, I understand. I don't read, either." Although I am certainly ready to admit that reading is difficult to do with the consistency, pleasure, and sense of purpose that drives one to relate it to the frequent opportunities for inspiration, guidance, information which make it a necessary professional activity, any decline in one's capacity for reading should be fought, not accepted. This is one time the supervisor probably should have offered a stone instead of bread. Frances Clarke Sayers, who has argued so brilliantly for librarians to become the belligerent profession, needs a counterpart to stress that with that belligerence about service, there should also be a kind of violent stubbornness to continue reading without--note well--in any way slighting the need to know the values of other media.

There are levels of sophistication in one's reactions to media other than the more traditional kinds. On one level, a librarian, like the one who has told me, "There can be no such thing as a good filmstrip," offers only a closed mind. Somewhere above that is the person who comments, "Oh, yes, we have a media center in our school. We have every film or filmstrip that relates to books--and the children love them!" One might call this the Weston Woods syndrome, or how to avoid having a media center while appearing to have one. Counter to these attitudes, but not much different in terms of sophistication, is the one which seeks variety in media formats for the sake of variety. Any librarian who has suffered through the familiar old assignments which required the use of at least six (or insert your own magic number) forms of information--e.g., newspaper, pamphlet, encyclopedia, book, map, and periodical--should recoil from this attitude. But some of them have adopted it themselves in a more contemporary form. They have been insensitive to the differences in quality, possible usefulness, and audience of various media, but have blithely assumed that the teacher or the student who wants a book on the Etruscans is also sure to want a slide, filmstrip, tape, film, and media kit complete with appropriate models or realia. In several media presentations about school library media programs, the magic moment comes when the librarian says, "... and that's not all! We also have a tape, a disc recording, and...!" Somewhere along the line, such a librarian has assumed that having the same information in several different formats is the goal of every learner. And that is not necessarily true. The difficult task, the one which calls for the librarian's best skills in terms of working with people and knowledge of media, is to recognize the most appropriate format, offer it, and not overwhelm the public with unwanted and perhaps only tangentially related media.

Evaluation Needed

Somewhere among these levels of sophistication is the point of view that a given form of media is always best for a given purpose. This is personified by the librarian who says, "To understand a rain forest, you have to see a rain forest." I chose that example because I have just seen, as one of the murkiest, least informative frames of a filmstrip, a picture of a rain forest which gives no sense of size, perspective, color, climate, or any other attribute of a rain forest. It is not as good as a good color picture in a book, perhaps accompanied by descriptive text, would be. And still another attitude comes into play here. Too many librarians assume that because a medium or format is new to them, it is guaranteed to have more up-to-date information than any print medium. Not so, of course. A film that shows antiquated equipment being used in a science laboratory or outmoded dress styles is perhaps easy to spot, but the information which has become wrong by being outdated (e.g., the statement that there are forty-eight states in the U.S., or that most of Africa consists of colonies of Europe, or that John XXIII is the reigning pope) is as wrong in a film or filmstrip as it is in a book, but less likely to be noted. Part of the reason for this is the greater difficulty of checking copyright dates on nonprint media, and part may be the problem of previewing a film before a showing, but part must be related to the guileless welcome librarians often extend to "the new media," while their every hackle rises as they evaluate new textbooks, which may be much more contemporary in tone and content.

For some time, some of the lack of evaluation of nonprint media might have been blamed on the problem of finding the media in the first place, and of finding good reviews in the second place. This has been alleviated, certainly, by such tools as the indexes coming from the National Center for Educational Media, by ALA Booklist's increased scope, and most recently by R. R. Bowker Company's Previews, which grew out of Library Journal reviews of other media. As a frequent reviewer, I am keenly aware of the practical and distinctive problems in reviewing nonprint media. One must have the necessary equipment. There is usually no way of skimming or re-checking a point passed earlier. Evelyn Wood herself would need twenty-eight minutes to view a twenty-eight-minute film. And the reviewer who is trying to check the accuracy and timing of beeps in a sound filmstrip endures a special kind of agony, as every interruption requires him to start from the beginning. I mention these kinds of problems, not to arouse sympathy for the reviewer, but to point out reasons why the evaluation of such media may have been slower to evolve in the first place and more difficult to conduct on a consistent basis.

Sometimes, it seems to me that librarians have underrated their skills and competencies by assuming that they need a whole new set of them if they are to deal with a variety of media. The techniques of organization, utilization, and evaluation, at least, are not all that different. But it has seemed easy to take the position that new media require new techniques, and that therefore, the newest person on the staff should be best able to handle all the nonprint media. Such an attitude was doomed to die in time, but it is a puzzling one.

There are probably as many different attitudes or perspectives about the growing kinds of media as there are librarians or media specialists. It seemed to me it might be useful to review some of them, if only to return to the point that any confusion, any lack of certainty about how to use or how to organize nonprint media should not be allowed to interfere with the concept of the librarian as someone committed to service to people in such a full and complete way that an expansion of the scope of a collection means, first and foremost, an expanded opportunity to serve the actual and potential users of that collection.

READING HABITS AND LIBRARY EXPERIMENTS IN SWEDEN*

Bengt Hjelmqvist

In 1968, the Swedish government appointed a committee to study the question of public support for literature. It is a long-established approach in Sweden to prepare reforms by having the problems analysed by special committees appointed by the government, but formally independent of it. The annually published series, Swedish Government Official Investigations (SOU), contains almost a hundred committee reports, and something over 3000 persons are currently employed in government work of this kind in the capacity of committee members, experts, secretaries and other officials.

The committee in question was named The Literary Commission (Litteraturutredningen). Its main purpose was to chart the conditions on which literature functions, and propose measures to promote consumption, distribution and production in the literary sector. This commission is thus not specifically geared to library activities, but its work is bound in the nature of things to touch upon the role of the library. The results so far reported by the commission are clear evidence that the importance of libraries for the book supply is if anything greater than supposed, and will tend to be still greater in the future.

The commission is not expected to present its final report until at the earliest the summer of 1973. What has been published to date is the preparatory work for this report, comprising four volumes of almost 2000 pages in total. These report the commission's studies on reading habits ("Reading and Book Habits in Five Swedish Communities," SOU 1972:20), library studies ("Experiments with Libraries,"

---

*Reprinted by permission from the volume 6, number 1 issue of the Scandinavian Public Library Quarterly, pages 2-8.

SOU 1972:61), and trade studies ("A Book about Books,"
SOU 1972:80). The fourth volume deals with literature in the
schools (SOU 1973:1). All four volumes include exhaustive
résumés in English.

Reading Habits

For the libraries, the studies performed on reading
habits and library activities are naturally of special interest.
These are mutually related in that both groups of studies
are linked to the same five communities in different parts
of Sweden, selected with a view to the government's directive that the commission should pay particular attention to
culturally underprivileged areas and population groups.
Three of the communities studied are districts in (by Swedish standards) large towns, two of them being new communities with new residential areas and a recently settled population, the third an old peripheral area with a certain proportion of slum buildings and a low level of education and
income. The two remaining communities are situated in
the northern part of Sweden, with its vast sparsely populated
areas and depopulation problems. In 1969, a large-scale interview survey was made of reading and book habits in these
five communities. In total, some 2000 persons between the
ages of 15 and 69 were interviewed. This study was supplemented by a questionnaire survey among school children
in these communities. It is the results of these two surveys that are reported in the study on reading habits, which
contains a wealth of statistical material, in which the observations made are related to age, sex, marital status, education, occupational group, income bracket, social allegiance, etc. This is the most thorough study of book and
reading habits made in Sweden. Leader for the project was
a well-known Swedish sociologist, Dr. Harald Swedner.

This is not the place to report the results of the
study in detail. Generally speaking, one can say that it
demonstrates the dependence of reading habits on environment, local industry, population structure, the supply of
leisure activities, traditions, and values. Certain details
can be mentioned from the interviews held with adults.
Those interviewed devoted on the average some ten hours a
week to reading, of which two to three hours were to the
reading of books. Noticeably enough, those in the most
typically underpopulated area devoted less time to reading
newspapers and more to television viewing. The order be-

tween activities was the reading of newspapers, books, magazines and periodicals. Men and women read the daily papers with equal frequency, while men were greater readers of periodicals and non-fiction, and women of magazines and fiction.

Of the books read by interviewees during the previous fortnight, something over one third had been purchased in conjunction with reading, slightly less than one third had been borrowed from a library, and again slightly less than one third had been acquired in some other manner, mainly by loans from acquaintances or as gifts. A study of the manner in which interviewees had learned of the books they read showed the most common source of information to be not the mass media--as one might have expected--but conversation with relatives and acquaintances. The next most common source was information in conjunction with visits to the library. Only after this came reviews, bookshop displays, advertisements, displays at sales points other than bookshops, television and radio (in this order).

The interviewers put certain questions designed to clarify the subjects' interest in books. It emerged--which is not in itself surprising--that people with a strong interest in books acquired a higher proportion of the books they read from a library. The relative role played by the book trade in the supply to interviewees failed to increase with a greater interest in books. In the opinion of the investigators, this is probably due to persons with a great interest in books not being able to afford to meet their needs by purchasing, and therefore using the library to a greater extent than others.

Of particular interest is the section on use of libraries. On the average, 59% had not visited any library during the previous twelve months. However, the percentage varied strongly between the different districts, between the sexes, and between different age groups. Obviously, educational background was also an important factor. The frequency of visits was highest in the lowest age bracket (15-19 years); those with a good education were more frequent users than the poorly educated; in the sparsely populated areas, library users were markedly fewer than in urban areas.

The most frequent visitors to libraries were the highly educated women living in the community with the best-off population: a full 92% had visited a library during the previous twelve months. At the opposite end of the scale were the poorly educated men living in the under-populated community: the figure here was 19%. These figures are not in themselves surprising. They agree very well with practical experience. Remarkable, rather, is that on the average a full 41% of the population in the communities studied--i.e., two fifths--had had contact with the library. At the same time, one must observe that the three fifths not reporting any contact included many who would have had profit and pleasure from books and libraries. If we try, on the basis of the study, to analyse the "non-user" group, we find--in highly generalised terms--that the non-user is poorly educated and thus poorly paid, not infrequently an immigrant or living in a sparsely populated area, often elderly, and often ignorant of the services offered by the library. A further cause of non-use is the library's inadequacy in various respects.

Library Experiments

The library's inadequacy and measures to overcome it are the subject of the second of the Literary Commission's studies, "Experiments with Libraries." In the five communities where reading habits had been investigated, a succession of library experiments were performed in 1970 to see whether it was possible to ready a new library public by increasing the libraries' resources and consciously directing efforts at the disadvantaged groups. The costs of these experiments were met largely from state funds. Activities followed a centrally designed plan, but the various libraries enjoyed great freedom in implementing the details. And indeed the five experimental libraries report an impressive, and richly varied catalogue of measures taken.

The planning of these experiments was based on six assumptions:

1. The degree to which libraries are used is dependent on the scope, diversification and level of difficulty of the supply.
2. The degree of use is dependent on the accessibility of the supply: the library's position and opening hours, how books are presented, and the opportunities of the staff to provide service.
3. The degree of use is dependent on the information

provided by the library.
4. The degree of use is dependent on activities over and beyond the distribution of books.
5. The degree of use is dependent on the integration of library activities with other cultural and social activities within the municipality.
6. The degree of use is dependent on the anchorage of library activities in the public mind.

I shall mention here only some of the many experiments performed to throw light on these six suppositions.

As regards the supply of books, experiments were made with light entertainment: books that could be classified as light entertainment were placed on special shelves; one of the libraries procured literature of the type customarily sold at newspaper stalls; and, for children, experimental purchases were made of series of condensed illustrated classics. Three of the communities studied had a high proportion of immigrants. (Sweden, like so many other industrial countries, has received large numbers of immigrants in recent years. The majority have been Finns but they have been joined by numerous Poles, Italians, Yugoslavs, Hungarians, Greeks and Turks.) Books in the immigrant languages were here acquired on a considerable scale, and contacts established with immigrant groups--in one case with such success that the library became something of a meeting point for local immigrants.

Longer opening hours, including on Sundays, the regrouping of stock to make it easier for users to find what they wanted, various types of outreach activity, and increased resources of staff were some elements of the experiment designed to make libraries more available. Particularly important were the experiments with libraries at places of work. Revolving book-racks were placed in the personnel dining rooms at factories and firms, and employees could loan books with practically no formalities. A librarian made regular visits to chat, and to take orders for books not included in the selection on the racks. Reports emphasized the advantages of a small selection that it was easy to look over. Another experiment that attracted great attention were the "pavement libraries." Two of the experimental libraries displayed books on the street, for instance outside the state liquor store. Anyone who wished could take a book and return it either to the same place, or to the library. A number of books, naturally, were never returned, but lending

functioned on the whole without friction, and many expressed
their satisfaction at being able to borrow books without a
complicated lending procedure. The measures tested included
also various experiments with bookmobiles, in both urban
and country areas. These experiments showed the strength
and weakness of bookmobile activities by comparison with the
service provided by a small lending station: on the one hand,
a greater supply of books, specially trained staff, and many
times more service points--on the other, fairly long intervals between visits, short stays, and times that many found
inconvenient.

Throughout the experimental period, the libraries involved ran a very intense information campaign. This mostly took the traditional forms, but more unusual approaches
like door-to-door canvassing and a talk on books over a department store radio system were also employed. Firsttime users were asked to give the reason for their visiting
the library: the most common source of information was
family members and acquaintances. Among direct measures
by the libraries, mailed information to homes and window
displays came high on the list.

An important and extensive aspect of the experiments
was "general cultural activities." The library was tested,
with favourable results, as a forum for art exhibitions, concerts and dramatic performances, meetings with authors
were arranged, and debates held on topical subjects. Activities with children were lively, and information was given
on local authority affairs--particularly interesting were the
debates arranged by a couple of the urban libraries on local
town planning, debates which clearly indicated the need for
communication between the local population and the council
representatives and officials. Certain social features were
incorporated: the libraries functioned as meeting-points,
and undertook arrangements designed to offer both children
and adults opportunities for meaningful leisure pastimes, and
active opinion-forming. Such activities by the libraries were
not intended to compete with any other cultural and social
institutions, but rather to supplement the activities of the
latter in fields where the library--thanks to its neutral
status--is particularly equipped to make a contribution, at
the same time creating an interest in and around library activities proper.

In these experiments, the libraries collaborated on a
broad front with a wide variety of institutions and organisa-

tions, at the local, regional and central levels. The experiments showed a need for more than collaboration: library activities need to be co-planned with other community action in, for instance, the cultural and social sector.

The experiments designed to anchor library activities more firmly in the public mind involved primarily the creation of "consumer councils" in connection with the libraries, loosely composed groups that were willing to discuss the library's problems with its administration and staff. Reference groups of this kind were set up at three of the libraries, and experience has been classified as positive.

Conclusions

The results of these experimental activities were measured in various ways. The difficulties were great. Many of the measurements planned proved impracticable, partly because no comparative material was available from previous years. Also, it quickly emerged that it was impossible to separate the various measures taken. This would have meant another experimental design, with a strict limitation on the number of experiments performed by each participating library, and extremely expensive--and for the public irritating--registration. Only naturally, activities resulted in greatly increased borrowing: more interesting, perhaps, is the fact that the lending figures of one participating library fell off sharply after the experimental period. Another interesting point is that experiments were successful in reaching culturally disadvantaged groups. This is indicated by the fact that social group III, which comprises mainly industrial workers and the equivalent, now notes a much higher percentage representation among library users than previously. The figures also show a percentage decline for children; young users have not declined in number, but adult users have strengthened their position--it is mainly among adults that the libraries can find new readers.
Other conclusions: more light literature is needed, as is an increased production of such literature; other needs include more copies of the books in demand, simplified library procedures, better guidance, less bureaucracy, more decentralisation, better information, more coordinated planning, better contacts, and more staff. The question of staff is particularly important: activities designed to reach new groups are personnel-intensive.

Two concepts, says the concluding summary, seem particularly important: integration and close-at-hand service. "Integration: the libraries must not be planned and must not function as isolated occurrences. They have their place in a larger context, they must be seen as one of many stages in society's services in various fields.... Close-at-hand service: proximity not only in the physical sense, short distances, external work, decentralisation. It also involves intellectual proximity, it means that the books supplied are of such form and content that they can be received by the new groups. And service--that involves the elimination of physical, psychological and economic handicaps to the utilisation of the libraries. It means information, staff with time, with a will to cooperate and with a positive attitude to service. It means premises where people can relax, where they can be active, where they can communicate with each other."

I noted by way of introduction that the task of the Library Commission is not to solve the problems of our libraries, but rather to find new paths for literature. However, one of these paths--and perhaps the most important--is via the libraries. In this way, the commission's studies, without comparison the most extensive ever to have been made in Scandinavia, will be of major importance also to the libraries. They show that the libraries need not only increased resources but also in many respects a new policy: within the framework of their present resources, they must revise their priorities if they are to reach the neglected groups. The volume on reading and book habits is a challenge to all concerned with libraries. The volume on library experiments is a case of samples, a catalogue of measures that every library has reason to contemplate. The Swedish title of this study, Försök med bibliotek, is ambiguous. It can be translated as meaning "Experiments with libraries"; it can also be read as a challenge in today's cultural debate--"Try libraries!"

IS TOMORROW A FOUR LETTER WORD?*

Jean Karl

>Billy and Bobbin and big bouncing Ben
>Could eat more meat
>than four-score men;
>Bill ate a cow, Bob ate a calf,
>Bill ate a church, Bob ate the steeple.
>Ben ate the priest and all the people.

   This rather hearty bit of verse, accompanied by a suitable three color picture showing Bill holding the church and eating it, Bob's hands holding the steeple, and Ben's hands gathering up the people, comes not from the distant past, when we might expect more earthy rhyme, nor from our much talked of modern approach to realism, but from a book published in 1929, designed as a textbook to teach the ABC's. <u>Jingling ABC's</u> also has charming verses on trains, geese, umbrellas, seaside bathing, and, in general, rather gentle pastimes. Yet there are Bill and Bobbin and Ben. We are not the only ones to have dealt in horror in one way or another. Yet sometimes there are those who think that "realism" and other "horrors" have been invented only in the last five years.

   Those who wrote children's books in the past were fully aware of the realities of life, perhaps more so than the author of <u>Jingling ABC's</u>. In a book of short rather preachy stories published in 1826, a young boy whose father is interested in chemistry hears a discussion on the make-up of gunpowder. Soon the boy is busy making gunpowder, only, eventually, to create an explosion and nearly kill him-

---

*Reprinted by permission from the winter 1973 issue of <u>School Media Quarterly</u>, pages 104-110. "This article is based on a speech given at the University of Tennessee, Knoxville, in May 1972."

self. Remember The Poor Little Rich Girl? Her story
might not have been typical. But for some, the realities of
life at Miss Minchin's establishment once one had fallen
from grace may not have been far from the truth in the
lives of a number of children. In David Copperfield, long
read by children and young adults, Dickens recounts some
of the horrors of his own childhood. E. Nesbit's Railway
Children have a father who is sent to jail--an innocent vic-
tim--but nevertheless in jail. Coming down to the present,
such books as Linnet on the Threshold drew a realistic picture of depression life for children of the 1930's. Linnet's
father and mother separate for a while in the course of the
book. Linnet has to leave school to get a job, working for
$8 a week. Though the ending is happy enough, the tale is
true to many lives. The Moffets are not rich and neither
is the heroine of The Hundred Dresses.

Though these books may seem commonplace, accepted
in our time, or passé because their time is past, they did
hold up to the eyes of their readers in the day they were
written, the more unpleasant things, as well as some of the
good things of life at that time. They may not have quite
the bite of our books today, but if that is true, it is true
because the thinking of people was different then, too. Authors live and write in a specific time, and their books contain, in essence if not in fact, the spirit of their times.
The means by which books accomplish this differ. Historical fiction will not reflect the present in the same way
science fiction does and neither of these will speak in the
same way as realistic fiction. To say this may seem to
repeat the obvious. Most people recognize this when they
look to the past. But too many forget it when they look to
our own time. Or else they wear rose colored glasses when
they look out at the world around them. They refuse to admit that what they see is what is really there. But children
who have not lived in any other time see it quite clearly.

Our world is not a pretty one. Take a look at your
local daily newspaper. In one day in a Knoxville, Tennessee, paper last spring the following headlines appeared,
among others not too different: Depot in Flames After Raid
Near House, Haiphong; Three British Soldiers Slain in Erin
Riots; Four Tots Die In Fire; Our Time Running Out on Nuclear Clock. In the same issue of the paper, Steve Canyon
(in the comic strip) gets a letter from his first wife. He
and his current wife are talking. "Steve," she says, "this
was a break. When we return to the suite--where the mi-

crophone can hear--I'll make a big row because you still hear from your first wife. Then I will throw you out--so I may get on with my spy job!" By coincidence, probably, Ann Landers writes to a man who asks what he should do when his wife beats him up. Should he fight back? "No," says Miss Landers, "just leave." Finally a column talks about the night club act of a man named Alice Cooper and his troupe. They chop up baby dolls, stage a mock hanging of Alice, work hard to get their audience stirred up, and are consistently drunk when they go on stage. This is one paper for one day and is only a part of what was there. Furthermore, it is not one of the nation's large city newspapers.

At about the time those articles were appearing in the one issue of the Knoxville newspaper, the magazine section of The New York Times carried an essay called, "An Eighteen Year Old Looks Back on Life." An eighteen year old girl, obviously very bright, a freshman at Yale; one of the first women admitted, discussed TV (I watch in earnest. How could I do anything else? Five thousand hours of my life have gone into this box). She was not bothered by repetition or dull, banal programs. "Boring repetition is itself a rhythm." In fact she confesses the world is so full of absurdities, of nonsequitors, that it is impossible to take anything too seriously. The things that seemed to have made the most impression on her were the realization of the power of the atom bomb, and pictures of unborn fetuses in a Life magazine. The church she turned to in 8th grade soon disappointed her. She did not smoke pot or take drugs, but had come to understand peer group pressure 1972 style in another area--"the embarrassment of virginity." Her dreams of the future? "As some people prepare for their old age, so I prepare for my 20's. A little home, a comfortable chair, peace and quiet--retirement sounds tempting."

This young woman may be retiring before she's begun to live, but one who in her childhood coped with death and the atom bomb, unborn fetuses, the boredom of repetition, the pressure of sex, and the problem of eluding drugs, and who has searched and found no meaningful pattern in life, is not about to be wooed into life by Elsie Dinsmore. She did not read much, she confessed. There was little encouragement to do so. True, books may not have made her twenties more attractive to her. They may not have penetrated the gray sameness of her days. But there again, the right book might have.

A book like Henry 3 perhaps. That girl would have understood Henry's preoccupation with keeping his intelligence a secret in order to stay one of the crowd. And she might possibly have been moved enough by Henry's unique problems to understand his breaking out of the crowd when life demanded it; she might then have come to share his concern with peace, with the meaning of life, and with human values. Precisely because it is a shocking book in places for some, but a book with enough reality to speak to the repetitious horrors of reality children find every day in their newspapers, on TV, and in school, it might have given life a more coherent pattern for her.

Or take A Nice Fire and Some Moonpennies, a not very gentle spoof of drugs, sex, and the whole "with it" culture. Decidedly shocking. Also terribly funny. And real enough to meet Steve Canyon, Ann Landers, and the daily headlines head on.

For children who can pick up a magazine and see photographs of fetuses, why should In the Night Kitchen be a shock? Nudity is a commonplace these days. Children cannot escape it. So why not encounter it in a true art form meant for the child. In a creative book where the nudity is a part of the whole, but only a part, where it is natural and seems right, not forced and vulgar like the centerfold in Daddy's and Mommie's magazines. Maybe a casual approach to sex and nudity occasionally in a children's book under the right conditions can some day make that centerfold less necessary.

And why not see life on the other side of the culture wall realistically, too. That suburban eighteen year old might have learned to resist the absurdities in life more if she had read The Planet of Junior Brown or His Own Where. Though such books may seem controversial to adults, they may be the essence of what life is like to the child or young person; they may be real enough to matter.

For any child of today whose daily existence is a ceaseless round of not necessarily stimulating activities and who is continually bombarded with too distant to matter news and rock and roll lyrics and TV comedies and tragedies, all of which may tend to blend horror into a routine pattern, a book that carries a powerful, close-up, emotion-filled look at some aspect of life may be a jolt, a needed jolt. We need to be aware of life to live life. And not until we have really felt it touch us can we respond. Today's children and young people, as has always been true, will respond best to the thing they must admit is true and that touches them. If even part is false or remote, the whole can be cast aside. And a chance at true awareness is lost.

And that is the heart of the matter. A book done for our own time, especially for the children of our time, cannot speak to them, cannot get past the continual barrage of TV, newspapers, and rock and roll radio (have you ever really listened to the words of some of these songs?) without being honest, even if some people would prefer not to see it that way. And the impact that books that try to present life honestly will have on the young will not be the same as the impact they will have on an older generation, who are looking at events from a different past.

Recently there have been protests about some of the words that have begun to appear in books for children and young adults. The words shock adults who see them. But for the most part they do not shock children and young adults. The free conversations of children in all parts of the country are filled with these words. And for them they have little meaning. Words, combinations of letters, have no inborn meanings. Connotations and denotations come from those who use them. Words we now would hesitate to say were once a part of common speech. And words we now say quite casually may one day be frowned upon. It is possible to say "Oh morning glory" or even "Oh coleslaw" with enough vehemence to make them sound truly hateful. At the same time it is possible for words that sounded ill on the ears of one generation to become gentle on the ears of the next.

And just as language changes, so life styles change. George Washington and Andrew Jackson had long hair. Ulysses S. Grant and Abraham Lincoln had beards. Teddy Roosevelt had a mustache. Franklin D. Roosevelt, Herbert Hoover, Dwight D. Eisenhower, and John F. Kennedy had short hair and no facial growth. Regardless of political affiliations, no one has ever judged the competence of these men in office by the amount of hair they allowed to grow on their heads. This is, of course, only a symbol for a larger truth. Dress is a symbol. Language is a symbol. And in many cases even the use or rejection of tradition is a symbol. The outside changes and the inside attitudes also change from generation to generation. What is accepted at

one time is not in another. For centuries women wore their
hair long. In the 1920's they cut their hair. Today young
girls have long hair. Sexual mores change from culture to
culture and generation to generation. Attitudes toward war,
peace and violence change and are still changing. The
crowding of our world, the ecological problems that confront
us, the greater awareness we have of other people and places,
all make attitudes different. And the young are the focus of
the change. They must change the most, for the world will
alter more rapidly for them than for people of an older generation. Furthermore, today's young will soon seem old
themselves, as their young cry out for still newer ideas.
And to some extent the human species, like other species,
will adapt or die.

This being the case it is a far greater crime to try
to inflict the superficial mores of a generation past on a
new generation than it is to break old shibboleths and let
old taboos be laid to rest. Never fear, new ones will grow
up. The young, once they begin seeking their own way,
crowd together in fear of open spaces. They leave their
parents, but cling to each other for support and create their
own boundaries, different, yet sometimes even more restricting than the boundaries they have left.

To seem honest to them, books must fall inside these
boundaries, not the boundaries created by others. Then how
can we do our duty and pass on the weight of civilization to
them? By digging deeper, by placing within the boundaries
of their external superficial surface culture, the deep truths
of life and of man's relationships to other men and to his
universe. Though the surfaces change, the deeper truths do
not change. This is why we can read books from other
generations and enjoy them, recognizing both the surface
differences and deep unchanging truths. We can do this,
and young people and children can do this, when the boundaries of time are clearly marked. But they will not accept
the past when someone tries to palm it off on them as today.

It may be necessary sometimes to get ahead of today,
to rush toward tomorrow if we are to make today's books
not only real but useful. So the writers, editors, and buyers of books for the young need to keep alert, to sense what
tomorrow's problems may be. Today we have sex, drugs,
poverty, war, and intercultural conflicts to contend with.
And books do contend with them. Tomorrow we may see
starvation, interplanetary exchanges in one form or another,

subtle forms of mind control that must be exposed to avoid 1984, and goodness knows what more. The children who as adults will cope best with any problems are those who have anticipated in advance their own response to problem situations and found a way to handle them. An article I once read said that the child who daydreams well and yet functions effectively in social situations handles unexpected and new situations better than the child who does not daydream, because in the daydreams he has anticipated such events and dealt with them before. Reading can be like daydreaming, only perhaps more effective. The girl today who reads books about girls who become pregnant, girls who take drugs, girls who drop out of school, will live these situations in a way harmless to her, and yet because she has experienced them vicariously, she may be able to face the actual situations, or the forerunners of such situations, with greater poise and knowledge. It is better to read about the mistakes of a teenage bride, than to have to become such a bride just to see what it is like.

Not that books for children and young people should preach. Far from it. Rather they must offer valid information on all sides of an issue in nonfiction and valid experiences in fiction. Preaching is negative. Experience is positive and allows the individual to exercise his own intelligence. Decisions become his and hence are more likely to be firm and strong and made without destructive fears.

Books for the young are changing. For some adults they are changing too rapidly. For some not rapidly enough. If they are to survive, they must change in ways that make sense. They must change to meet the needs of the generation they are written for. And they may need to change in form as well as content. Microfilm and microfiche are in their infancy today. Some day a book may never be a book on paper at all. It may only come in film, as the need for space increases and available space grows smaller rather than larger. Small portable viewers may even make it possible to read these rolls and cards in all the familiar places, including in bed. Or microscopic books, perhaps two inches by three inches in size, easy to carry and store, will be read with special magnifying equipment, itself small and easy to carry. Paperbacks will certainly overtake hard bound books in popularity, as much for convenience as for cost. Who can anticipate all that may happen? No one. But all of us must be ready to accept change or see the book as a written record, a written story, die.

Content changes will reflect not only changing life styles and vocabularies, but changing ways of presenting material. In a freer world, for example, we might be able to allow a reader more freedom in determining the outcome of a book. It might be possible to write a book in which at a certain point a reader makes a choice between several alternative directions in the plot and as a result turns to one given page or another. Somewhat further on, the reader makes still another choice, and so on. In this way a reader can make a new book every time he reads it, by changing his choices. He can try out different patterns of action and different consequences. Or books could be, as one adult book I saw was, completely shuffleable. Each page contained a complete incident and was loose. The reader could put the pages in any order he chose, trying out different patterns to see what struck him as being most appropriate and real. A book could be written with no real end, letting the reader end it, or perhaps circling back to the beginning. Books on tape could be a few seconds of moving pictures, perhaps to establish the look of a locale. Music might somehow be built into a book. If these ideas seem extreme, they are. Yet we must expect change in this or some other direction. We cannot be content. To be content is to move back, because the world is moving on.

Is tomorrow a four letter word? Yes, it may very well be. It may at least bring forth four letter words from normally staid individuals who are too set in their ways to accept the quickened flow of culture and technology. Those who accept change or at least realize it is here to stay will not be thrown, however. Instead, they will fight to be a part of the action.

All of which does not mean that the future is necessarily going to be less moral, less concerned, less well structured, or even less comfortable than the past. To some people all change is, by its very nature, evil. But change in children's books, as anywhere, brings both good and evil. There will be new things that will be better than anything we have ever had before, perhaps, although sex and drugs and "bad words" and a lot of other things some people feel are "bad" will continue to crop up. The way ideas are treated will not always be even the same as now. As the cultural attitudes in our society change, books will change. Watch the newspapers and you will be able to match the current of the times with the current in books. And when others protest, suggest that they too watch the newspapers and the television and think twice about what they are saying.

Surface differences then, must and will happen, but beneath these we, all of us, can work to see that the books we give to children reflect truths, both current truths and those truths we feel have always been: respect for life and for all who share the earth with us; beauty, not sentimental beauty, but the beauty that finds its way into every worthy corner of the universe. We must not let honor die, nor human dignity, nor a sense of individual and collective worth. No matter what the surface, we must hope that every book will be alive in itself and will let some of the deeper values of living live in it. If these are lost to our civilization then our hope for the future is indeed dim.

Adults write children's books, they edit them, and they buy them. But in the end children are free to accept or reject what they are given. How well we gear what we do to their particular surface world view, how much we respect them, and how much we give them to grow on--without preaching--may well determine the future of books and maybe the future of some other things we value as well.

BIOGRAPHY: THE BAD OR THE BOUNTIFUL?*

Patrick Groff

Biography about adults written for elementary school children† has long been heralded by authorities in children's literature. It is claimed, in so many words, by many of these writers that "no other reading can ever quite approach the effective moral implications of a good biography."[1] This life-model purported to be given by a biography is believed to become a part of a child's personality, specifically a constituent of his superego. As children "identify" with the adult figure's behavior in these books, it is asserted, this "may give them new models of greatness to emulate," and thus a succor from "disappointment or some temporary failure."[2,3]

Although they admit they know little about the nature of children's literature, experts in social studies instruction in the elementary schools readily echo these homilies about the extraliterary, or nonliterary, uses of a biography. In a typical example of this concurrence, one such authority contends "the power of identification" of children with adults "can frequently be created through the use of biography ... of persons whose own lives are worthy of emulation."[4]

These statements obviously are based on an assumption that children can understand the depictions of the lives of adults given in biographies. There seems little doubt to many commentators on children's literature that such comprehension takes place, even with children who are relatively young. One notable reviewer tells of a biography written for children seven to nine years old, in which she attests, "Fiorello La Guardia's blazing integrity and charm come

---

*Reprinted by permission from the April 1973 issue of Top of the News, pages 210-217.
†This kind of biography is meant whenever the term is used.

across," even though the book is "blandly done." Furthermore, "the book gives balanced attention to all the periods of La Guardia's life."[5]

There is increasing evidence to question such suppositions, however. The time is ripe, therefore, to challenge the veracity, and consequently the wisdom, of these previously unexamined contentions. Quite to the reverse of what is believed about children and biography, a careful inquiry into the information about this relationship reveals that biography has little chance of exerting the extraordinary moral or psychological influences on children credited to it. This inquiry questions whether true biography can be written for children. This study leads, indeed, in the opposite direction, to the question of what extent, if any, children can identify with adult figures in biographies, or understand the adult lives these books depict.

The conclusion that the common statements made about biography and children are often wrong, stems from several sources. First, it is important to remember that the bibliotherapy or identification (or whatever other psychological jargon that is used) supposedly takes place with good books of a relatively meager number. The judgments of one critic of children's literature indicates that only about one percent of the "good books for children" in the years 1950-1965 can be identified as biographies appropriate for children in grades one through six.[6] Similar data is available from the Children's Catalog. During these same fifteen years only about 3 percent of the superior books listed here were biographies readable by children of elementary school ages.[7] While it appears impossible to determine if a discrepancy exists between the percent of biographies published over these years for children and the percent that wind up on lists of good books, we would suspect (for the reasons to follow) that this also may be so. But it cannot be said, for sure, that this percentage gap is larger for biography than for children's books in general, however, since the figures on this are not available. In any case, if we are to believe those who claim that biography serves so well as psychological and moral therapy for children, they then must concede that this is largely done with mediocre or bad biography, since a relatively small total of good biographies are written.

Second, and as easily demonstrable a fact as the relatively small number of good biographies available, is the evidence that children cannot read biography, good or bad, in the ways that would be necessary if they were to "identify" with the adult figures of these books. The research evidence does not support the notion that children in such reading can take the roles of adults. Piaget, for example, found that before he is seven or eight the child thinks in egocentric ways.[8] That is, he has little notion of viewpoints different from his own--which, of course, he would need to have to "identify" with adults in biography. During the remainder of his elementary school years the child develops equality (cooperative, reciprocal) relationships with children of his age which allow him to interchange his viewpoint with his peers. It is not until adolescence, however, when the now young adult becomes eager to join the adult society as an active and equal partner, that adult roles are assumed and adult viewpoints are examined and tried out.

So, it is wrong to believe that elementary school children can exchange their points of view, needs, abilities, intelligence, intentions, purposes, traits, knowledges, experience, opinions, beliefs, etc., for those of adults. There is no present evidence, either, that a child by reading a biography can somehow develop the emotional, perceptual, and intellectual capacities that are used by one adult to empathize with the role of another adult. Specialists in child development warn us on this matter that "almost no one has set about trying to find out in a scientific manner what is the relationship between society, the family, child needs and the idols [from life and books] they set up and adore."[9] We know little, it is plain, as to whether, and/or how, a child could actively search out and identify the special differences between his own perspective and that of an adult figure, an introspection that would be required for him to identify with a biographical adult. As the keenest researcher into this matter has concluded, "Almost nothing is yet known about the early genesis of role-taking skills."[10]

There is still further evidence counter to the argument that children can identify with adult biographical figures. We can point to the conclusive findings that less than one-third of sixth-graders have a "reasonably accurate understanding" of the roles adults play as politicians.[11] These so-called "political primitives" also badly overestimate their fathers' roles in social activities, and have unrealistic conceptions of adult work in general.[12,13] It appears that children who later in life attained distinguished careers were much the same as any children. Very few of these "great men" recollect that they were influenced in their choice of career by a childhood identification with any adult member of their chosen field.[14]

A third reason biography more than likely cannot serve the psychological and moral functions attributed to it has to do with the proscriptions and traditions that are placed on this form of writing. It is an error to assume that biographical characterizations in children's books are true to life. A combination of influential taboos or prohibitions restrict the biographer for children from writing a scrupulously faithful, or truthful, account of his great man's life. He cannot deal with the infamous nature of his subject, nor with his misdeeds. He cannot consider, then, the whole man in the total of his various moods, behaviors, eccentricities, achievements, and weaknesses. For his book to be acceptable this biographer must perpetuate the American myth that our political, social, military, intellectual, creative, financial, and industrial leaders keep in view only the best interests of mankind as the guide to their behavior.

Children's biography is overrun with these conservative, establishment versions of the behavior of "great" men. An example of this is Daniel Boone, by James Daugherty.[15] The theme of Daugherty's biography is how Boone's "whole life and the blood of his sons had been spent opening up a promised land of untold wealth--for others." Boone's personality, as Daugherty's highly-politicized account describes it, is a symbol of the Manifest Destiny of "God's chosen people." Boone, in Daugherty's hands, becomes the metaphor for the nerve, strength, audacity, and relentlessness of those who thought it their divine right to displace the Indian from his lands.

But now we know of the damning case that can be made against the national belief that white men were ordained to rule this continent. Our present knowledge of the greed, perfidy, and malice of the white Americans against the Indians, as documented by such books as Dee Brown's Bury My Heart at Wounded Knee, causes one to read Daniel Boone as a consummate piece of irony.[16] For the sophisticated reader of Daniel Boone it is the Indians, protecting their lands and livelihoods by the only means they knew of, who become the heroes. Boone, and the settlers, by whom he was commissioned to kill Indians, become the villains. These conquerors were insatiable and avaricious in their desires for land, callously destructive of nature, reprobate in their deals with the Indians, and offensively abusive toward the Indian culture.

But to the child Daugherty tells a different story. This is that the Indians had no right to contest the settlers' advances. By fighting back the Indians became nothing but "raiders," a dreaded scourge of murderous, violent, terrorist "red varmints." "A doomed race," the Indians were best dealt with, according to Daugherty, when the settlers set to "burning their towns and destroying whole tribes," shooting them "like dogs."

As distressing as such writings should be, one must hurry to say that the reform of biographies like Daniel Boone, and the myriad of others like it, will be long in coming. If our history (including that of the Vietnam War) tells us anything, it says that Americans in power are loath, indeed, to admit their past mistakes. Under the influence of this continual and prevailing attitude from on high, it is hardly likely that publishers will risk setting forth biographies that bluntly reveal the errors of past generations. Thus, if children could identify with adults in biographies it would often be with surrealistic figures, rather than true supermen.

In all this we see the great reliance biographers for children have on the modes of what can be called "historical biography."[17] This perception of biography results, as illustrated, in the apologies made for a compromised social consciousness and the false sanctimony of Manifest Destiny. This "historical biography" also demands that the biography revert primarily to a commemorative purpose or hero worship, with ethical instruction its sought-after consequence. The biographers for children may cling to this predated notion of biography as laudatory portraiture for reasons out of their control, as has been suggested. In any event, it causes them to cautiously ignore the inner drives and motives of their subjects as they depend almost wholly on their trappings and the external appearances of the great man's honors, offices, and achievements. By this avoidance, however, the modern biographer for children is denied the use of much of the wit, innuendo, psychological interpretations, and epigrammatic flair that exemplifies twentieth-century biographers such as Strachey, men who defied the tenets of historical biography. Instead of the sprightly picture of the great man as a peculiar human given by Strachey and his twentieth-century followers, the writings of biographers for children mirror Victorian pomposity and restraints in their depictions.

A *final* reason to question the authenticity of the claims *made* for the effects of biography on children concerns the unfortunate manner in which this form of writing is often done. One social studies expert says that if biographies are "vivid and arresting" that "children quickly develop a strong identification ... with the heroic figures about whom the stories are written...."[18] While one could more properly insist that the reverse obtains, that is, *if* a child can identify with a truly heroic adult figure in a biography, *then* the book *may* become vivid and arresting, this does cause us to recall the shortage of biography of such "arresting" literary quality.

The reasons for this shortage are partly the manner in which these books come to be, the methods that many biographers use in their production. Many biographers for children can be said to belong to the "rewrite" school of production. These are the authors who cut-up-and-paste-back a previously written biography for adults. These writers go to an acceptable full-length, adult account of a great man's life and rewrite it into a brief narrative, and what now is hoped will be a narrative understandable by children. However, "the rewrite biographer does not make a committed search for truth and new information. His job is merely to simplify, often disastrously, the style of the original to make it suitable for children. Instead of a skillful recombining of prior elements, the rewrite biographer chooses a few characteristic incidents in the subject's life and combines them chronologically, losing whatever sense of continuity and transition the original work contained."[19] It can hardly be argued that mannerisms of writing, as this, can lead to vivid and arresting biography.

The careful reader of biographies written about the same person for both adults and children often is struck, when reading the child's version, with the oppressive feeling that he somewhere has read it all before. He soon learns this is not an illusion or déjà vu, but réchauffé in the form of a wholesale lifting of phraseology from the biography for adults by the rewrite biographer. For example, in *Nickels and Dimes*, Nina Baker "borrows" all of her events, chronology, and conclusions about Woolworth from *Five and Ten* by John Winkler.[20, 21] She also audaciously "borrows" his wording, barely changing it at times before fitting it into her book:

Winkler	Baker
... on his customary buying trip to New York, he went to Spelman Brothers and ordered a hundred dollars worth of five-cent goods. (p. 38)	On his summer buying trip to New York, he ordered a hundred dollars' worth of five-cent articles. (p. 67)
These included steel pens, crocheting needles, buttonhooks, watch keys, combs, book straps, safety pins, collar buttons, pencils, baby bibs, tin pans, wash-basins and dippers, turkey-red napkins, thimbles, soap, stationery, harmonicas. (p. 38-39)	There were pen points, pencils, safety pins, buttonhooks, collar buttons, tin washpans and dippers, writing tablets and some turkey-red napkins. (p. 68)
"Do you drink? Do you smoke? What do you do that's bad?" The country boy replied that he didn't drink or smoke and that he wasn't conscious of doing anything that was very bad. (p. 25)	"Do you drink? Do you smoke? What do you do that's bad?" "I don't drink, sir," Frank answered bashfully. "And I don't smoke. I go to the Methodist church every Sunday with my folks." (p. 40)

So, apparently when all it takes to write an acceptable biography for children is a scissors, a paste pot, and a flair for rhetoric (at least at the journalistic level), little wonder that even the staunchest supporters of the supposed bounties of biography become worried. As one such advocate is forced to admit, "The multiplicity of biographies is so overwhelming that one suspects they cannot all be excellent. Some may even be slipping back into the old stereotypes."[22] It is doubtless right that the numbers of biographies exceed their merit. There is much reason to assume, as well, however, that few biographies have never advanced to the upper level of literary distinction implied in this remark.

The pressures on writers inherent in the historical mode of biography, pressures to politicize their reader to worship the biographical figure, are much in evidence. The acceptance of this mode of writing also affects the quality of biography in other ways. It means the writer becomes preoccupied with trivial, external circumstances of his subject at the expense of providing his readers with a depiction of the essential nature or spirit of his subject. This often feverish depiction of the small and meaningless details of ordinary life is the antithesis of art, of course. It rules out any chance the writer has of writing a biography of literary merit.

Then, there is the biographer who feels he must use the historical approach or tries to cover his subject's life from cradle to tomb. In the rewrite versions of biography, which usually are highly truncated, this practice reminds one of an attempt to measure the depth of a pond by skipping a flat stone across its surface. For example, in Benjamin Franklin by Enid Meadowcroft, the author jumps across the tops of the icebergs of Franklin's life, with each succeeding leap leaving her reader less sure of his footing.[23] In her rush to get Franklin from his childhood to his deathbed in 184 large-print pages, Meadowcroft must strew her book with highly potent, yet unexplained phrases such as, "Franklin had been appointed to take complete charge of all American affairs in France," "Would the Penns permit the Pennsylvanians to make their own laws as William Penn had promised they should?" This inevitably causes her text to run far ahead of the typical child's comprehension of it, while making for literature of a very dubious quality.

In summary, the evidence presently available suggests that the badness of biography may very well outweigh any bounty to be gained from it. Why, then, the widespread acceptance of such books as literature for children by teachers and librarians? (One must not blame the children or the publishers. They read, or produce, what is available or what is asked for.)

The explanation for this apparently lies in the fallacy of the self-fulfilling prophesy, a self-deception, but one, nonetheless, shown of late to have a power over our minds we might not otherwise have imagined.[24] Under the "spell" of this phenomenon teachers and librarians who deeply and sincerely believe that some particular result will occur as children read biographies begin to actually see this happen. Thus, they testify they observe children become more ethical and more psychologically stable after reading biographies, just as they believed would be the case. Then, using this "evidence" as proof of their assumptions they restart the cycle, offering more biographies to children and encouraging them to read them--for the results they think this will accomplish (and later behold to occur).

The argument presented in this discussion obviously is aimed at breaking into this chain of events, to stop it by illuminating this shadowy thinking about children and biographies on which it rests. If this argument is successful two highly desirable goals may come within our reach: one, a diminution in the demand on publishers for biographies, and two, a reformation in the manner in which such books are written.

The alternative to the confrontation we have offered is to pretend that this problem (or biography, itself, for that matter) does not exist. One writer in children's literature would apparently have us do this (in the hope that biography will waste away if so ignored?).[25] Considering the strength of the convictions of those who trust biography to favorably affect the child's ethics and his psychological state of being, however, this simplistic maneuver is unlikely to achieve its desired objectives. The entrenched ideals about biography must be aggressively challenged if they are to be bent to the will of objective information.

REFERENCES

1. May Hill Arbuthnot. Children and Books. Glenview, Ill.: Scott Foresman, 1964; 553.
2. Charlotte S. Huck and Doris Y. Kuhn. Children's Literature in the Elementary School. New York: Holt, Rinehart and Winston, 1968; 247.
3. Constantine Georgiou. Children and Their Literature. Englewood Cliffs, N.J.: Prentice-Hall, 1969; 418.
4. Malcolm P. Douglass. Social Studies. Philadelphia: J. B. Lippincott, 1967; 288.
5. Zena Sutherland. "Children's Books for Spring." Saturday Review, 55 (May 20, 1972), 80-83.
6. Mary K. Eakin, ed. Good Books for Children. Chicago: University of Chicago Press, 1966.
7. Children's Catalog. New York: H. W. Wilson, 1956 (9th ed.), 1961 (10th), and 1966 (11th).
8. Jean Piaget and B. Inhelder. The Psychology of the Child. New York: Basic Books, 1969.
9. James H. Bossard and Eleanor S. Boll. Sociology of Child Development. New York: Harper and Row, 1966; 466.

10. John H. Flavell. The Development of Role-Taking and Communication Skills in Children. New York: John Wiley, 1968; 30.
11. Fred Greenstein. Children and Politics. New Haven: Yale University Press, 1965.
12. David Eason and Jack Dennis. "The Child's Image of Government." Annals of the American Academy of Political and Social Sciences, 361 (Sept. 1965), 43-57.
13. Phyllis M. Freeston. Children's Conceptions of Adult Life. Unpublished master's thesis, Univ. of London, 1945.
14. R. S. Illingworth and C. M. Illingworth. Lessons from Childhood. Baltimore: Williams and Wilkins, 1966.
15. James Daugherty. Daniel Boone. New York: Viking, 1939.
16. Dee Brown. Bury My Heart at Wounded Knee. New York: Holt, Rinehart and Winston, 1971.
17. William Anderson and Patrick Groff. A New Look at Children's Literature. Belmont, Calif.: Wadsworth, 1972; chapter 7.
18. Douglass, Social Studies, 396-7.
19. Anderson and Groff, A New Look, 192.
20. Nina Brown Baker. Nickels and Dimes. New York: Harcourt, Brace and World, 1954 (Voyager Book).
21. John K. Winkler. Five and Ten. New York: Doubleday, 1951.
22. Arbuthnot, Children, 518.
23. Enid LaMonte Meadowcroft. Benjamin Franklin. New York: Thomas Y. Crowell, 1941 (Scholastic Book Services ed.).
24. Robert Rosenthal. Pygmalion in the Classroom. New York: Holt, Rinehart and Winston, 1968.
25. James Steel Smith. A Critical Approach to Children's Literature. New York: McGraw-Hill, 1967.

BLACK ENGLISH: THE POLITICS OF TRANSLATION

June Jordan

We are in a political situation in America where, on the one hand, there are the powerful who control and, on the other hand, there are the powerless who pay the consequences. In America, we are knuckling under to the rapid loss of freedom of speech, freedom of the press. Too many people in this country deliberately seek to enforce a homogenized, complacent, barbarous society where standard means right, where right means White. Therefore, nonstandard means substandard, and means wrong, and means dangerous, and will be punished, even unto the death of the spirit.

We are talking about power; and poetry and books--history books, novels, what-have-you--none of these can win against the schools, the teachers, the media, the fearful parents, and the elite of this country, unless we understand the power of these politics.

In America, the politics of language has become obvious around the globe: it is American power that invented and imposed upon our minds the Vietnam vocabulary of "making peace by making war," of murdering people and calling that "pacification," of "advisory personnel," "protective reaction," and even the 1972 Twelve Days of Christmas "carpet bombing." There is an obscenely long list of the lies and the euphemisms that have been printed and telecast in perfectly standard, grammatical, White English.

---

*Reprinted by permission from the May 15, 1973 issue of School Library Journal (pages 21-24), published by R. R. Bowker Co., a Xerox Education Company. Copyright © 1973 by June Meyer Jordan. Adapted from a speech given at Prince George's County Library and the Enoch Pratt Free Library in Baltimore, February 1973.

In America, the politics of language, the willful debasement of this human means to human communion has jeopardized the willingness of young people to believe anything they hear or read. And what is anybody going to do about it? I suggest that, for one, we join forces to cherish and protect our various, multifoliate lives against pacification, homogenization, the silence of terror, and standards that despise and disregard the sanctity of each and every human life.

The Functions of Language

We can begin by looking at language. Because it brings us together, as folks, because it makes known the unknown strangers we otherwise remain to each other, because it is the naming of experience and, thereby, a possession of experience, and because names/language make possible a social statement of connection and lead these connections into social reality--for all these reasons, and more, language is a process of translation. Language is a process of translation whereby we learn and we tell who we are, and what we want, and what we need, believe, or why we tremble, or hide, or kill, or nurture and love. This is a political process, a process taking place on the basis of who has the power to use, abuse, accept or reject the words--the lingual messages--we must attempt to transmit to each other and/or against each other.

As a poet and writer, I deeply love and I deeply hate words. I love the infinite evidence and change and requirements and possibilities of language: every human use of words that is joyful, or honest, or new because experience is new, or old because each personal history testifies to inherited pleasures and/or inherited, collective memories of peril and pain.

But as a Black poet and writer, I hate words that cancel my name and my history and the freedom of my future. I hate the words that condemn and refuse the language of my people in America: I am talking about a language deriving from the Niger-Congo family of languages. I am talking about a language that joins with the Russian, Hungarian, and Arabic languages, among others, in eliminating the "present copula"--a verb interjected between subject and predicate. Or, to break that down a bit, I am talking about a language that will tell you simply, "They Mine." (And, incidentally, if I tell you, "they mine," you don't have no kind of trouble understanding exactly what I mean, do you?)

    As a Black poet and writer, I am proud of our Black verbally bonding system born of our struggle to avoid annihilation--as Afro-American self, community, and culture. I am proud of this language that our continuing battle just to be has brought into currency. And so I hate the arrogant, prevailing rejection of this, our Afro-American language. And so I work, as poet and writer, against the eradication of this system, this language, this carrier of Black-survivor consciousness.

The Politics of Black English

    The subject of "Black English" cannot intelligently separate from the subject of language as translation and translation as a political process distinguishing between the powerless and the powerful in no uncertain terms. Here are a few facts to illustrate my meaning:

    (1) Apparently, "Black English" needs defense even though it is demonstrably a language: a perfectly adequate, verbal means of communication that can be understood by any but the most outrightly standard racist.

    (2) On the other hand, where is the defense, who among the standard, grammatical, White English mainstreamers feels the need, even, to defend his imposition of his language on me and my children?

    (3) Thou know'st the mask of night is on my
        face
Else would a maiden blush bepaint my
    cheek
For that which thou has heard me speak
    tonight.
Fain would I dwell on form, fain, fain
    deny
what I have spoke: but farewell com-
    pliment!
Dost thou love me? I know thou wilt say
    'Ay.'
And I will take thy word; yet, if thou
    swear'st

Communication and Education

> Thou mayst prove false; at lovers' per-
> juries,
> They say, Jove laughs. [Romeo and Juliet Act II,
> Scene II]

Now that ain hardly no kind of standard English. But just about every kid forced into school has to grapple with that particular rap. Why? Because the powers that control the language that controls the process of translation have decided that Romeo and Juliet is necessary, nay, indispensable, to passage through compulsory, public school education.

> (4) You be different from the dead. All them tombstones tearing up the ground, look like a little city, like a small Manhattan, not exactly. Here is not the same.
> Here, you be bigger than the buildings, bigger than the little city. You be really different from the rest, the resting other ones.
> Moved in his arms, she make him feel like smiling.
> Him, his head an Afro-bush spread free beside the stones, headstones thinning in the heavy air. Him, a ready father, public lover, privately at last alone with her, with Angela, a half an hour walk from the hallway where they start out to hold themselves together in the noisy darkness, kissing, kissed him, kissed her, kissing.
> Cemetery let them lie there belly close, their shoulders now undressed down to the color of the heat they feel, in lying close, their legs a strong disturbing of the dust. His own where, own place for loving made for making love, the cemetery where nobody guard the dead. [His Own Where, first page]

Now that ain no standard English, either. Both excerpts come from love stories about White and Black teenagers, respectively. But the Elizabethan, nonstandard English of Romeo and Juliet has been adjudged as something students should take and absorb. By contrast, Black, nonstandard language has been adjudged as sub-standard and even injurious to young readers.

I submit that these judgments are strictly political and that they should be recognized as political and resisted, accordingly. But language and the politics of translation affect more than the censorship of literature: we are talking about power, and about the perpetuation of power.

White Power

In the compulsory public school situation, demonstration of such power is a daily event: Black and White children enter the so-called educational system. Once inside, the White child is rewarded for his mastery of his standard, White English--the language he learned at his mother's White and standard knee. But the Black child is punished for his mastery of his nonstandard, Black English. Moreover, the White child receives formal instruction in his standard English, and endless opportunities for the exercise and creative display of his language. But where is the elementary school course in Afro-American language, and where are the opportunities for the accredited exercise, and creative exploration, of Black language?

The two languages are not interchangeable. They cannot, nor do they attempt to communicate equal or identical thoughts, or feelings. And, since the experience to be conveyed is quite different, Black from White, these lingual dissimilarities should not surprise or worry anyone.

However, they are both communication systems with regularities, exceptions, and values governing their word designs. Both are equally liable to poor, good, better, and creative use. In short, they are both accessible to critical criteria such as clarity, force, message, tone, and imagination. Besides this, standard English is comprehensible to Black children, even as Black English is comprehensible to White teachers--supposing that the teachers are willing to make half the effort they demand of Black students.

Then what is the difficulty? The problem is that we are saying language, but really dealing with power. The word "standard" is just not the same as the word "technical" or "rural" or "straight." Standard means the rule, the norm. Anyone deviating from the standard is therefore "wrong." As a result, literally millions of Black children are "wrong" from the moment they begin to absorb and imitate the language of their Black lives. Is that an acceptable idea?

As things stand, consequences of childhood fluency in

Afro-American language are lamentably predictable; reading problems that worsen, course failure in diverse subjects dependent on reading skills, and a thoroughly wounded self-esteem. Afterwards, an abject school career is eclipsed by an abject life career. "Failing" English (Standard English) merely presages a "failure" of adult life. This, I submit, is a deliberate, political display of power to destroy the powerless.

Solutions

This punishment of Black children will continue until the legitimacy of Black language is fully acknowledged by all of us, Black and White. That will mean offering standard English as simply The Second Language. It will mean calling standard English studies "Second Language Studies" wherever that description accurately applies.

A sincere recognition of Black language as legitimate will mean formal instruction and encouragement in its use within the regular curriculum. It will mean the respectful approaching of Black children, in the language of Black children. It will mean an end to illegitimate, political use of language studies against Black life.

It is true that we need to acquire competence in the language of the powerful: Black children in America must acquire competence in standard English, if only for the sake of self-preservation. But I do not understand how anyone supposes that you will teach a child a new language by scorning and ridiculing and forcibly erasing his old, first language: all of his names for all the people and events of his Black life prior to his entry into school.

I am one among a growing number of Black poets and writers dedicated to the preservation of Black language within our lives, and dedicated to the health of our children as they prepare themselves for life within this standard, White America which has despised even our speech and our prayers and our love. As long as we shall survive Black, in this White America, we and our children require and deserve the power of Black language, Black history, Black literature, as well as the power of standard English, standard history, and standard, White literature.

To the extent that Black survival fails on these terms,

it will be a political failure; it will be the result of our not recognizing and not revolting against the political uses of language to extinguish the people we want to be and the people we have been. Politics is power. Language is political. And language, its reward, currency, punishment and/or eradication--is political in its meaning and in its consequence.

Recently, a White woman telephoned to ask me to appear on her television program; she felt free to tell me that if I sounded "Black" then she would not "hire" me; language is power. That woman is powerful if she feels free to reject and strangle whoever will not mimic her--in language, values, goals. In fact, I answered her in this way: "You are a typical racist." And that is the political truth of the matter, as I see it, as I hope you will begin to see it; for no one has the right to control and sentence to poverty anyone--because he or she is different and proud and honest in his or her difference and his or her pride.

There is a need to understand Black language, per se: a young friend of mine went through some scarifying times, leaving her homeless. During this period of intense, relentless dread and abuse, she wrote poems, trying to cope. Here are two lines from her poetry: "What have life meanted to me" and, "You are forgotten you use to existed."

There is no adequate, standard English translation possible for either expression of her spirit because they are intrinsically Black language cries of extreme pain so telling that even the possibilities of meaning and existence have been formulated in a past tense that is emphatic, severe.

I deeply hope that more of us will want to learn and protect Black language. If we lose our fluency in our language, we may irreversibly forsake elements of the spirit that have provided for our survival. Black language is not A Mistake, or A Verbal Deficiency. It is a system subsuming dialect/regional variations that leaves intact, nevertheless, a language that is invariable in fundamental respects. For example:

    (A) Black language practices minimal inflection of verb forms (e.g., I go, we go, he go; and I be, you be, we be, etc.). This is nonstandard and, also, an obviously more logical use of verbs. It is also evidence of a value system that considers the person/subject--the actor--more important than the act.

(B) Consistency of syntax: for example, in Black English/Black language, the imperative case, the interrogative case, and the simple declarative case all occur within the same structural pattern (e.g., You going to the store). Depending on tone, that is a statement of mere fact, or a command, or a question.

(C) Infrequent, irregular use of the possessive case. Therefore, in Black language, you say, "they house" at least as often as you might say, "their house."

(D) Clear, logical use of multiple negatives within a single sentence, to express an unmistakably negative idea (e.g., You ain gone bother me in no way at no time no more, you hear?).

(E) Other logical consistencies, such as: ours, his, theirs, and, therefore, mines.

Black language is a political fact suffering from political persecution. Black language and Black literature are political facts persecuted by the same powerful political people in this country who feel bold to say, in perfectly standard, grammatical, White English: "...let each of us ask not just what will government do for me but what I can do for myself."

(Of course that declaration is quite entirely at odds with another, perfectly standard, American concept: "...government of the people, by the people, and for the people.") As the President has since made plain, his standard English exhortation to self-help means the deadly reduction of government aid to every program against poverty, poor housing, inadequate education, and poor health.

This is a time when those of us who believe in people, first, must become political, in every way possible; we must devise and pursue every means possible for survival as the people we are, as the people we want to become. For Afro-Americans, this certainly means that we must succeed in the preservation of our language. Let us cherish its long service to us, as a people.

Let us halt the mutilation of abilities to manage the world through language. Let us cease the destruction of one language for the sake of another. Let us present standard English as merely a second language, whenever that is the case. And let us undertake these goals with full awareness that the stakes are truly the political stakes of the power to kill or the power to survive.

And, as for the children: let us welcome and applaud and promote the words they bring into our reality; in the struggle to reach each other, there can be no right or wrong words for our longing and our needs; there can only be the names that we trust and we try.

RECOMMENDED READING

Goodman, Kenneth. "Up-Tight Ain't Right!" SLJ, October 1972.
Labov, William. "Academic Ignorance and Black Intelligence." Atlantic Magazine, 1972.

MODERN TRENDS IN BOOK-COLLECTING*

Anthony Rota

As we look back over the world of rare books in the last ten or twenty years there are two great movements that stand out above all others, and every tendency and trend in book-collecting and book-selling is necessarily subservient to them. The first is the enormous growth in the volume of institutional buying. The second is the huge rise in prices. It can be argued that the second follows naturally on the first.

The so-called "learning explosion" has meant a vast increase in the spread and intensity of higher education, not least in the English-speaking world. In North America colleges have sprung up like mushrooms, and yesterday's colleges have become today's universities. For example there are now twelve universities on sixteen campuses in the Province of Ontario alone. With university status came a large library budget, providing the means of procuring, to go with the need for, a library of rare books.

Library buying on a substantial scale there has always been, but what we began to be faced with ten years ago was a complete reversal of the ratio in which the bookseller's sales to collectors and libraries used to be made. You will not need me to tell you that the chief significance of this is that a very large proportion of the rare books which have been sold in the last two decades have gone out of circulation forever: they have crossed that bourne from which no traveller returns. Thus, as we shall see in a

---

*Reprinted by permission from the Autumn 1972 issue of The Private Library, pages 148-158. This revision of an earlier address, to the Oxford University Society of Bibliophiles in 1970 that was printed subsequently in Antiquarian Bookman, was given to the Private Libraries Association general meeting, London, May 16, 1972.

moment, even the millionaire collector is faced with a situation in which avenues that were open to his father--and his father before him--are now firmly closed. Blank cheque or not, there are books which simply cannot be bought any more. This is not the time or place to debate whether this is a state of affairs without a single redeeming feature, but there is more than one side to the argument.

I spoke just now of libraries in North America and I want to stress that I did not intend North America as a loose synonym for the United States. I wanted most particularly to include Canada, for at last, in the past ten years, the Canadian libraries (with the active help of the Federal government--Lord Eccles please note) have begun to move forward. Two of their more spectacular advances have been in the acquisition of the Bertrand Russell archive at McMaster University and the purchase by University of British Columbia of the nineteenth century poetry collection formed by Norman Colbeck. The story of how Dr. Fredeman succeeded in buying not only that magnificent collection but also the services of its progenitor, that great and gifted bookseller Norman Colbeck himself, is in itself a fascinating one.

On a less spectacular scale the Manchester poet, Robin Skelton, who himself formed a respectable collection of William Butler Yeats, has persuaded the University of Victoria, where he now teaches English, of the merits of buying contemporary literary manuscripts. Victoria has made an enterprising beginning in this direction and with one or two others demonstrated that the University of Texas could not expect to have this field to itself for ever.

New antiquarian bookselling businesses, if you will forgive the paradox, are flourishing in Canada. Indeed two years ago the antiquarian booksellers there found it desirable and appropriate to form their first trade association. Both Sotheby's and Christie's have opened offices in Montreal and book sales are regularly conducted there. After a long slumber then, Canada has roused itself and is seeking to enrich its national and academic libraries. Where, one wonders, will the next great surge of institutional buying come from? Australia?

Institutional buying, from whatever quarter, has removed many rare books from the market. Institutional money has also been one of the factors leading to the inexorable and dramatic upward movement of prices. Let us look for a moment at precisely what has happened to the price of five famous books. I want to begin with the first edition of James Joyce's Ulysses, surely the one unassailable classic of the twentieth century. Ten years ago it was still possible to buy copies for £35. Today £350, ten times as much, is not an unreasonable price at all. A copy in really superlative condition in the original wrappers has brought as much as £700 at auction. More than that, one of the 100 copies signed by the author was recently sold in London for £2000.

A book which has always been a good indicator of the state of the book trade is the subscribers' edition of T. E. Lawrence's Seven Pillars of Wisdom, 1926. Ten years ago a copy might have cost £350. Today's price is closer to £2000, more than a five-fold increase. One of the most spectacular cases is that of Audubon's Birds of America. In 1966, a copy was sold at auction for some £21,000. The latest price at Sotheby's, admittedly for a spectacular copy, sold in 1969, was no less than £90,000--a four-fold appreciation in three years.

A book which I personally regard as the finest of all twentieth century illustrated books is the Golden Cockerel Press edition of The Four Gospels, where Eric Gill's wood-engravings are so splendidly married to the text. When I first joined my father's business in 1952, an early task was to write to a customer in Ohio who wanted to buy a Four Gospels for £30. I had to explain to him that the going price was £35. No, he said, that was too much; he wouldn't pay it. A year later he wrote relenting. Yes, £35 would be in order. I had to tell him that the book was then commanding £40. By the time he'd come round to the £40 figure, the book had moved up to £50. The same man missed the book at £75, at £100, at £150.... In fact to cut a long story short, this is today easily a £350 book and my man in Ohio is still struggling to reconcile himself to the current value.

My last example is again a private press book, this time the Kelmscott Press Chaucer, a monumental book in more ways than one and a book which has had a tremendous influence on standards of book design and production. It, too, is widely regarded as an indicator of book-trade health. I suppose that ten years ago £350 would not have been thought other than the right price. Just five weeks ago I sold a copy for £2000, a multiplication by 6 in the course of ten years.

Are these rises necessarily bad? They are in part
a correction following a long period in which books and
manuscripts were very seriously undervalued. Some readjustment was overdue. Then, too, today's prices are more
firmly based than those of the boom of 1929 and I for one
do not fear that the catastrophic slump in book prices which
obtained in the early 1930's will come again. In 1929 speculators, not collectors, were "investing"--their word, not
mine--in books whose scarcity was open to question. When
things went wrong with the economy and too many "investors"
tried to "unload" at once something had to give, and the
rare book market took almost two decades to recover! Today's high prices result from a genuine and growing rarity
factor. I cannot envisage a situation in which Yale's R. L.
Stevenson holdings, Texas's T. J. Wise collection or the
treasures of Indiana's Lilly Library will ever come flooding
on to the market.

The world's stock of rare books can be divided into
two classes: those in rare book collections, and those rarities which have not yet been discovered. High prices can
promote the process of discovery. Let me show you what I
mean. In 1962, for the first time in twelve years, W. B.
Years' rare first book, Mosada, turned up at auction. It
brought £820, four times what the experts had expected.
The high price attracted wide publicity and within twelve
months two more copies were brought on to the market.
This picture has been repeated scores of times with other
equally rare books.

I must be forgiven for what will seem like special
pleading when I say that one benefit of high prices has been
the bringing of greater prosperity to the book trade. A
more prosperous book trade is a more efficient book trade,
which can attract more able recruits capable of identifying
and tracking down the sorts of books which you as collectors
want to see on our shelves and in our catalogues. This is
a hobbyhorse that I could ride all night--but you might accuse me of straying from my subject and speaking about
"Modern Trends in Book-Selling" rather than "Modern
Trends in Book-Collecting."

The shrinking pool of rare books remaining outside
institutional libraries, and the higher prices that established
rarities command, have perforce driven collectors to seek
new fields. In the time that remains I should like to look
with you at some of those fields.

Mr. John Carter in his Presidential Address to the
Bibliographical Society in 1970 spoke of the greater emphasis
that was placed nowadays on the products of men's minds as
opposed to the products of their imaginations. His theme
was exemplified in the great Earl's Court exhibition <u>Printing
and the Mind of Man</u> in 1963. In that exhibition we saw in
their first edition an array of some four hundred and fifty
books which had made a significant impact on man's thinking
and ideas. These books ranged widely indeed. There is no
time now to do more than name a very few of them. What
I want to emphasize is their wide variety. There was
<u>Scouting for Boys</u>. There was <u>Das Kapital</u>. There was
Madam Curie's <u>On the Discovery of Radium</u>. There was
Harvey's <u>De Motu Cordis</u>, Ohm on the measurement of electricity and so on and so on. The original editions of most
of the books I have cited are rare and nearly all of them
are expensive. Interest in them continues to grow because
they are milestones in man's progress.

In line with the advancement of the cause of these
"high spots" humbler books move forward. Already there
are enterprising booksellers who have begun to seek out and
to offer to the discerning, books in what might loosely be
called the field of Industrial Archaeology: books about textile technology, about electric lighting, gas distribution and
fire protection, and about the early days of broadcasting.
The exciting thing is that these books are finding a new
market. Many of them are going, still at extremely modest
prices, to form the nucleus of new collections here in this
country, collections which are the property of graduates of
some of our newer universities, and not just the redbrick
ones, but those built of reinforced concrete. One of the
booksellers who is a pioneer in this field, William Duck of
Hastings, recently published a catalogue on water engineering and sanitation. I understand that he called it <u>Input and
Output</u>!

The merits of the first book printed from moveable
type have long been obvious to all. The advantages of owning the first book with illustrations have also been apparent
for a very long time. The significance of the first book
printed from type set not by hand, but by composing machine, has perhaps come home to us more recently. The
machine was Young and Deleambre's. The book was Edward
Binn's <u>Anatomy of Sleep</u>, 1842.

It is probably fair to say that the last twenty years

have seen greater and more far-reaching changes in the
printing industry than occurred in the previous five centuries.
Thus it is hardly surprising to find serious collecting attention being paid to milestones in the advance of technical
progress. There is a ready market now for: the first book
to be set on a linotype machine--The Tribune Book of Open
Air Sports in 1886; the first commercially published book
illustrated with photographs--Fox Talbot's Pencil of Nature,
1844. From there it is a comparatively short cry to the
first books produced by film-setting devices, that is processes dispensing entirely with the use of metal type at any
stage of production. Experimental work was progressing in
several countries using several different systems, but the
first book to be printed in the United Kingdom by film-setting
techniques was the edition of Eric Linklater's Private Angelo
which Sir Allen and Richard Lane issued to their friends in
January 1958. It can still be picked up for a modest sum.

The Times Literary Supplement has now recorded
another advance, if advance it be, which foreshadows the
end of the compositor. The American edition of V. C.
Clinton-Baddeley's book Death's Bright Dart was composed
entirely by machines. The text was read directly from an
ordinary, plain, unmarked copy of the British edition by a
Mergenthaler Optical Character Recognition System which
was linked to a computer-driven cathode ray tube type-setting
system. We are entitled to our own views on the desirability of this achievement, but we can none of us doubt its importance.

Before we leave the world of technology altogether
let us glance at some developments in the field of bibliography. Bibliographies are the tools of my trade and they
constitute the apparatus with which the wise collector builds
his library. Charles Harris, erstwhile head of the famous
firm of Francis Edwards, said when he retired recently at
the end of a long career, "Life is too easy for young booksellers nowadays. Everything is written down in bibliographies. When I was a boy we had to carry points in our
heads."

Certainly all of us have many more bibliographies on
our shelves. In the field of twentieth century English literature alone many more major writers have been treated in
definitive bibliographies in the last twenty years. I think of
Belloc, Chesterton, Eliot, Pound, Henry James, Lawrence,
Yeats, Forster, Virginia Woolf, Joyce, Brooke, Sassoon

and many another.

Moreover, there have been important advances in bibliographical technique. We are closer to agreeing on standard formulae. The Soho bibliographies have set a pattern which has won wide acceptance throughout the world. Our methods of measuring and describing bindings have become more exact. In this regard we all owe a debt of gratitude to Thomas Tanselle of the University of Wisconsin, who has suggested precise methods by which we can describe colours, for example. It is not many years since one Soho bibliography listed between its covers books in nine different shades of green: light green, blue green, sage green, olive green, moss green, dark green, and so on. The colours and some of the names for them seemed more appropriate, for knitting wools than book cloth and without a definite colour standard to work to, I, as a mere male, found myself completely lost.

Thomas Tanselle has also suggested that bibliographers should take greater care in defining their standards. In giving measurements for example, they should say whether they are working to the nearest quarter of an inch, to the nearest eighth, or to the nearest sixteenth. If a less precise bibliographer than Tanselle describes a book as being 7 1/4 inches tall we cannot be sure if a copy measuring 7 5/8 inches is or is not an unrecorded variant.

Another pioneer who is going to have an enormous effect on the development of modern bibliography is Warner Barnes of the University of Texas. Whether we should be grateful to him or whether we shall come to call down curses upon him, I am not yet sure. I remember his asking me earnestly some years ago, "Do you think any modern bibliography can be valid if it is not based on a comparison of at least six copies on an Hinman collating machine?" I confess that I had previously thought of Hinman as a tool for research among Shakespeare folios rather than among modern machine-made books, but when Professor Barnes produced his bibliography of Elizabeth Barrett Browning, practising what he preached and putting through the Hinman collator as many copies as possible of each title, he turned up such a profusion of variants as to lend considerable force to his argument. What he has chosen to call the "concealed editions" in Browning represent a challenge to bibliographers of the future and a nagging problem of conscience for those who thought their work was already complete.

Machine collation has recently brought to light an edition of Pendennis published fifteen years after the first but hitherto mistaken for it. Whether we like it or not, bibliography is ceasing to be an art and is rapidly becoming a science.

Now let us leave technology behind us and take a brief look at the world of creative writing. The field of late-nineteenth century fiction, the field of the three volume novel, the "three-decker," demonstrates particularly clearly how material is disappearing from circulation, thus causing prices to rise sharply. We had an interesting example of this in a sale at Sotheby's in the autumn of 1970, comprising four hundred and twenty-seven lots of Fictorian fiction in fine state. The average level of prices was high. What is significant however is that books of small literary merit by almost unknown writers were bringing prices akin to those fetched by the volumes of greater fame.

I remember when I first came in to the trade, making an arrangement with a bookseller in Lancashire under which I was to purchase all his three-decker fiction at 30/- per title. The calendar tells me that was only two decades ago, but it seems more like two centuries. At Sotheby's Victorian sale Alison by Beatrice Mary Butt fetched £32. Mrs. Chadwick's Rectitude; or, Virginia of the Wye was knocked down for £52. I wonder if anyone in this room or indeed anyone at Sotheby's would have predicted prices of this kind for such minor books even a month before.

One interesting and encouraging fact is that this particular collection was brought over from New York to be sold here in England. Of course most of the volumes concerned have probably crossed the Atlantic again by now to the benefit only of the Cunard steamship company, but certainly some of them will remain in the United Kingdom. It cannot be denied that the great flow of rare books across the Atlantic is in a westward direction, but I would like to emphasise that it is not completely a one-way traffic. I know a number of British collectors and British librarians who regularly order from American dealers' catalogues. I know too, that most British booksellers who visit the United States find themselves well able to make substantial purchases and bring back to England not only American books but English books originally exported ten, twenty and even a hundred years ago.

This would seem an appropriate point to talk about another form of trans-Atlantic traffic. In 1935 and 1936 Michael Sadleir published in his admirable Bibliographia series two volumes by the great American book scout, I. R. Brussel (who, alas, died two months ago at the age of seventy-four). They were called respectively <u>Anglo-American First Editions, East to West</u> and <u>Anglo-American First Editions, West to East</u>. For those of you who are not familiar with them I should explain that they constituted the first serious attempt to establish and codify the relative priorities of English and American editions of books which were published at roughly the same date on both sides of the Atlantic.

The sort of point Brussel made was that Thomas Hardy's <u>Far From the Madding Crowd</u> appeared in America two weeks before it was published in London, and that conversely Mark Twain's <u>Huckleberry Finn</u> was on sale in London nine days before the American edition went into the bookshops.

Brussel and his bibliographies were at the centre of the "Follow the Flag" controversy. Some said with Gertrude Stein that a first, is a first, is a first.... As first edition collectors they wanted the first appearance in book-form no matter where it was published. Perhaps they had logic on their side. Others "followed the flag" and sought only the English editions of English authors and the United States editions of American authors. If by some freak of publishing practice a book came out on the "wrong" side of the Atlantic first, then that accident shouldn't be allowed to interfere with the orderly accretion on a gentleman's shelves of, shall we say, William Heinemann's editions of Galsworthy.

Those collectors who acquired both forms, English and American, were in a distinct minority. And as for collecting transatlantic editions of books when questions of priority of issue were <u>not</u> at stake--why it was almost unheard of. How things have changed. Spurred on by the slow but steady publication of volume after volume of Blanck's <u>Bibliography of American Literature</u> and by the work of such textual scholars as James B. Meriwether and Matthew Bruccoli, librarians and collectors are at last realising the importance of assembling and comparing editions from both sides of the Atlantic.

The results of their researches--one often sees ex-

amples in Papers of the Bibliographical Society of America--
are interesting in the extreme. In a number of cases we
find that authors made corrections or even major changes
between the appearance of their work in England and its subsequent publication in America. Sometimes of course changes
were made in order to take account of the different mores in
the two countries.

Here I must confess to a personal interest in the
little-remembered publishing house of Boriswood which
flourished, if that is the word for an enterprise which never
made any money for its proprietors and eventually failed fi-
nancially, for a few years around 1930. Its authors included
Roy Campbell, Rex Warner and the highly controversial
James Hanley. Hanley's novel Boy and the moves to suppress it were largely responsible for Boriswood's failure,
and I was therefore moved to cause a comparison to be
made between the limited English edition of 1931 and the
American edition of 1932. This horrifying novel recounts
the experiences of a cabin boy on a tramp steamer who
finds himself the victim of a sadistic crew and who dies a
singularly unpleasant death. It is curious to note how examples of barrack-room, or rather fo'c's'le language were
treated on opposite sides of the Atlantic. "Bugger" was
perfectly acceptable in London but for the American edition
"sod" was substituted--on page 41 that is. At other points
in the American text no fewer than nine other synonyms
were used, either as verbs or nouns.

I could continue with other variant readings from this
unedifying text, but the presence of ladies in my audience
tonight persuades me to do to my script what the publishers
did to theirs for the English trade edition--expurgate it.

May I use this platform to attack one current mani-
festation of catering for a market? I refer to the publishing
of poster poems. You know the technique. One takes a
fashionable and hence expensive artist, persuades him or her
to make a hundred prints of an elegant design, gets a poet
to allow two quatrains, or if in generous mood, a sonnet,
to be printed on top of it. Author and artist sign each
double crown sheet--and Eureka! The result sells for 9
guineas a copy with no shortage of takers. But are they
eager takers? Are they even willing takers? My experience on the other side of the counter suggests not.

What is a book? Many people have tried their hand

Communication and Education

at a definition, with varying degrees of success. Is a poster poem a book? If it is the first separate publication of a poem by a "collected" poet, then perhaps it is. A serious collector of, say, the Poet Laureate's works feels that he must willy-nilly buy such a production from the Laureate's pen otherwise his collection will not be complete. The posters are attractive. They have a scarcity value, albeit an artificial one. Why then do I complain? It is really a matter of practicality. One poster poem looks well on the wall. The room in which I house my own library might perhaps afford hanging space for two--but the poets I collect have produced a dozen between them in the last two years alone! How do I store them? The drawer of my bookcase is not deep enough to take them flat. Rolled in a tube? What a wretched performance is involved in taking each poster out to show--or even to read! Think too of the damage to my purse. Twelve times 9 guineas would have bought a number of highly desirable books. Yes, <u>books</u>; with <u>pages</u> and <u>covers</u>; something to put on a shelf.

Pity the poor bookseller who has to stock and supply these irksome poster poems in order to oblige those of his customers who wish to make perfect and complete author-collections. Like the collector the bookseller finds the poster poems impossibly difficult to store or display--and the problems in attempting to send them by post are almost insurmountable. On top of that many buyers complain, with understandable irritability, that they feel obliged to purchase these productions when they would much prefer them not to exist. Loathing the things, the bookseller has to stand between the customer and the publisher, collecting all the kicks and precious few of the halfpence. Halfpence there are, and in plenty, for someone. Look at the economics of the thing. One drawing, one poem can yield close to a thousand pounds for its creators and the entrepreneur, with only the cost of printing one hundred single sheets at stake. The poster poem represents one trend which will, I hope, soon be on the wane.

A moment ago I invited you to pity the bookseller, but perhaps there is no real need for you to shed a tear for him since in times of change there is much that for him remains unchanging.

The bookshop is one of the last citadels of the individualist. The bookseller, more than almost any other man, has control of his own destiny. His income and his way of life reflect directly the energy and skill he puts into his work. He can choose. He can pick the kinds of books he wishes to handle. He can, if he wishes, pick his customers. He can certainly see that his best books, like his favourite puppies, go to good homes. He can ensure the preservation of rare materials that might, but for his knowledge, his keen eye and his nose for a good book, have lain undiscovered or even been sent for pulp. At the end of the day he can sit back and reflect on solid accomplishment and the part he has played in the advancement of learning.

  The bookseller is a fortunate man for he can indulge in the hobby of book-collecting vicariously. Moreover, he can do it regardless of limitations of cost and space. He is richer than Huntington and Hoe, richer than Abbey and Mellon--for by his skill and devotion in aiding and abetting the formation of great collections he makes each of them uniquely his own.

WHY WE HARDLY HAVE ANY PICTURE BOOKS IN THE CHILDREN'S DEPARTMENT ANYMORE: A Brief Fantasy*

Eva Nelson

A college student came into the children's room the other day and said she needed some books for the children's literature course she was taking. "Fine," I said. "May I help you find the books?"

She pulled out a hectographed list. "I need to read at least four Caldecott Medal books. Is <u>Drummer Hoff</u> in?" "I'm sorry," I said, "but we discarded all our copies of <u>Drummer Hoff</u> because some patrons objected to the fact that the whole book is about loading and firing a cannon. They felt it might make militarists of preschoolers."

"But," the student protested, "the prof had a copy in class and I remember that on the last page the cannon is abandoned in a field and covered with flowers." "Your memory is correct," I said, "but the part the children remember is the line repeated over and over again ... 'but Drummer Hoff fired it off.'"

"Well, then, how about Maurice Sendak's <u>Where the Wild Things Are</u>?" she asked. "Oh, the 1964 Caldecott winner," I said. "We did have several copies of that book but a grandmother came in and said she thought the wild things would frighten children. She felt it was an extremely objectionable book. We dropped it."

The girl again consulted her list. "Let's see, the 1953 winner was Lynd Ward's <u>The Biggest Bear</u>. Is that in?" "I really regret not having that one for you," I said.

---

*Reprinted by permission from the November 1972 issue of <u>Top of the News</u>, pages 54-56. The Library portrayed is not Ms. Nelson's.

"It's one of my personal favorites and in the past I often used it in preschool story hours. Then one day an animal lover objected strenuously to the biggest bear being hauled off and caged in the zoo. He feels it's wrong to confine wild animals in any fashion. So we reluctantly withdrew all our copies of the book."

"Well," the student said, a bit truculently I thought, "How about Ludwig Bemelmans' Madeline's Rescue?" "All the Madeline books were banned some years ago. It was insinuated in Time that Mr. Bemelmans had some rather nasty implications in mind when talked about 'ten little girls.'"

"Do you have the 1970 Caldecott winner? With all this controversy the recent committees must have screened the books pretty thoroughly and come up with noncontroversial selections." "Are you nuts?" I said. "We never ordered the 1970 Caldecott Medal winner at all. William Steig's prize winning illustrations had pictures of pigs wearing policemen's uniforms. As a result policemen all over the country may no longer permit their children to use public libraries!"

"How about The Snowy Day by Ezra Jack Keats? I've heard that's marvelous." "We liked it very much," I answered. "Keats made a hit with that and with his subsequent books about Peter but then only last week a mother complained to me about it, and I immediately withdrew all the books in that series."

"Was it a white mother objecting to her child reading about a black boy?" "Oh, no, no! It was nothing like that. It was because Peter's mother in the book is rather large and comfortable looking. This mother felt that mothers should be represented in children's books as being small, neat, and trim. Rather an odd case," I trailed off uncertainly.

She frowned a minute and then said, "I do have some picture books listed here that aren't Caldecott Medal winners. Perhaps I'll read some of those. I member liking Lois Lenski's books myself. How about Papa Small?"

I turned pale. "Nothing could make us have Papa Small on the picture book shelves anymore. Let me quote from memory: 'Papa Small has a family. There is Mama

Communication and Education

Small and Baby Small. There are the small Smalls, Paul and Polly.' Count the Smalls! Three of them! With the Zero Population Group this town has it would be worth my job to let the little impressionable two and three year olds take that book home!"

She took a step backwards--probably at my vehemence--but again looked gamely at her list. "How about <u>A Visit from St. Nicholas</u> illustrated by Paul Galdone?" "We used to have a lot of copies of that one--the poem <u>The Night Before Christmas</u> I mean--illustrated by a variety of outstanding artists, but we haven't replaced them as they've worn out and the last copy fell apart the Christmas before last. You would be surprised at the number of parents who are extremely opposed to the association of Santa Claus with Christmas. So I'm not replacing it again no matter who might illustrate it."

"I know one picture book you'll have," she challenged me, "It's not on my list but maybe it would be an acceptable substitute." "What is it?" I asked suspiciously. "<u>The Tale of Peter Rabbit</u> by Beatrix Potter," she crowed triumphantly.

"Wrong!" I said. "It was a standard item on picture book shelves before Dr. Spock's famous baby care book came out a couple of decades ago. You will remember Peter is sent to bed for being naughty. Dr. Spock parents do not want their children to hear about things like that."

"Well," she said rather feebly, "I'll take a picture book by Dr. Seuss. Please just give me any Seuss book." "This children's room doesn't stock Dr. Seuss because some years ago a mother opposed our having him. She didn't feel he was elevating and, as she pointed out, her taxes help to buy the books and if she detested Dr. Seuss, why should we spend tax money on his books?"

She shuddered slightly and looked at her list again. "Alphabet books? Do you have any ABC's?" "We have several," I said cheerfully. "Among them are <u>ABC</u> by Bruno Munari, <u>ABC</u> by Brian Wildsmith, <u>ABC</u> by Thomas Matthiesen, <u>The ABC Book</u> by Charles Falls and <u>The ABC Bunny</u> by Wanda Gag. Lovely books!"

She smiled, a trifle ruefully I thought, and asked, "You mean no one who uses this children's room has objected to any of the letters of the alphabet?" "Not one," I answered, but as I went to the picture book shelves to collect the alphabet books for her, I murmured to myself, "Not one. As yet...."

AUDIO-VISUAL AIDS:
FALLOUT FROM THE McLUHAN GALAXY*

William R. Eshelman

The orbiting of Sputnik in the fifties was viewed in the United States as a kind of handwriting on the sky: our educational system must be thoroughly reformed. Among those who hastened to make the most of the crisis were the advocates of audio-visual aids. Claiming successes with military training films and language labs during World War II, they intensified their campaign to revolutionize teaching methods. It was old hat to require students to use their imaginations while reading, they argued. Such devices as slides and filmstrips, films and television would motivate students to read and increase their appreciation of literature.

The A-V proponents based their claims on research, usually summarized like this: Learners retain about 10 per cent of what they read, 20 per cent of what they hear, 30 per cent of what they see. Of what they see and hear the retention is 50 per cent, of what they see as they speak 70 per cent, of what they say as they participate in activities fully 90 per cent.

In the sixties the McLuhan galaxy swam into our ken, creating a new cultural shock. We were informed that the long dominance of print had forced us into being linear creatures. Print is made up of words strung together in sentences and paragraphs, separate elements that can be arranged only in linear chains. Thus we think step by step, a clumsy, time-consuming method when contrasted with what is possible through the means of the new electronic media. Now, according to Marshall McLuhan, because of TV, com-

---

*Reprinted by permission from the May 6, 1973 issue of the New York Times. Copyright © 1973 by The New York Times Company.

puters and other such gear it behoved everyone to become an involved, simultaneous thinker.

The argument raised questions and problems that Mr. McLuhan and his followers never got around to answering. Who can think in TV's split images? How many can speak in film or slides? Are computer programs the language of love? The development of TV's instant replay technique is a concession to the linear process. Like print, it allows the viewer to "re-read" and so to comprehend.

The individual uses language internally to encode ideas and to communicate them. Thus he is both a sender and a receiver of verbal messages. The vast majority of people never encode ideas in filmic terms, nor do they interact with others who do. We may receive nonprint messages, but seldom if ever are they our tools of thought. Where are the enduring classics of the filmstrip? Who quotes them? Who remembers them?

The chief characteristic of the multi-media techniques used in teaching (the simultaneous presentation, for example, of slides, films and filmstrips) is over-stimulus without time for response. Without interactions, there can be little learning. One rises from such a presentation battered and bemused, having tried to drink, as it were, from a fire hydrant. Where is the grammar of this new A-V language? What is its syntax? Is there an electronic Fowler to rail against the blurring of useful distinctions?

The McLuhan rage produced a dramatic change of heart among American schools and libraries in 1969. In that year, the National Educational Association (which had absorbed the national visual aid group back in 1923) and the American Library Association (which had urged its members to collect films as early as 1925) jointly published a "set of standards," the effect of which was to upgrade the educational importance of A-V software and hardware and to substitute the phrase "school media center" for the word "library."

Typical of the new media packages now currently being urged upon school librarians by their two national associations is one made up of eight filmstrips plus cassettes which claims to put "the civil rights movement into meaningful perspective." The two-hour show consists of more than 900 color frames, with the narration highlighted by the voices of Mar-tin Luther King, Medgar Evers, Orval Faubus, John F. Kennedy, George Wallace, among others. The school library possessing plenty of copies of books by Claude Brown, Malcolm X, Angela Davis, Eldridge Cleaver, plus a collection of the views of Spiro Agnew, Barry Goldwater, William F. Buckley and the John Birch Society will find the set a useful aid in achieving the aim of every worthy school and public library--an increase in the number of thoughtful, independent citizens. If it can afford the $142 the package costs.

Anyone who thoughtfully examines the two associations' school media standards inevitably finds himself weighing the relative priorities of books and A-V materials. If one filmstrip title costs $142, the cost of reaching the minimum standard set for A-V materials in a 2000-student high school library would be $71,000. This to complement a book collection of 40,000 volumes, in itself a completely unrealistic goal!

In less than 20 years the mystique of A-V has grown from a helpful aid to reading and learning into a titan that threatens to supplant reading entirely. Equipment sales in 1971, the latest year for which figures are available, reached $544-million, while sales of films, filmstrips, recordings and the like totaled $887-million. For the same year, sales of textbooks to all elementary and secondary schools came to $448-million.

The growing drain of A-V purchases on library budgets may well have a secondary but equally disquieting effect: Book publishers, discouraged by the sagging market, will publish fewer books. They will take fewer risks in making selections for publication. The chances for manuscripts espousing dissident views will grow dimmer. The present reading generation loses, the oncoming generation never learns to read.

A recently published research study contradicts the earlier findings that A-V aids are effective with the general run of students. It shows that filmstrips are not effective even for learning by rote and that films improved the learning of a skill only by students whose verbal reasoning ability was underdeveloped. For those who scored high on verbal reasoning tests, the films were a hinderance; the "spoonfeeding" interfered with their performance.

Libraries--the ideal tool for self-paced instruction

and life-time learning--are the chief targets of the Nixon Administration's fusillade against social programs. In cutting off federal funds, the President suggested that the worth of libraries was so self-evident that he was confident the states and local governmental units would deal them a portion of their revenue-sharing dollars. Librarians, who recall that the federal programs were initiated in 1956 precisely because these governmental units had failed to support library service, are understandably less sanguine.

Most libraries in this country have always been undersupported; they have never been financed well enough to show what they could really do to help the mass of the people. If you doubt this, make a little experiment. Compile your own list of books that have changed the world, that should be in every library, and then go look for them in your local library. Do not be satisfied that the titles appear in the card catalogue; are the books actually on the shelf? That is the test of a library collection--are the books available when you need them?

Librarians who participate in children's story hour programs are frustrated and saddened by a situation that occurs all too frequently. At the end of a typical hour, they find a dozen children clamoring to take "the book" home. But no. The librarian is forced to favor only one or two of the children. There just aren't enough copies of any book to go around.

Libraries have not been tried and found wanting; they have not been tried. It is in this context that the demands for libraries to give priority to films and filmstrips, games and realia, must be examined. Some non-print media are needed, of course--to attract non-readers, to stimulate latent readers, to supplement and enrich. But A-V must not become the end, it is an aid; indispensable but auxiliary.

Part IV

THE SOCIAL PREROGATIVE

KID PORN v. THE BURGER FIVE*

John Leonard

You are Pat "Average" Garrett, sheriff of Swamp Statistic, West Garble, D.C. You are probably un-young, un-poor, un-black, Protestant, with 2.5 children--the <u>real</u> majority. Although 10 per cent of you is over 65, your median age is 28.1. You are, according to Chief Justice Burger, neither "particularly sensitive" nor "totally insensitive." But you're the boss now, buddy! It's sundown, and Kid Porn hasn't boarded the train for Las Vegas. Kid Porn, instead, is exposing himself in front of the saloon. You whip out your Burger-gun and go bang-bang. Kid Porn is dead. Community standards are safe again.

Of course, you don't exist. You are a composite, a statistical inference, the invention of census analysts and advertising agencies. Network TV programs, political campaigns and bathroom tissues are all designed for the mythical, "average" Mr. You. And now five consenting adults on the U.S. Supreme Court--four of them appointed by our incumbent President--have put you in charge of deciding which books, movies and plays don't deserve the protection of the First Amendment. It couldn't happen to a nicer inference. If enough of you get together in Albany or Little Rock, you can even turn your average "unprovable assumptions" into laws.

What the Supreme Court did last month was to say

---

*Reprinted by permission from the July 8, 1973 issue of the <u>New York Times</u> (the Sunday Book Review regular column, "The Last Word"). Copyright © 1973 by The New York Times Company.

that books, movies and plays are no longer to be presumed
innocent of obscenity until proven guilty. In Roth v.
United States (1967), the Warren Court held that three elements
must "coalesce" to prove obscenity: (a) the dominant theme
of the material taken as a whole appeals to a prurient interest in sex; (b) the material is patently offensive because
it affronts contemporary community standards relating to the
description or representation of sexual matters; and (c) the
material is utterly without redeeming social value. The
item that counts is (c). In Memoirs v. Massachusetts (1966),
the Court took a closer look at (c) and decided that it must
be "affirmatively established." In other words, somebody
had to prove in court that the material was "utterly without
redeeming social value."

    Well, the Burger Five say nonsense to this. Whereas the "community" was considered by the Warren Court to
be a national one, it's considered by the Burger Court to
consist of states and localities. Its "standards" will be applied by "the average person." Whether material is patently
offensive will be determined by "the applicable state law."
Chief Justice Burger believes that "It is neither realistic
nor constitutionally sound to read the First Amendment as
requiring that the people of Maine or Mississippi accept public depiction of conduct found tolerable in Las Vegas or New
York City." Gone are all the "utterly withouts," affirmatively established. Only your State Legislature knows for sure,
being full of averages.

    I suppose it's hopelessly civil libertarian to protest
that my desire to go to a movie or buy a book without the
state's permission doesn't "require" anybody to "accept"
anything except my freedom of choice. Kid Porn must be
gunned down, and the "utterly without" proviso inconveniences that end. Get rid of it. Justice Burger holds, vividly, that "a 'live' performance of a man and woman in a
sexual embrace at high noon in Times Square" is not protected by the Constitution even though the couple might
"simultaneously engage in a valid political dialogue." A
little humor. He also objects to patently offensive "representations or descriptions of ultimate sexual acts, moral or
perverted, actual or simulated" and "representations and
descriptions of masturbation, excretory functions and lewd
exhibition of the genitals." I guess breasts are okay. But
who defines which description of what "ultimate," "normal"
sexual act is patently offensive, or lewd? "The average
person," of course, as certified by state legislators, simu-

lating intelligence.

Nor does it matter that "there is [sic] no scientific data which conclusively demonstrates [sic] that exposure to obscene materials adversely affects men and women or their society." For, says Burger, "from the beginning of civilized societies legislators and judges have acted on various unprovable assumptions." Ah, yes: like racial superiority, for example.

So the First Amendment has been parceled out to 50 states for 50 different glosses according to 50,000 community standards arrived at by 200-million average inferences. Imagine the mostly-male State Legislature of Georgia deciding whether the raft of new books on female sexuality is obscene, no matter how important such explorations are to women, including Georgia women, for a rehabilitated consciousness. Imagine the differing perceptions, in Baton Rouge or Trenton, of what's patently offensive in a novel featuring black-white sexual relations. Suppose Al Carmines's new musical, "The Faggot," were to tour: okay, maybe, in New Orleans, but in Lubbock or Pierre? We've seen what California did to its textbooks to keep kids from being brainwashed by the theory of evolution. Yahoos everywhere are already telling us we can't mention "Mafia" and that "Huckleberry Finn" is racist. Librarians, bar the doors: here come your average vigilantes.

Art isn't "average." It tends toward extremes. It's been trying for more than a century to make us uncomfortable. (Unlike, say, TV.) To return the sanctioning of what's permissible in art to those very communities it may be trying to discomfit is to ensure censorship and mediocrity. We are back inside the frontier mentality. In the old frontier days, each town had its own law, and that was considered democratic because the communities were heterodox. Even then dissent didn't have much of a chance because, as John Roche pointed out in The New Republic years ago, each community was its own inflexible orthodoxy, its own totalitarianism.

But now we can't even move to our own orthodoxy. More than 73 per cent of Americans live on just 1.5 per cent of the land. The average overwhelms. Those who service it uncritically produce sitcoms. In a wired nation, a Galileo or a Joyce could appear only on the public-access channels of cable TV, and not even then for long. Stern

Justice Burger disapproves of "totally unlimited play for free will," which means reading books or seeing movies he thinks are lewd. Off permissiveness! Only the S.E.C. and the Committee to Reelect the President are allowed to be permissive. This Government is rated "X," because nobody above average will be admitted without the permission of the President, and how would he know?

BOOK SELECTION IN PHILADELPHIA*

S. J. Leon

The "Survey of the Handling of Certain Controversial Adult Materials by Philadelphia Area Libraries" was conceived in the fall of 1969 and executed in the spring and summer of 1970. The Social Responsibilities Round Table book list, therefore, inevitably reflects the social scene and literary politics of that time.

It was decided to study all major libraries in the area. In selecting academic libraries for study, we wanted to include a Catholic Institution, a college whose administration was liberal, and an institution whose student body was predominantly black. In selecting public libraries for study, we weighed the general economic level and general social and political orientation of the community served and the size of the system. Here our aim was to contrast an urban system with a small town library and a library that serves a working-class clientele with one that serves more affluent readers.

In shaping our adult book list, it was obvious that the major areas of controversy in our culture today are psychosexual and sociopolitical. We wanted to include fiction of unquestioned merit as well as creative work of more questionable durability and finesse. Inevitably, we included imaginative writing that probes homosexual behavior, interracial sex, and political violence since these are hot issues

---

*Reprinted by permission from the April 1, 1973 issue of Library Journal (pages 1081-1089), published by R. R. Bowker Co., a Xerox Education Company. Copyright © 1973 by Xerox Corporation. "Editorial work ... was done by [the author] with the special assistance of Miriam Crawford of the Temple University Libraries, and Jeremiah Post of the Map Division of the [Philadelphia] Free Library."

in today's social scene. Some of the nonfiction titles deal
directly with sociopolitical unrest, and we tried to represent
the radical right as well as the splintered left. We also included certain books written by practitioners whose work for
different reasons is not accepted by their professions.

Among our periodicals is a local underground paper,
Thursday's Drummer, and publications on the red and violet
end of the social rainbow.

In constructing our questionnaire, we aimed to get
as many statements of institutional book selection policies
as we could. We also wanted a description of how restricted books are made available to patrons and what
closed shelf procedures have been adopted by various institutions surveyed. Hopefully, we asked for specific descriptions of pitched censorship battles and, again hopefully, we
tried for some indication of how censorship attacks have affected institutional book selection practices. Finally, we
solicited administrative evaluation of anticensorship apparatus
existing within the profession and suggestions for making the
apparatus more effective. We tried to ask questions which
were specific but not so complicated as to discourage
answers.

In order to elicit a better response we decided to
omit the names of the 12 institutional libraries involved.
Rather than attempt direct interviews with library administrators, we decided to concentrate on a mailing piece. However, we also decided to supplement the mailing piece by
sending members of the Intellectual Freedom Committee on
independent surveys of institutional holdings and practices.
Of the 12 institutions surveyed, 11 were scrutinized independently by committee members before the questionnaires
were sent through the mail.

Four Public Libraries

The urban system surveyed reports a book budget of
approximately $953,000 for the fiscal year 1970. In that
year fully 61 percent of its book money came from local
taxes; the remainder came from state and federal monies
and private donations.

The library has adopted an official book selection
policy. The director has final authority on all book selec-

The Social Prerogative

tion matters, and that is delegated to him by the Board of Trustees. Standard book selection tools are used in building the collection, and staff reviews supplement commercial reviews in arriving at decisions.

The library maintains restricted collections of books and magazines. Restricted materials are shelved near the service desks but are closed to public access. They may be borrowed by persons 18 years of age or older. Restricted books are so listed in the public catalog, but no symbols are used in the catalog to show the location of any of these books.

The library reports that it has no formal program for the reevaluation of restricted or rejected titles. It adds, however, that "a responsible request for reconsideration of both rejected and restricted titles will be considered after a reasonable amount of time has elapsed following the initial decision."

During the past decade this library system has been hit by five significant censorship attacks. In 1961 the local District Attorney's office ordered all copies of Henry Miller's Tropic of Cancer withdrawn, but in 1964, after the Supreme Court had ruled the novel was not obscene, all copies were returned to circulation and placed in restricted collections. Soon after publication, James Baldwin's Another Country was attacked by individual readers, but no copies of this novel were withdrawn or restricted. In 1963 Nikos Kazantzakis' The Last Temptation of Christ was attacked by individual citizens, but no copies were withdrawn or restricted.

In 1968 Evergreen Review was attacked by the local Constitutional Party, a local Chamber of Commerce group, and smaller community groups. As a result of this attack, two of the library's four subscriptions were cancelled and all copies are now placed on closed shelves. More recently the same groups attacked Jerry Rubin's Do It, demanding variously that it be removed from the library's collection or placed under restriction. The library, however, has not withdrawn or restricted any copies of this title.

The three smaller area public libraries studied vary in size and scope. The largest of the three serves a borough and adjacent county. Another serves a smaller residential community and is an autonomous unit in a county system. The third is a minisystem which serves a township and consists of six suburban libraries.

In 1970 the county system was given a book budget of $67,620 to serve 622,376 people. Its money comes almost entirely from local and state funds. In this system book selection is controlled by the director. Standard book selection tools are used, though staff reviews are not a factor in the selection process. In contrast to the large urban system surveyed, this library has no official restriction policy. However, books that are frequently stolen and mutilated are placed in a locked case, and there is evidence that this amounts to de facto restriction. The locked case is in the public service area and has glass doors so that restricted items are reviewed periodically in the same manner as all titles in the collection. The library further reports that no serious censorship controversies have developed in recent years.

In 1970 the autonomous unit in the larger county system was given $28,830 in county funds to buy books for more than 141,204 people. Selection in this library is controlled by the director and a lay advisory committee. Standard book selection tools are used, and staff reviews are a factor in making decisions. This library also has no official restriction policy, but books that are habitually stolen or mutilated are placed in reserved stacks, and there is evidence that some controversial material is placed in the librarian's office. Reserved or restricted books are available to readers 14 years old or older who have adult cards. The library reports that when restricted material is stolen or worn out its repurchase is considered. It also reports that no serious censorship controversies have developed in recent years.

In 1970 the township system was given $66,600 in local and state funds to buy books for 68,000 persons. Selection in the six community libraries that comprise this system is controlled by the director. Standard book selection tools are used, but staff reviews do not figure seriously in the selection process. The library reports no official restriction policy, emphasizing that all books circulate freely. It indicates that lost, stolen, or worn out copies of controversial books are replaced. In recent years the township system reports that Gore Vidal's Myra Breckenridge was challenged by individual citizens but adds that this novel continues to circulate on open shelves.

The Social Prerogative   335

Three College Libraries

   The three college libraries surveyed vary in size and function. One serves a Quaker-affiliated liberal arts college in the Philadelphia area; another serves a coeducational satellite campus in the Philadelphia area; and the third serves a community college with a two-year program.

   None of the three college libraries has written book selection policies, and none reports significant censorship incidents or attacks in recent years. In every case selection is controlled by the head of the library, and none of these administrators reports any special restriction policy.

   The Quaker-affiliated liberal arts campus has a population of approximately 2000. In 1970 its library was given a book budget of $124,500, which came from the overall college budget and private donations. The book selection process involves the head librarian, staff members, and faculty. Standard reviewing media are used, and staff reviews play a role in selection. The library reports that "collections are built on pertinence and prospective usefulness without regard to controversy." It adds that books are restricted only because of their rarity and vulnerability to theft.

   The satellite campus library serves a population of approximately 1600. In 1970 its book budget was $17,500, representing $1500 in state funds and $2500 in federal funds. Selection is a collaboration between the head of the library and faculty members. The standard book reviewing tools are used, but staff reviews do not figure in selection. This library reports that its selection is motivated by "courses taught, the ethnic composition of the student body, and the interests of the student body." It lists student requests as a significant factor in determining selection. This library reports that it restricts "only those materials placed on reserve for use in specific courses at faculty request or to discourage theft." It adds that repurchase of lost, stolen, or worn copies of controversial materials is considered if the materials "are still of current interest or significance."

   In 1969-1970 the community college library received a book budget of $75,000, exclusive of periodicals and films, to serve a population of approximately 7000 persons. Its money came from local, state, and federal funds. In this library selection is described as a collaboration between li-

OWNERSHIP AND CIRCULATION OF CONTROVERSIAL PERIODICAL TITLES

Periodical Title	Four Public Libraries				Five University Libraries					Three College Libraries		
	PL1	PL2	PL3	PL4	UL1	UL2	UL3	UL4	UL5	CL1	CL2	CL3
American Opinion	X	O	X	O	X	X	X	O	O	O	X	O
Distant Drummer (Thursday's Drummer)	R	O	O	O	X	R	R	R	O	O	R	O
Evergreen Review	X	O	X	O	X	R	X	X	X	O	O	O
Human Events	X	O	O	O	O	X	O	X	O	O	X	O
Journal of Black Poetry	X	O	X	X	X	R	O	X	X	X	O	X
Liberator	X	O	X	X	X	X	O	O	X	O	X	O
Ramparts	O	O	X	O	X	X	X	X	X	O	X	O
Realist	X	O	O	O	X	O	O	O	O	O	O	O

X = Library has   R = Library restricts   O = Library does not have   * = In Spanish

NUMBER OF CONTROVERSIAL PERIODICAL TITLES OWNED

Periodical Title	Public Libraries			Academic Libraries		
	C	R	N	C	R	N
American Opinion	2	0	2	4	0	4
Distant Drummer (Thursday's Drummer)	2	0	2	3	0	5
Evergreen Review	0	1	3	3	3	2
Human Events	1	0	3	6	0	2
Journal of Black Poetry	1	0	3	2	1	5
Liberator	2	0	2	4	0	4
Ramparts	4	0	0	6	1	1
Realist	0	0	4	1	0	7

C=Number that circulate title   R=Number that restrict title   N=Number that do not own title brarian, faculty, and students. The standard reviewing tools are used, but staff reviews are not used as checks on them. This library reports that "we do not purchase titles because they are controversial but rather we purchase to support the curricula primarily. If a controversial title is requested, we judge each request on its merit." Aside from regular reserved collections, the library reports that it restricts only "titles which tend to disappear from open stacks."

Five University Libraries

The five university libraries studied vary in size and function. All serve coeducational institutions. Two of the universities involved are large urban institutions. A third urban university has a heavy technological and business emphasis. The fourth is a suburban university with a predominately Catholic faculty and student body, and the fifth is biracial but predominately black.

None of the five university libraries involved has a written book selection policy, and none reports significant censorship confrontations or controversies in recent years. Selection practices vary slightly, but in every instance selection seems to be controlled by the library administration. None of the university libraries reports official restriction policies, restricting only for rarity or vulnerability to theft.

Perhaps because it was between administrations, one large university library responded to the Intellectual Freedom Committee's questionnaire in so fragmentary a fashion that information on budget and book selection practices is not available. This library indicates that it has no special restrictive practices; however, it does maintain special collections in its closed stacks, and one of the titles on the committee's controversial list does not circulate at all.

The second urban university library serves approximately 45,000 persons. In 1970 the book budget for the main undergraduate library was $700,000, of which approximately 50 percent came from state funds. Selection is accomplished by a bibliographical department of 13 persons; in addition, faculty and students participate in the process, but final authority rests with the director of libraries. The library reports that it has a blanket order for all current books in the English language, with some minor exceptions. Restricted collections are found in a rare book room and a

restricted area in the stacks. Rare books can be used only
in the room by any legitimate reader, and books in the restricted
stacks can be used in the library. The library
maintains a Contemporary Culture Center, which amounts to
a special collection of periodicals, underground papers, and
leaflets housed in a seminar room on the second floor.
This arrangement is "because of the fragility of most of
these publications." The library makes provision for replacing
lost, stolen, or worn copies of controversial materials.
Regarding censorship pressures, the director reports:
"No sweat."

  The third university library serves a "technological
university with limited Humanities and Social Sciences collecting."
Its population exceeds 11,000, and in 1970-1971
its book budget amounted to $80,000. Of this amount, 91
percent represented university appropriations; eight percent
was federal funds; and one percent was gifts. Selection is
accomplished by library staff members and faculty, and final
authority rests with divisional librarians. Restricted
collections amount to "archival and special collections and
reserve books." This library circulates acquisitions lists
in order to keep its clientele informed. Lost, stolen, or
worn copies of controversial materials are replaced as funds
permit.

  The fourth university library serves a Catholic-related
institution, with a population of approximately 8000
persons. In 1970 its book budget was $325,000, all of
which came from church funds. Book selection in this library
is handled by staff members and faculty, and final
authority rests with the head of the Acquisitions Department.
This library orders all university press books on a special
approval plan. It also uses staff reviews to supplement the
commercial reviewing media. The library reports that it
has no special restrictive policies other than those customarily
found in university libraries. Lost, stolen, or
worn copies of controversial materials are replaced "if requested."

  The Negro university library serves 1000 students,
125 faculty, and some 500 borrowers from adjacent local
communities. In 1970 it received $50,000 for books from
state and federal funds, private donations, and endowment.
Selection is a collaboration between the head librarian, library
staff, and faculty members. The standard reviewing
media are used in selection, and staff reviews are a factor.

The library reports that it restricts only rare books. Periodicals are kept in a locked stack, but there is an attendant on duty during library hours and access to them is freely given. Also a Special Negro Collection and an African Collection are shelved in a special room. The library reports that the repurchase of lost, stolen, or worn copies of controversial materials is periodically considered.

Public Libraries' Report

Reviewing the reports of the four public libraries surveyed, we find a few striking facts. The urban library system predictably holds the most controversial titles on the list--32 of 33--but it also restricts the most--nine. The other three libraries restrict relatively few of the controversial titles on the list, but the number of titles they hold is almost balanced by the number of titles they do not own. The county library system circulates 16 of the titles, restricts four, and does not own 13. The semi-autonomous unit of the larger county system, where selection is controlled by the director and a community advisory group, also circulates 16 of the controversial titles on the list, restricts two, and does not own 15. The township minisystem circulates 18 of the titles, restricts none, but does not own 15.

The urban library system reports five significant censorship confrontations during the past decade, but the other three public libraries maintain that there have been no significant confrontations with elements in their respective communities in the recent past.

When we examine the handling of specific titles by the four public libraries surveyed, a few patterns emerge. The books that are either significantly omitted and/or heavily restricted include William Burroughs' Naked Lunch, Jean Genet's Our Lady of the Flowers, Henry Miller's Tropic of Cancer, the Marquis de Sade's Selected Writings, Hubert Selby's Last Exit to Brooklyn, Le Roi Jones' Dutchman and the Slave, Timothy Leary's The Psychedelic Experience, Wilhelm Reich's Selected Writings, Arlo Tatum's Conscientious Objector's Handbook, and The Kama Sutra by Vatsyayana. Among the periodicals, the Realist, Evergreen Review, and Human Events are conspicuously either not owned or restricted.

Of the writers omitted or restricted in impressive

quantities, Burroughs, Genet, and the Marquis de Sade deal explicitly with homosexual behavior on fictional, autobiographical, and other levels. Henry Miller and Hubert Selby deal more freely and less compulsively with sexual behavior. Wilhelm Reich is an orgonomist, therapist, and philosopher whose work in the sexual area has become more influential in our own day; The Kama Sutra, though a classic, deals explicitly with sexual techniques. Of the heavily restricted and/or thinly represented writers, Leary is a spokesman for the liberating effect of drugs, and Le Roi Jones, of course, focuses on the racial conflict in America and its implications.

NUMBER OF CONTROVERSIAL BOOK TITLES OWNED

Author and Title	Public Libraries			Academic Libraries		
	C	R	N	C	R	N
Baldwin, J., *Another Country*	3	0	1	7	0	1
Burroughs, W., *Naked Lunch*	1	1	2	6	0	2
Donleavy, J. P., *Ginger Man* (Unexpurgated, Delacorte)	4	0	0	5	0	3
Genet, J., *Our Lady of the Flowers*	1	1	2	5	0	3
Lawrence, D. H., *Lady Chatterley's Lover*	3	1	0	7	0	1
Mailer, N., *Why Are We in Viet Nam?*	4	0	0	7	0	1
Miller, H., *Tropic of Cancer*	2	2	0	4	1	3
Roth, P., *Portnoy's Complaint*	3	1	0	7	0	1
Sade, D. A. F., *Selected Writings*	2	2	0	2	0	6
Selby, H., *Last Exit to Brooklyn*	0	1	3	4	0	4
Ginsberg, A., *Howl and Other Poems*	2	0	2	7	0	1
Jones, L., *Dutchman and The Slave*	1	0	3	7	0	1
Cleaver, E., *Soul on Ice*	4	0	0	8	0	0
Fanon, F., *Black Skin, White Masks*	4	0	0	8	0	0
Guevara, C., *Diary*	4	0	0	5	0	3
Guttmacher, A. F., *Planning Your Family*	3	1	0	4	4	0
Leary, T., *The Psychedelic Experience*	1	1	2	3	0	5
Lester, J., *Look Out, Whitey!*	3	0	1	6	0	2
Little, M., *The Autobiography of Malcolm X*	4	0	0	8	0	0
Masters, W. H., *Human Sexual Response*	3	1	0	8	0	0
Reich, W., *Selected Writings*	1	0	3	3	1	4
Tatum, A., ed., *Conscientious Objectors Handbook*	1	0	3	1	1	6
Vatsyayana, *The Kama Sutra*	1	1	2	3	1	4
Velikovsky, I., *Worlds in Collision*	4	0	0	6	0	2
Welch, R., *Blue Book of the John Birch Society*	2	1	0	1	1	6

C = No. that circulate   R = No. that restrict   N = No. that do not own

But Jones alone, of all the writers on the racial conflict, is relatively ignored or rejected. Particularly well represented are Eldridge Cleaver's Soul on Ice and The Autobiography of Malcolm X. All four public libraries hold titles in multiple copies and circulate them freely. Also fairly well represented are Franz Fanon's Black Skin, White Masks, circulated freely by all four public libraries; James Baldwin's Another Country, held and circulated by three of the four public libraries; and Julius Lester's Look Out, Whitey!, also listed and circulated by three of four public libraries.

The Social Prerogative   341

Norman Mailer's Why Are We in Viet Nam?, which mixes political and sexual iconoclasm, is freely circulated by all four public libraries surveyed and does not seem to fall into the pattern of sexual restriction suggested by the above noted holdings. On the other hand, Philip Roth's popular Portnoy's Complaint, which is circulated by three of the four public libraries, is restricted by the urban library system, which makes all 140 copies available only to readers 18 years of age or older upon proper identification.

Among the gingerly handled periodicals mentioned above, both the Realist, which is totally unrepresented in all four collections, and Evergreen Review, which only the urban public library makes available and that on a restricted basis, stand for political and sexual iconoclasm, while Human Events, represented in only one of the four collections, deals with political and social currents from a particularistic conservative point of view.

Although all 12 of the libraries surveyed were invited to give reasons for purchase or rejection of specific titles, only two of the four public libraries responded to the invitation. Regarding this matter, the county library system replied: "No records are kept since all items purchased meet our library's book selection policy. Rejection of a title is on the basis of published reviews or examination of the book." The library noted that it has not purchased Le Roi Jones' Dutchman and the Slave because it is out of print; also, it has not purchased Tatum's Conscientious Objector's Handbook both because it is out of print and because it owns that author's Guide to the Draft. The library subscribes to Ramparts because it is indexed in Reader's Guide to Periodical Literature. Regarding restrictions, the library explains that it restricts Lady Chatterley's Lover, Tropic of Cancer, Guttmacher's Planning Your Family, and Welch's Blue Book of the John Birch Society because of repeated theft.

Of the four public libraries surveyed, only the township system, comprising six community libraries, attempted to comment on the literary or social value of specific titles. A closer examination of some of these comments is illuminating. One librarian replied: "Many books were not purchased by my predecessor, and I cannot give reasons for her." Since the titles so annotated included Burroughs' Naked Lunch, Miller's Tropic of Cancer, Ginsberg's Howl, Jones' Dutchman, Reich's Selected Writings, and The Kama

Sutra, we can assume that this particular community library does not periodically reconsider rejected titles on the basis of shifts in critical attitude and general literary and social influence. Another community librarian had three of the 33 listed titles in her collection and justified their presence as follows: Baldwin's Another Country: "representative of our times"; Roth's Portnoy's Complaint: "popular demand"; Guttmacher's Planning Your Family: "very much needed in this day of population explosion."

Still another township librarian wrote cryptically of Naked Lunch, de Sade's Selected Writings, and Look Out, Whitey!: "Not needed." Her comment on Genet's Our Lady of the Flowers, generally regarded as that author's most powerful fiction, was: "Have other Genet." And her comment on Che Guevara's Diary: "Have other Guevara." However, this same librarian's comment on Lady Chatterley's Lover, which was well represented in her collection, was: "Classic." And she promised to pick up copies of Ginsberg's Howl and The Kama Sutra. Such positive reactions were rare among the commentators.

A colleague supported her rejection of Why Are We in Viet Nam? with the following comment: "Not even author's earlier reputation could redeem. Literary quality nil." Of Wilhelm Reich she wrote: "But Reich's thesis highly suspect. Unacceptable in standard medical circles. Therefore not acceptable for this library." However, she called the absence of Our Lady of the Flowers in her collection a "simple oversight" and said that The Tropic of Cancer was missing "through oversight, not design." A survey that can generate even a few instances of retrospective self-criticism has something to be said for it.

Comments by several of the community librarians in this township system would indicate that demand is the strongest single factor in shaping their periodical collections. As one librarian wrote regarding the eight periodicals: "Do not have any of these in our holdings. Up to the present, no demands or requests concerning these editions. Ramparts is the only one indexed in Reader's Guide Index, but have not found it to be in demand."

All four public libraries surveyed have book selection policy statements which they have forwarded, but the eight academic libraries do not. Since the four libraries do not comment on their statements, we can only assume that they have adopted them because they feel more susceptible to direct community pressures and feel more secure with guidelines.

A closer look at the four policy statements is useful. The urban library system's statement is the only one that explicitly provides for restriction. It reads in part: "... the Library is obligated to select works, often experimental, whose themes run counter to community mores, when these books have literary quality, represent a recognized development or trend in literature, or are of sociological importance. When suitable material is available, representative viewpoints of significant, though controversial, issues and questions are considered for the collection. Though antisocial in nature, certain publications of current or historic importance and examples of propaganda may be included for informational and educational purposes. The Library exercises judgment in restricting circulation of this material."

The restriction procedure is more explicitly explained elsewhere: "Two types of books are contained in these restricted collections. They are: (1) Books which are continually stolen or mutilated, e.g., books on automotive mechanics, marriage manuals, etc. (2) Books likely to be regarded as pornographic by many patrons and which are predominantly unsuitable for persons under 18 years of age. Examples: <u>Memoirs of a Woman of Pleasure (Fanny Hill)</u> by John Cleland and <u>My Life And Loves</u> by Frank Harris.

> In the case of the first category it is up to the head of the agency to determine what titles should be restricted.... Books in the second category are designated for restriction only by the Office of Work with Adults and Young Adults following administrative discussion. These titles are restricted in all agencies and circulated on 'pink pass' to patrons 18 years and over....

The statement further provides that young adult books are to be restricted only if they are repeatedly stolen or mutilated and stipulates that restricted books are to be reviewed periodically by the Coordinator's Office. However, the frequency of such review is not specified, and there is evidence that reviews of restricted materials are only sporadic at best.

The other three libraries do not mention restriction

OWNERSHIP AND CIRCULATION OF CONTROVERSIAL BOOK TITLES

Author and Title	Four Public Libraries				Five University Libraries					Three College Libraries		
	PL 1	PL 2	PL 3	PL 4	UL 1	UL 2	UL 3	UL 4	UL 5	CL 1	CL 2	CL 3
Baldwin, J., *Another Country*	X	X	X	X	X	X	X	X	X	O	X	X
Burroughs, W., *Naked Lunch*	R	X	O	O	X	X	X	X	O	O	X	X
Donleavy, J.P., *Ginger Man* (Unexpurgated, Delacorte, 1965)	X	R	X	X	X	O	X	X	X	O	X	O
Genet, J., *Our Lady of the Flowers*	R	O	X	O	X	X	X	X	X	O	X	X
Lawrence, D.H., *Lady Chatterley's Lover*	X	R	X	X	X	X	X	X	X	O	O	O
Mailer, N., *Why Are We in Viet Nam?*	X	R	X	X	X	X	X	X	X	O	X	X
Miller, H., *Tropic of Cancer*	R	X	X	X	X	X	X	X	X	X	O	X
Roth, P., *Portnoy's Complaint*	R	X	R	X	R	X	X	X	X	O	O	X
Sade, D.A.F., *Selected Writings*	R	O	O	X	O	X	O	O	X	O	X	X
Selby, H., *Last Exit to Brooklyn*	X	O	O	O	X	X	X	O	X	X	O	X
Ginsberg, A., *Howl and Other Poems*	X	X	X	X	X	X	X	X	X	O	O	X
Jones, L., *Dutchman and The Slave*	X	X	X	X	X	X	X	X	X	X	X	X
Cleaver, E., *Soul on Ice*	X	X	X	X	X	X	X	X	X	X	X	X
Fanon, F., *Black Skin, White Masks*	X	X	X	X	X	X	X	X	O	O	O	X
Guevara, C., *Diary*	X	R	X	O	X	X	O	O	X	X	X	O
Gutmacher, A.F., *Planning Your Family*	X	X	O	X	X	X	X	X	X	X	X	X
Leary, T., *The Psychedelic Experience*	R	R	X	X	X	X	X	X	X	X	X	X
Lester, J., *Look Out, Whitey! Black Power's Goin' Get Your Mama!*	X	X	X	X	X	X	X	X	X	X	X	X
Little, M., *The Autobiography of Malcolm X*	X	X	X	X	X	X	X	X	X	X	X	X
Masters, W.H., *Human Sexual Response*	X	X	R	X	X	O	O	O	O	X	X	O
Reich, W., *Selected Writings*	X	O	O	O	X	O	O	R	O	X	O	O
Tatum, A., ed., *Conscientious Objector's Handbook*	R	X	X	O	R	R	R	O	X	X	O	O
Vatsyayana, *The Kama Sutra*	X	X	X	X	X	X	O	X	O	O	O	O
Velikovsky, I., *Worlds in Collision*	X	X	X	X	X	X	X	X	X	R	O	O
Welch, R., *Blue Book of the John Birch Society*	X	R	X	O	X	X	X	O	O	O	X	O

The Social Prerogative   345

in their policy statements, but we have noted that they practice it. However, they do have something to say, and sometimes in considerable detail, about what they will not buy. The autonomous unit in a larger county system indicates that it will not buy materials inconsistent with current obscenity laws. "The library subscribes to the present laws dealing with obscenity and believes they should be vigorously enforced." The county library states: "Special efforts will be made to provide the best books on all sides of controversial issues, and those written in a sensational or inflammatory manner will not ordinarily be selected." The township library system's statement runs to considerable length, largely because it goes into forms and categories of materials, and it is heavily adjectival. It notes two areas in which exclusion may be necessary: "first, books which seem offensive to good taste or contrary to prevailing community moral and ethical standards, and second, books on public questions presenting one side of a question only, when written in a violent, sensational, inflammatory manner."

The township system's statement further provides: "The libraries may exclude from their collections a majority of the books representing views that are regarded by a consensus of responsible opinion--civic, scientific, religious, and educational--as unsound and have been so regarded over a period of years." Concerning fiction specifically, it notes: ... it may be said that the libraries' policy is to acquire fiction, whether serious or amusing, realistic, or imaginative, which is well written and based on authentic human experience and to exclude weak, incompetent, or cheap sentimental writing, as well as the solely sensational, morbid, or erotic."

Three of the four statements explicitly mention censors and censorious pressures as facts in a public library's existence. The autonomous unit in a larger county system observes that "there is no place for extra-legal efforts to coerce the taste of others, to confine adults to reading matter considered suitable for adolescents, or to inhibit the efforts of writers to achieve artistic expression. We will resist efforts of individuals or groups to deny access to materials on the part of other sections of the community whether in the name of political, moral, or religious beliefs. We believe it is against the public interest to force the reader to accept with any book the prejudgment of a label characterizing the book or author as subversive or dangerous."

The county system's statement reads more succinctly: "The librarian is responsible to the board for the selection and development of the collection and will not act as a censor for adult materials." The township system's statement reads diplomatically: "The libraries are opposed to the withdrawal, at the request of any individual or group, of books which have been chosen by the above principles. The librarian welcomes the opportunity to discuss the interpretation of these principles with representatives of such groups." It is the only one of the four libraries to provide that complaints about its acquisitions be filed in writing on standard forms provided by each of its six community branches.

As we have seen, one book selection policy statement cites two factors in restricting adult materials: frequency of theft and mutilation and the unsuitability of some adult materials for use by minors and adolescents. Obviously these factors frequently coalesce; it is precisely those adult materials that some deem unsuitable for minors and adolescents that are most frequently stolen or mutilated. This state of affairs enables some administrators to take or keep controversial materials off the shelves, citing theft and mutilation when they are actually more concerned with anticipating censorious pressures, real or imagined, in their communities. It is difficult sometimes to tell where safeguarding against theft and mutilation shades off into caution, fear, and self-censorship unless one knows intimately the library in question, its clientele, and the specific materials involved.

We have also seen that one of these policy statements gives detailed descriptions of materials that it will not purchase, but these details inevitably become adjectives which can be subjectively interpreted. Is <u>Naked Lunch</u> morbid?

TABLE ON USE OF REVIEWING MEDIA

Title	Public Libraries					Academic Libraries						
	1	2	3	4	5	1	2	3	4	5	6	7
Kirkus	X	O	X	X	X	X	X	O	O	X	O	
Library Journal	X	X	X	X	X	X	X	O	X	O	O	
ALA Booklist	X	X	X	X	X	X	X	X	O	O	X	
Choice	X	X	X	X	X	X	X	X	X	X	X	
New York Times Book Review	X	X	X	X	X	X	X	X	X	X	X	
Saturday Review	X	X	X	X	X	X	X	X	X	X	X	
New York Review of Books	X	X	X	X	X	X	X	X	X	X	X	
New Republic	X	X	X	X	X	X	X	X	O	X	X	
Commentary	X	X	X	X	X	X	X	X	O	X	X	
Paris Review	X	X	X	X	O	X	X	O	O	X	O	
Times Literary Supplement	X	X	X	X	X	X	X	X	X	X	X	
Other		X	X	X	X	X	X	O	O	O	X	

X = Library uses   O = Library does not use   — = Information not forwarded

The Social Prerogative

Is Our Lady of the Flowers erotic, and if yes, is it more erotic than Lady Chatterley's Lover? Is Last Exit to Brooklyn cheap and sensational? If one were to judge by holdings alone, at least one public library in this survey would seem to think that all of this is so.

College Libraries' Report

Closer scrutiny of the holdings of the three college libraries surveyed reveals a pattern of acceptance, rejection, and unawareness that sometimes coincides with and sometimes deviates from the public library pattern. To begin with, a few titles are well represented. All three academic libraries have Ginsberg's Howl, perhaps because of its influence on the Anglo-American poetic scene during the sixties, and two of three hold Le Roi Jones' Dutchman and the Slave, whereas only one public library has that title. There are also several titles which are held with the same frequency as public libraries, notably Burroughs' Naked Lunch, which two of three college libraries have, and Evergreen Review, which one college library holds and restricts.

RELATION OF OFFICIAL BOOK SELECTION POLICIES OF FOUR PUBLIC LIBRARIES TO THEIR ACTUAL HANDLING OF CONTROVERSIAL BOOKS

	PL 1	PL 2	PL 3	PL 4
Director Selects	X	X	O	X
Director and Community Group Selects	O	O	X	O
Official Restriction Policy	Yes	No	No	No
No. of Selection Tools Cited Used	All	10 of 11	All	All
Staff Reviews Used in Selection Process	Yes	No	Yes	No
No. of Titles on Controversial List Circulated	23	16	16	18
No. of Titles on Controversial List Restricted	9	4	2	0
No. of Titles on Controversial List Not Owned	1	13	15	15
No. of Censorship Controversies Reported	5	0	0	0
Librarian believes professional organizations should be more active in censorship controversies	Yes	Yes	Yes	Yes
Librarian believes profession needs a supportive agency in censorship controversies	Maybe	Yes	Yes	Yes

On the other hand, some of the holdings are almost inexplicably thin. Lady Chatterley's Lover is held by two of the three libraries, whereas all the public libraries hold it, some openly, one cautiously. Two of the three college libraries surveyed have Mailer's Why Are We in Viet Nam?, but Miller's Tropic of Cancer, which has grown in stature through the past two decades, is held by none of these libraries. The Kama Sutra, generally regarded as a classic of its kind, is also ignored, and Welch's Blue Book is held by one college library. Whereas two of the four public libraries surveyed have Leary's The Psychedelic Experience, only one college library has it. Likewise, de Sade's Selected Writings is held by none of the three college libraries, though it can be argued that a complete work might have fared better than an anthology. Among the periodicals, Ramparts is held by two of three college libraries, whereas all four public libraries have it. And the Realist is completely ignored, even as it is by the public libraries surveyed.

The fiction and nonfiction that focuses on race seems fairly well represented in these college collections, and the fiction and nonfiction that explores human sexual behavior seems less well represented even as it was in the public library collections. There is virtually no restriction of access to materials reported--the Evergreen Review and Welch's Blue Book being two exceptions--but it is obvious that these college libraries show their negativism, not by restricting materials but by not buying them, whether through a process of deliberate rejection or blithe lack of awareness.

Since none of the college librarians surveyed gave specific reasons for acceptance or rejection of specific works, we do not know what book selection values were operative in these cases. However, a few of their comments are ironic.

The librarian who serves a Quaker-affiliated campus reports that "collections are built on pertinence and prospective usefulness without regard to controversy." This collection does not have Tropic of Cancer, Guevara's Diary, The Psychedelic Experience, or Wilhelm Reich's Selected Writings.

The librarian who serves a satellite campus located in the Philadelphia area reports: "Books not purchased were not actively rejected. None of these titles was requested by anyone--library staff, faculty or students." And regarding the periodicals, she notes: "We have none of these.... We have had no requests to add them to our collection." We are asked to suppose an undergraduate institution which offers courses in modern literature where no student or faculty member asks the librarian for Our Lady of the Flowers, Lady Chatterley's Lover, Tropic of Cancer, Portnoy's Complaint, The Psychedelic Experience, Dutchman and the Slave, Ramparts, and Evergreen Review.

The Social Prerogative   349

The librarian who serves a community college reports that his library has a book selection policy, "but not on paper." He adds: "... we purchase to support the curricula primarily. If a 'controversial' title is requested, we judge each request on its merit." His collection does not have Our Lady of the Flowers, Tropic of Cancer, Look Out, Whitey!, Welch's Blue Book, Evergreen Review, and the Journal of Black Poetry among other titles.

In all these cases, curriculum support and lack of requests are suggested as strong reasons for not including some controversial materials in collections. But in one or two instances one is sorely tempted to ask if the librarian's initiative and sensitivity both to modern letters and the current scene are not also legitimate factors in book selection.

University Libraries' Report

Closer scrutiny of the five university libraries surveyed shows that they hold more controversial titles than the college and in many cases the public libraries. They are apparently more alert to contemporary literary values and to social problems, though in some instances they are more restrictive, perhaps for security reasons.

Four of five university libraries have Naked Lunch, which is the best group showing for that particular novel. Also four of the five university libraries have Our Lady of the Flowers, again a better group showing than the college and public libraries. All five university libraries have Lady Chatterley's Lover, and they all circulate it. All five university libraries have Tropic of Cancer, and though one library restricts it, the treatment of available copies is freer than it is among the public libraries. All five university libraries have Portnoy's Complaint, which shows more responsiveness to contemporary fiction than the college libraries evidence. Two of the five university libraries have Leary's The Psychedelic Experience, again a better showing than one finds among the college libraries. Four of the five university libraries hold The Kama Sutra, a better showing than the college or public libraries. All university libraries surveyed have Velikovsky's Worlds in Collision despite the scientific attacks leveled against his work.

Of the periodical titles, all five university libraries hold the Evergreen Review and, though two libraries restrict it, the group showing is better here than among the college or public libraries. Three of the university libraries have the Journal of Black Poetry, whereas only one college and one public library have it. All five university libraries carry Ramparts, whereas two of three college libraries carry it. And an urban university library is the only one among 12 surveyed to carry the Realist.

On the other hand, a few titles are not as well represented as they are in college and public library collections. Four of five university libraries have Ginsberg's Howl, whereas all three college libraries have that title. Three of five university libraries have Donleavy's Ginger Man, whereas two of three college libraries have that novel. Three of five university libraries have Guevara's Diary, and one of these copies is in Spanish, whereas two of three college libraries have that title. Only one university library has Welch's Blue Book, and only two have the Selected Writings of the Marquis de Sade. Both titles emerge as public library items.

Though the university libraries hold more controversial titles on this list than the other libraries, they do not duplicate as heavily as the public libraries do, a practice which might reasonably be expected. The fiction and nonfiction which deals with racial problems is relatively well represented. Of the fiction and nonfiction that concerns itself primarily with sexual behavior, only the Selected Writings of the Marquis de Sade and Donleavy's Ginger Man are relatively weakly represented: on the political front only Guevara's Diary and Welch's Blue Book are comparatively overlooked or rejected.

Since none of the university librarians offered specific comments on specific titles on our list, we cannot evaluate more closely the selection and rejection processes involved. Whether the university libraries duplicate in sufficient quantities to meet their particular demands is a pertinent question, but we cannot answer it conclusively since that would require a familiarity with all five campuses and the internal operations of all five libraries beyond the scope and resources of this survey. There is some evidence that they do not duplicate some of these titles in sufficient quantities.

The library that serves a university with a strong technological and business emphasis reports divisional autonomy operating in book selection with this statement:

"Our selections are left to the discretion of our librarians whose decisions are based upon funds available and priorities in their divisional collections."

The library that serves a Catholic-related university reports that there is no restriction in the handling of its materials, but this particular library does not have Donleavy's Ginger Man, Genet's Our Lady of the Flowers, de Sade's Selected Writings, Selby's Last Exit to Brooklyn, Ginsberg's Howl, Guevara's Diary, Leary's The Psychedelic Experience, Wilhelm Reich's Selected Writings, Welch's Blue Book, and the Journal of Black Poetry among other titles. In this library final selection authority rests with the Acquisitions Department head, and faculty recommendations are particularly important.

One urban university library has a blanket order for all current books in the English language, with some minor exceptions, which means that controversial materials in English arrive as a matter of course. The selection process is operative primarily with foreign language materials. In this library selection is handled by a bibliographical department of some 13 librarians supplemented by faculty and student recommendations. The library has an interesting Contemporary Culture Collection of more than 425 items. These titles are kept in a Contemporary Culture Center, which is open two hours every afternoon. Among the titles are The Militant, New Left Notes, and Youth International Party News, representing the radical left; the Dan Smoot Report and Storm Trooper, representing the radical right; Thursday's Drummer, East Village Other, Los Angeles Free Press, Philadelphia Free Press, and Rat, representing the underground papers; Black Panther and Up From Under, representing the Women's Liberation movement.

Conclusions

"The nightingale sings with its fingers," a line in Cocteau's film Orpheus reminds us. Moving from poetry and the literary history of the early 20th-Century to librarianship now, we are reminded that librarians sing with statistics and file with their fingers. However, sheer statistics have their crudities, and vital half truths are often hidden underneath, between, and around them. Figures don't lie: they merely make half statements much of the time, and much depends on how they are presented.

Given the ineradicable accomplishment of D. H. Lawrence, is it impressive that only one of the 12 libraries surveyed does not have Lady Chatterley's Lover and only one restricts it? Shall we say that 92 percent of the libraries we surveyed have Lady Chatterley, or shall we say more accurately that one library does not have and one library restricts a significant novel by one of the major novelists of this century dead these past 40 years? Given the reputation of Naked Lunch, at least among many specialized critics, shall we say that only seven area libraries make freely available one of the significant avant-garde novels of our time? Shall we say that 75 percent of the libraries we surveyed have Tropic of Cancer, or would it be more exact to say that three libraries do not have and three libraries, including one university library, restrict a novel that is taught in American Literature classes in a steadily increasing number of academic institutions?

One of the limits of such a study as this is the absence of expansive statements to explain the responses. Are the four libraries that do not have the two plays by Le Roi Jones making evaluative judgments on the merits of these plays? Are they even aware of them? Are they reacting partially to the author's reputation as a militant in Newark's recent ghetto wars? Or are they reacting, perhaps, to his anti-Semitic diatribes disguised as poems? All these factors are separable, but only in the minds of knowledgeable collection builders.

As we moved from the sixties into the seventies, the following controversial areas dominated the thinking of our citizens and inevitably affected the judgments of librarians: (1) racial tensions, (2) radical politics and the war in Vietnam, (3) changing sexual mores, and (4) drugs. Reviewing overall holdings in these respective areas, we find first that certain titles which deal with racial problems, heavily publicized because of their substance and rhetorical force, are fairly well represented. All of the libraries surveyed have Soul on Ice, Black Skin, White Masks, and The Autobiography of Malcolm X, and some have them in quantity. When we move to the books that try to make literature of our racial problems, the showing is less impressive: one public library and one college library do not have Baldwin's Another Country, and three public libraries and one college library do not have the two plays by Jones. Among the periodicals, the showing is also less impressive: only four libraries carry the Journal of Black Poetry, and only half the

The Social Prerogative

libraries surveyed have the Liberator.

In the area that can be roughly designated as radical politics and Vietnam, the holdings are spottier, suggesting more caution and sharper differences of opinion. Of the 12 libraries, 11 have Ginsberg's Howl and Guevara's Diary, and one of these holds Guevara in Spanish only. Since Tatum's Conscientious Objector's Handbook is a title that is not widely known, the fact that only three libraries have it and one of the three restricts it may not seem particularly surprising, but only five libraries have the Blue Book of the John Birch Society, and only three of them circulate it freely--a curious statistic that invites closer scrutiny.

12 PHILADELPHIA LIBRARIES' OWNERSHIP OF 33 CONTROVERSIAL BOOK AND PERIODICAL TITLES

	Public Libraries				Academic Libraries						
Ownership of 25 Book Titles:	1	2	3	4	1	2	3	4	5	6	7	8
No. of titles owned, no restrictions	17	15	13	16	20	24	15	15	8	15	21	15
No. of titles restricted	8	4	2			1		1	1			1
No. of titles not owned			6	10	9	5		10	9	16	10	4	9
Ownership of 8 periodical titles:												
No. of titles owned, no restrictions	6	1	3	2	6	5	4	3		5	4	2
No. of titles restricted	1					3		1		1		
No. of titles not owned	1	7	5	6	2		4	4	8	2	4	6
No. of combined titles owned:												
(unrestricted)	23	16	16	18	26	29	19	18	8	20	25	17
Owned, with restriction	9	4	2			4		2	1	1		1
Totals, all ownership:	32	20	18	18	26	33	19	20	9	21	25	18

Only one public and one academic library have all book titles. No public library, and only one academic library (the same one) have all periodical titles. Only seven of the 25 book titles are owned by all four public libraries, unrestricted. An additional 12 book titles are owned, used with restrictions. Twelve book titles are lacking in at least one of each of the four libraries.

Only four of the 25 book titles are owned by all eight academic libraries; only four additional titles are owned, restricted. Twenty-one book titles are lacking in at least one of each of the eight academic libraries.

Only one of the eight periodical titles is in all four public libraries, unrestricted. Only one of the eight periodicals is not in any of the four public libraries, but another is in only one, and then restricted.

Total of 73 titles is owned by the four public libraries, making the average total 18.25, or 15.25 book titles. Total of 162 titles is owned by the eight academic libraries, making the average total 20.3, or 16.6 book titles.

Among the periodicals that belong in the area of radical politics, only Ramparts, which is held by 11 of 12 libraries, is well represented. Evergreen Review, which combines New Leftism with its own idiosyncratic version of sexual freedom, is held by seven libraries, four of whom restrict it for security reasons. Two conservative periodicals, American Opinion and Human Events, are held by six and seven of the libraries surveyed respectively, and the

Realist is held by one university library only.

Turning to the fiction and nonfiction that probes our sexual mores, usually critically, the holdings reflect a clear-cut pattern of caution, restriction, and rejection mixed with unawareness. In this area the highly publicized Masters and Johnson study is the only widely held title; all libraries have it, and 11 circulate copies freely. Of the creative works, Portnoy's Complaint, another highly publicized book, is held by 11 of 12 libraries holding the title in some quantity.

But the other titles fare feebly. Naked Lunch is freely circulated by six libraries who have single copies of the novel. The only library that holds it in quantity restricts it. Donleavy's Ginger Man, less influential and less iconoclastic, is freely circulated by nine libraries. But Our Lady of the Flowers, evocative autobiographical fiction by one of the most forceful novelists and playwrights since 1940, is freely circulated by six of 12 libraries studied, and the one library that holds it in quantity restricts it. Lady Chatterley, as already noted, is not held by one college library and restricted by one public library. Tropic of Cancer, freely circulated by six libraries and restricted by three, apparently still gives cause for professional anxiety almost 40 years after it was written. And Selby's Last Exit to Brooklyn, more dubious because of its one-dimensional realism but a representative novel nevertheless, is freely circulated by four libraries and restricted by one.

In the nonfictional area, the Selected Writings of the Marquis de Sade is freely circulated in small doses by four libraries and restricted by one. The handling of Howl has been noted. Wilhelm Reich is a catalytic influence on the sexual thinking and therapeutic techniques of the sixties and early seventies, but his Selected Writings are freely circulated by four libraries and restricted by one. And The Kama Sutra is freely circulated by four libraries and restricted by two. Among the periodicals, the handling of Evergreen and the Realist, which are anti-establishment in both sexual and political fronts, has been noted.

The one title that deals directly with the drug scene, Leary's The Psychedelic Experience, is freely circulated by four libraries and restricted by one. Only one university library makes it freely available in quantity.

We conclude from this mathematics that books that

challenge conventional sexual mores meet with more caution, anxiety, and defensiveness from our selecting and/or administrative librarians than books that challenge prevalent political values and practices. Soul on Ice, Guevara's Diary, and The Autobiography of Malcolm X will make their way more readily into our collections than Tropic of Cancer or Our Lady of the Flowers. Established novels, like Lady Chatterley and Tropic, which one might have hoped would be fully represented, are not, and creative works, like Our Lady and Naked Lunch, which are now tunneling their way into modern letters, are handled nervously or cavalierly. Also, recent censorship attacks have told us clearly that it is the bisexuality and the nudity in Evergreen Review much more than its New Leftism that sticks in the craws of our moralistic citizens and librarians.

We conclude further that the puritanical heritage we read about in our social and cultural histories still lives in Philadelphia area libraries.

One would find it difficult to assign an overall adjective to describe this state of affairs. Is the state of intellectual freedom in Philadelphia area libraries as reflected by the handling of these titles good, bad, or indifferent? The answer obviously depends on the values of the investigators making the judgment. One might reasonably have hoped that most, if not all, of these titles would be held by all 12 libraries surveyed, but such was far from the case. Only one public library and one university library had all of the book titles, and only one university library had all the periodicals. One would opt for a descriptive adjective like indifferent rather than good to describe the situation.

In extenuation of the mediocre showing these collective libraries make in the area of contemporary writing particularly, one might argue that each institution has its unique function and some, because of budget limitations alone, would give lower priority to such luxury items as Our Lady and Naked Lunch. One might argue further that the capacity of our student and adult masses to assimilate esoteric and arcane fiction is not as great as their supposed social and political sophistication, that they can more readily connect with a Cleaver, who is out on the street speaking colloquial Afro-English, than with a Genet, who weaves his sexual fantasies in dense symbolist prose. One suspects, however, that unawareness is a sizeable factor in the neglect of several of these absent or thinly held titles. The survey afforded occasional glimpses of indifference to certain authors and titles and suspicion regarding positive censorship stands that are far from reassuring to the members of this Committee and do not particularly augur well for the future. We can only conclude that librarians who care about contemporary letters, experimental approaches in art and social action, and the right of radical voices to be heard have cause for continued concern and ample reason for using their professional wits to try to improve this unimpressive situation.

Unawareness covers a wide stretch of territory, ranging from ignorance to indifference. The unawareness uncovered by this survey reflects, among other things, a professional overemphasis on administrative matters. Particularly does our professional literature prefer to dwell on bureaus rather than ideas, perhaps because furniture is more maneuverable and less explosive.

Even if differences in function and book buying potential are taken into consideration, some libraries are obviously more sensitive to controversial materials than others. We have seen that university libraries have a wider spread of titles but do not duplicate heavily. We have also seen that there are two modes of behavior in the public libraries surveyed: a few reject or ignore much controversial material, and one or two will add it, but often on a restricted circulation basis only. We see further that a few libraries with relatively large budgets tend to hold most, if not all, of these titles. The university library with a $700,000 budget has all 33 titles and circulates more of them than any other library surveyed--29. Two other university libraries, one with an undisclosed budget and a Negro university library with a $50,000 budget, circulate the next largest number of titles--25. The public library with a $953,000 budget has all but one of the 33 titles but circulates 23 and restricts nine. This same public library has multiple copies of all 23 titles that it owns, more multiple copies than any other library surveyed. But that is consistent with its function as a large distributing agency.

On the other end of the spectrum we find that the weakest showing is made by the area state college library with the smallest book budget--$17,500. This library holds nine of the 33 titles on our list, circulates eight, restricts one, and holds only one of these titles in multiple copies. On the other hand, the second and third weakest showings are made by libraries with relatively substantial book budgets. The community college library, with a book budget of $75,000, holds 18 titles on the list, circulates 17, restricts one, and holds only one title in multiple copies. And although it has the third largest budget reported in this survey--$325,000--the Catholic-related university library holds 19 of the 33 titles, circulates all of them, but holds none of them in multiple copies.

If we compare the community college library, which has a $75,000 annual book budget, with the Negro university library, which has a $50,000 annual book budget, we find that the library with the smaller budget holds more of the controversial titles on our list--25 against 18--circulates more of them--25 against 17--and holds more of them in multiple copies--seven against one.

We conclude that relatively favorable book budgets are no guarantee that the library's collection will include controversial materials in any significant quantities, that the values of the institution and the librarian inevitably come into play, and that some librarians with modest budgets and a sense of social and artistic adventure are building more contemporary and provocative collections than others, who have more money at their disposal but suspect or dislike the unorthodox or feel compelled to ignore it because of institutional policy.

At the close of our survey we asked the 12 librarians to evaluate existing anticensorship apparatus in the profession and comment on the supportive role of existing professional organizations and agencies in censorship controversies. Nine librarians, a clear majority, thought that existing professional organizations should play a more active role in supporting libraries or librarians in censorship controversies. One Catholic university librarian did not. One college librarian hedged, answering: "I'd like to know more." And one university librarian did not reply.

All four public librarians spoke for stronger supportive organizational action in censorship confrontations, perhaps because public libraries are more vulnerable to direct attack by organized community elements, whereas college and university censorship problems are usually internal and frequently unpublicized. One supportive college librarian thought the recently established Freedom To Read Foundation proper. However, none of the eight who answered af-

I.F. SCORES OF 12 PHILADELPHIA LIBRARIES

I.F. Rating	UL $700,000 Bk. Budget	PL $953,000 Bk. Budget	UL Undisclosed Bk. Budget	UL $50,000 Bk. Budget	PL $66,600 Bk. Budget	UL $80,000 Bk. Budget
No. Controversial Titles Owned	33	32	26	25	18	20
Plus No. Controversial Titles Circulated	29	23	25	25	18	18
Plus No. Controversial Titles Circulated in Multiple Copies	18	23	9	7	9	5
Minus No. Controversial Titles Restricted	4	9	1	0	0	2
Equals Intellectual Freedom Rating	76	69	59	57	45	41

I.F. Rating	CL $124,500 Bk. Budget	PL $28,830 Bk. Budget	PL $67,620 Bk. Budget	PL $325,000 Bk. Budget	CL $75,000 Bk. Budget	CL $17,500 Bk. Budget
No. Controversial Titles Owned	21	18	20	19	18	9
Plus No. Controversial Titles Circulated	20	16	16	19	17	8
Plus No. Controversial Titles Circulated in Multiple Copies	1	8	7	0	1	1
Minus No. Controversial Titles Restricted	1	2	4	0	1	1
Equals Intellectual Freedom Rating	41	40	39	38	35	17

firmatively were very specific or chose to elaborate on their views.

Eight of the 12 librarians surveyed thought that the profession needs an agency to give financial, legal, and moral support to a library or librarian with a censorship problem. One college librarian in this group thought that the Freedom To Read Foundation was the probable answer and could do the job. Also, one vacillating public librarian said that such an agency was needed only if existing agencies do not begin to do an effective job. However, one college librarian dissented from the majority view, stating: "Some librarians, I think, want a confrontation and create a situation which produces such." The inference here is that censorship confrontations are often devised by opportunistic librarians who are guilty of self-dramatization and self-aggrandizement, even though they sometimes risk their jobs. The Catholic university librarian again dissented, and one other university librarian did not reply.

Without overinterpreting these answers, we can say that most of the librarians surveyed seemed aware of the censorship problem, though some were tepid and none were particularly expansive. Dissenting voices among a few college and university librarians could mean that either they do not regard the issue as important or they regard themselves as removed from the censorship arena. Particularly does the militant dissent from the college librarian remind us that some professionals suspect or resent censorship fighters in their midst and continue to see intellectual freedom as a synthetic and manufactured issue as we move towards the Orwellian millenium.

THE CONCEPT OF "NATIONAL SECURITY" AND ITS EFFECT ON INFORMATION TRANSFER*

I. M. Klempner

The idea of restricting the flow of information for reasons of "national security" can, of course, be traced and attributed to many a political system. Freedom of information, however--the free expression and communication of ideas--whether accomplished through interpersonal communication or recorded media, represents one of the most fundamental cornerstones of the U.S. constitutional system of government. Fundamental also is the notion that a democratic government ought to govern with the consent of the governed. It follows, then, that such consent would be essentially worthless if it were based on ignorance or on incomplete or inadequate information.

And yet, many are aware that there exist today huge collections of documents which cannot be freely disseminated and whose content, under dire penalty of law or administrative directive, cannot be freely disclosed. What is the magnitude of these collections which, for practical purposes, encompass both security-classified and so-called unclassified, "limited distribution" documents? No one within the Federal government, and certainly no one outside of it, can give a definitive answer to this question. There are, however, a number of estimates available.

How Many Are There?

A former Air Force security classification expert indicates that within the Department of Defense there are at least 20 million classified documents, including reproduced

---

*Reprinted by permission from the July 1973 issue of Special Libraries, pages 263-269.

The Social Prerogative

copies.[1] As of last year and prior to the issuance of the 1972 presidential executive order[2] relating to classification policies for government documents, estimates are that there were 31,000 individuals within the Department of Defense who were authorized to exercise original classification.[3] Within the Department of Defense military departments alone, there were more than 100 classification managers, apparently a new profession, whose purpose it was, and still is, to manage and administer the security classification program.[4] Incidentally, in October 1964 a National Classification Management Society was formed with a current membership of over 200 and a journal which began publication in 1965.[5]

Estimates are that the National Archives holds 160 million pages of classified documents from World War II which are under review for declassification, and over 300 million pages of classified documents for the years 1946 through 1954.[6] At 100 pages per document, we were dealing here with close to 5 million documents. The Atomic Energy Commission, excluding contractor holdings, has in its possession close to 8 million documents.[7] William D. Blair, Jr., Deputy Assistant Secretary of State for Public Affairs, Department of State, indicates that over 150 million documents are in custody of the Department of State in Washington, D.C.[8] No one knows what portion of this collection is classified. For just one segment of the foreign policy file, comprising about 5 million documents issued prior to 1971, estimates are that a review of this file for purposes of declassification would require $300,000 annually and that with this "modest approach," it would take the Department of State 10 years to complete its review.[9]

Of course, in the interim, new millions of documents would have been created. Hundreds of thousands of people, in and outside of the government, have been given authority to exercise so-called derivative classification, i.e., a procedure whereby the citation or reference to a classified document could result in the creation of a new classified document.[10] There were, as of last year, a total of 13,000 security-cleared contractors[11] and their thousands of cleared employees who could assign original or derivative classification. The overall estimate is that approximately 1 million people have the authority to classify information.

Thus it should become obvious that there exists today a vast bureaucratic mechanism encompassing inspectors and inspections, security clearances and cleared facilities, "need to know" and certificates of destruction, paper-shredding machines and approved surveillance systems--a mechanism which seems to have developed a life of its own, supported by federal funds, having every attribute for self-perpetuation, and, of course, based on the rationale of "national security."

This vast security mechanism has been functioning with great efficiency. The occasional surfacing of the Pentagon papers or the Anderson disclosures have merely been indications of the internal effectiveness of the system. It should also be noted that the publication of the Pentagon papers and similar disclosures triggered administrative measures for even tighter control of the classified document collections.

Classification Results

A fundamental question that is increasingly being raised, not just by the Ellsberg case, but by individuals such as Harold C. Urey, a Nobel laureate, by Edward Teller, one of the prime developers of the H-bomb, by Harold M. Agnew, Jr., director of the Los Alamos Scientific Laboratory, and many others, is whether our nation's security is, indeed, enhanced by the present system of safeguarding information. A distinguished group of military men, scientists, engineers, and scholars formed a Department of Defense Task Force on Secrecy, which, under the chairmanship of Frederick Seitz, president of Rockefeller University and former executive president of the National Academy of Sciences, considered security classifications both from the short and long range viewpoints. Some of its basic findings, published in July 1970 in a classified report which has since been declassified, may be summarized as follows.

1. It is unlikely that classified information will remain secure for periods as long as 5 years, and it is more reasonable to assume that it will become known by others in periods as short as 1 year through independent discovery, clandestine disclosure, or other means.

2. In addition to the dollar costs of operating under conditions of classification and of maintaining the information security system, [security] classification establishes barriers between nations, creates areas of uncertainty in the public mind on policy issues, and impedes the flow of useful information within our own country and abroad.

3. More might be gained than lost if this nation were to adopt--unilaterally, if necessary--a policy of complete openness in all areas of information; but the Task Force agreed that, in spite of the great advantages that might accrue from such a policy, it is not a practical proposal at the present time. The Task Force believed that such a policy would not be acceptable within the current framework of national attitudes toward classified defense work.

4. Security classification is most profitably applied in areas close to design and production, having to do with detailed drawings and special techniques of manufacture rather than research and most exploratory development.

5. The amount of scientific and technical information which is classified could profitably be decreased perhaps as much as 90% by limiting the amount of information classified and the duration of its classification.[12]

Freedom of Information

It is not the purpose of this paper to advance the argument that the government ought to operate in a fish bowl, i.e., that all of its documents and decision-making processes be visible and accessible to the public. Of course there are documents and information that ought to be kept secret. In recent and past Congressional legislation, in the Freedom of Information Act, the Congress recognized the need to keep certain categories of documents from general public scrutiny. Invariably, however, the legislative authorizations to withhold documents from the public, the exemptions under the Freedom of Information Act, were meant to be interpreted in a narrow and limited sense. The intent of the provisions of the Freedom of Information Act was to maximize disclosure of information. Yet, as Congressional testimony reveals, almost the very opposite seems to have taken place: the provisions of the Freedom of Information Act are often used as justification for withholding information.

The point to emphasize here is that the atmosphere of secrecy engendered by the overzealous application of the concept of "national security," the withholding of information within this society, from its own citizens, carries over into a much broader category of documents which have not been given a "national security" label. A variety of 60 markings, ranging from "addressee only" to "U.S. Government use only," i.e., markings other than "confidential," "secret," or "top secret," were discovered to be in use within federal government agencies.[13]

Moreover, federal agency bureaucrats have learned rather well not only to withhold documents under the various exemptions of the Freedom of Information Act--which are supposed to be permissive rather than mandatory--but have also learned to make use of a variety of delaying administrative techniques, have applied new and excessive document copying charges and searching fees, and have practiced, what may be called, "negative or blank bibliographic control" on a vast array of documents which are often withheld from the public for other than "national security" reasons. The following will elaborate somewhat on some of these bureaucratic techniques and procedures.

Delays in Responding to Requests. If an agency, for whatever reason, is reluctant to release a document, it may drag out its response in the hope that the passage of time will render the information obsolete or will lessen, if not completely eliminate, the initial requester's interest in the information. A study done by the Congressional Research Service of the Library of Congress for the Foreign Operations and Government Information Subcommittee reveals that the major government agencies took an average of 33 days to just respond to a request for information under the Freedom of Information Act. When an initial decision to withhold information was made and that decision appealed, the agencies took an average of 50 days for a subsequent response.[14] As is substantiated also by a study of the Los Angeles Regional Technical Information Users Council, from 10 to 22 weeks were required, or an average of 100 days, to acquire a report having a "limited distribution" marking.[15] For these requests the contractor's "need to know" could easily be ascertained. At an East Coast meeting of a number of defense contractor librarians, it was indicated that, just to obtain sponsoring agency approval signatures for "limited distribution" documents, 30 days to 6 months were needed.[16]

Meaningless, Obstructive or Nonsubstantive Responses. Another mechanism which federal agencies employ to thwart the flow of information is to respond to a request by sending back a blank form which calls for the information provided in the initial request. In addition, for some agencies, the

The Social Prerogative 365

completed form must be returned with a fee which is nonrefundable, even if no information or documents are subsequently made available. Of course, by far the most common ploy is to send a copy of a press release or a bland pamphlet only remotely related to the inquiry.

Information and Publication Pricing Policies. One other less sinister, yet quite effective, way of throttling or impeding the information transfer process is by instituting excessive charges for information or document services. The information derived from government-sponsored research, the information held by federal government agencies, may be considered to be a national resource to be made accessible to all U.S. citizens. Yet it seems that only the very rich library or the very rich individual may be able to afford certain information held by federal agencies. The problem will be illustrated here as related in Congressional testimony by Reuben B. Robertson III and Harrison Welford of the Center for Study of Responsive Law, and others.

A student requests from an official of the Federal Aviation Administration the names of the 26 inspectors who report directly to that official. The student is asked and had to pay a search fee for that information.[17]

A scientist reaching at the University of Georgia requests certain information on pesticides from the Department of Agriculture. The response is that the scientist give some assurance that he could pay a search fee of at least $100 before the department would go to the trouble of locating the information.[18]

An additional fee for photocopying the requested data may be imposed ranging from $.05 per page at the Department of Agriculture to as much as $1.00 a page at the Selective Service System.[19]

On not quite the same subject, yet somewhat related, is the policy of NTIS to raise the cost of its 1972 Government Reports Index to $250 and to price the 1964-1967 cumulation at $500. There is a trend among federal agencies to do away with the gratis distribution of reports to contractors and potential contractors, first of hard copy, then of microfiche, then of some of the abstracting and indexing services. Support for OTS depositories has been withdrawn for a number of years and NASA and AEC depository collection funding has been curtailed and is further threatened. Late last year, without public announcement, the Government Printing Office ordered a sweeping increase in charges for government documents averaging 80% of present costs.[20] Thus the annual subscription rate for NASA's STAR went up from $54.00 in 1972 to $118.00 in 1973, for the AEC's Nuclear Science Abstracts from $42.00 in 1972 to $75.50 in 1973. If information gathered at taxpayer's expense can, indeed, be considered a national resource and if lack of information or mal-distribution of information can have profound sociopolitical and economic effects on the citizens of the U.S., should concern be shown that only certain libraries, that only certain individuals will be in the advantageous position of putting public knowledge to work? While security classification may not be a question here, what may need analysis and concern is whether the government's niggardly policy of publication subsidy and support tends to make its information more or less easily accessible to the general public.

Negative or Blank Bibliographic Control. Another way to impede and obstruct the information transfer process is for a federal agency to withhold the bibliographic information that a particular document or documents exist. The general axiom may be stated as follows: if an existing publication is not listed, or if it is listed in a secret source, it does not necessarily exist for the general public. Thus, not only the private citizen, but elected officials in Congress bemoan the fact that frequently they are unable to determine whether a particular document is extant at all so that it could be requested or sought out for declassification and release.[21]

Under the Freedom of Information Act, and this provision is certainly implemented in executive procedures, it is first necessary to identify the document requested. Requests that lack specificity or which do not provide adequate bibliographic detail may be returned to the requester unfilled. Typical of federal agency regulations is the following one from the Atomic Energy Commission.

> Requests need not be made on any special form but shall, as specified in the Executive order, describe the document with sufficient particularity to enable AEC personnel to identify and obtain the document from AEC records without expending more than a reasonable amount of effort.[22]

Of course, the most desirable report may be an unclassified, "limited distribution" document which will be found listed only in an abstracting and indexing service which bears a "secret" or "confidential" national security classification. Certainly the AEC Index of Limited Distribution Reports, formerly called Abstracts of Classified Reports, bears a "secret" security label and about 20% of its listings comprise unclassified, "limited distribution" reports.

The listing of unclassified "limited distribution" reports in the issues of the Defense Documentation Center Technical Abstract Bulletin rose from less than 10% in 1964 to more than 50% in 1969.[23] The Technical Abstract Bulletin (TAB) was given a "confidential" security marking in 1967. Is it simply a coincidence that TAB went underground the very year the Freedom of Information Act came into effect? "Negative bibliographic control" resulting in fewer requests and curtailed use of federally generated information was further advanced by the Defense Documentation Center in 1971 when it placed a "confidential" security label also on the indexes to TAB.

Of considerable concern to all should be that documents of a number of federal agencies are not to be found listed in any open and accessible bibliographic service. For example, the White House staff increased from 8 presidential advisers in 1941 to a 1971 staff of 5,395 in the Executive Office of the President, plus 600 additional White House staff employees, plus 45 presidential advisers.[24] Which abstracting and indexing service provides bibliographic access, classified or unclassified, to the document products of the White House bureaucracy? Which abstracting and indexing service lists the memoranda of the National Security Council? As is well known from recent events, even oral testimony sought by Congress from White House officials is often refused since the total White House staff considers itself responsible directly to the President and invokes "executive privilege," when asked to testify before Congressional committees.

To reiterate, it is the author's conviction that the often deliberate practice of negative or blank bibliographic control, that the broad and expanding interpretation and application of the concept of "national security" are incompatible with free and democratic processes. There is, indeed, strong evidence to suggest that these practices may be inimical to our development as democratic people and a democratic society. While secrecy may be effective and may be practiced with impunity in a totalitarian system, it is likely to wield a destructive influence in an open society. Many a thoughtful individual has advocated an atmosphere of openness as one of the strongest weapons at our disposal, a weapon effective from a socio-political and economic point of view and, in the long run, from a military point of view. It is the atmosphere of openness that engenders and accelerates mutual understanding and provides the basis for maximum social interaction and collective and individual well-being. The idea of openness forms the very essence of the First Amendment to the Constitution of the United States.

The Librarians' Role

Thus a basic task for special librarians, who are often caught between demands for maximum security and maximum interchange of information, is to strive for a balance by counteracting the present trend toward secrecy. Prior to the Watergate investigation, one of the expert witnesses before the House Committee on Government Operations stated:

> The first problem [that we need to be aware of] is the intransigence of government officials. Basically they do not believe in freedom of information. They believe that the public's business is their business, and not the business of the public. Until there is a fundamental change in the attitude on the part of government officials, either by process of education, or by a process of some kind of court sanction, I do not believe that the Freedom of Information Act is going to be administered as the Congress intended it to be administered. 25

Let the process of awareness and education, barely begun with the public at large, deepen and expand within the membership of the library profession.

REFERENCES

1. U.S. Congress, House, Committee on Government Operations. Foreign Operations and Government Information Subcommittee. <u>U.S. Government Information Policies and Practices.</u> Hearings, 92nd Cong., 1st-2nd Sess., June 23, 1971-June 1, 1972. Wash-

ington, D.C.: Government Printing Office, 1972; 8 pts., p. 97.
2. Executive Order No. 11652, Mar. 8, 1972.
3. Ref. 1, p. 683.
4. Ref. 1, p. 681.
5. Congressional Record, Mar. 21, 1972; p. E2774.
6. U.S. Congress, House, Committee on Armed Services. Special Subcommittee on Intelligence. Hearings on the Proper Classification and Handling of Government Information Involving the National Security. 92nd Cong., 2nd Sess., Mar. 8-10, 13-14, 16, 22, 24, and May 9, 1972. Washington, D.C.: U.S. Government Printing Office, 1972; p. 17512.
7. Ref. 6, p. 1716.
8. Ref. 1, p. 2464.
9. Ref. 1, p. 912.
10. Ref. 1, p. 96.
11. Ref. 1, p. 684.
12. Ref. 1, p. 3144-3151.
13. Ref. 1, p. 2494.
14. Ref. 1, p. 1332.
15. Los Angeles Regional Technical Information Users Council. User Problems Associated with the Services of Federal and Quasi-Federal Technical Information Producing Agencies. LARTIUC report no. 1, June 1970-July 1971. Los Angeles, Dec. 1971; 32.
16. Proceedings of the Fifth Scientific and Technical Information Seminar, New Haven, Conn., April 9, 1970. New Haven: Southern Connecticut State College, Mar. 1971; 90.
17. Ref. 1, p. 1252.
18. Ref. 1, p. 1253.
19. Ref. 1, p. 1245.
20. Gannon, James P. "U.S. Printing Office to Boost Document Prices Average 80%." Wall Street Journal, Dec. 22, 1972; 15, col. 2.
21. Ref. 1, p. 52.
22. Federal Register, 37:15624, Aug. 12, 1972.
23. Ref. 16.
24. Ref. 1, p. 3021.
25. Ref. 1, p. 1394.

FREEDOM OF THE PRESS--AMERICAN STYLE*

Harriet F. Pilpel

... what it means, what it should mean ...
some of the ways it is threatened

All of us reading this magazine are apt to agree that the First Amendment guaranteeing freedom of the press should be "first in the hearts of our countrymen" and that from a variety of sources that freedom is in danger today. The trouble is we talk about freedom of the press as if it were one and indissoluble whereas, in fact, like other generalities, it is composed of a large number of specifics.

Perhaps what we have and what we try to keep would be clearer if we bore those specifics in mind. Indeed, there is a school of thought which believes that the first order of business in the solution of any problem is the application of the technique of fragmentation--the ability to talk and think in terms of the component parts that together make up our large lump concepts--love, peace, war, truth, goodness, and, of course, freedom of speech and the press which the First Amendment forbids the government to abridge. (I shall refer throughout to "freedom of speech" as including all forms of expression, including, of course, freedom of the press.)

It is necessary to define "abridgment" as well as "freedom." Clearly, it can take many forms which break down under two main headings: "prior restraint," which usually means an injunction against speech, or "subsequent

---

*Reprinted by permission from the March 12, 1973 issue of Publishers Weekly (pages 26-29), published by R. R. Bowker Co., a Xerox Education Company. Copyright © 1973 by Xerox Corporation.

punishment," which can be a fine, a jail sentence or even in extreme cases a loss of life (e.g., as in treason--cf. Ethel and Julius Rosenberg). Often, however, the abridgment takes much more subtle forms. A "prior restraint" can inhere in a requirement that in order to receive certain types of mail from abroad you must put your name on a list. A "subsequent punishment" need not be criminal--it may "merely" mean you lose your job for something you have said (e.g., the "Hollywood 10").

Now, let us look at the constituent parts of the freedom itself. It breaks down into at least eight categories:

(1) First, there is freedom to speak, the right to communicate freely and without restraint.

(2) Second is the right to listen, the freedom to read, to watch and to hear.

(3) Third is the right not to speak or write, to refuse to communicate.

(4) Fourth, there is the right not to be forced to listen or see, which has been said to be part of another basic constitutional right, the "right of privacy." In this context, "privacy" means the right of the individual not to be subjected to sight, sound or smell which he wishes to avoid but has no way of avoiding.

(5) Fifth is the right of anonymity, the right to communicate and receive communications anonymously.

(6) Sixth is the right to know, the right not to have government keep secrets from us, except those absolutely necessary to the security of government itself.

(7) Seventh, and in a way part of the first, is the "right of access." It is not enough to have freedom to speak if all the effective media of communication are unavailable either as the result of government action or of action or non-action on the part of "private interests" which control the media.

(8) And, finally, we come to the question: Against whom does this constitutional guarantee apply? Is only government forbidden to abridge freedom of expression? Can the Constitution be read to guarantee that freedom against non-governmental forces as well?

1. Freedom to Speak

Freedom to speak, in the sense of the right to communicate, was no doubt paramount in the minds of those who first promulgated the First Amendment. Yet this freedom has perhaps the most exceptions grafted upon it today. We are all familiar with and accept the fact that one's speech may be prohibited because it threatens what the courts call a "clear and present danger." As Mr. Justice Holmes, himself a true apostle of freedom of speech, put it, no one has the right to cry "Fire" in a crowded theatre. Recently, however, the government has tried to suppress freedom to communicate in situations where no "clear and present danger," no matter how defined, was present. There are, for example, the "Pentagon Papers" actions, both the original attempts to prevent the New York Times and the Washington Post from printing the Pentagon material and the later controversies such as the one involving Senator Mike Gravel and the Beacon Press. Even more recently, there have been the efforts of the CIA to prevent former employees from writing about it at all.

Less generally recognized as limitations on freedom to speak are such civil actions as those for libel and violation of the right of privacy. With reference to libel, the rule of New York Times v. Sullivan and its offspring has been in the direction of permitting greater freedom of speech in the libel area. Today there is greater freedom of speech about public officials, candidates for public office, public personages and persons in the context of public issues as far as libel is concerned than ever before. As to these categories of persons, there is actionable libel only if they can prove that what was said about them was knowingly or recklessly false. However, the mere existence of this exception, so deplored by Justices Black and Douglas, has resulted in many cases being brought by such persons, and while it seems that they lose more often than they win, the continued danger of exposure to a libel suit--which is expensive and time-consuming--remains something of a throttle on free discussion about public issues. Since public officials themselves are absolutely immune from libel liability for any statements they make in their capacity as public officials, a rule of absolute immunity for those who libel them in that capacity may well be called for.

Today, oddly enough, the threat to freedom of expression on the civil side--that is, in the form of private

suits--comes much more from actions alleging violation of
the right of privacy than from suits claiming libel. Since
the United States Supreme Court has held that the test is
substantially the same with reference to the same categories
of people, there is far more risk of violating someone's
right of privacy than there is of libel. Almost anything said
about a person, even a public person, and even though not
libelous, can be made the basis of a successful privacy suit
if the plaintiff alleges and proves that there was a "substantial" deliberate falsification or a reckless disregard of the
truth. And again, even if the plaintiff loses a privacy suit,
he can, by bringing it, subject a publisher or broadcaster or
producer or distributor to such enormous expense in defending the suit that they may be seriously damaged even if they
win. Perhaps in libel and privacy cases the law ought to
allow the courts to award costs against the plaintiff if he
loses, as is the situation in unsuccessful copyright infringement suits today.

Then there are the obscenity laws. Almost no attention is being paid to the Report of the Commission on Obscenity and Pornography which, based on extensive study,
recommended that there be no law proscribing obscenity for
adults and a very limited one as to children. A few groups,
such as the Committee on Civil Rights of the Association of
the Bar of the City of New York, have called for the enactment of these recommendations into law in New York State;
the probability of this being done anywhere in the present
climate of public opinion is remote. On the contrary, much
of the pending legislation would tighten the present Supreme
Court definitions of obscenity by, for example, eliminating
"redeeming social importance" as part of the test and/or
by declaring that the "community standards," by which a
work attacked as obscene is to be judged, are to be solely
the standards of the particular local community where the
case is brought. An effort along such lines was defeated in
November by popular referendum in California, but nonetheless Congress and many state legislatures are contemplating
tightening controls on obscenity and thus further restricting
the freedom to speak.

Especially disquieting are recent attempts of the
Federal and state governments to "get" underground newspapers for publishing, for example, abortion referral ads.
By and large, these efforts have been defeated in the lower
courts but such suits against publications with dissident
points of view have caused considerable concern.

There are many more restrictions on the freedom to speak which, by and large, are not recognized as such. In addition to the Post Office laws and regulations, there are the civil laws against fraud, the Federal Trade Commission, the SEC, the increasingly frequent bans on "abusive language," epithets and "insulting words," the imposition of license requirements for news vendors and theaters, and many others. Finally, there are entire groups of people whose freedom of expression, at least until recently, has been totally abridged and which even today have very little: persons in the military service, persons in mental institutions, and to considerable extent minors. Yet these are "persons" too, entitled, within limits that must surely be definable, to the First Amendment's guarantee of the right to speak.

2. Freedom to Listen

We come now to the second aspect of the basic constitutional guarantee of freedom of expression, the right correlative to the right to speak, namely, the right to listen. This is a freedom the contours of which are only now beginning to be drawn, primarily with respect to radio and television. The United States Supreme Court, in the Red Lion case, specifically held that the constitutional guarantee exists not only for those who wish to speak but also for those who wish to listen. In sustaining the Fairness Doctrine for broadcasters, the Court said, "... It is the right of the viewers and listeners, not the right of the broadcasters, which is paramount.... It is the right of the public to receive suitable access to social, political, esthetic, moral, and other ideas and experiences which is crucial."

It has been suggested that this freedom of the receiver as well as the transmitter of speech should also be recognized with respect to the print media, but no such recognition has yet been accorded or even seriously considered as law.

3. The Right Not to Speak

The right not to speak has been very much in the news because of the Caldwell and like cases, involving the right of newsmen to refuse to disclose their sources or to reveal material which they choose not to publish. Because of the United States Supreme Court decisions in the recent newsmen subpoena cases, this right at the moment appears to be on somewhat shaky ground. However, many states have already passed shield laws to protect the confidentiality of news sources and material, and proposals for such laws are presently pending in many state legislatures and before Congress.

To some extent the right not to speak is closely related to the right to listen since, as the United States Supreme Court pointed out in the Red Lion case, the real point of the First Amendment guarantee is not only the protection of the reporter and his source but the public itself, which will inevitably be deprived of important information if the sources of that information dry up because of forced disclosure.

4. The Right Not to Listen

This right is also not clearly delineated. It is part of the rapidly evolving doctrine of the "right of privacy." This doctrine is still so amorphous that, as Justice Stewart said with respect to hardcore pornography: "I can't define it but I know it when I see it." The "right of privacy" today already stretches all the way from contraception and abortion to protection against electric eyes, computerized personal dossiers, and knowingly false statements (see item 1 above). In the context of the affirmative constitutional guarantee of free expression, the right means that no one should be exposed to having "thrust" upon him material he doesn't want to see. This concept figured largely in one of the recent key United States Supreme Court obscenity cases, the Redrup case. Under the view expressed in that case, the criterion of obscenity seemed to be not the content of any material which people, in the exercise of a free choice, choose to see, but whether it is distributed in such a manner that it is forced upon those who choose not to see it. Examples are outdoor signs, window displays and sounds in public places or facilities from which there is no escape. Obviously, one man's right not to listen may conflict with another man's freedom to speak, but the Redrup limitation on public display and "thrusting" may be moving toward the necessary balance.

5. The Right to Speak Anonymously

The right of anonymity is claimed infrequently in the context of oral speech, although even here it can be in issue if a speaker chooses not to be seen or identified. However, when it comes to printed matter in the mails or otherwise, it is argued that the constitutional guarantee to be meaningful must embrace the right to be anonymous. Exponents of unpopular points of view may well be "chilled" into silence if they are not permitted to circulate their views without having to attach their names to it. Similarly, it has been held by the United States Supreme Court that those who wish to receive certain types of mail from abroad must have a right to receive it without having to notify the Post Office in order to have it delivered to them. Except for this decision, there would have been in Post Office hands a rapidly lengthening list of those seeking material which in the eyes of the Post Office or some other government agency might be considered "subversive."

6. The Right to Know

This aspect of freedom of the press is also today very much in the news. It is what the Freedom of Information Act is all about. In a sense, it, too, was involved in the Pentagon Papers case. It poses the distinct and separate question: how much can the government keep to itself and what are guiding criteria? It looks as if the recent decision of the Supreme Court upholding government secrecy classifications may have struck a serious blow at this concept of the right to know, but, clearly, the last word has not yet been spoken.

7. The Right of Access

In the past few years, it has been suggested that perhaps there are situations where, if the government does not intervene to assure access to the press, this failure may be a violation of the First Amendment. The argument is that non-action by government can infringe the basic freedom. What good does it do for a person to have the right to speak, it is asked, if private individuals control the arteries of speech and block access to them? A partial right of access to the electronic media is assured by the Fairness Doctrine promulgated and enforced by the FCC. Under that doctrine, a person attacked on the airwaves has a right to reply. In addition, the doctrine imposes on all broadcast licensees the obligation to air a variety of different viewpoints on controversial public issues. The Communications Act itself requires all licensees which permit any candidate to use their facilities to accord equal time to all other candidates for the same office. It also calls for every licensee to devote some of its broadcast time to issues of public importance. It is the duty of the Federal Communications Commission thus affirmatively to make possible the exercise of free speech on the air at least to this extent. The Fairness Doctrine is grounded on the First Amendment and the fact that the airwaves constitute public property as to which the government has the right and the obligation to insure access for persons attacked and for different points of view on controversial issues.

As mentioned above, it has recently been suggested that a similar obligation should be imposed to implement the First Amendment with regard to the print media. Here there is, theoretically, no scarcity element as there is in the case of the still limited number of available air channels, a scarcity, incidentally, which is apt to disappear as cable TV comes into its own. On the other hand, theoretically, anyone can publish a newspaper or a magazine or a book.

Actually, however, there is realistically in the case of the print media even a greater scarcity of channels, dictated not by technology but by economic realities. Thus, while in New York City there are only three general daily newspapers, there are more than 35 radio and television stations. It is true that anyone can distribute handbills expressing their opinions and many people may be able to hire halls in which speeches can be made. In these days of mass media covering our "global village," however, it is hardly realistic to say that such limited right of access to the print media creates any real right of access on the part of most of us. The proponents and opponents of establishing "right of access" to the print media are equally on both sides. The ultimate resolution even with respect to the airways, now that we have virtually unlimited cable potential with a requirement of public access channels, is far from clear.

8. Against Whom the Guarantee Applies

So much for a brief indication of the major components of the constitutional guarantee of freedom of expression here and now. Equally important is the question against whom, in all its various meanings, it applies. Primarily, it applies against the government itself in all its branches--the prohibition of abridgment of freedom of speech and the press extends to the legislative, executive and judicial departments of government, to federal, state and local officials, down to the town dog catcher and the ski instructor in a national park. In addition, there are other so-called private groups which in effect exercise governmental power which should be, and in some respects have been, held also to be bound by the guarantees of the First Amendment. Thus, the United States Supreme Court has held that where a private company "owns" a town, lock, stock and barrel--its streets, its parks, its playgrounds and public buildings--then, for purposes of the First Amendment, that company is the government and subject to the same inhibitions against abridgment of free speech. Similarly, when a shopping center prohibits picketing relating to a labor controversy involving one of its stores, the United States Supreme Court has applied the First Amendment guarantee to the shopping center. More recently, the present Court has stepped back a little from this position and has held, for example, that anti-Vietnam forces did not, under the First Amendment, have the right to protest inside a shopping plaza.

On occasion, the freedom of expression guaranteed by the First Amendment can be asserted even against private individuals although they are not exercising the prerogatives of government, as did the company in the company-town case and the shopping center in the labor dispute. The Federal Civil Rights Act prohibits private persons from conspiring to deprive others of their civil rights, one of which, of course, is freedom of expression. Generally, however, the guarantees of free speech and free press do not apply against private individuals. If, however, a "right of access" to all the media is recognized, the government might have an affirmative obligation to insure freedom of expression against the private interests which control the media, and in that sense the scope of the First Amendment may come to apply to those who own and control the mass media.

The Battleground Today

Many commentators and students of the First Amendment today discern what may be a many-pronged attack by the government on freedom of expression in many of its aspects. They point to an apparent government effort to fragment each medium of the press. Looked at from one point of view, this might not be such a bad idea. The three major networks have dominated and continue to dominate the airwaves and, like such newspapers as the New York Times and the Washington Post, have enormous influence on millions of Americans. Theoretically and ideally, the more diverse and numerous the sources of the press, the greater the freedom of each one of us to arrive at our own conclusions. In fact, however, this hypothesis may not hold up in the face of a big government getting bigger, with more power concentrated in the Chief Executive.

In an article published in the Harvard Law Review some years ago, the writer reluctantly concluded that, bad as big networks may be in terms of their competitive effect on individual station licensees, it may well be that they are the only effective defense against big government in the area of freedom of speech. By its attacks on the major news media, electronic and print, the stand of the present Administration that the networks are too powerful has had an appeal for those who would like to see more newspapers, more radio and TV stations, and more mass magazines. However, it may well be that only giants can fight giants. The result of a diminution of the power of the giants in the media is all too likely to be an increase in the power of the government. The government's present efforts to break up the public broadcasting service is another example of its apparent effort to divide the media into small ineffective fragments, which individually could not possibly represent a counter-force to government pressures.

There is no question, as Mayor Lindsay pointed out as recently as January 26, 1973, that "... the press has an obligation to examine its own biases and to review constantly 'its own efforts to separate fact and opinion.' In this area of self-criticism, the media could do a great deal more to gain public confidence. But the most serious threat to the goal of an informed public comes from government itself."

It has been said that the power to tax is the power to destroy. In a much more fundamental and important sense, the power to control the media is the power to destroy a democratic society. As was pointed out recently in a Civil Liberties publication, in banner headlines, "CONTROL THE MEDIA AND YOU CONTROL THE MINDS." Now must be the time for all good men to come to the aid of the media and demonstrate, as the good citizens of California did by rejecting Proposition 14 (the anti-obscenity provision), that freedom of the press continues to be our "first freedom" and that here, as elsewhere, eternal vigilance is indeed the price of liberty.

NOTES ON CONTRIBUTORS

Henry BEARD is a well known American humorist.

Verner W. CLAPP died on June 15, 1972. He was a member of the Council on Library Resources, Washington, D.C.

Raleigh DePRIEST is the humanities librarian at Mansfield State College, Pennsylvania.

Robert B. DOWNS is dean of library administration emeritus and university librarian, University of Illinois, at Urbana.

William R. ESHELMAN is the editor of the Wilson Library Bulletin.

D. J. FOSKETT is the librarian of the University of London Institute of Education.

Patrick GROFF is professor of education at San Diego State University, San Diego, California.

Dick HIGGINS is the owner and editor of the small press, The Something Else Press.

Bengt HJELMQVIST, former head of the State Public Libraries, Sweden, has been linked to the Swedish Literary Commission as its library expert.

Edward G. HOLLEY is dean of the Graduate School of Library Science at the University of North Carolina.

Ada Louise HUXTABLE is the architecture critic of the New York Times.

June JORDAN is a poet and author who has written both a novel and a history book all in Black English.

Jean KARL is vice-president and editor of children's books for Atheneum. Her editorial work includes a Caldecott Award winner, several Newbery and Caldecott honor books and the 1972 Newbery Award book.

I(rving) M. KLEMPNER is a professor of library and information science at State University of New York at Albany.

Richard KLUGER is president and publisher of Charterhouse Books, a new, small, independent trade house.

S. J. LEON is the librarian-in-charge of the Northeast Regional Library of the Philadelphia Free Library.

John LEONARD is a novelist and editor of the New York Times Book Review.

Herman LIEBAERS is the president of the International Federation of Library Associations.

John MAASS, the author of several books, serves as an information officer for the City of Philadelphia.

Arthur McANALLY was the director of libraries at the University of Oklahoma, Norman.

Joseph McDONALD is the assistant director for Reader's Services at Stocton State College in Pomona, New Jersey.

S. D. NEILL is an associate professor at the School of Library and Information Science at the University of Western Ontario, London.

Eva NELSON is the children's librarian at the Great River Regional Library, St. Cloud, Minnesota.

Harriet F. PILPEL is a contributing editor to Publishers Weekly.

Anthony ROTA is a bibliographer and owner of Bertram Rota book store in London, England.

Arnold P. SABLE now lives on the kibbutz Kabri near Haifa. He was formerly the director of Adriance Memorial Library in Poughkeepsie, New York.

Notes on Contributors

Peggy SULLIVAN is the director of the Office of Library Personnel Resources, and executive secretary of the Library Education Division, American Library Association.

Robert VOSPER is the former director of libraries at the University of California at Los Angeles.

Oscar M. TRELLES is an assistant professor of law and assistant law librarian at the University of Toledo (Ohio) Law School Library.

Caroline E. WERKLEY is currently at the University of Pennsylvania Department of Anthropology.

Denis WOOD is affiliated with the Graduate School of Geography at Clark University in Worcester, Massachusetts.

Z
671
L7024
#4
1973

AUG 21 1974